Irish Foreign Policy, 1919–66

Irish Foreign Policy, 1919–66

From Independence to Internationalism

EDITED BY
Michael Kennedy and Joseph Morrison Skelly

FOUR COURTS PRESS

Set in 10.5 on 12.5 Adobe Garamond for
FOUR COURTS PRESS LTD
Fumbally Lane, Dublin 8, Ireland
e-mail: info@four-courts-press.ie
and in North America by
FOUR COURTS PRESS
c/o ISBS, 5804 N.E. Hassalo Street, Portland, OR 97213.

© The various contributors and Four Courts Press 2000

A catalogue record for this title
is available from the British Library.

ISBN 1–85182–404–9 hbk
ISBN 1–85182–560–6 pbk

All rights reserved. No part of this publication may be reproduced, stored in or introduced into a retrieval system, or transmitted, in any form or by any means (electronic, mechanical, photocopying, recording or otherwise), without the prior written permission of both the copyright owner and publisher of this book.

Printed in England
by MPG Books, Bodmin, Cornwall

Contents

ACKNOWLEDGMENTS 7

ABBREVIATIONS 9

Foreword 11
Patrick Keatinge

1 The Study of Irish Foreign Policy from Independence to
  Internationalism 13
  Michael Kennedy and Joseph Morrison Skelly

2 Taking the World Stage: Creating an Irish Foreign Policy in the 1920s 25
  Gerard Keown

3 'Mr Blythe, I Think, Hears from him Occasionally': The Experiences
  of Irish Diplomats in Latin America, 1919–23 44
  Michael Kennedy

4 'Weird Prophecies': British Intelligence and Anglo–Irish
  Relations, 1932–3 61
  Eunan O'Halpin

5 Inter-war Irish–German Diplomacy: Continuity, Ambiguity and
  Appeasement in Irish Foreign Policy 74
  Mervyn O'Driscoll

6 Ireland, Vichy and Post-liberation France, 1938–50 96
  Robert Patterson

7 'Benevolent Helpfulness'? Ireland and the International Reaction to
  Jewish Refugees, 1933–9 116
  Katrina Goldstone

8 'The Virtual Minimum': Ireland's Decision for *De Facto* Recognition of
  Israel, 1947–9 137
  Paula Wylie

Contents

9 A Larger and Noisier Southern Ireland: Ireland and the Evolution of Dominion Status in India, Burma and the Commonwealth, 1942–9   155
Deirdre McMahon

10 Anti-partitionism, Irish America and Anglo–American Relations, 1945–51   192
Troy Davis

11 Integration or Isolation? Ireland and the Invitation to Join the Marshall Plan   203
Bernadette Whelan

12 The Enthusiastic Response of a Reluctant Supporter: Ireland and the Committee for European Economic Cooperation in 1947   222
Till Geiger

13 'A Wider Perspective': Ireland's View of Western Europe in the 1950s   247
Gary Murphy

14 Irish Neutrality and the First Application for Membership of the EEC, 1961–3   265
Dermot Keogh

15 National Interests and International Mediation: Ireland's South Tyrol Initiative at the United Nations, 1960–1   286
Joseph Morrison Skelly

16 *Raison d'État* and the Evolution of Irish Foreign Policy   308
Ronan Fanning

SELECT BIBLIOGRAPHY   327

NOTES ON CONTRIBUTORS   339

INDEX   343

Acknowledgments

The editors wish to express their appreciation to the staff of the National Archives in Dublin, without whose efforts this volume would not have been possible. We are grateful to Professor Patrick Keatinge for his contribution of an eloquent Foreword. We would also like to thank Mr Seamus Helferty of the University College Dublin Archives Department, Dr Susannah Riordan, Combined Departments of History, University College Dublin, Professor Richard Sinnott, Department of Politics, University College Dublin, and Professor Joseph Coady, Department of History, College of Mount Saint Vincent. Annette Keogh and Colin Knightly provided essential word processing and editorial assistance. The friendship and hospitality of Moira Palumbo and Shane Barry are greatly appreciated. Finally, the entire team at Four Courts Press has, once again, set the standard in Irish academic publishing and, especially, in the field of Irish diplomatic history.

Abbreviations

TEXT

BIS	British Information Service
CFLN	Comité Française de la Libération National
CEEC	Committee for European Economic Cooperation
CIU	Congress of Irish Unions
DAAD	Deutscher Akademischer Austauschdienst
ECE	United Nations Economic Commission for Europe
ECSC	European Coal and Steel Community
EEC	European Economic Community
EFTA	European Free Trade Area
ERP	European Recovery Program
GATT	General Agreement on Tariffs and Trade
GC&CS	Government Code and Cipher School (UK)
ISC	Irish Situation Committee (UK)
ITO	International Trade Organisation
ITUC	Irish Trade Union Congress
KPD	Kommunistische Partei Deutschland (German Communist Party)
MP	Member of Parliament
NATO	North Atlantic Treaty Organization
NSDAP	Nationalsozialistische Deutsche Arbeiterpartei (National Socialist Workers' Party or Nazi Party)
OECD	Organization for Economic Cooperation and Development
OEEC	Organization for European Economic Cooperation
SPD	Sozialistische Partei Deutschland (German Social Democratic Party)
TD	Teachta Dála (member of the Irish parliament)
UN	United Nations
WEU	Western European Union

FOOTNOTES

Dáil Deb.	*Dáil Éireann, Parliamentary Debates*
NAI DE	National Archives of Ireland, Dáil Éireann
NAI DF	National Archives of Ireland, Department of Finance
NAI DF F	National Archives of Ireland, Department of Finance, Finance Division
NAI DFA	National Archives of Ireland, Department of Foreign Affairs, Central Registry Files
NAI DFA BE	National Archives of Ireland, Department of Foreign Affairs, Bern Embassy

NAI DFA CM	National Archives of Ireland, Department of Foreign Affairs, Common Market Series
NAI DFA DPG/IFS B	National Archives of Ireland, Department of Foreign Affairs, Dáil Provisional Government/Irish Free State Files, Berlin Series
NAI DFA ES	National Archives of Ireland, Department of Foreign Affairs, Early Series
NAI DFA LN	National Archives of Ireland, Department of Foreign Affairs, League of Nations Series
NAI DFA PE	National Archives of Ireland, Department of Foreign Affairs, Paris Embassy Series
NAI DFA PMUN	National Archives of Ireland, Department of Foreign Affairs, Permanent Mission to the United Nations Series
NAI DFA SF A	National Archives of Ireland, Department of Foreign Affairs, Secretary's Files, A Series
NAI DFA SF P	National Archives of Ireland, Department of Foreign Affairs, Secretary's Files, P Series
NAI DFA SF PS	National Archives of Ireland, Department of Foreign Affairs, Secretary's Files, PS Series
NAI DFA SF S	National Archives of Ireland, Department of Foreign Affairs, Secretary's Files, S Series
NAI DT CAB	National Archives of Ireland, Department of the Taoiseach, Cabinet Minutes
NAI DT G	National Archives of Ireland, Department of the Taoiseach, Government Minutes
NAI DT S	National Archives of Ireland, Department of the Taoiseach, Files Series
NAI ICTU	National Archives of Ireland, Irish Congress of Trade Unions, Congress Archives
PRO	Public Record Office, London
PRO CAB	Public Record Office, London, Cabinet Office
PRO DO	Public Record Office, London, Dominions Office
PRO FO	Public Record Office, London, Foreign Office
PRO HW	Public Record Office, London, Government Code and Cipher School Series
PRO KV	Public Record Office, London, MI5 Series
PRO T	Public Record Office, London, Treasury
UCDA P4	University College Dublin, Archives Department, Hugh Kennedy Papers
UCDA P24	University College Dublin, Archives Department, Ernest Blythe Papers
UCDA P80	University College Dublin, Archives Department, Desmond FitzGerald Papers

Foreword

Patrick Keatinge

At the end of the twentieth century, and not yet eighty years in existence, the Irish state has an assured and, arguably, privileged 'place among the nations'. As a member state of the expanding European Union, Ireland offsets the unavoidable limits of size and location through participation in the world's most complex diplomatic coalition. Relations with its larger neighbour are still central, but more readily managed within this shared context. The conduct of diplomacy now reaches beyond the scope of the professional diplomat and is subject to the (somewhat erratic) attentions of parliamentary committees and non-governmental organisations.

The path towards this outcome has rarely been straightforward and often not clearly understood. Some thirty-five years ago when, as a political scientist, I first came to study Irish foreign policy the state of affairs described above was far from realisation. My chosen subject was problematic; indeed, for many colleagues in my field it was by no means obvious that small states actually had foreign policies. More worrying, I found myself making all too many grand generalisations on the basis of frequent leaps of faith rather than established evidence. There was a good deal of anecdotal 'noise in the system', but the limited amount of scholarly writing – mainly the pioneering work of Nicholas Mansergh – was presented in the context of the history of the British Commonwealth rather than of its onetime slightly awkward member. For many years even the prospect of a national archive to allow a full analysis of the Irish position seemed remote. Both parliamentary and administrative cultures combined to defend the notion that foreign policy, past as well as present, was best left to consenting adults in Iveagh House.

Happily, the few academics working in this environment included some historians with a mission. In the 1960s David Harkness of the Queen's University of Belfast steered the state's Commonwealth experience into home waters. In University College Dublin Ronan Fanning, encouraged by Desmond Williams, developed his interest in Anglo-Irish relations. In University College Cork Joe Lee and Dermot Keogh explored European connections. They and their students, both in Ireland and beyond, came to develop a critical mass of historical writing on Irish foreign policy, of which – as a political scientist – I am rather envious. They successfully lobbied for the long-overdue Irish National Archives, and the Royal Irish Academy has recently launched a major series of official documents. Diplomatic history, Irish style, is here to stay.

That achievement is further demonstrated in this volume. The editors, who have recently published important monographs on Irish policy at the League of Nations and the United Nations, have gathered a team of contributors who are steadily filling out the gaps in a story more complex, diverse and nuanced than that suggested by the pioneering works. At last a central facet of the history of the Irish state is receiving no less than the attention it deserves, for no democracy can operate successfully on the basis of collective amnesia about its foreign relations.

This collection of essays brings us from 1919 up to the mid 1960s, a period when independent Ireland moved through an 'heroic age' of contested statehood, constitutional revision and survival in the most terrible of Europe's internecine wars. The state's involvement in the growing multilateralism of the post-war international system was still tentative, and the conduct of diplomacy remained on a much smaller scale than we have become accustomed to. However, historians of Irish foreign policy will soon approach an archival threshold when their subject matter proliferates, with the great increase in activity associated with membership in the European Community and the conflict in Northern Ireland. The paradox of the last thirty years is that while more evidence of policymaking appears more quickly in the public domain, what is not revealed may be more difficult to trace as technology changes the way in which internal debates are conducted and recorded.

I look forward to seeing how the present and future generations of historians meet this challenge. On the evidence of the professionalism and imagination shown in this volume, I am confident that they will do so successfully.

Dublin, 9 July 1999

The Study of Irish Foreign Policy from Independence to Internationalism

Michael Kennedy and Joseph Morrison Skelly

A REVOLUTION IN THE STUDY OF IRISH FOREIGN POLICY,
1989-99

The application of the term 'revolution' to the writing of Irish history is somewhat over-used, but over the past decade a revolution has definitely taken place in the study and writing of Irish foreign policy and, more particularly, of Irish diplomatic history. When Joseph Lee published his seminal volume *Ireland 1912–85: Politics and Society* in 1989 he could, in all truth, write that Ireland:

> has chosen to ignore the study of international relations, including the study of neutrality, to an extent unparalleled in any other small Western European neutral. Were it not for the efforts of a handful of individuals, the study of Irish foreign policy, not to mention wider issues of international politics, would be wholly neglected.[1]

Now, ten years later, the arrival of many young researchers has swollen the ranks of that initial 'handful of individuals' – Patrick Keatinge, Ronan Fanning, Dermot Keogh, Deirdre McMahon, David Harkness – and a much more vibrant environment exists for the study of Irish foreign policy. This collection of essays is a reflection of that milieu, and the authors who have written chapters for it represent a broad sweep of established and upcoming scholars in the field of Irish diplomatic history. This school is still small by international standards, but within it there is a palpable desire for further development, an aspiration that is shared by the contributors to this volume.

The above quote from *Ireland 1912–85: Politics and Society* does, perhaps, miss one crucial point: the history of Ireland since 1916 is, in many respects, the history of Irish foreign policy. The origins of the modern Irish state lie in its foreign policy, with the desire of Sinn Féin strategists to find a place amongst the nations for an independent Ireland and, before them, the hope of John

---

[1] Joseph Lee, *Ireland, 1912–85: Politics and Society* (Cambridge, 1989), p. 605.

Redmond that a Home Rule Ireland would play its part within the British Empire.² The negotiation of the Anglo–Irish Treaty from October to December 1921 was the major foreign policy *démarche* of the Dáil Eireann administration, an administration which, as one of its first steps, sent Irish representatives to Paris in 1919 to call for Ireland's admission to the Versailles Conference and later sent envoys such as its President, Eamon de Valera, to the United States to rally support for Irish independence. These recurring themes – the desire for international recognition and the assertion of an international role for Ireland – persisted after the Irish state achieved independence in 1922 and animated Irish diplomacy up to, and beyond, the end of Seán Lemass' tenure as Taoiseach in 1966.

Although the narrative of twentieth-century Ireland is inextricably bound up in its foreign affairs, a major problem confronted researchers and writers interested in Irish diplomatic history: for many years this subject was largely inaccessible to them. The archives of the former Department of External Affairs (renamed Foreign Affairs in 1971) remained closed until the early 1990s, a fact not helped by the lack of any national archives legislation nor any concomitant official archival system in Ireland. Legislation had been promised by successive governments since 1973, but did not materialise until the mid 1980s. In the meantime, research into Irish foreign policy was carried out in foreign archives, where Irish diplomatic material was assiduously hunted down and imaginatively used to compensate for the absence of equivalent Irish sources.³

Meanwhile, some Irish government departments, most notably the Department of the Taoiseach, had been selectively releasing files since the mid 1970s, and a few scholars had gained limited access to archival material from the Department of Foreign Affairs.⁴ But in January 1991 a major breakthrough took place as thousands of boxes of material from the Department of Foreign Affairs were released under the National Archives Act (which had been passed in 1986) and made available to the public at the National Archives in Dublin. This was a defining moment in the study of Irish foreign policy: now, for the first time, it was possible to view through primary documents the development of Irish foreign policy from its first principles and follow the actions of Irish diplomats as they defined and implemented that policy. Accordingly, a new body of individuals emerged from these papers. Through their letters, minutes and notes person-

---

2 See Ronan Fanning, Michael Kennedy, Dermot Keogh and Eunan O'Halpin (eds), *Documents on Irish Foreign Policy: Volume I, 1919–22* (Dublin, 1998) and Paul Bew *Ideology and the Irish Question* (Oxford, 1994), respectively, for further details. **3** As examples, see Deirdre McMahon, *Republicans and Imperialists: Anglo–Irish Relations in the 1930s* (New Haven and London, 1984) or John Bowman, *De Valera and the Ulster Question* (Oxford, 1982). **4** See, for example, Dermot Keogh, *The Vatican, the Bishops and Irish Politics, 1919–39* (Cambridge, 1986).

alities such as Joseph Walshe, the long-serving secretary of the Department of External Affairs, his second-in-command, Seán Murphy, and a host of other diplomats, including Seán Lester, Michael MacWhite, Denis Devlin and Leo McCauley, took on central roles in the conduct of Irish diplomacy. Indeed, the history of Irish foreign policy could finally be written from Irish sources.

This first significant step in revolutionising the study of Irish foreign policy was augmented by a second, equally important development: the fortuitous union of readily available research material with a steady supply of postgraduate students eager to trawl through these new sources. These students, generally working under the supervision of the 'handful of individuals' Professor Lee referred to above, claimed their share of this new archival territory, and slowly, but surely, the wider perspectives of Irish foreign policy since 1922 came into view. This progress at the post-graduate level was matched by a corresponding advance at the undergraduate level as, by the mid 1990s, courses on Irish diplomatic history started to appear on university syllabi. In recent years many Irish universities have gone a step further and developed international relations as a field of teaching and research at both the undergraduate and post-graduate levels. Their efforts have been complemented by the growing number of conferences and seminars on Irish foreign policy taking place under the auspices of bodies such as the Royal Irish Academy and the Institute of European Affairs. These academic meetings mirror a growing public interest in Irish foreign policy, particularly over several pressing issues: immigration into Ireland; Ireland's role as a member of the European Union; its future defence and security disposition; neutrality; peacekeeping; international trade; and the country's desire to develop an image abroad as an international good citizen.

An important spin-off from these welcome trends is that more material than ever before is now being published on Irish foreign policy, especially by Irish publishers such as Four Courts Press, Cork University Press, Irish Academic Press and the Institute of Public Administration. Also reflecting this growth is the new dynamism of the Royal Irish Academy's journal *Irish Studies in International Affairs*, which is edited by Professor Michael Cox. The tables of contents of each successive issue of this premier academic publication comprise articles covering a wider and wider array of topics on Irish foreign policy and international relations.

* * *

The chapters in this volume likewise explore a broad range of issues, a panopoly of subjects unimaginable previous to the opening of the Irish National Archives. As such, this collection presents a snapshot of research into Irish foreign policy in the decade following the systematic release of official records. The contributors have written essays within their fields of expertise. Each chapter explores a significant episode, or era, of Irish diplomatic history. In the process, several essential themes emerge: the aspiring role of the newly independent Irish state in the world system and the League of Nations; its nascent diplomatic contacts with the world beyond Europe; its maturing bilateral relations with inter-war Germany, Vichy France and post-war Italy and Austria; the Irish government's attitudes towards Jewish refugees before World War II and the new state of Israel after the war; Ireland's post-war interaction with multilateral economic organisations such as the Marshall Plan, EFTA and the EEC; its pursuit of national interests at the United Nations; and how the principle of *raison d'état* has guided Irish foreign policy from independence to internationalism.

Whereas in 1969, 1979 or even 1989 historians generally felt that Anglo-Irish relations constituted the most important dimension of Ireland's external affairs, it can now be seen that a far wider range of interests commanded the attention of Irish diplomats from 1919 to 1966. That said, Anglo–Irish relations always remained – and, indeed, remain – a most important area of their work. Consequently, another compelling theme surfaces in this collection: Irish foreign policy as a factor in British diplomacy. This motif is developed in essays by Eunan O'Halpin, Troy Davis, Deirdre McMahon and Ronan Fanning that explore, *inter alia*, British intelligence and inter-war Anglo–Irish relations; the Irish American factor in post-war Anglo–American relations; the subtle effect of Irish precedents on the constitutional development of the British Commonwealth; and how Irish neutrality affected British security policy. These chapters, as well as all of the essays in this book, underscore an essential dynamic about international relations that is worth recalling in a volume focusing on one state: the interrelationship of national foreign policies. No country's foreign policy is conducted in a vacuum; diplomats, instead, must constantly assess the international environment. This fact of international political life holds true not only for small states, but large ones like Britain, which, on numerous occasions, had to integrate the behaviour of its smaller neighbour into its own foreign policy calculus.

Overall, the chapters in this volume show how Irish foreign policy in the first fifty years of the state's existence has shifted from asserting Ireland's place in the international system to engaging in that system at bilateral and multilateral levels. They also evince a significant historiographical development: Irish diplomatic history has reached a mature, more sophisticated plane. Scholars in this field are no longer preoccupied with navigating the flood of primary sources let loose in the early 1990s, but are now engaged in a healthy debate about various stages of Irish foreign policy. This trend is evident in essays in this collection that assess the performance of Charles Bewley in Berlin, Ireland's pre-war Jewish refugee policy, its response to the Marshall Plan and the place of national interests in the conduct of Irish foreign policy. This maturation of Irish diplomatic historiography is most welcome. It deepens and broadens our understanding of Ireland's relations with other states, permits a more subtle understanding of Irish statecraft and encourages a more nuanced interpretation of Ireland's engagement with the wider world. It also mirrors a corresponding process underway in the broader historiography of independent Ireland, where, in the wake of new research, scholars are challenging standard interpretations of the Irish past.

THE HISTORIOGRAPHY OF IRISH FOREIGN POLICY, 1919-69

A broad-brush review of the historiography of Irish foreign policy up to the present day will place this book in its proper scholarly context. The mapping of the landscape of Irish foreign policy since 1919 is far from complete, but the process has already covered major areas: Anglo–Irish affairs; neutrality and security policy; Irish–American relations; Church–State relations in an international context; and Ireland's membership in international organisations.[5]

Up to the late 1960s, however, it is impossible to speak of any separate 'historiography' of Irish diplomatic history. Undoubtedly, material exists that could be put into this category, but for the period from the 1920s to the late 1960s it was widely scattered, and no identifiable grouping of foreign policy analysts or writers existed. Frank Pakenham's 1935 study, *Peace by Ordeal*, still the standard account of the 1921 Anglo–Irish Treaty negotiations, T. Desmond Williams' writings on Irish neutrality in *The Leader* and the numerous writings of Nicholas Mansergh on Anglo–Irish relations spring to mind as the main works of note.[6] Articles on Ireland's position in the international system did occasionally appear in journals such as the *Irish Statesman*, *Studies* and, later, *Administration*. Also, while they were not foreign policy journals, publications such as the short-lived *Ireland Today* in the 1930s, *The Bell* in the 1940s and *Christus Rex* in the 1950s carried articles on world affairs and their relation to Ireland. Favourite topics of Catholic journals such as *Christus Rex*, *Irish Monthly* and the *Capuchin Annual* were events in Spain and in Salazar's Portugal. These publications had a relatively small circulation, however, and informed comment on Irish foreign policy remained outside the mainstream.

---

5 See Robert Fisk, *In Time of War: Ireland, Ulster and the Price of Neutrality, 1939–45* (Dublin, 1983); Patrick Keatinge, *A Singular Stance: Irish Neutrality in the 1980s* (Dublin, 1984); Deirdre McMahon, *Republicans and Imperialists: Anglo–Irish Relations in the 1930s* (New Haven and London, 1984); Sean Cronin, *Washington's Irish Policy, 1916–1986: Independence, Partition and Neutrality* (Dublin, 1987); Dermot Keogh, *The Vatican the Bishops and Irish Politics, 1919–39* (Cambridge, 1986), *Ireland and the Vatican: Politics and Diplomacy of Church–State Relations, 1922–60* (Cork, 1995); Michael Kennedy, *Ireland and the League of Nations, 1919–46* (Dublin, 1996); Joseph Morrison Skelly, *Irish Diplomacy at the United Nations, 1945–65* (Dublin, 1997).
6 See *Nationalism and Independence: Selected Irish Papers* (Cork, 1997) for a survey of Mansergh's writings.

Usually, foreign relations received short chapters in general works or, more commonly, went unnoticed. In general, the Irish public showed little interest in Irish foreign policy, except, to use Sean T. O'Ceallaigh's infamous phrase, when it came to 'whipping John Bull'. Diplomacy was viewed as a luxury which the Irish Free State could scarcely afford; indeed, it was frequently equated with imperialism, and it was felt that since the Free State had no empire, by corollary it had no need of a foreign policy.

One can point to the closed nature of the Irish administrative system and the particularly secretive environment of the Department of External Affairs under Joseph Walshe as a reason for this lack of academic interest in Irish foreign policy. Walshe's minister, Eamon de Valera, agreed with his secretary and discouraged the public discussion of foreign policy. Quite simply, information did not leak out from the corridors of power. It is noticeable that one figure writing about Irish foreign policy in the 1950s, T. Desmond Williams, had an inside line to Iveagh House and carried on a confidential correspondence with diplomats Michael MacWhite and Conor Cruise O'Brien. Joseph Lee notes that Williams' articles on neutrality in *The Leader*, 'though unannotated ... were clearly based on an extensive command of archival material'; it would be fair to say that contacts with Iveagh House were also an important source.

This lack of interest in Irish foreign policy at a public level continued into the 1960s, despite the fact that Ireland had by then developed a distinct international personality. Ireland's high profile in the United Nations, particularly the deployment of Irish troops in the Congo as part of the ONUC peacekeeping mission, marked the first time that many Irish people began to take an interest in Ireland's external relations. The death of Irish soldiers in the Congo, particularly at the Niemba ambush, brought home to many in Ireland the fact that their country had developed a role for itself on the world stage and was active in the United Nations.

THE HISTIOGRAPHY OF IRISH FOREIGN POLICY, 1969-99

The publication of two pioneering studies, David Harkness' *The Restless Dominion* in 1969 and Patrick Keatinge's *The Formulation of Irish Foreign Policy* four years later, marks the real beginning of dedicated writing on Irish foreign policy. Harkness' book was written without access to official Irish sources, but by using the private papers of former Irish foreign ministers and through widespread interviews his book reconstructed the role played by the Irish Free State in the transformation of the British Empire into the modern Commonwealth. Whereas Harkness' work was historical, Keatinge took the understanding of Irish foreign policy in a different direction and applied the techniques of political science to the first fifty years of Irish diplomacy. The result was the first full length study of the process by which Irish foreign policy was made.

On 1 January 1969 the British fifty year rule covering the release of state papers was relaxed to thirty years. Papers from the Colonial Office, Dominions Office and Foreign Office, all ministries which played a key role in Anglo–Irish relations, were now available up to 1939. This was of major importance to Irish historians. Deprived of access to Irish archives, they descended on the British Public Record Office to discover new and important material relating to Irish foreign policy. At the same time, American archives were also revealing new insights into Ireland's external relations. From 1969 and through the 1970s a steady stream of studies on various aspects of Irish foreign policy began to appear. In addition to Harkness' and Keatinge's works, five equally important texts were published throughout the decade: T. Desmond Williams and Kevin B. Nolan's *Ireland in the War Years and After, 1939–51* (1969); Joseph Carroll's *Ireland in the War Years, 1939–45* (1975); T. Ryle Dwyer's *Irish Neutrality and the USA, 1919–47* (1977); Patrick Keatinge's *A Place amongst the Nations: Issues in Irish Foreign Policy* (1978); and Ronan Fanning's *The Irish Department of Finance, 1922–58* (Dublin, 1978). While the Williams and Nolan volume was not strictly a work on foreign policy, William's 'Conclusion' was of considerable importance to the field. Fanning's volume, a political and administrative history of the most senior Irish government department, was, crucially, based on previously unseen material from the department's archive and remains a groundbreaking assessment of the creation and functioning of the Irish administrative system. By looking at the role of the Department of Finance during the Emergency it added greatly to the understanding of wartime policymaking in Ireland. Thus World War II and Irish neutrality were the first areas of Irish foreign policy outside of Anglo–Irish relations where progress was made towards an understanding of the wider context.

Important works on Anglo–Irish relations continued to appear, such as Patrick O'Farrell's *Ireland's English Question* (1975), John Peck's *Dublin from Downing Street* (1978) and Tom Jones' revealing account of the years 1918 to 1925 in volume three of *Whitehall Diary* (edited by Keith Middlemass, 1971).

Throughout the 1970s several Irish academics, most notably David Harkness at Queen's University Belfast, Ronan Fanning at University College Dublin and Patrick Keatinge at Trinity College Dublin, continued to specialise in the study of Irish foreign policy. During the 1973–77 coalition government, an attempt was made to bring these developments together in an Irish version of the British Royal Institute of International Affairs. The plan fell through in its original form, but the proposed research body reemerged in the shape of the Royal Irish Academy's National Committee for the Study of International Affairs, which was formed in 1977. The National Committee brings together representatives from academic and government organisations and provides a forum for the study and discussion of important questions relating to Ireland's participation in international affairs.

The National Committee published the first volume of its journal *Irish Studies in International Affairs* in 1979. Now entering its third decade, it is the only Irish journal dedicated to covering Irish foreign relations. In its first ten years it published many important articles on various aspects of Irish foreign policy, such as Ronan Fanning's 'Irish Neutrality – an Historical Perspective' (1982) and Dermot Keogh's 'Eamon de Valera and Hitler: an Analysis of International Reaction to the Visit to the German Minister, May 1945' (1989), as well as articles by diplomats and civil servants, including Con Cremin, Noel Dorr, Padraic MacKernan and Tadhg Ó Cearbhaill. The journal proved to be an important source of new material and provided a focus for the slowly developing academic field of Irish foreign policy.

* * *

The limited release of official records by some Irish departments of state, most notably cabinet minutes and associated files by the Department of the Taoiseach from 1973, greatly helped diplomatic historians in Ireland. So, too, did the increasing availability of private papers, a process in which the University College Dublin Archives Department played an important role.[7] By the mid 1980s the research into Irish diplomatic history carried out in London, Washington – and now Dublin – was beginning to appear in print. John Bowman's *De Valera and the Ulster Question* (1982), Deirdre McMahon's *Republicans and Imperialists* (1985) and Trevor Salmon's *Unneutral Ireland* (1989) showed just what could be done with a mix of Irish, British and American sources. A general text which had important implications for the study of neutrality was Ronan Fanning's *Independent Ireland* (Dublin, 1983). By using British material augmented with newly released records from the Department of the Taoiseach, this book showed for the first time the facilities that Ireland had granted to the Allies during the Second World War.

A 'big picture' study of the history of Irish foreign policy awaited its author, but other scholars continued to illuminate parts of the overall scene. Dermot Keogh's *The Vatican, the Bishops and Irish Politics* (1986) and John Duggan's *Neutral Ireland and the Third Reich* (1985) were clear evidence of this trend. Thus the monograph, showing the fruits of concentrated research, remained the main outlet for Irish diplomatic historians.

The publication in 1989 of Dermot Keogh's *Ireland and Europe, 1919–48* marked a new departure in the writing of Irish diplomatic history. Here was the first historical survey of Irish foreign policy written with unparalleled access to the archives of the Department of Foreign Affairs. The book was republished in 1990 with extra chapters covering the period from 1948 to 1989. With its wide

---

7 For example, the papers of Ernest Blythe, Richard Mulcahy, Hugh Kennedy and Patrick McGilligan are deposited in the University College Dublin Archives Department.

scope, this book identified many new themes and moved the study of Irish foreign policy further beyond Anglo–Irish relations and Irish neutrality. It became a key text for younger researchers setting out after 1991 into the unknown territory of the Department of Foreign Affairs collection at the National Archives.

* * *

As a glance at the select bibliography at the end of this volume shows, research, writing and publishing on Irish foreign policy have expanded exponentially in the 1990s. Works dealing with Ireland's relations with India and Latin America, as well as the publication of new research into areas like neutrality, censorship and inter-war diplomatic history, show how widely diversified the field has become.[8] The decision in 1995 by the Department of Foreign Affairs and the Royal Irish Academy to proceed with the Documents on Irish Foreign Policy series, and the appearance of volume one of the series in October 1998, marked another milestone in the study of Irish diplomatic history. As the 1990s end it is safe to say that after many precarious years of merely existing rather than developing, Irish diplomatic history is now firmly established in its own right as an important sub-section of modern Irish historiography. Specialists in the field exist in most Irish universities and they are publishing regularly; undergraduate and postgraduate programmes on international relations and European studies are thriving; research through the plentiful archives of the Department of Foreign Affairs continues apace; and scholars based abroad offer their own fresh perspectives on Irish foreign policy.

THE DEPARTMENT OF EXTERNAL AFFAIRS, 1919–69

A review of the first fifty years of the history of the Department of Foreign Affairs will provide useful context for the chapters that follow. Today it is one of the primary administrative departments of the Irish government, but in the 1920s it fought an uphill battle to maintain its existence. From 1919 to 1922 the current department's predecessor, then entitled the Ministry, or Department, of Foreign Affairs, had sent representatives around the globe to secure Ireland's request for international recognition, and its members had participated in the negotiations that led to the 1921 Anglo–Irish Treaty. This high point of Irish diplomacy quickly became its nadir as the split over the Treaty and the descent into Civil War tore the fledgling department apart.

---

8 See, for example, Dennis Holmes and Michael Holmes, *Ireland and India: Connections, Comparisons, Contrasts* (Dublin, 1997); Peadar Kirby, *Ireland and Latin America* (Dublin, 1992); Donal Ó Drisceoil, *Censorship in Ireland, 1939–45: Neutrality, Politics and Society* (Cork, 1996); Mervyn O'Driscoll, *Irish–German Relations* (forthcoming).

It fell to Joseph Walshe, who first was its acting secretary and later its secretary, to rebuild the shattered department, now called the Department of External Affairs. With a staff of about twenty he directed the first steps the Irish diplomatic service took on the world stage. Throughout the 1920s External Affairs remained small, under-funded and constantly under the threat of absorption into the Department of the President. Walshe fought continual battles with the Department of Finance to secure funding. In May 1927 he could write to H.P. Boland at Finance that the 'Washington and New York [legation] staffs are sadly in need of attention, and our whole system of representation in Europe requires re-organisation. But it would be stupid to submit proposals concerning our foreign establishment until our position at home has been placed on a solid basis'.[9] This quote succinctly encapsulates the position of the department in the mid 1920s.

Walshe was finally promoted to secretary in August 1927. A small expansion took place in the late 1920s, as legations were opened in Berlin, Paris and the Holy See, thus augmenting existing missions in London, Geneva and Washington and a small number of overseas trade representatives. For its size, the department had achieved much by the time Eamon de Valera took over from W.T. Cosgrave as President of the Executive Council in March 1932. Two Ministers for External Affairs, Desmond FitzGerald (1922–7) and Patrick McGilligan (1927–32), had overseen Ireland's admission to the League of Nations, undertaken a virtual revolution in the development of the Commonwealth through the Balfour Declaration (1926) and the Statute of Westminster (1931) and expanded the Dominion status granted to the Irish Free State in 1921 to such an extent that the state now had the right to exchange diplomatic representatives, to negotiate and sign treaties in her own right and to issue separate Irish passports for her citizens.

* * *

The 1930s, a decade during which Eamon de Valera was both Minister for External Affairs and President of the Executive Council (Taoiseach from 1938), was a much more secure period for the Department of External Affairs. Though the department was still under-resourced, Walshe and the legal section in the department (John Hearne and Michael Rynne) played a key role in de Valera's Anglo–Irish policy, as did Ireland's High Commissioner in London, J.W. Dulanty. At the League of Nations Ireland's permanent representative, Seán Lester, was seconded to the League of Nations staff as High Commissioner in Danzig. The first intake of cadets into the department included a number of rising stars, foremost amongst them Freddie Boland, Con Cremin and William Warnock. Opening missions at Ottawa and Rome in 1938, Ireland's diplomatic service entered its third decade in a much stronger position than it had started its second.

9 NAI DFA SF A 247/1, 5 May 1927.

It would not be unfair to say that the Department of External Affairs was the major weapon Ireland employed to protect her neutrality in the Second World War. Unable to rely on a credible display of military power, Ireland's diplomats became her first line of defence against both Allied and Axis threats. De Valera and Walshe, ably aided by Freddie Boland and John Dulanty, twisted and turned Ireland's policy of ambiguous neutrality to ensure that threats were countered. But hidden by a fire-wall of censorship, Ireland's apparently pristine neutrality was, in fact, extremely favourable to the Allies. And despite the department's achievements, the wartime experience was a trying one. Many historians have interpreted Walshe's actions during the war years as verging on support for the Axis powers. To other observers, however, he seems to have suffered from a period of prolonged despair after the fall of France and his pro-Axis outbursts may have been symptomatic of a growing fear that Britain would be defeated by Germany.

* * *

Ireland's foreign service faced a daunting task in the post-1945 world. Wartime neutrality had wiped out much of the good-will that had accrued to the state during the inter-war years: her stand at the League of Nations was forgotten and had been replaced by the memory of de Valera's visit to sign Hitler's book of condolences in May 1945. While correct in terms of complete neutrality, de Valera need not have signed the book, but may have done so in order to send an unsubtle message to the Allies, who had attempted to interfere with Irish neutrality in 1944 when they demanded the removal of all Axis diplomats from Dublin. Whatever the reasons for de Valera's visit, it certainly did not appeal to the Soviet Union, which vetoed Ireland's application to join the United Nations in 1946.

The years from 1946 until Ireland's admission into the United Nations in 1955 tend to be seen as 'wilderness' years. But they most certainly were not. They witnessed the widespread restructuring of the Department of External Affairs, with Frederick H. Boland taking over from Walshe as secretary and the internal framework of the department being revamped to take account of the new economic-based interests of Irish foreign policy. These years saw Ireland appoint her first ambassador (heretofore foreign diplomatic representatives had not held ranks higher than minister plenipotentiary and envoy extraordinary), as Joseph Walshe became the Irish ambassador to the Vatican in 1946. New offices in Buenos Aires, Stockholm, the Hague and Canberra were also opened, epitomising Ireland's desire to adopt a more global foreign policy.

This aim was also reflected in Irish participation in the European Recovery Programme (the Marshall Plan), the Council of Europe and in other multilateral organisations such as the Food and Agriculture Organisation and the International Civil Aviation Organisation. These events are normally crowded out by the repeal of the 1936 External Relations Act in 1948, the declaration of the Irish Republic in 1949 and Ireland's refusal to join NATO (also in 1949), but they remain important landmarks on Ireland's journey to reintegration into the world system, which was now dominated by the Cold War.

* * *

Between the wars the Department of External Affairs had acquired the tag of the 'Cinderella' department, unwanted and underfunded by the Department of Finance. In the post-war years the Department of External Affairs developed in stature to rival Finance as one of the primary departments of state. Foreign policy became based much more on economics and less on the politics of international recognition. Ireland's involvement in the Marshall Plan began this process, and it was augmented by the widespread adoption of economic planning by Irish economists and officials in the late 1950s. Most notably exemplified by T.K. Whitaker, this policy exhorted export-led growth in order to build up the Irish economy. The Department of External Affairs began to play a vital part in the international development of the Irish economy, and this process was paralleled within the department as the old Commercial Matters Section was reformed into the Economic Division and the Political and Treaty Section was split to become a separate Political Division and an International Organisations Section.

Admission to the United Nations in 1955 commenced what has sometimes been seen as the 'Golden Age' of Irish diplomacy, as Frank Aiken, Minister for External Affairs from 1957 to 1969, raised the Irish delegation's profile in the General Assembly to new heights. Certainly, the state relished its role in the United Nations as one of the small, independent nations, but as the 1950s gave way to the 1960s Ireland was drawn more closely into the Western sphere of influence through a mixture of her anti-communist stance in the Cold War and the desire of the Taoiseach, Seán Lemass, to secure Irish admission into the European Economic Community (EEC).

The years from the early 1960s to the end of the Lemass era in 1966 saw External Affairs retain its position as one of the top three government departments along with Finance and Industry and Commerce. With Hugh McCann as its secretary, the department played a key role in Sean Lemass' economic policy, particularly as Ireland steered towards Europe and applied for membership of the EEC in 1961. The rejection by France of the Irish and British applications in 1963 was to remain a blot on the diplomatic landscape until 1973, when Ireland eventually became a member of the organisation, but it did not in any way reduce the scope of the department's operations. If anything, the work of the Department of External Affairs continued to increase in the mid 1960s as Ireland embarked on trade negotiations with Britain that led to the 1965 Anglo–Irish Free Trade Area Agreement. Thus by 1966, after almost a half century of pursuing Ireland's national interests, the Department of External Affairs had not only secured a place for independent Ireland in the world order, but had promoted peace and progress abroad in the finest tradition of Irish internationalism.

Taking the World Stage:
Creating an Irish Foreign Policy in the 1920s

Gerard Keown[1]

INTRODUCTION

In the ninth century take of the voyages of Saint Brendan there is the story of two Irishmen who boarded a ship for France. When they arrived after their long and arduous journey they headed for the fair, where they stood amidst the other merchants and shouted that they had wisdom for sale. When Irishmen set out for France a thousand years later it was not as merchants that they went, but as spokesmen for a newly independent state. When it convened in January 1919 one of Dáil Éireann's first acts was to appoint a foreign minister and despatch envoys to argue the case for Irish independence in foreign capitals. The immediate goal was to win international support for the campaign for independence from Britain, but there was also the desire to breach what Sinn Féin founder Arthur Griffith had described as the paper wall which had been erected around their country in the hundred years after the Act of Union. While Sinn Féin was ultimately unsuccessful in securing international recognition for an Irish republic, the outside world learnt a little about Irish aspirations through the efforts of these envoys. More significantly, perhaps, the experience confirmed the belief of those nationalists predisposed to contemplate an Irish foreign policy that the country could develop a distinctive relationship with the outside world once it had achieved self-government.

After independence in 1922 it became the responsibility of the Department of External Affairs to communicate the fact, and the particular form, of the new Irish state's existence to foreigners. But as Desmond FitzGerald, the first Minister of External Affairs of the Irish Free State, explained to the Dáil, this would be no easy task, for 'Ireland is not only an unknown quantity in a neutral form, but in a negative form'.[2] The new state would have to market itself abroad and build up recognition of the symbols it had chosen to represent itself with. It would also have to communicate to a well disposed, though largely ignorant,

---

[1] The views expressed in this essay are the author's alone; he is writing here in a personal capacity. [2] *Dáil Deb.*, 7, 799, 15 May 1924.

world the values for which it would stand. These twin objectives occupied Irish diplomats for the first years of the Free State and, in seeking to realise them, they would find time and again that their task was made all the harder by the ill-defined nature of the state's independence and its continuing links with Britain.

* * *

The Irish Free State came into existence at a time of change, when the domestic powers of the Dominions were gradually increasing, and thus received the same status within the British Commonwealth as Canada. But while internal autonomy had already been secured, the Commonwealth states were not free to pursue an independent line in the field of foreign relations. Like the other Dominions, the Free State was entitled to a High Commissioner in London, and trade commissioners elsewhere, but neither enjoyed real diplomatic status. British embassies represented the Dominions in third countries, the British empire acted as a diplomatic unit and the British Foreign Office determined policy after consultation with Dominion premiers – as and when it saw fit. Finally, because of the diplomatic unity of the empire, Commonwealth agreements were not regarded as international treaties, and international treaties were not held to be binding on internal Commonwealth relations. It was against this backdrop that the Free State appeared on the world stage.

The Dominions, however, were individual members of the League of Nations, and this would do much to bring about the formal equality of the Commonwealth states. At a series of Imperial Conferences in the 1920s the Dominions cooperated to secure freedom of action on the world stage. The story of this development, and the leading role played by the Irish Free State, has been described elsewhere.[3] It was a remarkable transformation. In 1922 none of the Dominions had a diplomat accredited in a foreign capital. In 1920 the Canadians had secured the right to appoint a representative in Washington, but had not exercised that right. It was the Irish who established the first of many precedents by appointing a minister to Washington in 1924.[4] He was subsequently joined by a Canadian and a South African colleague. By 1932, ten years after independence, the Free State had established diplomatic relations with the United States, France, Germany and the Holy See; had been elected to a seat on the Council of the League of Nations; was concluding its own political and commercial treaties; and enjoyed complete freedom of action in the Commonwealth as a result of the Statute of Westminster, which was passed in 1931.

---

3 For an account of this development, see D.W. Harkness, *The Restless Dominion* (London, 1969). **4** In the period before World War II only major states exchanged ambassadors; other countries were represented abroad by ministers plenipotentiary, who operated from legations rather than embassies.

THE FOREIGN POLICY OF SMALL STATES

There has been a tendency in studies of Irish foreign policy to concentrate on relations with Britain and the constitutional development of the Commonwealth, to the exclusion of other foreign policy arenas. In such narratives, centre stage is occupied by constitutional lawyers in smoke-filled back rooms at Imperial Conferences. However, having accepted a nationalist impetus to push Commonwealth bonds as far as they would stretch, this approach to Irish foreign policy then relegated such considerations to the sideline, conveying the impression that reform of the Commonwealth was an end in itself. While there is no denying the centrality of Anglo–Irish or Commonwealth relations, it is now generally accepted that they represent but one aspect of a wider policy, in which both the League of Nations and bilateral relations with other states featured just as prominently.

In particular, focusing on the Commonwealth has meant that a number of similarities with other newly independent European countries have been overlooked. In 1923 the Free State was one of a number of states that had achieved independence following the upheavals of World War I. Many of these states were small in both size and population, commanded limited resources and supported dependent economies. Along with Eastern European countries such as Finland, Czechoslovakia and Estonia, in the decade after its independence Ireland embarked upon a programme of creating a separate and distinct image, using the recognised vocabulary of statehood. In its adoption of a flag, anthem, and national emblems, and in issuing its own passports, for example, the Free State had more in common with these countries than it did with many of the Dominions. And because of their good voting record at the League of Nations, it was countries such as Denmark and Norway which were frequently held up as examples to be followed. It might, accordingly, be helpful to consider early Irish foreign policy in small state terms.

There are a number of general observations that can be made about the foreign policy interests of small states. Firstly, they tend to have fewer vital interests than their larger neighbours, which can be accommodated with greater ease. They likewise tend to be more interested in a stable international environment and, accordingly, set store by the rule of law governing as many aspects of their external relations as possible. These three basic characteristics of the small state predicament governed much Irish thinking about foreign affairs in the years after independence. For instance, the Free State was an enthusiastic advocate of the codification of international law throughout the inter-war years. Desmond FitzGerald's successor as foreign minister, Patrick McGilligan, told the Dáil in 1931 that 'we are recognised at Geneva as one of the main upholders of the complete independence of the smaller states'.[5] In

---

5 *Dáil Deb.*, 39, 1281, 1 July 1931.

this there was a dual objective – extending international law would benefit the country, just as it would help all small states. It would also strengthen Dublin's hand in constitutional negotiations within the Commonwealth. Irish politicians were also committed to a pacific approach to conflict resolution and to collective efforts to reduce injustice in international relations. As FitzGerald told the Dáil in 1925, the view of the small nations would 'always be nearer the ten commandments than the point of view of the big nations'.[6] Although these convictions also reflected small state interests, they were, nonetheless, sincerely held.

INDEPENDENCE AND FOREIGN POLICY

It is, perhaps, unremarkable that a newly independent state should seek to use its foreign policy to bring itself to notice, particularly when not only the fact, but also the form, of that independence was unclear. With Cumann na nGaedheal maintaining that the Treaty was an international instrument, it would have undermined this position to have conceded that there was no need for a foreign policy. As Leo Kohn observed in 1932, the existence of a foreign ministry exemplified 'more than any other functional innovation the new political status of Ireland'.[7] Early Irish policy towards both the League of Nations and the Commonwealth was driven by the need to stress the country's legal status as a platform from which to pursue a fuller foreign policy. The ability to invoke League opinion in its support would prove invaluable as the Free State pushed the boundaries of Dominion status to their fullest extent during the 1920s. An early example of this was the registration of the Anglo–Irish Treaty with the secretariat of the League of Nations in 1924, which was achieved in the face of stiff British opposition. By securing recognition of the Treaty as an international instrument, the Free State reinforced its status as a sovereign state before the rest of the world.

Ireland's insistence on status was not a narrow nationalist preoccupation, however; practical benefits of an economic, political and security nature flowed from the assertion of full sovereignty. For example, the power to conclude separate commercial treaties and appoint trade and diplomatic representatives abroad was seen as being central to the development of a more balanced economy. Government departments did not believe that British embassies would adequately promote the country's economic interests abroad. The Canadians shared this view, and this was also one of the reasons why they opened their own

---

6 *Dáil Deb.*, 11, 1452, 13 May 1925.   **7** Leo Kohn, *The Constitution of the Irish Free State* (London, 1932), p. 318.   **8** See, in particular, H. Gordon Skilling, *Canadian Representation Abroad* (Toronto, 1945), p. xv.

missions in foreign capitals.[8] At the same time, the Irish had to be careful not to prejudice their position in other spheres when asserting their rights at international fora. When the government exercised its right in 1927 to attend a naval disarmament conference, for instance, it did not want any intervention it might make to be used by the British to extract a contribution to the cost of running the British navy.[9] It was often a fine line that delegates had to walk.

* * *

The forging of a separate foreign policy also formed part of a broader campaign of identity building which the new state engaged in after independence. In this regard, a primary ambition was to follow what might be described as a prestige policy, one designed to make the Free State a respected international unit. From the outset, Dublin aspired to a responsible and disinterested foreign policy. Successive governments aimed to increase the country's status by behaving as an exemplary international actor. This was possible largely because there were no major issues outstanding with other countries, apart from Britain. It was also based on a calculation that being an international good citizen was the most effective means of advancing Irish interests where they coincided with those of other small states. As an official memorandum put it in 1927, 'conciliation and cooperation are the surest means of strengthening our position within and without the Commonwealth. That is the road to national prestige and prosperity'.[10] It was hoped that this role would bring with it influence: other states would see in Ireland a disinterested and committed member of the international community and therefore seek its counsel on issues which might touch its interests. Irish policy at Geneva, for example, was influenced by this assumption, and demands for Commonwealth liberties were often couched in these terms, too. This reading of the international system dovetailed with a desire to pursue a high-profile presence on the world stage, if only to advertise the country's independence. It bore fruit in a policy of attending conferences in which the country had no substantial interest and in the signing of agreements which it was unlikely to be in a position to break. This policy was also intended to make other states more likely to uphold Irish rights should they ever seriously be challenged by Britain. Thus we can say that Ireland's good neighbourliness was also a response to its continuing link with Britain, as each time the Irish voted against a British interest, or ignored a joint Commonwealth position, they further illustrated their independence. As a Belfast newspaper ruefully observed, 'it is curious how at every turn this League of Nations comes up to hit us in the eye'.[11]

9 NAI DFA BE, box 5, Walshe to MacWhite, 17 June 1927. **10** National Library of Ireland, Free State Papers, 21, 817(I), Walshe memorandum, Status of the *Saorstát* Summarised, August 1927. **11** *Morning Post*, 17 December 1924.

THE LEAGUE OF NATIONS

Like other small states at the time, the Irish were helped in their efforts to map out a foreign policy by the League of Nations. Possessing few resources, and even less clout, a small state is generally able to pursue an active foreign policy only when the international system provides an opportunity for it to do so. The League of Nations not only strengthened the Free State's sovereignty by admitting it in 1923 as a full and equal member, it also provided an arena in which it could purse a multilateral foreign policy in spite of its limited resources. Geneva gave the Free State access to a network of information on global issues and allowed it to interact with over fifty different states without having to use British embassy channels. As one newspaper put it, the Irish representative to the League was quite literally the country's 'ambassador to the rest of the world'.[12]

The Irish Free State joined the League in September 1923. The country was voted in unanimously, and its delegates took their seats to a standing ovation. It was widely believed at the time that because it was perceived to have no international ambitions or axes to grind the Free State would be able to facilitate agreement between rival European states – and thereby aspire to a particular role. Desmond FitzGerald told the Dáil that 'we have only one small voice, but I think we will use that voice to good effect'.[13] As the 1920s progressed the Free State spoke out on a number of issues at Geneva, voting against British interests at the 1925 opium conference and again voicing its support for naval disarmament in 1927 in the face of an agreed Commonwealth position that the terms on offer were unsatisfactory. Among the first acts of the new state were to remove reparations taxes on German imports and to support German membership of the League, even to the extent of supplying League documents to the Germans prior to the country's admission in September 1926.

Belief in the Free State's ability to take a lead in advancing a liberal agenda was widespread. The country was elected to a non-permanent seat on the League Council in 1930 due to its record as a disinterested member state and having acquitted itself well in its first, unsuccessful bid in 1926. Even the secretary general of the League, Sir Eric Drummond, felt that Ireland could make a contribution greater than its size might indicate.[14] Membership of the League Council, however, would expose many of the constraints on a small state as much as it offered new opportunities to pursue a principled position, such as during the Manchurian crisis of 1931.[15] Still, Irish diplomats strove to base inter-

---

[12] *Connacht Tribune*, 19 January 1929. [13] *Dáil Deb.*, 16, 259, 2 June 1926. [14] NAI DFA 217/44, Lester to Walshe, 23 April 1929. [15] See Michael Kennedy, '"Principle Well-Seasoned with the Sauce of Realism": Seán Lester, Joseph Walshe and the Definition of the Irish Free State's Policy towards Manchuria', *Irish Studies in International Affairs*, vol. 6 (October 1995), pp 79–94.

ventions, wherever possible, on disinterest, and this independent stance reached its peak in 1932 when Eamon de Valera's critical speech as president of the League Council was greeted in stony silence by the big power delegates.

THE GENEVA PROTOCOL AND THE COURT OF INTERNATIONAL JUSTICE

If the League of Nations enabled the Free State to develop a broader based foreign policy than would otherwise have been possible, it also brought into focus the limitations posed by the continuing link with Britain and the Dominions. Just how constraining this was became apparent in 1925. In that year the government was invited to sign the Geneva Protocol for the Pacific Settlement of International Disputes. Among other things, signatories would be bound to apply military and economic sanctions against an aggressor state if it refused League offers of arbitration. While sanctions could be imposed by a two-thirds vote of the Council, it would require a unanimous vote for them to be lifted. Britain opposed the measure, wishing to preserve its freedom to protect its imperial possessions around the world. The Dominions were prepared to follow the British lead, with the exception of the Free State. The ideals underpinning the Protocol, after all, were in keeping with Irish policy at Geneva; rejection would cause lasting damage to the country's image as a model League member and foster suspicions that the Irish would always dance to a Foreign Office tune. But there were other factors to consider. It was unclear whether a Dominion could be at war without automatically involving the rest of the Commonwealth, including Ireland. If Britain itself was the aggressor, Free State sanctions would be potentially disastrous to Irish trade. The government was also anxious, with Northern Ireland in mind, to avoid having to impose sanctions on a country that had acted in support of a minority in a neighbouring state. Thus the Irish found themselves in a difficult position. To accept the Protocol would be to alienate Britain and could result in potentially disastrous consequences. To reject it would be to undo much of the good work achieved so far at the League. As it was, forthright statements of support in the Dáil, coupled with judicious inaction, averted a no-win scenario, since the Protocol was dealt a fatal blow by Britain's rejection before the Free State had to declare its position at Geneva. Although the government escaped with its policy largely intact, the conclusions drawn by the Department of External Affairs were not encouraging. A postmortem report concluded that, with regard to the Geneva Protocol, the Free State 'was not in the position of an independent state'.[16]

[16] UCDA P24 179, Department of External Affairs memorandum on the Geneva Protocol, 6 March 1925.

The situation had changed four years later, when the Free State was invited to sign the optional clause of the Permanent Court of International Justice in 1929. By then the Irish had secured the right to conclude their own treaties, the Dominions were appointing diplomats in foreign capitals and Irish legations had just opened in Paris, Berlin and the Vatican. Furthermore, along with the other Dominions and the great powers, the country had been invited to sign the Kellogg–Briand Pact for the renunciation of war; the other small states were invited to accede to the pact at a later date. The government had also grown in experience and had an eye on securing those final concessions that would result in the Statute of Westminster. Again, there was an agreed Commonwealth position that the Court of International Justice's jurisdiction should not cover disputes within the Commonwealth. The Department of External Affairs advised that the only way to put an end to the diplomatic unity of the empire would be to sign the clause without this reservation – and to do so first.[17] Acting on this advice, Patrick McGilligan, the Minister for External Affairs, signed the clause before Britain and the Dominions and defied the Commonwealth position by stipulating that he was doing so without reservation. As far as Dublin was concerned, a dispute with one of the Dominions, or even Britain, should be adjudicated in the same way as a dispute with any other state. Thus by acting so forthrightly the government ensured that the Free State once more appeared as an exemplary League member less than a year before it successfully stood for election to the League Council in 1930. McGilligan was careful not to burn his bridges, however, and told the Dáil upon his return from Geneva that the government would first exhaust Commonwealth tribunals before bringing a dispute with Britain before the international court.[18] Once again the Free State had preserved its right to independent arbitration, even if it might choose not to exercise that right.

NATIONAL SECURITY, ECONOMICS AND FOREIGN POLICY

Self interest and principle alone did not enable the Irish to aspire to a disinterested line on international issues and develop a new tradition of international good citizen. The country was also fortunate in its geographical location. Under the terms of the Anglo–Irish Treaty the Free State effectively found itself in a British naval exclusion zone and, with British garrisons stationed in Northern Ireland, any potential aggressor could be sure that Britain would not stand idly by. Thus, apart from some concerns about a possible German or British invasion

---

17 NA DFA BE, box 5, MacWhite memorandum, n.d., 1929.   **18** *Dáil Deb.*, 33, 893, 26 February 1930.

in 1940, the Free State could rest assured that its territorial integrity was not at risk. The British military umbrella also enabled the country to maintain a small army for purposes of defence alone, and in condemning the arms trade, for example, or supporting calls for disarmament, Irish governments did not risk compromising the state's security. Dublin could also claim that it had disarmed after the Civil War, thereby acquiring a degree of moral standing. More importantly, because its security was never seriously in doubt, the Free State could afford to adopt a more principled line in its foreign policy than other small states. The contrast with the Baltic States is striking. As an Estonian minister lamented in a 1923 interview with *Studies*, while the Free State might not enjoy complete sovereignty, his own republic's unfettered independence was no defence against the predatory intentions of Berlin or Moscow.[19]

The Free State was also influenced by its vulnerable economic position. The Irish economy was heavily dependent on the British market, with the vast bulk of exports destined for the United Kingdom. At one level, Irish foreign policy can thus be interpreted as an attempt to reconcile conflicting political and economic interests. Economic dependency dictated a certain Commonwealth orientation, so, when Britain conceded in 1926 that the Dominions were 'international units individually in the fullest sense of the term', the Department of External Affairs was careful to insert a clause into commercial treaties to protect the preferential tariffs Irish goods enjoyed in Commonwealth markets. Similarly, although nationalist economics envisaged a growth in markets outside the United Kingdom, Free State manufacturers benefited from the substantial advertising budgets of imperial trade promotion agencies once 'Buy British' had been removed.[20] The currency link with sterling was also of great importance, meaning the Free State's credit was guaranteed by the British Treasury, allowing it to weather financial storms where other new states foundered.

THE IRISH DIASPORA

One of the most significant factors affecting foreign policy calculations was the Irish diaspora. The idea of Ireland as a mother country ran through nationalist and, subsequently, government thinking on foreign policy. Throughout the 1920s small state rhetoric was paralleled by talk of the diaspora, the tens of millions of Irish and their offspring who had settled around the world, which led successive Irish governments to believe they could punch above their weight. As Treaty signatory and former foreign minister George Gavan Duffy put it in

19 Francis McCullagh, 'The Baltic States from an Irish Point of View', *Studies*, vol. 12, no. 14 (March 1923), pp 7–25. **20** NAI DT S 5198, Ó hEigeartaigh to McDunphy, 10 November 1926.

1923, 'we are a world race with a unique opportunity as a link between the old world and the new'.²¹ Memoranda to London frequently reminded the British that Ireland was also a mother country, as did speeches in the Dáil, and diplomats at times purported to represent the interests of the entire Irish race as much as the Irish state. The pro-government weekly, the *Star*, went so far as to state in 1929 that the new Irish minister to the Vatican would speak for Irishmen around the world.²²

This 'global' potential had been vividly illustrated by Eamon de Valera's tour of the United States in 1920. Although Washington had not recognised the Sinn Féin government, it was largely American money which funded the propaganda effort elsewhere around the world. The failure of Sinn Féin to secure United States recognition of Ireland in 1921, however, revealed an important gap between American sentiment and American self-interest. But once independence had been achieved it was hoped that this would change. The United States was the most important of all the countries in which the Irish had settled in large numbers. It was in Washington that the Free State opened its first legation in 1924, an act the Americans reciprocated two years later, and the United States was the site of the first Irish state visit in 1928. When discussing Ireland's place in the world, Dáil deputies made frequent, and sometimes florid, references to its supposed influence in the United States: the Fianna Fáil TD Patrick Little, for example, called for the government to set an example to the rest of the world by bringing about a rapprochement between Britain and America over naval disarmament in 1929.²³ The belief persisted that the country could act as a bridge linking America with Europe and the Commonwealth, and this idea was used in 1930 when canvassing support for a seat on the League Council.

* * *

Apart from the substantial influence which Britain commanded in American political circles, hopes for close cooperation with the United States received two early setbacks. First, attempts to organise a World League of the Irish race, based in Dublin and funded by the Irish government, collapsed in acrimony before they got off the ground. Without this network Irish governments lacked a means of organising opinion among the diaspora. More importantly, the United States did not join the League of Nations. In response to this situation Irish diplomats proposed, somewhat improbably, that they seek to represent American interests at Geneva. The strength of the Irish constituency in American elections had led many to assume that it could be used to influence United States government policy. The fact that Washington had not recognised an Irish republic in 1921 should have been evidence that this was not so, but it was in Irish interests to

---

21 *Dáil Deb.*, 3 (ii), 2389, 25 June 1923. **22** *Star*, 9 February 1929. **23** *Dáil Deb.*, 2818, 297, 21 February 1929.

cultivate the idea. Reports from Geneva suggested the beliefs among League officials that Irish thinking on international issues closely followed that of Washington and that Dublin might be able to influence the Americans favourably towards the League.[24] Even when this did not occur the feeling persisted that the Free State somehow represented more than the sum of its parts when it spoke at international fora. This was one of the reasons why its League membership was looked upon with such interest. The influence of the diaspora, and the Irish influence on the diaspora, may have been intangible, but these phenomena lent the Free State a leeway which it would not otherwise have enjoyed.

COMMONWEALTH AND CONTINENTAL DIMENSIONS

Ironically, much of the importance other states attached to Irish opinions derived not so much from the diaspora as from the country's Commonwealth membership. The French and German governments believed the Irish were privy to British policy considerations, and Irish diplomats sought to exploit this in their dealings with both countries. The French were also concerned with furthering their relations with the United States by cultivating links with Ireland. But this association in foreign eyes hampered attempts to generate a separate Irish identity. Commonwealth membership, Irish presence at Imperial Conferences and the joint briefings Commonwealth delegates held before League meetings confused the country's position in continental eyes. Diplomats were told that 'new customs and precedents would have to be created to meet new situations'.[25] In order to establish that the Crown in Ireland acted on the advice of the Irish government alone, legations were flagged on the King's birthday and 'Amhrán na bhFiann' ('The Soldier's Song') was played during royal toasts. Although this was constitutionally correct, it clashed with the image of separateness that was being constructed at the same time. Anomalies abounded, and even when they had been largely removed the impression persisted that they remained. A report concluded in 1927 that for all of the gains of the previous five years the impression persisted that the Free State was not fully regarded as 'a unit in international affairs in no way subservient to Britain'.[26] One way to address this problem was to open legations in European capitals, but even then the link remained as Irish diplomats were accredited abroad in the name of the crown.

* * *

Attitudes to Ireland were also shaped by the interests of its European neighbours during the 1920s. The French consul in Dublin, Alfred Blanche, was concerned

---

24 NA DFA, ES, miscellaneous files, MacWhite memorandum, May 1922. **25** NA DFA PE, letter book, 1923–24, Walshe to Murphy, 1 March 1923. **26** NAI DFA D 1983/4, Department of External Affairs memorandum, 11 July 1927.

to counter what he believed to be a growing German influence in Ireland when the firm of Siemens Schukert won the contract to construct the Shannon hydroelectric plant in 1927. 'We can say today, without exaggeration', he reported to Paris, 'that the Free State is set to become a sort of German province, a bridge head in the Anglo–Saxon world'.[27] The same officer described the National University of Ireland as a 'hotbed of ignorance and Germanism' and believed a 'German fleet would soon be anchored off the Limerick coast'.[28] His successor, Charles Alphand, shared a belief that France had a role to play in Europeanising the Free State and maintained that government circles would be receptive to an extension of French influence.[29]

But such concerns did not typify official attitudes. The Quai d'Orsay, like other foreign ministries, carefully weighed up the impact on Britain before making any overture to the Irish and, on occasion, ran ideas past the Foreign Office first. This was to be expected. Power politics naturally influenced the way other states related to Ireland, as did lingering notions that the Free State was still 'a part of *Angleterre*', as one diplomat complained in 1930.[30] This was so despite the fact that the government repeatedly described itself in European terms: the Irish were one of the oldest nations in Europe, had spread Christianity there and had kindled the light of learning during the Dark Ages. It had long been assumed that an Irish state would promote a European identity abroad. Whilst conscious of the 'moral bond' with the overseas Irish, government leaders were anxious to impress upon the rest of the continent that Ireland was part of the European fold. As the government deputy Hugh Law put it, 'we shall prove not the less good Irishmen for being also good Europeans'.[31] Nationalist histories, with their emphasis on Ireland's past links with the continent, implicitly supported a European-oriented foreign policy as more natural than remaining within the British orbit, as did foreign policy enthusiasts at the time. This was the most significant difference, in Irish eyes, between the Free State and the other Dominions.

ANGLO–IRISH RELATIONS

Throughout the 1920s tension existed between aspirations towards an independent and principled line in foreign affairs and the need to avoid alienating Britain, from whom, it was hoped, further concessions in the constitutional field would be secured. The continuing constitutional link with Britain, how-

27 Quai d'Orsay, *Correspondence Politique et Commerciale Europe 1918–40, Irlande*, vol. 15, pp 152–66, Blanche to unknown (Herriot?), 4 April 1925.   **28** Ibid., vol. 13, p. 26, Blanche to Briand, 12 May 1925.   **29** Ibid., vol. 20, p. 11, Alphand to Briand, 1 September 1930.   **30** NA DFA PE, letter book, O'Kelly to Walshe, 3 April 1930.   **31** Hugh Law, 'The Irish Free State in 1929', *Review of Reviews*, September 1929, p. 194.

ever fluid, meant that the Free State frequently found itself unable to pursue issues which many nationalists held dear. Prior to independence it had been a commonplace of much nationalist thinking that the campaign for separation from Britain mirrored that of other subject peoples. But independence inevitably transformed attitudes to such issues, for a revolutionary movement had greater scope to espouse international injustices, or adopt idealistic positions, than a newly independent small state. In 1922, before the Free State was legally established, Arthur Griffith refused to meet a delegation of Egyptian nationalists in Dublin, despite the fulsome support he had offered them only a year before. Likewise, in 1930 the government decided not to support Iraqi membership of the League of Nations nor receive Gandhi on a visit to Ireland lest such acts damage relations with Britain ahead of the crucial Imperial Conference of that year. Such caution was an early feature of Irish diplomacy.

By refusing assistance to separatists elsewhere, Irish leaders found themselves in the reverse position to earlier generations of nationalists, an irony which cannot have been lost at the time. Questions continued to be asked in the Dáil about the treatment of nationalities within the British empire, but concern was as much to ensure that the Free State could not be held responsible in any way. Desmond FitzGerald told the house in 1924 that they could protest to Britain only as much as they could to Japan about conditions in Korea.[32] This did not satisfy some, especially republicans who frequently denounced alleged British injustices or imperialism *per se*. Fianna Fáil, when it entered the Dáil in 1927, accused the government of turning its back on the very peoples whose cause they had championed before independence. But under the circumstances it is difficult to see what could have been done, and when Fianna Fáil took power in 1932 there was no significant shift in policy. Despite these sincerely held convictions, there were too many outstanding issues in Anglo–Irish relations to risk championing the rights of others.

However, the very act of carving out a separate identity and role was the one thing designed to alienate the authorities in London. The Foreign Office remained implacably hostile to the Dominions developing a separate foreign policy and, in particular, to Irish claims in this sphere. Irish diplomats were instructed to be on their guard against moves by British officials to speak for the Free State abroad, precedents that might prove damaging. The Dominions Office, which dealt with the Free State as a Dominion, was inclined to be more sympathetic. But even while it was facilitating the establishment of an Irish legation in Washington in 1924, the Foreign Office placed obstacles in the way. And once it became clear that an Irish minister would be appointed in spite of its efforts, the Foreign Office turned its attention, ultimately without success, to getting a Canadian minister appointed first.

32 *Dáil Deb.*, 8, 829, 9 July 1924.

***

Difficulties were also experienced in dealings with British embassies overseas, most of which resented encroachment on their patch by a parvenu diplomatic service. International sporting fixtures illustrate the problems faced in promoting the state abroad. Foreign visits by sports teams were occasions of vigilance for Irish diplomats lest the British flag and anthem feature on the programme. Here the Free State was at a disadvantage against the superior resources of the Foreign Office, with British consuls making a point of showing up to local stadia armed with flag and score. But the presence of an Irish diplomat did not always guarantee that the correct procedure would be followed, as Count Gerald O'Kelly, the Irish envoy in Brussels, discovered during an athletics tournament in 1926. A veteran of the flag wars, he had had the foresight to send in advance a tricolour and the score of 'Amhrán na bhFiann' to the organisers. He was taken aback, however, to see the Union Jack raised and hear the British anthem greet the arrival of the Irish team, all the more so as he was a guest in the royal box. After much embarrassment on the part of the Belgian organisers the correct flag was found, but the music was not. As the Belgian army band did not know the tune, and O'Kelly was unable to hum it, the victorious Irish athletes took their lap of honour to the bars of the Norwegian anthem, it being hoped that no one present would know the difference.[33]

***

Because the Cumann na nGaedheal administration did not make an issue of Northern Ireland in its dealings with Britain at either Commonwealth gatherings or the League, partition did not impinge significantly on foreign policy, despite the emotiveness of the issue. Still, External Affairs took an interest in minority problems at Geneva and closely followed attempts at arbitration in analogous situations. Abroad, diplomats treated the North as an 'anomaly' and strove to remove all mention of partition from official references to Ireland.[34] From an early date care was taken to present the anti-partitionist case, and official publications attempted to cover the whole island. Speakers at international gatherings largely confined themselves to referring to Ireland and the Irish people, to the chagrin of British diplomats, and in 1930 the plaque outside the mission in Paris referred simply to the Légation d'Irlande. However, the very name of the state posed difficulties, and the Foreign Office insisted that the Irish Free State, and not Ireland, become international usage. At a bilateral level the issue impinged even less, with foreign governments eschewing interest in the subject. The unionist press in the North paid scant attention to Free State diplomatic endeavours, whilst nationalists could only look on wistfully. In the end

[33] NAI DFA EA 3–1, O'Kelly to Walshe, 13 April 1926.   [34] NA DFA PE, letter book, 1925–27, Walshe to Dempsey, 3 December 1925.

governments did not want to draw attention to unionists or the North, and a belief that economic and other factors would eventually lead to reunification disinclined them to make an international issue of partition, though this would change when Fianna Fáil came to power.

RELIGION AND IRISH FOREIGN POLICY

The idea of a foreign policy inspired by religious values had been a staple of nationalist pamphleteers and continued to influence attitudes after independence. Religious journals, such as the *Irish Monthly*, hoped that Ireland would be 'a beacon shedding the light of holiness in the world', while the *Church of Ireland Gazette* urged the country to 'forget her own little troubles in contemplation of the vast distress of mankind'.[35] A 1931 External Affairs review recommended that Christian values should guide Ireland's foreign policy.[36] The Catholic formation of many in government and civil service circles ensured that their outlooks closely mirrored that of the Catholic Church: the number of ministers undertaking private and official visits to Rome is just one testament to this. With the secretary of the department, Joseph Walshe, being a former Jesuit, and William Cosgrave, the President of the Executive Council, a frequent guest of the papal nuncio in Dublin, one might argue that there was little need for overt clerical intervention in foreign policy. On occasion the state did give weight to religious considerations before adopting a particular policy. In 1930 Walshe advised against becoming involved in a dispute between Britain and the Vatican over Malta, despite potential advantages in doing so, because it 'would not be good for religion'.[37]

For some, the two identities, Catholic and Irish, may have been close to synonymous, such was the emphasis placed on Christian values. But it would be wrong to speak of a specifically Catholic foreign policy. Although the government condemned religious persecution in Mexico in 1928, the motive was also to distance the country from Britain, which had not done so. Similarly, although officials took an interest in the appointment of Irish clerics around the world, this was seen as a low-cost means of extending Irish influence abroad. Cosgrave's young government strongly resisted an unsolicited papal peace mission towards the end of the Civil War in 1923, resenting Vatican intervention in its affairs, and Eamon de Valera refused to assist Franco's nationalists during the Spanish Civil War despite enormous public and clerical pressure to do so. Neither did religious convictions prevent the government from considering

---

35 *Irish Monthly*, July 1926; *Church of Ireland Gazette*, 2 June 1922. **36** NAI DT S 2220, report on the Department of External Affairs, April 1931. **37** NAI DFA 7/32, Walshe to Bewley, 24 June 1930.

diplomatic and commercial relations with the Soviet Union, and support for trade links with Russia persisted during the 'red scare' of 1930, despite denunciations of the communist threat from the pulpit.

INDEPENDENCE AND IRISH IDENTITY

Independence inevitably dictated a change in identities, too, and as new interests developed, old images were dropped. An early example was that of the 'fighting Irish', which evoked unpleasant memories of the Civil War, while clashing with the idea of a new, pacific Ireland. The country strove to lose the image of the begging bowl, too. William Cosgrave turned down offers of help from abroad after reports of famine appeared in the international press in 1925. The government was particularly concerned to remove the impression in America that Irish politicians regarded the country as little more than a source of funds, though it did hope to attract American investment. Cosgrave paid a state visit to America in 1928 to promote the image of the Free State as a modern European nation able to pay its own way, although this was somewhat undermined by Desmond FitzGerald's party fundraising visit the following year.

Modernity was seen as central to the state's efforts to portray itself abroad, opting for consciously modern pavilions at international exhibitions. This was at variance, however, with the imagery of a Celtic idyll which nationalists had popularised and which the tourist board inherited from them. Tourist posters of misty Connacht hills by Paul Henry exemplified this contradiction, as did those designed by Seán Keating in 1929 to advertise Irish farm produce in Britain. Featuring a group of Hispanic-looking peasants surrounded by hens and ramshackle farm buildings, the campaign sat awkwardly alongside the image of modernity and financial probity which the state strove to promote abroad. Moreover, no real attempt was made to act upon the pledge made at Geneva in 1923 to protect and promote Celtic culture overseas, and officials discouraged interest in the pan-Celtic movement in case it should impact negatively on relations with France and Britain. Simply put, the Irish had to establish themselves as responsible members of the club of independent states. This meant turning their backs on those independence movements with which Irish nationalism had previously identified itself.

* * *

Attitudes towards Britain had to change to a certain extent, too. It was necessary to avoid creating the impression that the Free State was animated by anglophobia. A report in late 1922 warned of the dangers in continuing to predicate international positions solely on opposition to British interests, and throughout the 1920s diplomats were instructed to base interventions at conferences 'on general principles so clearly that no suspicion of hostility to Great Britain may exist'.[38]

This was necessary for a number of reasons. Apart from the obstacles Britain could place in the path of Irish development, on matters of trade and security the two country's interests often overlapped. In addition, the other Dominions would not follow an Irish lead if it were seen to be anti-British. Above all else, Britain was too powerful an international actor to have as an enemy. The small countries with which the Free State sought to associate would have little to do with it under such circumstances. But Sinn Féin thinking on foreign policy was always more sophisticated than Arthur Griffith's over-quoted dictum that he would first ascertain where Britain stood on any issue and then support the other side. These words were uttered in the middle of the campaign for independence, but it was accepted that after independence Ireland would be free to pursue a policy of friendship towards her neighbour. England's difficulty would no longer be Ireland's opportunity, but the reverse would be true, as de Valera had told the Dáil in 1919.[39] The Treaty negotiators accepted that concessions would have to be made to British security interests and that some form of military association would even be desirable. Even Document Number 2 listed defence as a 'matter of common concern' between the two islands. Fianna Fáil urged that cooperation with Britain could only be on a normal footing when outstanding nationalist demands had been met, and its policy in government was influenced by this position. The Cumann na nGaedheal administration of William Cosgrave felt differently, seeing in the Commonwealth a path to fuller freedom.

A PLACE AMONG THE NATIONS

Regardless of this difference, an important strain in nationalist self-perception was the contribution Ireland could make to the rest of the world, and this strongly influenced attitudes to international relations. Before independence the idea had developed that Ireland would be a force for good on the world stage. De Valera famously referred to Ireland possessing the 'might of moral beauty'.[40] These beliefs were held across the political divide and persisted after independence. Eoin MacNeill told the Dáil in 1923 that it was their destiny to be a teaching nation, setting an example to the rest of the world.[41] The Labour leader, Thomas Johnson, believed the country should 'take a distinctive part in the work of international peace', a sentiment shared by the young Seán Lemass, who believed his co-nationals had 'a desire for peace deeply ingrained ... to an extent which probably does not exist in any other race on earth'.[42] The more urbane

---

38 NAI DFA, letter book, League of Nations 1923–25, Walshe to MacWhite, 27 March 1923. **39** *Dáil Éireann Official Reports*, 19 April 1919, p. 38. **40** *Eamon de Valera States his Case* (Boston, 1918). **41** Brian Farrell, 'MacNeill and Politics', in F.X. Martin and F.J. Byrne (eds),

League of Nations Society urged that 'if Ireland is to stand high in the eyes of the world it must be by moral and intellectual attainments', language not so far removed from that of republicans during the Treaty debates. This belief in a higher calling was perhaps best captured by the journalist P.S. O'Hegarty, when he wrote that 'Ireland's position is unique. By virtue of our special history, our special position ... We can become a pivot for Europe and for America as well'.[43]

Some of this rhetoric had origins in a dimly held belief in a communal Celtic past, despite scholarship to the contrary. The country's long-standing missionary tradition was also influential in shaping approaches to the international environment, with echoes in the contribution Irish monks and scholars had made in the past. It was hoped that Ireland might aspire once more to such a role. We might dismiss these ideas as over-blown romanticism, but they had a wide currency both before and after independence. When combined with a conviction that the country's historical experience, as nationalists saw it, should incline it to a compassionate and principled stance, we can see some of the contours of Irish aspirations emerge.

* * *

How to translate aspiration into action was what confronted Irish leaders, and their efforts during this period can be divided between a need to preserve and advance the new state's position, on the one hand, and an attempt to develop a national identity through the elaboration and performance of international roles, on the other. Before independence nationalists had been concerned to differentiate Ireland from Britain. After 1922 it became important to differentiate the Free State from the other Dominions by stressing its distinct identity, just as it was important to differentiate the Commonwealth as a group from the British empire. But scope for action on issues of substance was severely limited, not only by the incomplete nature of independence, but also by the constraints imposed on the freedom of action of any small state. The former would be gradually removed in the course of Commonwealth evolution and, naturally enough, this formed a foreign policy priority. The second constraint, a function of the small state predicament, could not so easily be resolved.

Irish nationalists sought to change not only the way the Irish interacted with the outside world, but also the way the rest of the world perceived the Irish. It is this, as much as national self-interest and the desire to advance the constitutional settlement of 1921, that motivated Irish attempts to forge a foreign policy in the decade after independence. These efforts were sometimes successful, more often not, and the Free State was not able to live up to its earlier hopes of being

---

The Scholar Revolutionary (Dublin, 1973), p. 194.   **42** *Dáil Deb.*, 28, 297, 21 February 1929.
43 UCDA P4 860, O'Hegarty memorandum, 15 September 1922.

the 'first of the small nations'.⁴⁴ But it was, perhaps, more successful than the country's small size and resources might have indicated, and in this the Free State drew on its European identity, its links with the diaspora and its membership of the Commonwealth. It was this multiple identity which allowed Irish diplomats to base some of their policy on the principles which they held to be important or, in the words of Patrick McGilligan, seek to 'tell the world something worthy of ourselves at last'.⁴⁵

44 NAI DFA ES Box 1 File 13, Gavan Duffy, report of Minister for Foreign Affairs to Dáil Éireann, April 1922. 45 NAI DT S 2220, McGilligan, report on the Department of External Affairs, April 1931.

'Mr Blythe, I Think, Hears from him Occasionally': The Experiences of Irish Diplomats in Latin America, 1919-23

Michael Kennedy

INTRODUCTION

This chapter examines and assesses the four-year period from 1919 to 1923, during which Ireland had a diplomatic presence in Latin America with envoys in Argentina and Chile. These Sinn Féin envoys were not officially accredited to the governments of their host countries. Yet they were 'official' envoys to the Irish communities in Latin America. These representatives, Eamon Bulfin in Argentina and Frank Egan in Chile, have been viewed rather disparagingly by historians of Irish foreign policy, because the two envoys are best known as the subject of Diarmuid O'Hegarty's ire when he wrote: 'I have never heard from him [Egan]. With regard to Mr Bulfin, he is more a Trade Consul than a diplomatic representative. Mr Blythe, I think, hears from him occasionally.'[1] The Minister for Foreign Affairs, George Gavan Duffy, wrote in similar terms when he referred sarcastically to 'our very wide awake representative in Chile Mr Frank W. Egan'.[2] Both Chile and Argentina had significant Irish populations and were considered by contemporaries to be, along with Brazil (where there was only a handful in the Irish community), 'the only three South American states which can be said to count seriously as yet in international politics'.[3] Britain had strong economic and financial interests in both Argentina and Chile; Sinn Féin propagandists constantly reiterated this and saw their own

---

1 NAI DFA ES 105, 16 March 1921. O'Hegarty was the Secretary of Dáil Éireann. 2 NAI DFA ES 114, 7 March 1922. 3 NAI DFA ES 216, report by Simpson, October 1921. Simpson had been recommended to Sinn Féin as 'a man who could be safely relied on to act loyally and capably in the interests of the Republic': NAI DE 2/526, Brennan to de Valera, 11 May 1921. Simpson was a friend of President Allessandri of Chile, and in the summer of 1921 his wife's business interests brought him to Chile with her. Before undertaking this trip he contacted Sinn Féin leaders in Dublin to see if he could act as an Irish representative. He was told of Egan's appointment and urged to give Egan assistance.

position in Ireland reflected in microcosm in Latin America. There were other active Irish supporters in Latin America, though Blythe and Gavan Duffy had probably never heard of Jasper Nicholls in Bolivia, Donal Buckley in Brazil or the elusive Mr O'Durnin in Paraguay.

At its second meeting, on 26 April 1919, the Dáil cabinet voted five hundred pounds to Eamon Bulfin in Argentina.[4] Bulfin thereafter kept a low profile, though Arthur Griffith announced Bulfin's appointment in the Dáil on 17 June 1919, and the following day the Dáil voted Bulfin another one hundred pounds to set up a consulate in Buenos Aires.

Frank Egan was appointed as honorary Irish representative in Chile on 14 September 1920. He was resident in Chile and operated a mining business alongside distributing Sinn Féin propaganda.[5] He had to devote much time to his business and was only a part-time diplomat. But with business and political contacts in Chile and his in-laws related to the Chilean President, Egan could bring the Irish case to the attention of those with influence in Chilean society.

EAMON BULFIN AND MICHAEL COLLINS

On 24 September 1919 Michael Collins wrote to Eamon Bulfin asking for 'an account of things in the Argentine as they affect Ireland' and mentioning that Eamon de Valera, then in the United States, wished to contact Bulfin. Collins told Bulfin about the beginning of the Dáil loan. Bulfin was to contact de Valera or Harry Boland before making a start, as 'the issue would naturally come under the U.S.A. flotation'.[6] The letter reveals much about Dublin's attitude to Latin America. Though Bulfin was specifically accredited to Argentina by the Dáil, his mission was apparently a subset of the mission to the United States for the purpose of collecting the Dáil loan. The use of the Sinn Féin mission in the United States to coordinate the progress of the Latin American mission removed control from Dublin by one more step. It is therefore understandable that Egan and Bulfin should seem so remote to Dublin that Dublin could even question their existence.

In reply, Bulfin wrote that he did not get Collins' letter until mid January 1920. Such communication problems are worth mentioning. If Bulfin was unable to keep up regular correspondence with Collins it is likely that he sent as few letters as possible, and this provides some insight as to why he periodically vanished from view. No established channel of communication existed with the

---

4 NAI DE 1/1. **5** Egan was the son of Patrick Egan, a former treasurer of the Land League and a colleague of T.M. Healy (of the Irish Parliamentary Party) during the 1880s. **6** NAI DE 5/21.

Irish in Latin America. Representatives were unable to benefit from the regular Paris to Dublin messenger service that could forward all diplomatic correspondence to Dublin from the envoys in Europe in about three days. Collins illustrated this problem when he wrote to Bulfin on 13 February that he had not 'heard anything whatever of you except in the most remote hearsay manner'.[7] That was because Bulfin's letter of 26 January 1920, replying to Collins' of 24 September 1919, did not arrive in Dublin until 19 March 1920. It may be labouring the point, but understanding this barrier to communication is essential when examining the development of Irish relations with Latin America.

The loan and simply keeping in touch with Bulfin were Collins' main objectives. He wrote of how 'it is important to hear from you ... to know that something is being done in Buenos Aires ... [and] that you are in touch with President de Valera'.[8] Bulfin was not yet receiving propaganda material such as the Sinn Féin Bulletin, and the disarray in the Argentinean mission was evident. Collins wrote of how he would look forward to Bulfin's next letter 'as you will have got yourself more settled since you last wrote'.[9] Bulfin eventually replied to Collins' letter of 3 April 1920 on 14 December 1920. He 'had no opportunity to answer it before now, at least a chance was offered to me, but circumstances prevented me from availing myself of it'.[10] This may be a reference to Bulfin's arrest under Argentina's military and naval service acts. Bulfin seemed to be feeling the distance from Ireland when he spoke of feeling 'pretty much like a deserter myself' and he revealingly told Collins that 'so little has been done here'.[11] What Bulfin had accomplished was to draft a scheme for setting up an active Irish interest group in Argentina, but he suggested that the messenger had delivered it to the wrong person in Dublin and so he had got no reply. Through this diplomatic response to Dublin's inaction Bulfin tried once again to elicit an answer from Collins.

In the more practical sense Bulfin had been making attempts to procure ammunition for the IRA. He sent on 1,000 rounds of forty-five calibre revolver ammunition and, despite its expense at thirty shillings for one hundred rounds, was willing to secure a stock and make arrangements to ship it to Ireland should Collins desire. Procuring this ammunition was Bulfin's most active *démarche* to date.

Bulfin had organised propaganda for Sinn Féin in Argentina. In a report dated June 1921, though delivered to the Dáil in August 1921, under-secretary for foreign affairs, Robert Brennan, passed on that Bulfin emphasised 'the urgent need that exists of educating the whole people of the Argentine – as distinct from the Irish there – to the true position of Ireland'.[12] The report sheds some

---

7 Ibid. **8** Ibid., Collins to Bulfin, 13 February 1920. **9** Ibid., Collins to Bulfin, 3 April 1920.
10 Ibid., Bulfin to Collins, 14 December 1920. **11** Ibid. **12** NAI DE 2/269.

light on the position of the Irish community in Argentina. They had split into two factions in 1911 and there was still bad blood between the two parties. This split reduced the power of the Irish in the Argentine and Bulfin felt that effective propaganda could overcome this split. As we will see later, the ferocity of this split was to prove detrimental to overall Irish efforts to create a viable support base in Argentina. There were some good channels to use, though: Bulfin commented that the President of Argentina was disposed to the Irish cause, as were a number of papers. These were most useful connections; Brennan had already made clear to Bulfin 'the vital necessity of being in a position to refute English publicity and to put Ireland's case in a true perspective before the peoples of South America'.[13]

* * *

It is unfortunate that more of the Bulfin–Collins correspondence has not survived. But the use of a specific 'Collins to Bulfin channel' shows a distinct cleavage in the Sinn Féin organisation. Whilst de Valera, O'Hegarty and the nominal Minister for Foreign Affairs, Count George Plunkett, received the bulk of communications from envoys abroad, certain envoys wrote only to Collins. Another case is Donal Hales in Genoa. Hales and Collins were both from the same part of West Cork, and Collins also knew Donal's brothers Tom and Sean, who were active in the West Cork IRA. The Hales and Bulfin correspondence did not reach the Ministry of Foreign Affairs; it remained with Collins in the Ministry of Finance.[14]

Collins made a revealing remark to Bulfin about his own position in Ireland. Bulfin had written congratulating Collins of his rise to fame and was glad that 'from all accounts it has not changed your scowl or sweetened your tongue'.[15] Collins replied that 'nothing is due to me, it is all due to the persons who made me do it. On the whole I cannot grumble with the form. Of course I am beginning to feel myself getting old'. The guerrilla war against the British was taking its toll on Collins. He revealed himself not as the fearless guerrilla leader, but, instead, as bewildered by the events of 1919 and 1920. There was, Collins continued, 'little chance of getting one's thoughts sufficiently collected now-a-days to write a really clear view of things'. The strain was again evident in Collins' words; the only silver lining on the dark clouds was that 'things have changed a good deal since you left. Notwithstanding everything, they have improved, and the people are better than ever'. Collins did not write of himself as the master of events; rather he seemed to be aware that the guerrilla war against the British was a genuinely popular event. Collins seemed to perk up at the thought of

---

13 NAI DFA ES 216/4. **14** See NAI DE 5/56 for the Collins–Hales correspondence. **15** NAI DE 5/21, Bulfin to Collins, 14 December 1920.

Bulfin sending on supplies of ammunition. It was 'the solution of the whole case ... we do want it badly ... no stuff is more acceptable'. And with that Collins left Bulfin to close the deal and concluded the letter.

The specific nature of the Collins–Bulfin correspondence goes some way to explain why Diarmuid O'Hegarty could find no mention of the elusive Bulfin or, indeed, the equally intangible Egan. In Egan's case, the newly appointed under-secretary for foreign affairs, Robert Brennan did not know until a month into his appointment that the Dáil had a representative in Chile. Both representatives could go to ground very easily. In Bulfin's case it was because he remained throughout very much under Collins' remit of operations.

TRACKING DOWN THE ENVOYS

By the spring of 1921 Robert Brennan and Eamon de Valera were beginning to regularise the control and communication mechanisms of the Ministry of Foreign Affairs. Count Plunkett had been sidelined and Brennan took the widely spread Dáil missions under his own control, reporting on their actions directly to Eamon de Valera. Brennan then carried out a search for the Republic's two wayward envoys in Latin America.

By late March some details were beginning to emerge. Ernest Blythe, the Minister for Trade, claimed that 'he has never had a communication from him [Bulfin]' and all that could be found were three or four reports on the position of the Irish in the Argentine.[16] This is not surprising: the evidence outlined above suggests that the channel by which Bulfin communicated to Dublin was routed primarily to Collins.

Bulfin's 'personal' role can clearly be seen when Collins wrote to Brennan that 'I do not think from the records I have that Mr Bulfin's position is quite the same as our other Foreign Agents'.[17] Bulfin did not receive a regular salary from the Department of Finance, and so Collins concluded 'there was no reason for this Department being in touch with him'. Collins jokingly commented that the last communication he had had with Bulfin was 'a note of sympathy on the death of the present writer'. Again, it is clearly seen that Collins saw Bulfin as a personal and private contact in Argentina; possibly this was related to the ammunition shipments which Bulfin was negotiating.

The position was somewhat worse with regard to Frank Egan. Brennan had never heard of Egan, and O'Hegarty could only say that he had heard of Egan's existence, but never received any reports from the elusive Irish representative in

---

16 NAI DFA ES 128, O'Hegarty to Collins, 24 March 1921. **17** NAI DFA ES 217/1, Collins to Brennan, 30 March 1921.

Chile. As the queries degenerated into farce even Arthur Griffith put in his point: he had, Collins believed, mentioned 'the name of somebody in Chile'.[18] Eamon de Valera was of the opinion that Egan held a purely honorary position and seemed to use this fact to explain Egan's low profile. In fact, once Egan began reporting on his activities in Chile he began to show some quite effective results.

FRANK EGAN: THE CHILEAN PROPAGANDA OFFENSIVE

Writing to Harry Boland, Frank Egan blamed Dublin for his lack of communication which 'was owing to the absence of instructions from headquarters'.[19] Despite speaking of his 'poor endeavours', Egan acted without instruction from Dublin in a reasonably competent manner. He was flying an Irish republican flag from his offices as 'an eyesore to the British Legation' and was actively using Irish propaganda. Egan also reported how he had come out top in a newspaper contest with the British minister in Santiago, commenting that 'I think I floored him all right with a knock out at [the] first round'. The British minister had since become, according to Egan 'the laughing-stock of his English colony and an object of ridicule'. Egan's other activities had included a propaganda initiative in the Chilean press against the League of Nations.

Like Bulfin in Argentina, Egan had good connections in Chilean society. He was married to a Chilean and the President of Chile, don Arturo Alessandri, was a first cousin of his brother's wife. Egan commented that he was friendly with the President and that he might prove a useful contact in the future. Another series of contacts Egan was developing was amongst the members of the Chilean National Assembly. Egan hoped he could get them to make a declaration in favour of recognising the Irish republic. Such an action would, it was felt, lead the Argentineans and, perhaps, the Brazilians to make a similar declaration. In order to spur this policy on Egan was founding a ginger group amongst the Chilean-Irish, the 'Irish Colony of Chile'.

There were about 300 Irish in Chile at the beginning of the 1920s. According to a report from a Mr J. Simpson on the Irish organisation in Santiago, the number in this city was about forty strong and hardworking. The Irish were 'in influential positions, and some of them in direct contact with the President and the American legation'; however, the Irish did not take a direct part in the political life of the Chilean state.[20] In the coastal city of Valparaiso there was no organised Irish community. Simpson said that this was because the Irish were 'mostly the superior officials of the great British importing houses and in fear of

---

18 Ibid. **19** NAI DFA ES 216/1, 26 May 1921. **20** Ibid., undated report, October 1921.

losing their positions'. This group was also deeply mixed in British social circles and this also muted any Irish nationalist sympathies. There were 'about twenty Irish "of the right colour" in Valparaiso', according to Simpson. It was Simpson's contention that the Irish in Chile were absorbed quickly into Chilean national life due to the similarity of Irish and Chilean temperament, and that this accounted for the quiescence of the Irish population in the country.

* * *

Several of the leaders of the Chilean independence struggle had been Irish, and this fact, allied to public opinion generally supporting the underdogs, made the Chilean populace very supportive of Ireland. Simpson remarked that Chile had 'been pro-Boer, pro-Japanese and pro-German'. But British influence in the Chilean nitrate and borax mining industries, and control of railways and coastal trade, made this support less vocal than it could have been. The well-to-do Chilean, according to Simpson, was guilty of Chilean 'West-Britonism': 'The British have earned a reputation in Chile for reliable and honest dealing, which makes it hard for Chileans to believe accounts of their dealings in Ireland. Chileans like to hear themselves described as "the English of Latin America".' There was a counterweight to this trend through increasing United States influence in the banking and financial sectors. Similarly, British management of the Chilean nitrate industry through price fixing, political interference by Britain and Chilean plans to reassert domestic control over her coastal shipping all could create a more pro-Irish climate, at least in the sense that public opinion could become increasingly anti-British. Simpson was not optimistic about the practical political value of these issues, as opposed to their rhetorical value for the Irish cause: 'recognition of the Republic by Congress could not be expected at present, nor is a successful loan'.

* * *

Judging from Simpson's report, Egan had a hard task ahead of him. Yet Egan appears to have been more of a natural diplomat than Bulfin. He brought to Boland's attention the need to send clear instructions to Santiago as to his status and position. Egan was clearly conscious of his 'non-recognised' position and wanted instructions from Dublin to make him 'more secure' and give him 'tone, respectability [and] gloss to representation'.

Egan's reports for the middle of 1921 show him trying to follow basic diplomatic procedure. He was diligent in replying to Dublin and was using his contacts to distribute Sinn Féin propaganda 'to all the leading and commercial people [and] to Legations, Consulates, Spanish Clubs and Societies'.[21] Writing

---

21 Ibid., 8 July 1921.

before the truce in the Anglo–Irish War, but with the hint of negotiations in the air, Egan was almost a model example of the rules for diplomatic procedure set down by Brennan. Egan had been asked about the agenda in any negotiations with Britain. He replied, quoting de Valera, that 'the fundamental question at issue between the two countries is the question of Ireland's right to chose freely and independently her own government and political institutions at home and her relationship with foreign nations as well'.[22] Egan made clear that he would take this line until told otherwise and asked to be let know of any developments by cable. Egan was hoping for some developments from Ireland, as the Irish question had slipped out of the columns of the Chilean press. Domestic politics and relations between Chile and Peru held the attention of the press, and Egan had scaled down his active propaganda policy. Egan's propaganda had been a success; he immodestly described a pamphlet he had translated into Spanish on the Irish appeal for recognition from Washington as 'a sensation in Spanish circles'.[23]

LAURENCE GINNELL BEGINS THE BOND DRIVE IN LATIN AMERICA

Under the auspices of the Irish mission in the United States Sinn Féin director of publicity, Laurence Ginnell set out in the summer of 1921 to extend the Irish republican bond drive to the Irish communities in Latin America. Ginnell arrived in Buenos Aires on 25 July 1921, staying until April 1922. He was given 'full and unrestricted powers ... to do whatever [he] found advisable in the local circumstances'.[24] Ginnell made contact with 'the best and the wealthiest Irish Argentines' and reported that they were ready and willing to subscribe to the bond drive. However, he was up against an obstacle: the wealthy Argentines he targeted would leave Buenos Aires for the 'health resorts' until March. Ginnell feared he might not be able to get 'the same people interested [again], and a loan was the only way of raising money consistent with the dignity of the young republic'.[25] Dáil diplomats had not taken account of the summer months in the Southern Hemisphere. It also turned out that the Dáil mission had to face a slump in the cattle market, a trade in which many of the Irish community were involved.

A start had to be made immediately, and Ginnell called for personnel support from the Irish in the United States in order to undertake the bond issue and register it correctly with a reliable local bank. Silence from Dublin and Irish

---

22 Ibid.   **23** Ibid.   **24** Ibid., Ginnell to O'Mara, 1 September 1921.   **25** Ibid., Ginnell to Collins, 13 September 1921.

America led Ginnell to appoint Bulfin as registrar of the Dáil loan. He hoped at this stage to collect about half a million pounds. Ginnell was somewhat diffident about the progress of the loan. 'Most people', he wrote, 'are surprisingly friendly, even people whom no one expected to be'; but Ginnell was doubtful what a popular Irish Argentine organisation could achieve, preferring to wait until the bond drive was over before commenting in detail on the Irish Argentine community.

Writing of his mission in retrospect in March 1922, Ginnell said there had been a 'want of knowledge, want of interest, extreme apathy, and a positive horror of one person who claimed that he alone represented the Republic, and publicly outraged the rest as knaves and renegades'.[26] Ginnell had to get around this individual (unnamed, though possibly faction leader Padraic MacManus) and set about his task through a series of appearances at public functions. He was now taking sides in the faction ridden Irish Argentinean community. He presented a reply to a welcome by the Comite Argentino pro Libertad de Irlanda and laid wreaths at many Argentine patriotic festivals where Irish dead in the Argentine revolution were remembered. He was also interviewed by some of the larger papers such as the *Southern Cross*. Other larger papers, such the *Buenos Aires Herald* and the *Nación*, were controlled by British interests and proved more timid in advocating the Irish cause, refusing to advertise the Dáil loan.

Perhaps Ginnell's greatest triumph was afforded by British propaganda backfiring. In late August 1921 an official British press statement was issued in London on the severe consequences for Ireland if the Irish did not accept British terms in the ongoing peace negotiations. Ginnell took the report and reissued it as a poster under the heading 'What England offers to Ireland: submission or destruction'. The poster, issued under the name of the Irish Argentine committee, was posted in public and the British minister 'was silly enough to denounce the poster in a public speech'.[27] This action opened up a correspondence in the press and lead to the poster being copied in other newspapers. 'Thus', Ginnell reported, 'the whole country was prepared for my propaganda'.

A SNAPSHOP: PATRICK J. LITTLE'S REPORT ON THE
ARGENTINE IRISH

On 17 September 1921 Patrick J. Little arrived in Buenos Aires from South Africa and set about compiling a report on the Irish community in the country. The report remains an illuminating account of the constituency Ginnell was operating in. Little reckoned there were 40,000 or 50,000 individuals of Irish

26 Ibid., Ginnell to Gavan Duffy, 3 March 1922. **27** Ibid.

extraction in Argentina, but very few of Irish birth. These Irish immigrants came mainly from the Midlands and Southeast of Ireland. The figure was about 0.65 percent of the entire population of 7.75 million and almost twice as big as the reported figure of 27,000 for those of English origins. However, the Irish community was, as noted above, split, and the much smaller English community controlled the railways and, through the banks, Argentina's foreign loans. As a précis of Little's report put it, 'enormous amount[s] of English capital [are] invested in exploiting this country'.[28] Little noted that South Africa (where he had worked on the Sinn Féin mission) had a much more organised Irish community, but that, nonetheless, Ginnell's bond drive 'was very well received by rich people connected with our cause'. The report downplayed Ginnell's optimistic figure of £500,000 in subscriptions and spoke of collecting merely ten or fifteen thousand pounds. Little founded his lower figure on the basis of a lack of interest in government loans in the past and unfavourable economic conditions.

Little reported that the President of Argentina, *Senor* Irregoyen, a member of the Radical Party, was favourable to Ireland, but 'would not involve the country in diplomatic entanglements by recognising [the] Republic'. Britain's economic grip was judged by Little to mitigate against any recognition, but he thought that lobbying in the Argentinean Congress might secure a resolution in favour of Ireland. The Irish in the country seemed politically to have gravitated towards the Democrats, with Little reporting that 'many of our best (Irish) friends are in it'. Despite a pro-British Conservative Party made up of landowners, overall, the Argentine citizens 'dislike the English because of their superior airs and their efforts to force English ways, language, etc., on them. Also they make money and *spend* [it] *in England* ... Another sore point is the taking of one of the Falkland Islands by England for strategic purposes'. Little could merely have been paraphrasing a Gaelic League pamphlet and putting in some 'local gloss', referred to by Little as 'the principle, "Argentine for the Argentines"'.

Reading his report, it is evident that he was selectively drawing details from the Argentinean political climate that would go down well in Dublin. His conclusion was that public opinion was generally favourable to Ireland, but the interested Argentinean Irish knew very little of what was happening in Ireland. He forcefully concluded that *'propaganda badly needed.* Those of Irish extraction have the right spirit but practically no work done'. He was putting a rather lacklustre situation in the best possible light. The underlying trends of the report made clear that the Argentinean Irish community was unprepared for propaganda and fund raising work and that British power was strong and supported by elements of the Irish community. On a wider scale, 'the Irish question is not intensely alive among [the] general public and working classes'. Organisation, propaganda and the promotion of trading links were Little's proposed remedy

---

28 Ibid.

for the lacklustre response of the Irish in Argentina. The Irish Argentineans did not like this kind of outside interference in their factionalised world.

GINNELL'S PROGRESS

'The loan is now fairly well launched', Ginnell told Arthur Griffith on 15 October 1921. It was, however, slow progress through Argentina's towns and cities. He was coming up against some opposition from the suspicious Irish Argentine organisations, and 'in this country of mañana ... one cannot do things too hastily'.[29] Ginnell was setting up trustees for the loan and holding public meetings to publicise the finance drive. It was a task that involved 'infinite trouble, patience and perseverance'.[30] Ginnell also hoped to send a good contingent from Latin America to the Irish Race Conference scheduled to open in Paris in January 1922. Staffing was Ginnell's main problem. Eamon Bulfin was meant to be in charge of the bond issue but he was forced to undertake other tasks because of the lack of a reliable typist. The Irish office had 'a very reliable Spanish secretary', but Ginnell wanted another typist, a Miss Myles, sent from Dublin in order to release Bulfin to more effective duties.

Little wrote pessimistically to Dublin in December 1921; he was disillusioned with the Irish of Latin America. Commenting on the problems facing him, he bluntly asked to be brought home from his mission: 'I came to the conclusion that it would be far better for me to go home as much more can be done by returning than by staying'.[31] Little spoke obliquely of difficulties with the work of the Buenos Aires mission in the past, but finished by saying that 'now things are much better'. Little gave a poor impression of the 'very rich Irish [who] would be friendly to-day and tomorrow would be indifferent or have misunderstandings'. Little had fewer constraints to his mission than Ginnell and Bulfin and he spent much time meeting Irish Argentineans. He found that he 'was continually obliged to get these people to keep up interest ... it is very hard to work up enthusiasm amongst the Irish who are born out here, so the work is very uphill'. Yet, by the end of 1921, a Spanish version of the *Irish Bulletin* was being produced to the standards of that in Dublin and drama was being used to convey the message of Sinn Féin.

* * *

Little was trying to counter the heretofore uncommented upon negative side of Ginnell's mission. The Irish in Argentina felt 'that we only come here for money

---

29 NAI DFA ES 216/4. **30** NAI DFA ES 216, Ginnell to Gavan Duffy, 3 March 1922. **31** Ibid., 4 December 1921.

and we don't care a jot what happens to the Irish'. Little was far more perceptive than Ginnell and more receptive to the feelings of the Irish Argentineans. Perhaps his own experiences in South Africa forewarned him of possible trouble. Ginnell had fallen foul of the factionalism of the Irish community and was the target of much criticism from the Hennessy faction. To try to overcome this factionalism a Federation of Irish Institutions met on 29 November 1921. But though it was a success in terms of numbers attending, Little felt that it had fallen at the first fence by lacking a clear plan of organisation and structure. It had, however, appointed an Argentinean delegation to the Irish Race Conference.

Little's long letter of 4 December provides the most realistic appraisal of the Irish position in Latin America. Buenos Aires was the only place of importance, as elsewhere travel costs, local interests, changing economic and political conditions and the sparse population of Irish people made travel pointless. Other countries in the continent could only provide a handful of Irish people. The Irish in Uruguay had made no attempt to contact Buenos Aires. Paraguay was 'very poor and is in an unstable condition as they had a revolution not long ago and expect another', and in Peru 'there is one doubtful Irishman actually discovered [but] owing to unstable conditions not much can be expected from there at present'. To concentrate on Argentina and Chile was Little's advice: 'there is no use wasting money on the other Republics'. Little also advocated another line of approach: 'in all the chief centres in Europe our representatives should try and get on terms with the representatives of all these republics'.

This latter was the policy Ireland adopted. At the League of Nations from 1923 Ireland's representative, Michael MacWhite, intensely cultivated Irish–Latin American historical links. He was successful in this policy, so much so that by 1930 MacWhite's successor, Seán Lester, was able to canvas support from the Latin American republics at Geneva for votes in Ireland's successful election to the League of Nations Council as a non-permanent member.

THE TREATY AND LATIN AMERICA: RELATIONS WITH THE PROVISIONAL GOVERNMENT

Chile
In Chile the Irish community backed the December 1921 Treaty. Describing themselves as 'auxiliaries abroad', they said it was 'their bounden duty to abide by whatever decisions our leaders at home may think it advisable to come to'.[32] Unhindered by the burgeoning split in Ireland over the Treaty, Egan graciously thanked all those in Chile who had helped the Irish cause. After consulting rep-

---

32 UCDA P80 261, letter from leaders of the Chilean Irish community to FitzGerald, 20 January 1922.

resentatives of the Irish colony he gave a series of lunches under the auspices of the committee for the proprietors of the major newspapers that supported Ireland. It was an astute move and created a 'public topic very friendly to future relations'.[33] Egan again played the diplomat by building up the importance of Chile to Ireland. At a reception in Santiago he mentioned how the Minister for Foreign Affairs, George Gavan Duffy, had referred to Chilean support in a Dáil speech. Egan successfully played on the role of the Chilean Irish in the Sinn Féin struggle. He ended with a toast to the Chilean press.[34] The reception received strong coverage in Chilean newspapers.

The Chilean Irish were content with the treaty of 1921 probably because they were a small and united group firmly led by Egan. He seems to have avoided splitting the small Irish community and worked well with local interests to build up the Irish cause. In a newspaper interview Egan made sure that the Chilean people would continue to have an interest in Ireland. He appealed not to their romantic notions of Ireland, but to their pockets: 'Ireland ... will become a big consumer of Chilean nitrate for agricultural usage, and Chile will need many Irish products, I have no doubt that in the near future a productive interchange will be initiated'.[35] The journalist took his leave of Egan, calling him 'a true son of Erin'; as we will see below, it was a far cry from the position facing Laurence Ginnell and Eamon Bulfin in Argentina.

Bulfin was forced to tender his resignation as Irish envoy due to ill health in February 1922, but Gavan Duffy seems to have prevailed on him to stay on in a semi-official capacity. Egan continued to report in passing on events in Chile and on irregular propaganda after the outbreak of the Irish Civil War, but he never undertook any sustained diplomatic work for the Free State. Joseph Walshe, the secretary of the Department of External Affairs, kept in touch with Egan and in August 1922 was in the process of making sure that Egan was reimbursed for his propaganda work over the previous year.[36] Egan's position is hard to work out in the months leading up to the establishment of the Free State. Walshe wrote to Egan on this matter, speaking of Egan's 'somewhat equivocal position'.[37] Egan had no official credentials and was instructed to keep his actions confined to trade matters, though he reported frequently to both the Department of External Affairs and the Department of Trade. In August 1923 Egan was finally officially appointed Honorary Irish Trade Agent in Chile.

Argentina
The success of the Dáil loan was the most pressing item in Irish–Argentine relations in January 1922. George Gavan Duffy wrote to the accountant general,

33 Ibid., Egan to FitzGerald, undated, December 1921.   **34** A report of this speech is contained in UCDA P80 261.   **35** UCDA P80 261, newspaper interview by Egan, 8 December 1921.   **36** NAI DFA ES 216, 2 August 1922.   **37** NAI DFA ES 219, 25 October 1922.

George McGrath, that 'it concerns your department alone and not this department'.³⁸ Gavan Duffy requested that the 'immediate recall to Ireland of Mr Ginnell is in contemplation' and that if it was appropriate McGrath should stop the loan.

Following a cabinet meeting on 27 January, Gavan Duffy wrote to Ginnell requesting that he return home and meet the cabinet. The inexact position of the loan in Argentina was clear, as Gavan Duffy wrote that the Minister for Finance (Michael Collins) 'seems to be in the dark as to the exact position'.³⁹

The 'exact position' was far from promising, and once news filtered back to Dublin the ruinous position of Ginnell in Argentina was clear. The timing of the signature of the Treaty was disastrous from Ginnell's perspective. By the end of November 1921 the preparatory work was completed and the selling of bonds was to commence. Ginnell had slowly prepared the ground and, he wrote later, 'had foundation for my confidence'.⁴⁰ Then the news of the signature and passage of the Treaty reached Argentina and proved the death knell of Ginnell's mission.

In Argentina the trustees of the loan met to consider their position 'as affected by recent events in Ireland'.⁴¹ Erroneously, the trustees unanimously agreed that when the Treaty was passed the republican government ceased to exist and so the trustee's power to raise the loan lapsed. Clearly this was different to the pro-Free State Irish in Chile. The Argentinean committee spoke of 'the uncertainty and discouragement consequent on the Anglo–Irish negotiations'. Despite the unsatisfactory outcome in Argentinean eyes, twenty people had subscribed to the loan and it had raised $19,155. This figure was not much greater than Little had expected to be collected. Expenses had come to $11,280 and subscribers who wished would be reimbursed a proportion of their initial subscription out of the remaining $7,875. It was felt that full expenses should be paid, as had the loan run its full course these expenses would have been acceptable. The money could also go to another Irish use. Any remaining money would be banked in the name of the new Irish Argentinean organisation.

This whole action was based on a misunderstanding of the relationship between the Dáil administration and the provisional government. The provisional government had no remit over external matters. As Gavan Duffy made clear to Frank Egan, 'This Department [Foreign Affairs] is not connected with the provisional government, and Foreign Affairs will remain in the domain of the Republican Government until such time as that government is superseded by a Free State government'.⁴² This was not to be until December 1922. But in Argentina 'once it became known that the treaty had been signed, no Irish Republican Bond could be sold; and once Dáil Eireann had adopted the treaty

---

38 NAI DE 2/357, 25 January 1922. **39** NAI DFA F.S 216/4, Gavan Duffy to Ginnell, 30 January 1922. **40** NAI DFA ES 216, Ginnell to Gavan Duffy, 3 March 1922. **41** NAI DE 2/357, minutes of meeting dated 3 February 1922. **42** NAI DFA ES 229.

the Republic was universally regarded as at an end'.[43] Ginnell was made aware by local interests that 'my obvious duty [was] to close up and leave the country as soon as possible'. He told Gavan Duffy that though he could, if requested, represent the Republic in other states, 'it would be quite impossible in this state'. Ginnell wisely decided to leave by issuing a farewell address 'which will ensure a friendly reception for any other representative of Ireland'.

Gavan Duffy hoped that Ginnell would stay on in Latin America and complete his mission by going to Chile, where the Irish community had come out in favour of the Treaty. The Dáil ministry granted that Ginnell could return home immediately a general election was called. Ginnell stayed on in Argentina. Only in March 1922 did reports filter through to Argentina that representatives in foreign countries still represented the Republic. This delay had destroyed Ginnell's work. His 3 March report to Gavan Duffy made clear that an earlier announcement:

> would have modified my action, and enabled me to carry on the work, at least temporarily, just when everything was ready to carry it on vigorously. No hint of it appeared in the press, and no one in this country imagined ... anything else than that the Republic had been definitely overthrown and was at an end.[44]

The events since December had wrecked Ginnell's work, the loan was dead, the bulletin moribund and the Irish community unwilling to support the Treaty.

Ginnell and Bulfin closed the Irish office in Buenos Aires and duly liquidated the loan. Like Ginnell, Bulfin felt 'that my services can be of no further use to the Government' and he also tendered his resignation.[45] He went so far as to say that 'no representative can be of practical use to the Irish Government at the present moment in this country. The political situation at home and the position of affairs in this country are the main reasons I have for this belief'. Bulfin intended to sail for Britain, but the British consul refused to issue him with an appropriate visa. In a letter of 15 May Bulfin went one step further; he said that even if arrangements had been made for continuance of representation he would 'have felt obliged nevertheless to adhere to my resolution'.[46] The reason for this forthright statement soon became clear.

* * *

With Ginnell and Bulfin about to depart, a faction amongst the Irish Argentines who had been opposed to Ginnell's work tried to get their own representative, their 'leader' Padraic MacManus, accredited by Dublin as official republican representative in the country. The faction seems to have been composed of the

---

[43] NAI DFA ES 216, Ginnell to Gavan Duffy, 3 March 1922. [44] NAI DFA ES 216. [45] Ibid., 19 March 1922. [46] Ibid.

Irish Republican League and the Irish Catholic Association. It was a strange about turn, but it seems to have been directly related to Ginnell's departure. A letter to Collins and Gavan Duffy from Edmund Flannery and Carlos Brady, representing the MacManus faction and written on Irish Republican League notepaper, called for a representative of 'competence and recognised patriotism who would have a knowledge of the conditions in this country'.[47] The letter was little more than a thinly disguised attempt by the MacManus faction to gain the upper hand in Irish Argentinean domestic politics by appealing to the Dublin government. MacManus was credited with maintaining Irish principles in Argentina and resisting the Anglicisation of the Irish colony. The authors wasted little time getting to their main point: to attack Ginnell. They spoke of 'the deplorable results of the mission [which] should be sufficient to show you the advisability of confiding Irish interests to persons acquainted with the conditions here and with the personality acceptable to the critical character of the Argentine population'. Ginnell was little more than a British dupe, according to this faction; he had stayed in British hotels, spent his money with British friends and then left on a British ship. The conclusion was that he was 'managed from beginning to end by the British legation'. Needless to say, he had treated the MacManus faction 'with marked discourtesy and inattention'. This kind of treatment was 'to be avoided in the future'. The obvious solution, from MacManus' perspective, was the appointment of Padraic MacManus to deal officially with Irish interests in Argentina. There was no response from Dublin to this selfless offer of support to the Irish diplomatic service.

It was only in his later reports that Ginnell seemed fully aware of the intense factionalism of the Irish Argentineans. Perhaps he walked into the arena without proper knowledge, or perhaps he felt that he had sided with the stronger faction, who would be buoyed up by support from Dublin. Dublin, it seemed, was of little importance to the factions amongst the Buenos Aires Irish. Control of their own patch was more important, and outsiders like Ginnell were not welcome, especially if they came looking for money about a faraway place about which the Argentinean Irish knew next to nothing: Ireland.

It was not until after World War II that Ireland again ventured towards Argentina. In 1947 a chargé d'affaires represented Ireland in Buenos Aires. The mission was upgraded to ambassadorial status in 1964.

CONCLUSION

Sinn Féin's 'moment' in Latin America was not very successful either financially or in terms of support. It seems that Dublin felt that simply using the same tac-

47 Ibid., 3 April 1922.

tics as were successful in the United States and Europe would succeed in Argentina and Chile. The Irish community in both these countries was a more isolated body, made up of the sons and daughters of emigrants rather than those who had immediate memories of Ireland. So it is not surprising that Sinn Féin envoys came up against suspicion and were the victims of factionalism.

Frank Egan appears as the most effective of the Sinn Féin envoys. Perhaps this was because he was a native of Chile and was not perceived as a 'blow-in' like Ginnell. Ginnell was simply unaware of the bear-pit he was descending into and was then caught off guard by the nature of Argentine Irish politics. It is really only with Egan's effective propaganda that Sinn Féin could be said to be have made any headway in Latin America.

It has become fashionable lately to try and build up the role of the Irish Diaspora and to see it as a kind of Irish empire of the spirit. However, the case of the Irish in Latin America shows the dangers of this idealistic perspective. Time and distance break down all but emotional links. It is little surprise that it was in drama and culture that the Irish envoys were the most successful in their Latin American missions. When it came to practical involvement in Irish affairs the Irish in Latin America, especially in Argentina, showed the negative side of the Irish 'empire of the spirit'. They viewed the Irish missions from their own perspective and wanted either to obtain power, as seen by the MacManus faction in Argentina, or to play at being Irish without the responsibility, as seen through Ginnell's experiences through the bond drive. It was only in Chile that the Irish community saw themselves in perspective and waited for a response from Dublin over the Treaty. The Irish in Argentina simply jumped headlong into the debate and rejected the Treaty. It would seem that failing to judge and understand the nature of these more isolated Irish communities was at the heart of the lack of success of the Sinn Féin envoys to Latin America from 1919.

'Weird Prophecies': British Intelligence and Anglo–Irish Relations, 1932–3

Eunan O'Halpin

INTRODUCTION

This chapter discusses the sources of political intelligence on Irish affairs available to the British government during Eamon de Valera's first turbulent administration (1932–3) and speculates on the reasons why policymakers were so consistently misinformed about Irish political conditions. It throws light on the benefits and the limitations of diplomatic cryptanalysis (decryption or codebreaking) as a source of information on de Valera's aims and plans and also sets the decision to read Irish diplomatic traffic in the wider context of Dominion relations after the Statute of Westminster, as Britain began to make the painful adjustment from proprietorship of an empire towards partnership in a commonwealth. Finally, it brings back by nine years the date from which it can be stated with certainty that the British government decrypted Irish diplomatic traffic: hitherto, this could only be demonstrated from 1941, the year in which Irish material first appears in the selection of intercepted and decrypted military and diplomatic messages supplied daily to Prime Minister Winston Churchill.[1] It is also clear that the British took some interest in foreign diplomatic traffic to and from Dublin at least from 1930 onwards.

BRITISH REACTIONS TO THE COMING OF DE VALERA, 1932–3

On 18 January 1932 J.W. Dulanty, the Irish High Commissioner in London, received the Great Seal of the Saorstát from King George V. Coming so soon after the passage of the Statute of Westminster in December 1931, this modest ceremony was of considerable symbolic importance, marking the Commonwealth's unequivocal recognition of the Irish Free State as an equal with Britain

---

[1] Eunan O'Halpin, '"According to the Irish Minister in Rome ...": British Decrypts and Irish Diplomacy in the Second World War', *Irish Studies in International Affairs*, vol. 6 (1995), pp 95–105.

and the other Dominions and confirming that, like the other Dominions, it now engaged with the British Commonwealth on an entirely voluntary basis. What appeared to be the final maturation of Anglo–Irish relations within a mutually-agreed framework was, however, haunted by the enigmatic spectre of Eamon de Valera. Brushing aside the diplomatic pleasantries appropriate for such an occasion, the King instead spoke his mind. 'What', he indelicately asked Dulanty, 'are we to do if Mr de Valera is returned' in the impending Irish general election? Dulanty, whose own prospects in such an eventuality did not look too rosy, sagely counselled a wait-and-see approach.² Shortly after the election, but before the Dáil met to select a new administration, Tom Jones, a retired cabinet official and a veteran of the lengthy negotiations which culminated in the signing of the Anglo–Irish Treaty on 6 December 1921, had a conversation with Stanley Baldwin, leader of the Conservative Party and Lord President of the Council in Ramsay MacDonald's recently formed National Government. Baldwin, normally the most equable of men, had alarming news. He told Jones that, following de Valera's victory, 'anything might happen'. A journalist had returned to London from Ireland

> with weird prophecies. The gunmen were expecting to be set free and made generals in the Free State Army ... When de Valera would be put up for President Labour would combine with Cosgrave and defeat him; then a dark horse would be trotted out in the shape of John Dillon's son and he would be elected.³

This bizarre analysis suggests two things: firstly, that just a decade after relinquishing control of the affairs of the twenty-six counties the British government was comically ill-informed about the realities of Irish party politics; and, secondly, that even in the face of the election result British ministers preferred to remain in denial, so appalling was the vista of turmoil conjured up by the thought of a de Valera government. There was no area of Anglo–Irish and Commonwealth affairs, from constitutional matters to defence and to economic relations, where this unbalanced extremist might not run amok. What were his political intentions in Ireland? What was he going to do about those aspects of the 1922 constitution which he abhorred as intolerable symbols of imperial subordination, such as the oath of allegiance to the monarch required of members of the Oireachtas before taking their seats and the role of the Governor General? How was he going to behave in Commonwealth affairs, where the other Dom-

---

2 Quoted in Nicholas Mansergh, *The Unresolved Question: The Anglo–Irish Settlement and its Undoing, 1912–72* (London, 1991), p. 282. **3** Thomas Jones, *A Diary with Letters, 1931–50* (Oxford, 1954), p. 31 (27 February 1932). Senator Maurice Manning, whose authoritative biography of James Dillon will appear shortly, expressed astonishment at this story.

inions might conceivably find some common cause with him? What were his military ambitions and intentions? What wild line might he adopt in the League of Nations, where Ireland was, inconveniently, due to hold the rotating presidency of the Assembly between September 1932 and January 1933?[4] Such issues had resonances not simply for bilateral Anglo–Irish relations, but for Commonwealth development – in May Geoffrey Dawson, the influential editor of *The Times*, 'talked Ireland mainly' at a Round Table dinner and there was considerable apprehension that the Imperial Economic Conference due to open in Ottawa in July would be deliberately thrown off course by the Irish delegates.[5]

A fortnight after de Valera became President of the Executive Council the British cabinet removed its head from the sand sufficiently to establish a powerful Irish Situation Committee (ISC) under the chairmanship of Prime Minister MacDonald. Its brief was to ride out the storm anticipated from de Valera's likely depredations, to afford him no easy triumphs by hasty overreaction and to find a way forward which would protect the interests, respectively, of the Commonwealth, of Britain and of responsible politicians in Ireland. The ISC became the decisive forum in the determination of British policy. During its first year in operation, its deliberations were bedevilled by straightforward and fundamental problems: profound ignorance of the nature and pace of political development in the Irish Free State; and an utter failure to appreciate the tactics and strategy of the new regime in Dublin. The Free State formally enjoyed exactly the same official links to Britain as did Canada, Australia and South Africa, but Dominion status allied to contiguity had created a curious paradox, where, precisely because Ireland was so near, London had neither the processes nor the personnel in place there to collect political information, to take soundings or to offer informed assessments of affairs to Whitehall. The only British official accredited to Dublin in a remotely diplomatic capacity was the Trade Commissioner, William Peters. While he did what he could to report on political affairs – proving himself, in Deirdre McMahon's words, 'a reliable and perceptive informant' – by so doing he was acting outside his remit and, as an official of the Department of Overseas Trade, his views carried little weight in the more august reaches of Whitehall, where those responsible for trade relations ranked even below consular officers.[6] In the face of these unauspicious circumstances, what other sources of advice and guidance were available?

Thanks largely to the logic of the Treaty, and in part to Cosgrave's polite but firm emasculation of the office since 1922, the Irish Governor General was no

---

4 Michael Kennedy, *Ireland and the League of Nations, 1919–46: International Relations, Diplomacy and Politics* (Dublin, 1996), pp 164–5. **5** Bodleian Library, MS Dawson 36, Dawson Diary, 5 May 1932. **6** Deirdre McMahon, '"A Transient Apparition": British Policy towards the de Valera Government, 1932–35', *Irish Historical Studies*, vol. 22, no. 88 (September, 1981), p. 338.

more than a cipher, entirely the prisoner of the government of the day. Furthermore, unlike other Dominion Governors General who customarily maintained informal links with Whitehall and the armed services through their personal secretariats and *aides de camp*, the Irish incumbent, James MacNeill, had only a small office staff, all of whom were Irish without any ties to London. In any case, he had limited experience of Irish politics and no contacts in the Fianna Fáil camp, having spent the bulk of his career in the Indian civil service before becoming the Irish Free State's first High Commissioner in London in 1922 and being appointed Governor General in 1928. He was, consequently, ill-placed to appreciate the subtleties of the policy of a party – Fianna Fáil – and of a politician – Eamon de Valera – hostile to the very existence of his office, let alone in a position to open informal lines of communication with the new regime which might shed some light on its real intentions.[7]

Another possible source of guidance on the tide of affairs in Ireland were the British intelligence and security services. However, because of both contiguity and Irish sensitivities, the security service, MI5, had no liaison arrangements with Dublin along the lines maintained with the other Dominion capitals – what few Anglo–Irish exchanges there were from time-to-time on security issues of common concern, such as republican activities outside of Ireland and the ramifications of international communism, were conducted between Scotland Yard and Garda headquarters. Moreover, Britain's main security concern after the Irish Free State came into being in 1922 had been the continued effectiveness of the passport control system which it had developed as a shield against espionage and Bolshevik subversion throughout the Empire. Ever since the Irish Free State began issuing its own passports and visas for foreigners in 1924, the Irish had been exemplary collaborators in the maintenance of tight controls on people seeking to enter the British Isles, both because this allowed for the maintenance of a common Irish–British travel area, thus facilitating the unfettered movement of people between Ireland and Britain, and because it was an extraordinarily effective and cost-free means of preventing immigration to the state from the continent or further afield. Precisely because it worked so well, operational aspects of Anglo–Irish passport control could be managed sufficiently by correspondence at departmental level and so never required the stationing of a British liaison officer in Dublin.[8]

Furthermore, MI5 had no obvious expertise on Ireland in 1932 – its Irish section was only established as war loomed in 1939 – and this may explain why its head, Sir Vernon Kell, 'after consideration declined' an invitation following de Valera's election to begin collecting information.[9] The British secret intelligence

---

7 Brendan Sexton, *Ireland and the Crown, 1922–36: The Governor Generalship of the Irish Free State* (Dublin, 1989), p. 118.   8 Eunan O'Halpin, 'Intelligence and Security in Ireland, 1922–45', *Intelligence and National Security* [hereafter *INS*], vol. 5, no. 1 (January, 1990), pp 57–8.   9 PRO KV 4/9, History of the MI5 Irish Section, 1939–45, p. 3.

service (SIS or MI6) proved more responsive. Although it had no presence in the Irish Free State in 1932, it and other departments did provide odd scraps of intelligence relating to Ireland from the United States and Europe – in August reports from naval intelligence about rumoured arms shipments from Hamburg and Antwerp to Ireland, at a time when there were fears that de Valera might be planning a military strike against the British forces in the Treaty ports or even against Northern Ireland, caused the ISC considerable alarm – although there was precious little useful material available from such sources.[10] SIS also established 'not an intelligence service, but a very restricted information service' in Ireland. This, however, never did more than 'give a limited cross section of private opinion on current events of political or public interest in Eire'.[11]

The residual British army presence in the Free State also offered some reporting opportunities – this may have been what the Chief of the Imperial General Staff had in mind in August when he undertook to investigate the possibility of 'obtaining information as to activities in the Irish Free State, both from the point of view of military intelligence and also of political intelligence'.[12] But officers in charge of care and maintenance parties in the Treaty ports had neither the training nor the contacts to act as informed analysts of Irish politics. Furthermore, the involvement of such officers in clandestine information gathering would inflame an already difficult diplomatic situation should such activities ever come to light.

There were, however, other sources of information and opinion on de Valera to hand in 1932: people who were directly involved in Irish affairs. Those on whom the British came largely to rely, in addition to members of the press, were casual visitors to Ireland; members of the Anglo–Irish ascendancy fearful lest de Valera turn on them; and, most significantly, supporters and members of the defeated Cumann na nGaedheal administration. In April Cumann na nGaedheal sent two emissaries to London to advise the British government on how best to deal with de Valera, whose bill to abolish the oath of allegiance was before the Dáil and who had already made clear his intention of withholding the land annuities payable to Britain under the Treaty. One of those sent was a senator; the other was, outrageously, a serving public official (Donal O'Sullivan, Clerk of the Seanad and later the author of an illuminating, though venomous, account of Irish Free State politics).[13] Ignoring the foolishness, let alone the

---

10 Bodleian Library, Sankey Papers, MS Eng. Hist. C. 286, Sankey Diary, 24 August 1932 (Sankey was Lord Chancellor and a member of the ISC); McMahon, '"A Transient Apparition"', p. 338; John Bowman, *De Valera and the Ulster Question, 1917–73* (Oxford, 1982), pp 110–14. 11 F.H. Hinsley and C.A.G. Simkins, *British Intelligence in the Second World War: Volume 4: Security and Counter-Intelligence* (London, 1991), pp 8–9; History of the MI5 Irish Section, p. 3. 12 PRO ADM 178/91, extracts from minutes of Irish Situation Committee, 5 August 1932. 13 Donal O'Sullivan, *The Irish Free State and its Senate* (London, 1940).

obvious impropriety, of clandestine discussions with representatives of a recently defeated political party in a new and volatile Dominion, British ministers accepted the analysis of their Irish visitors without reservation or adjustment. The picture presented was at once disturbing and reassuring. De Valera was, predictably, an impetuous, egocentric demagogue in hock to the IRA, not a man with whom anyone could ever do serious business. Accordingly, Cumann na nGaedheal above all urged Britain not to compromise – in pursuit of temporary calm – on the big financial and economic issues arising in Anglo–Irish affairs; rather, the policy should be to let de Valera destroy his own prospects by his reckless folly. This would, they reasoned, soon produce an economic crisis for the minority Fianna Fáil administration, resulting in an election in which the majority of the people would return to their senses and vote Cosgrave back into power. The ISC was so much at a loss to understand de Valera that for almost a year they subscribed to this puerile theory. British policy towards de Valera's government was formulated, accordingly, on the premise that the interests of the United Kingdom were coterminous with those of Cosgrave, and that nothing should be done which would lessen Cumann na nGaedheal's chances of securing power once more. This extraordinarily proprietorial attitude towards Cosgrave and his party came to underpin British policy for the duration of de Valera's first government; indeed, in September the ISC dismissed a proposed Anglo–Irish compromise on a financial issue, explicitly stating that it was 'unthinkable in Mr Cosgrave's interests, as well as our own', because de Valera's domestic audience would see it as a victory.[14]

Throughout the autumn, as Anglo–Irish tensions intensified on financial, trade and constitutional matters, the basis of British calculations remained the safeguarding of Cosgrave's prospects. Even when de Valera offered extreme provocation through his clumsily managed ouster of James MacNeill, the Governor General, Geoffrey Dawson counselled Buckingham Palace against 'the King giving Dev any excuse for a general election on an anti-King ticket' by refusing to accept his formal advice on MacNeill's replacement.[15] The futility of this strategy was exposed in early January 1933, as Dawson ruefully noted in his diary: 'Rather a desperate afternoon & still more desperate evening over de Valera's dissol[ution] of the Dáil announced in the early hours of the morning.' Three weeks later he recorded 'a bad time ... in London. Groans on de Valera's now assured victory', which put Fianna Fáil in a much stronger parliamentary position and put paid to any hope of Cosgrave's early return to power.[16] The basic premise which had underlain British policy since March 1932 – that de Valera's blunders, coupled with

---

14 McMahon, '"A Transient Apparition"', pp 336–7; ISC minutes, 27 September 1932: quoted at ibid., p. 344.   15 Bodleian Library, MS Dawson 36, Dawson Diary, 1 October 1932; Sexton, *Ireland and the Crown*, pp 131–41.   16 Bodleian Library, MS Dawson 37, Dawson Diary, 3 and 27 January 1933.

British firmness, would cause domestic support to shift back to Cosgrave, with a resultant restoration of Anglo–Irish harmony – was shown to be completely false.

In retrospect, it is clear that what Whitehall and the ISC needed, but did not have in 1932, were British officials on the ground in Dublin who could take political soundings and offer sensible appraisals of de Valera's activities and likely intentions. This crucial lacuna in Anglo–Irish diplomacy was only filled seven years later when the exigencies of war sufficiently outweighed the reservations of the two governments and the conventions of Dominion status to allow for the appointment of Sir John Maffey as the 'British Representative', in effect High Commissioner, in Dublin. Even then, it took some time for Maffey to come sufficiently to grips with Irish affairs to be able to read de Valera with any degree of confidence.[17]

DIPLOMATIC CODEBREAKING AND IRISH AFFAIRS, 1932–3

It is now clear that in 1932–3 the British government had one other potentially useful source on Irish policy and intentions: diplomatic cable traffic to and from Dublin. The records of the Government Code and Cipher School (GC&CS), the British codebreaking agency, are now available for the period from 1919 to December 1933. The inter-war GC&CS was a small, underfunded and highly secret government department which attempted to intercept and to read the encoded military and civilian cable and wireless traffic of foreign powers – both potential enemies and old friends. As part of the British government's understanding with the Post Office and the companies operating the international cables, GC&CS received copies of all encoded traffic on cables passing through British territory. It is also clear that all encoded traffic carried on the direct Ireland–North America cables was, similarly, supplied to GC&CS by the cable operators, a quiet luxury denied inter-war American codebreakers because of stringent federal laws prohibiting all disclosure of wireless and cable traffic in the United States to third parties, including the government.[18] It is a fair guess that Irish diplomatic traffic, sent in a straightforward code which appears to have been left unchanged for years, was amongst GC&CS's easier targets.

Included in the GC&CS records are sequentially-bound bundles, starting in 1926, of many thousands of sheets of intercepted and decrypted diplomatic cables (and occasionally wireless messages) from various countries whose communications were of interest to Britain. Some foreign code and cipher systems were studied for years without yielding any breakthroughs, while others were

---

17 Mansergh, *The Unresolved Question*, pp 309–10.   **18** Robert Angevine, 'Gentlemen Do Read Each Other's Mail: American Intelligence in the Interwar Era', *INS*, vol. 7, no. 2 (April, 1992), p. 18.

broken within days of the first investigations and could easily be read for years thereafter – success depended upon their complexity, the coding procedures followed, the amount of intercepted traffic available for analysis and other factors. If they were thought to contain anything of possible interest, decrypted (and usually translated) messages were circulated to appropriate customer departments in Whitehall – most frequently the Foreign Office, the three armed service ministries, the Colonial Office, the Dominions Office, the India Office and the Department of Overseas Trade – and copies were kept in GC&CS. Depending on the complexity of the code involved, the date and quality of interception and other variables, decrypts might only be partial or might be completed long after the message under attack had been sent and acted on. Furthermore, many decrypts were so anodyne that they were not issued to departments, and in such cases it is assumed that no copies were kept by GC&CS.[19]

The diplomatic decrypts so far released not only cast a little additional light on Britain's conduct of its relations with other states, but also undermine some of the received wisdom about British codebreaking in the inter-war era. The intercepts show that British inter-war cryptoanalytic activity was somewhat more widespread than previous accounts have suggested (such as those based largely on the recollections of codebreakers who naturally thought their organisation was grievously underfunded).[20] The new releases appear to be a full set of GC&CS's surviving copies of all diplomatic cable and wireless traffic successfully intercepted, decrypted, distributed and stored between 1926 and 1933. They make interesting reading for students of both Anglo–Irish and wider Commonwealth relations. They also command the attention of those interested in the phenomenon of 'intra-allied intelligence' – less delicately, spying on one's friends – which has only recently begun to receive systematic scholarly analysis.[21]

Amongst the GC&CS intercepts up to 23 March 1932 there are no Irish messages and no inter-Dominion messages. This suggests that prior to the election of de Valera, the Free State was treated no differently than the other Dominions, whose communications traffic was apparently sacrosanct. His advent evidently caused a double departure from established practice: not only did GC&CS, presumably acting on the request of interested departments, sometimes decrypt Irish messages and the traffic of foreign missions in Ireland, but it also read, stored and circulated to its customers bilateral exchanges between Ireland and the Dominions – the intercepts include inter-governmental messages from

---

19 I am grateful to Michael Herman, author of *Intelligence Power in Peace and War* (Cambridge, 1996), for comments on these and other points. **20** Robert Denniston, 'Diplomatic Eavesdropping, 1922–44: A New Source Discovered', *INS*, vol. 10, no. 3 (July, 1995), pp 423–6. **21** Martin Alexander, 'Introduction: Knowing your Friends, Assessing your Allies – Perspectives on Inter-Allied Intelligence', *INS*, vol. 13, no. 1 (Spring, 1998), pp 12–14.

Dublin to Pretoria, from Dublin to Canberra and from Ottawa to Dublin. This presented no technical difficulties, as Britain supplied the standard codes used for inter-Dominion communications. Nevertheless, the practice carried particular risks for Britain's relations with the overseas Dominions, on whose cooperation in signals intelligence gathering around the world GC&CS and the armed services were largely dependent. Although the contents of the messages were not particularly significant – they deal with arrangements for the Ottawa Imperial Economic Conference – Canada, Australia and South Africa would presumably have regarded British decryption of their confidential bilateral communications with Dublin as a serious breach of the spirit of Commonwealth cooperation embodied in the Statute of Westminster.[22]

The intercepted and decrypted telegrams relating to Ireland released in the GC&CS records fall into five categories (the number in each is indicated in brackets): communications from the Irish government to the governments of other Dominions (2) and communications from the governments of other Dominions to the Irish government (1), as discussed above; communications from External Affairs to Irish missions or representatives abroad (4); communications from Irish missions abroad to External Affairs (6); and communications from foreign missions in Dublin – the Italian, the Belgian and the American – to their national capitals (5). All the cables were despatched in the period between March and July 1932, when British policymakers were struggling to understand the new Irish regime. Cumulatively, they raise questions about both the usefulness and the limitations of such sources in diplomatic affairs.

The External Affairs messages to missions abroad which survive in the GC&CS records – two to Washington, one to Paris and one to Geneva – deal with a miscellany of matters. The first, sent to Washington on 23 March, enjoined the Irish minister to 'keep Press informed unofficially ... that there has not been for many years such peace, harmony and goodwill amongst our people at home', a remarkably sanguine description of the prevailing political ferment. The second concerned a proposed trade mission to the United States. The third sought urgent action on a press report that French officials were making 'difficulties in inducing the police authorities to accept "Irlandais" as a definition of nationality. It is stated that officials substitute "Anglais" therefor'. The fourth was a brief reply to a request for instructions from Sean Lester, the Irish representative at the League of Nations in Geneva.[23] None are of particular importance. The decoded original of only one of these messages has been traced in the

---

[22] PRO HW 12 157 and 157, Walshe, secretary, Department of External Affairs, Dublin to Bodenstein, South African government, Pretoria, 30 May 1932; Dublin to Prime Minister's Department, Canberra, 5 July; Minister for External Affairs, Ottawa, to Minister for External Affairs, Dublin, 8 July.   [23] PRO HW 12 154, 155 and 157, decrypts of External Affairs to Washington, 23 March and 28 April, to Paris, 5 July, and to Geneva, 6 July 1932.

Department of External Affairs records, in a file dealing with what was clearly considered a routine enquiry rather than a matter of high policy.²⁴

The six messages from missions abroad to External Affairs are similarly anodyne: indeed, the only two original decodes of such cables traced in External Affairs records, messages from the New York consulate of 2 and 4 May, are rather less interesting than many others in the same file. The only message of any substance is that from Sean Lester in Geneva, which gives some details of negotiations between the representatives of Britain and of the Dominions about an imminent disarmament resolution. This was decrypted too late to have any bearing on Britain's handling of the matter.²⁵ That the decrypted messages are so unexceptional may be, perhaps in part, because serving Irish diplomats treated the new regime in Dublin with considerable circumspection. As C.S. Andrews – the forthright IRA veteran and public servant – later recalled, most Fianna Fáilers in 1932 regarded the civil service as 'a crowd of Free State bastards' and 'anti-national' and expected a major clean-out once de Valera took office; likewise, some government officials themselves undoubtedly feared a blood-letting.²⁶ It is also possible that other Irish decrypts have been withheld, although it is hard to think of a reason why, or that GC&CS in fact kept copies of only some intercepts for illustrative purposes. However, the main reason why the Irish messages are so unexceptional is surely this: from the time he took office de Valera played his cards very close to his chest and did not confide his intentions to officials at home and abroad, save in the most general sense, until action was imminent. Further, the Irish external communications which mattered most in 1932 were between Dublin and High Commissioner Dulanty in London and these could be maintained more securely by courier rather than by cable. This may explain why there are no Dublin–London messages amongst the surviving intercepts.

Of the five messages from foreign missions in Dublin, those from the Belgian and Italian missions report government approaches to improve bilateral trade in order to lessen Irish dependence on the British market. The intercepts were duly sent to the Department of Overseas Trade and may conceivably have been of some use in assessing Irish trade policy.²⁷ The cable from the United States mission to Washington reports the 'situation regarded here as very serious' because of the Anglo–Irish trade war looming on foot of the land annuities dispute, but it conveys nothing more than could be gleaned from newspapers or other open sources.²⁸ One of many American diplomatic intercepts – the British had broken

---

24 NAI DFA Pre-100 Series, 5/33, originals of External Affairs to Paris and reply, both of 5 July 1932.   **25** PRO HW 12 157, text of Lester, Geneva, to External Affairs, 6 July (decrypted 9 July) 1932.   **26** C.S. Andrews, *Man of No Property: An Autobiography: Volume II* (Dublin, 1982), pp 120–1.   **27** PRO HW 12 157, texts of Mariani, Dublin, to Rome, and of Goor, Dublin, to Brussels, both 19 July 1932.   **28** Ibid., Sterling, Dublin, to Washington, 2 July

some, if not all, of the State Department's encoding systems in use at the time – it was, nevertheless, duly circulated to the Foreign Office and the Department of Overseas Trade, which could scarcely have been shocked by its contents.[29]

The GC&CS records also contain some American intercepts pertaining to Ireland dating from the W.T. Cosgrave era. These include exchanges in 1930 between Washington and the United States embassy in London and two between Washington and the American legation in Dublin. They concern the delay in Irish accession to the London Naval Treaty. As such, they disclose the straightforward explanation which the Irish government offered to the American consul general in Dublin and to the State Department in Washington and which Patrick McGilligan, the Minister for External Affairs, gave to the British government during discussions in London. This was that the treaty had first to be ratified by a resolution of the Dáil, which was not due to sit for several weeks. Because of the subject matter the Admiralty was included on the distribution list for this material.[30] As it would take some weeks' work to go through all the many thousands of surviving foreign diplomatic decrypts between 1926 and 1933, it may be that other decrypts relating to Ireland exist, but have not yet been found in the GC&CS collection. It is also highly likely that inter-war Irish intercepts appear in the records of other states which invested in codebreaking: this is certainly true of France, where some Paris–Dublin material has survived in the archives.[31]

The release of this set of GC&CS intercepts presents other problems for the historian. Did the British not bother to read Irish traffic before March 1932, or was it simply that the contents were so unexceptional that no decrypts were issued to departments or copies kept by GC&CS? Although relations with Cosgrave had generally been good, his administration had a record of unwelcome innovation in both Commonwealth and League of Nations affairs from 1923 which had seen the progressive redefinition of the status of Dominions on lines which the British had not favoured. For example, there must have been considerable temptation to have a look at inter-Dominion traffic in the run-up to the Imperial Conferences of 1926 and 1930 to see whether the Irish were stirring the pot. Yet it appears that Irish government traffic was put on a par with that of the other Dominions and regarded as inviolable until March 1932 (unless, that is, potentially embarrassing records of Dominions' intercepts were destroyed once issued or are still being held back in a separate class).

1932. **29** Kathryn Brown, 'Intelligence and the Decision to Collect it: Churchill's Wartime American Diplomatic Signals Intelligence', *INS*, vol. 10, no. 3 (July, 1995), pp 449–50. **30** PRO HW 12 136, Sterling, Dublin, to State Department, and Dawes, London, to State Department, both 21 October 1930. **31** France, *Ministère des Affaires Étrangères, Collection de Telegrammes Interceptes*, vol. 1. I am grateful to Dr. Peter Jackson of the Department of International Politics, University of Wales, Aberystwyth, for this reference.

There are other questions to be answered. Why did GC&CS bother to store and to circulate such generally anodyne intercepts in the spring and summer of 1932? The answer may be that this was done simply to show that Irish traffic was not worth the bother of breaking. What use, if any, were the Irish intercepts to British policy makers in 1932? Despite the release of the Irish intercepts, the answer to this crucial question may never be known. This is because the copies supplied to the departments concerned with Irish affairs, together with all references to such secret sources, were removed from the relevant policy files before they were transferred to the Public Record Office. With some series of records – for example the vast Foreign Office class FO371, which is bound into volumes – a researcher can at least tell from the bindings where material has been excised; with others, including Dominions Office files, this cannot be done because the papers are in looseleaf files and are only held together with Treasury tags. This problem applies not only to decrypts, but related sources of information which British policymakers may have used, such as telephone taps, stolen documents, agent reports or whatever.

It may be that further releases of GC&CS intercepts covering the period from January 1934 up to the outbreak of war in September 1939 will disclose a similar pattern of activity, with occasional outbursts of interest at times of Anglo–Irish crisis, whether constitutional, economic, political or related to defence – for example, during the negotiations to end the economic war and to settle the question of the Treaty ports in 1937–8 – interspersed with long stretches when no one in London troubled to decrypt whatever messages came to, and went from, Dublin. It is also to be hoped that the British government will soon follow the example set in 1991 by the Irish Department of Foreign Affairs and Department of Defence. They have released various documents from the 1939–45 period showing the realities of the Irish state's surveillance of its foreign diplomatic community in a period of crisis. Included are transcripts of telephone conversations, clandestine photostats of diplomatic correspondence, documents purloined from diplomatic wastebaskets and other material, all of which was channelled to policymakers in External Affairs.[32] If a small state could mount such successful surveillance operations, how much more thorough a watch through telephone intercepts, hidden microphones, suborned servants and the like could the British have kept on Irish diplomacy at times of Anglo–Irish tension? To take a crucial example, when, if ever, will historians see whatever evidence remains of surveillance of the Irish Treaty delegation in London – Sir Basil Thomson's Directorate of Intelligence spied enthusiastically on other diplomatic missions in that era, and it defies belief that his or some other British

---

[32] Eunan O'Halpin, 'Army, Politics and Society in Independent Ireland, 1932–45', in T.G. Fraser and Keith Jeffery (eds), *Men, Women and War: Historical Studies XVIII* (Dublin, 1993), pp 170–1.

agency would not have done their best to follow as closely as possible the debates in 22 Hans Place. Only when such documents become available in association with the relevant policy files will historians have a clear picture of the material on which key assessments and decisions were based. The British government's gradual acknowledgement that it did indeed read other countries' messages in peacetime, and its ongoing programme of releasing diplomatic intercepts from the inter-war period, bring that still distant day somewhat closer.

CONCLUSION

British government policy towards Ireland during de Valera's first year in power was characterised by a remarkable dearth of reliable information and assessment on Irish political affairs, coupled with extraordinary reliance on the prospect of an early return to power for Cosgrave and Cumann na nGaedheal. While a prolonged period of Anglo–Irish tension was unavoidable once de Valera took office – as even the ISC recognised, he had strong domestic reasons for wanting a row – British policymakers were undoubtedly hampered in their calculations by the fact that they had so little insight into his aims and objectives. The main reasons for this are obvious enough: undue reliance on his domestic enemies for advice and guidance on how to deal with him, and the absence of officials on the ground in Dublin who could provide a more dispassionate and professional analysis of Irish affairs. It is, however, also clear that Britain attempted to gauge what de Valera was really up to by the simple expedient of reading some of his diplomatic communications. It is unfortunate that such decrypts, unexceptional though they are, have still to be studied in isolation from the policy files of which they were undoubtedly once part.

Inter-war Irish–German Diplomacy: Continuity, Ambiguity and Appeasement in Irish Foreign Policy

Mervyn O'Driscoll

INTRODUCTION

Inter-war Irish–German diplomacy has escaped sustained examination, despite the central role of the 'German question' in modern European history. This oversight is conspicuous considering the subsequent importance of Irish–German relations during the Emergency. In addition, just as many of the new post-Versailles European states shared common traits, superficial similarities existed between inter-war Germany and Ireland.[1] Immediately after the Great War, for example, both countries experienced revolutions, reluctantly signed domestically divisive treaties and witnessed the birth of indigenous parliamentary democracies. In the 1920s they faced the challenges of new statehood in an adverse international climate, while their international status remained ambiguous and uncertain. Then the Wall Street Crash adversely affected their economies and fuelled the rise of anti-treaty political parties – Fianna Fáil and the National Socialist Worker's Party (the NSDAP or Nazi Party) – whose election manifestos set out an agenda for foreign policy revisionism and autarchy. These parties ultimately gained power in the early 1930s and then implemented their election promises. Arguably, both regimes adopted authoritarian political styles, although Fianna Fáil did so within the democratic fold, while the Nazis acted in an openly dictatorial manner. This distinction is crucial and it means that the resemblances in international situations, regime changes and economic policies, while significant, should not obscure the profound contrasts between Germany and Ireland after Versailles.

The ensuing analysis of inter-war Irish–German diplomacy focuses on key Irish policymakers, notably Eamon de Valera, the Taoiseach and Minister for External Affairs, Joseph Walshe, the secretary of the Department of External Affairs, and the diplomats on the ground in Berlin: Dr Daniel Binchy, Leo T. McCauley and Charles Bewley. It concentrates on the unsuccessful efforts of

---

[1] Hubert Sturm, *Hakenkreuz und Kleebatt: Irland, die Allierten und das Dritte Reich, 1933–1945* (Frankfurt, 1984).

Irish envoys to secure recognition for the new state in the early 1920s and the subsequent collapse of their nascent diplomatic presence in Berlin amidst a welter of acrimony and confusion. The Irish Free State and the Weimar republic eventually established formal diplomatic relations in 1929. Irish representatives, therefore, were witnesses to key German domestic events throughout the late 1920s and the 1930s, and their confidential reports provide significant insights into this crucial era of German history as well as the development of Irish foreign policy.[2]

Coincidentally, the first Irish ministers in Berlin – Binchy and Bewley – were both in Germany during the early stages of the Weimar Republic, although in different capacities. In the early 1920s Binchy was a student in Munich and Bewley was Ireland's unofficial trade representative in Berlin. Later, in his capacity as Ireland's official envoy to Germany between 1929 and 1932, Binchy experienced first-hand the disintegration of Weimar parliamentary democracy. Leo McCauley, who represented Ireland at the rank of chargé d'affaires after Binchy's departure, was an able commentator on the final, decisive phase of the Weimar Republic's demise. His successor, Charles Bewley, witnessed the economic, political and social consolidation of the Nazi regime. Economic self-sufficiency, the Hitler cult, *Gleichschaltung* (the extension of Hitlerite control over domestic organisations), the elimination of political rivals, Nazi racial policies and Hitler's revisionist foreign policy are all covered in Bewley's diplomatic reports. Owing to his anti-Semitism, proto-fascism and his disastrous relationship with his Irish colleagues, Bewley was the most controversial Irish diplomat of his generation and, probably, of the first seventy years of the Irish diplomatic service; for this reason he is an interesting character worthy of deeper analysis. So, too, are the tenures of Binchy and McCauley and the attitudes of Irish policymakers towards Germany.

This analytical exercise yields a variegated interpretation of Irish diplomacy in Berlin during the inter-war era. Irish–German relations during this period were characterised by continuity, ambiguity and appeasement. In terms of diplomatic personnel, Bewley and Binchy were constants in the Irish–German relationship. Another significant element of permanency was the German foreign policy perspective. In the German national interest, German attitudes towards the new Irish state between the wars displayed marked official indifference to Irish nationalist sensitivities. Under both the Weimar and Nazi regimes, Germany was determined to ameliorate Anglo–German relations to counteract French *revanchisme*. Irish–German intimacy potentially threatened Anglo–German friendship. Therefore, Germany inevitably subordinated Irish–German relations to greater German strategic and diplomatic considerations.

---

2 A more comprehensive interpretation is available in Mervyn O'Driscoll, *Irish–German Relations* (forthcoming, 2000).

Conversely, Berlin's official attitudes were suffused, to a certain degree, by an unconcealed empathy with Irish nationalism. Ambiguity similarly permeated Eamon de Valera's and the Irish government's postures towards pre-war Nazi Germany, as the forthcoming analysis establishes. On one hand, the Irish government, newspapers throughout the country and the Catholic Church deplored certain unfolding Nazi internal policies. Though sections of Irish society were anti-communist, latently anti-Semitic and disillusioned with parliamentary democracy, the rabid anti-religious, anti-Semitic and totalitarian nature of Nazism, particularly as it developed in the mid 1930s, was offensive to Irish eyes. On the other hand, the historical record also shows that although de Valera, other Irish decision-makers and opinion leaders harboured substantial reservations about the domestic extremes of Nazism, they, nonetheless, were well disposed to the German revision of the Treaty of Versailles. According to the Irish nationalist interpretation, the Treaty of Versailles unjustly denuded Germany of her national sovereignty, territory, wealth and population. Thus nationalist empathy with German national degradation combined with the Irish government's staunch support for the League of Nations and collective security to produce an Irish appeasement policy. Its rationale was that nationalist slights against Germany should be admitted and corrected in order to transform Hitler's Germany into a contented European state, an outcome that would avoid future European conflict.

PRE-1929 IRISH–GERMAN RELATIONS

Roger Casement's efforts to forge an Irish–German alliance during World War I were instrumental in uniting a segment of the Irish population with sympathisers in Germany and led to the creation of the German–Irish Society (Deutsche–Irische Gesellschaft). The society outlived Casement and later provided part of the basis for Irish attempts to forge diplomatic links with the Weimar Republic. This aim was crucial to Dáil Éireann, which established missions abroad during the Anglo–Irish War to demonstrate Irish independence from Great Britain and to seek diplomatic recognition for the nascent Irish state.[3] The enthusiastic report of a peripatetic Irish envoy who visited Berlin in early 1921 (probably George Gavan Duffy), stimulated the Dáil's interest in Germany. The Irish representative was:

> tremendously impressed by the spirit and determination of the people and by the anti-Ally feeling generally prevalent despite official efforts at a

[3] Mervyn O'Driscoll, 'Irish–German Diplomatic Relations, 1922–39: An Examination of Irish Diplomatic Performances in Berlin, 1922–39' (unpublished MA thesis, University College Cork, 1992), chapter 1.

pro-English policy. I have not in any of the war countries come across anything like the cool confidence and assurance with which the Germans view the future and many of their leading men are willing to be pro-Irish because England is our enemy ...⁴

Two of the staff in the Dáil's Berlin mission, Dr Nancy Power and her assistant, Michael O'Brien, were students of the Berlin University Professor of Celtic, Julius Pokorny, who was an active member of the German–Irish Society.⁵ The leader of the Irish political operation in Berlin, John Chartres, a trusted acquaintance of Michael Collins, had played a key role during the Anglo–Irish negotiations of 1920 as secretary to the Irish Delegation.⁶ Together the Irish mission and the Irish–German Society resurrected the *Irish Bulletin* (*Irisches Bulletin*) that the society had produced during the latter half of World War I. The *Bulletin*, targeted at a German audience, promoted the Irish independence movement and counteracted British accounts of the Anglo–Irish War.⁷

In early December 1921 Charles Bewley arrived as the Irish trade representative. He and his assistant, Cornelius Duane, were accountable to Ernest Blythe, the Minister for Trade, and not to George Gavan Duffy, the Minister for Foreign Affairs. This twin-track organisational approach led a to lack of coordination and an unnecessary division of duties between the two offices.⁸ The situation was further complicated by professional jealousy between Chartres and Bewley; indeed, the latter coveted Chartres' post.⁹ Exacerbating this already tense atmosphere was a third Irish faction: the gunrunners of the IRA. Technically, they were unconnected to the Irish political and trade offices: it would be improper for a diplomatic mission seeking German recognition to involve itself in weapons procurement. However, Robert Briscoe, an IRA arms agent linked with Michael Collins, crossed paths with Charles Bewley on the night of 19 January 1922 in the Tauenzien Palast in Berlin, where Bewley hurled a variety of anti-Semitic insults at him.¹⁰ George Gavan Duffy, who knew that Bewley was 'mad on the Jewish question', considered the incident 'inexcusable'.¹¹

---

4 NAI DFA DPG/IFS B (1921–2), Subject File: Germany, memorandum to External Affairs, 10 February 1921.   **5** Martin Elsasser, *Germany and Ireland: 1000 Years of Shared History* (Dublin, 1997), p. 39; Dermot Keogh, *Jews in Twentieth-Century Ireland: Refugees, Anti-Semitism and the Holocaust* (Cork, 1998), p. 103.   **6** Brian P. Murphy, *John Chartres: Mystery Man of the Treaty* (Dublin, 1995), chapters four and five.   **7** NAI DFA DPG/IFS B (1921–22), Subject File: Germany, memorandum on Germany by Power, 25 March 1921.   **8** NAI DFA DPG/IFS B (1921–2), Subject File: Germany, Charles Bewley Folder, Bewley to O hAodha, 2 September 1922.   **9** Charles Bewley, *Memoirs of a Wild Goose* (Dublin, 1989), p. 76; NAI DFA DPG/IFS B (1921–2), Subject File: Germany, Charles Bewley Folder, Bewley minute, 21 March 1922.   **10** NAI DFA DPG/IFS B (1921–2), Subject File: Germany, Charles Bewley Folder, Briscoe to Chartres, 21 January 1922; Robert Briscoe, *For the Life of Me* (Boston and Toronto, 1958), p. 259.   **11** NAI DFA DPG/IFS B (1921–2), Berlin Office Folder, Gavan

In retrospect, the Tauenzien Palast incident signalled the terminal decline of the mission. It also further poisoned the Chartres–Bewley relationship. A 'regrettable' and 'unnecessary coolness' developed between the two men as Chartres supported Briscoe's version of events. He informed Duffy that:

> such behaviour in a public place by a gentleman known to represent officially a department of the Irish Government reflects injuriously upon our country's reputation here. Moreover, an anti-Semitic outburst by an Irish official in a country where Jews are very numerous and very influential was an extraordinary indiscretion from the point of view of Irish material interests.[12]

Nonetheless, this episode was not investigated further, because the Irish Free State was spiralling towards civil war. In fact, the Provisional Government, which supported the Anglo–Irish Treaty, viewed Briscoe as 'an undesirable person' because of his anti-Treaty views.[13] A few months later Bewley, who backed the government, alerted Dublin to John Chartres' alleged anti-Treaty sympathies. As a result, Chartres and Power were recalled from Berlin, and Dublin closed the political mission.

The matter of Irish passports and visas was largely taken over by the British consul in Berlin, and visas were granted in consultation with the English authorities. Bewley, who had remained in Berlin to manage the trade mission, became frustrated by what he perceived as Irish subordination to the British authorities.[14] Disillusioned, he resigned in February 1923, and Cornelius Duane took over as consul. Meanwhile, the Weimar economy entered a state of hyperinflation,[15] and the Wirth government defaulted on its reparations payments, which provided France with the justification she had long desired to occupy the Ruhr. The resultant German 'passive resistance' in the region made German economic collapse imminent. Europe had moved from a total war of attrition during World War I to a Franco–German economic war of attrition in 1923, an outcome that almost destroyed the German economy. The economic crisis forced the Irish trade mission to close in November 1923. Duane pessimistically, but presciently, commented at the time:

> The political structure of Germany has been shattered and the economy has been in agony since 1918. The very obvious signs of hunger and want

Duffy to Chartres, 29 March 1922. **12** NAI DFA DPG/IFS B (1921–2), Subject File: Germany, Charles Bewley Folder, Chartres to Gavan Duffy, 30 January 1922. **13** Ibid., Blythe to Gavan Duffy, 27 March 1922. **14** NAI DFA DPG/IFS B (1922–4), German Numerical File: Consuls no. 1, Ó Lochlainn's Report on Brussels and Berlin, November–December 1922; Bewley, *Memoirs*, p. 88. **15** Graham Ross, *The Great Powers and the Decline of the European States System, 1914–1945* (Harlow, 1983), p. 46.

moving side by side with luxury cannot but create a despondent feeling ... Generally speaking such universal unrest does not contribute anything in the nature of economic or industrial progress, but it cannot last indefinitely, and a distracted Europe must make up its mind to secure order as a preliminary to progress ... Germany remains in the melting pot ...[16]

WEIMAR'S DEMISE AND HITLER'S RISE TO POWER, 1929-33

From 1923 until 1929 Ireland had no official diplomatic representation in Berlin. In January 1929, though, Irish–German relations were placed on a firmer footing when Professor Daniel A. Binchy became the Irish Minister Plenipotentiary and Envoy Extraordinary to the Weimar Republic and the German Consulate General in Dublin was upgraded to a legation.[17] This was a difficult era, however. The death in 1929 of Gustav Stresemann, the German Foreign Minister, had left Weimar without a statesman of sufficient stature to deal with the economic and political effects the Wall Street Crash had on the US-funded German economy. Indeed, the subsequent political failure to deal with the economic crisis created the circumstances that fuelled Hitler's rise in popularity.

While studying in Munich in 1921 Professor Binchy had his first encounter with Adolf Hitler and the NSDAP when a fellow student took him to a meeting of this 'new freak party' in the Burgerbraukeller. Writing about the experience over a decade later, Binchy adjudged that this 'commonplace-looking man' was 'a natural born orator' who seemed to 'take fire' as he launched into his address.[18] Despite Binchy's dismissal of the content of Hitler's speech (extremely repetitive and conspiratorial, an attack against Marxists, 'the October criminals' and Jews), he acknowledged Hitler's magical power over his 'audience of down and outs' and ex-soldiers. Portentously, Binchy's colleague had commented that 'no lunatic with the gift of oratory is harmless'.[19]

Nine years later, after Binchy had attended a meeting celebrating the Nazis' success in the September 1930 elections, he noted that the content of Hitler's speech had not changed.[20] Now, however, the NSDAP had emerged as the second largest party in the Reichstag. Binchy loathed the Hitlerite movement and attacked it in print after he had resigned as Irish minister to Germany, a move that made him very unpopular in Nazi circles and in the Foreign Office in Berlin.[21] Analysing *Mein Kampf*, Binchy astutely stated that 'anything [Hitler]

16 NAI DFA DPG/IFS B (1922–4), Numerical Copies of Correspondence: Germany, 08, Duane to External Affairs, 13 November 1923. **17** NAI DT S 5736/A, Amery to McGilligan, 22 November 1928; Decision of the Executive Council, 8 January 1929. **18** Daniel Binchy, 'Adolf Hitler', *Studies*, vol. 22 (March, 1933), p. 29. **19** Ibid., p. 30. **20** Ibid. **21** NAI DFA 5/88B,

tells us about himself is merely introduced as a peg on which to hang some political or ethnological dissertation'.[22] He proceeded to give a detailed critique of the tract's various contradictions and 'absurdities'.[23] According to Hitler's outlook, the Jews were 'equally responsible for the curse of parliamentary government and for the dictatorship of the proletariat which has abolished it'.[24] Binchy understood that anti-Semitism was a fundamental feature of the Nazi movement and was troubled by the potential consequences if they gained power.[25] Despite the astuteness of his diplomatic reporting, however, Binchy internalised the prejudices of the German haute bourgeoisie and never foresaw the Weimar Republic's downfall. When Hitler became Chancellor in January 1933 Binchy optimistically concluded: 'before being entrusted with the Chancellorship he has had his wings firmly clipped by the President. He has had to accept as colleagues most of the "Government of Barons" which he was hysterically denouncing a few months ago ... He can hardly expect these men to swallow his programme'.[26]

* * *

Hitler confounded such complacency by acquiring unlimited powers in the succeeding months, a process tracked in the lucid reports of Leo McCauley, who represented Ireland in Berlin at the rank of chargé d'affaires from April 1932 until July 1933. His commentary is a valuable record of the transition from the Weimar Republic to Nazi dictatorship. He read the unfolding political situation almost flawlessly. It was clear to McCauley, for example, that Hitler was simply awaiting the appropriate opportunity to seize power. In an April 1932 dispatch he thus interpreted the ageing and ailing Hindenburg's recent reelection as President as a desperate effort by Chancellor Brüning to keep Hitler out of the President's office, a vehicle that would have enabled him to rule by presidential decree – in effect, as a constitutional dictator. McCauley commented that Hitler was waiting 'for the time when Hindenburg will no longer be his rival'.[27] The Irish envoy also delineated the polarisation of German politics during the numerous federal and state elections of 1932, whereby smaller, marginal parties lost support and the two ideological rivals, the Nazis and the communists, gained strength.[28]

McCauley chronicled the resignation of Chancellor Brüning and his cabinet in May and the difficulty Hindenburg faced in forming non-extremist coalitions in the Reichstag and in the Prussian Landtag. In June 1932 he prophetically speculated that the 'Prussian problem will probably be solved by the appointment of a Reichskommissar; *and the same problem, should it arise for Germany as a whole, would probably be solved by dictatorship*'.[29] McCauley correctly predicted

Bewley to Walshe, 9 September 1933. **22** Binchy, 'Adolf Hitler', p. 31. **23** Ibid., p. 38. **24** Ibid., p. 39. **25** Ibid., p. 40. **26** Ibid., p. 46. **27** NAI DFA 34/125, McCauley to Walshe, 7 April 1932. **28** Ibid., 25 April 1932. **29** Ibid., 9 June 1932.

that the Nazis, though capable of making substantial electoral gains in the federal elections now scheduled for July (and necessitated by the fall of the Brüning government), would:

> not command an absolute majority [in the Reichstag]. The situation would then be that a party organised for violence and committed to an extreme programme will be in the position of having either to compromise, in which case it would lose many of its followers, or else disregard the constitution and install a dictatorship by force.[30]

He realised that the future of Weimar democracy was at a delicate stage: ever since Brüning's resignation, 'there has been no pretence whatever at parliamentary government; and even before that date the government had been carried on by decree'.[31] 'Presidium' dictatorship had replaced parliamentary democracy and was dependent on the whim of an old right-wing President who was not a democrat by instinct. In retrospect, McCauley's recounting of political events during this crucial transition period is exemplary.

Following another round of federal elections in late 1932, Hitler finally became Chancellor on 30 January 1933 after forming a coalition government with Franz von Papen, a well-respected member of the conservative establishment, with close links to the Catholic Centre Party, who was named Vice Chancellor. On 27 February 1933 McCauley astutely remarked that 'one of them is the cuckoo in the nest …' He foretold that if the coalition failed to gain a majority in the elections scheduled for 5 March it would 'continue to hold office, if necessary by force'.[32] That evening the Reichstag fire conveniently provided Hitler with the justification he needed to fight the elections on his own terms, making 'no pretence whatever at impartiality'. Hitler used the charge that the Reichstag had been burned by a Dutch communist to proscribe public meetings of the German Communist Party (KPD) and the German Social Democratic Party (SPD) and to outlaw their election campaigns. A situation 'bordering on a state of terror now prevails among the communists and the socialists', McCauley wrote.[33] During the next several days, the governing coalition monopolised the wireless service, but even in these artificially advantageous conditions the Nazi Party failed to achieve an overall majority in the Reichstag. Undeterred, Hitler destroyed German democracy by forcing the Reichstag to commit 'political suicide', that is, he coerced it into passing the Enabling Bill on 23 March 1933, which made him the dictator of Germany.[34]

Despite his political acuity, McCauley's reports during the initial months of Hitler's dictatorial rule betray, like many other observers of the early years of the

---

30 Ibid., 29 June 1932.   **31** Ibid., 28 February 1932.   **32** Ibid., 27 February 1933.   **33** Ibid., 6 March 1933.   **34** Ibid., 27 March 1933.

Nazi regime, a degree of ambivalent admiration for it.[35] He was impressed by the Nazi's success in revolutionising the government overnight after a decade of political paralysis. His dispatches, in fact, captured this new-found dynamism: 'New history is being made daily', he wrote in March 1933.[36] It 'would be difficult to find a parallel in history for such a burst of administrative energy ... [the] government's energy shows not the least sign of dissipation'. Assessing Hitler's seizure of the SPD's funds, he tentatively likened the action, in its 'boldness and magnitude', to a situation whereby 'a dictator in Great Britain seized the funds of the Liberal Party'.[37]

CHARLES BEWLEY, THE HITLER STATE AND NAZI–CHURCH RELATIONS

Beguiling Nazi successes also affected McCauley's successor in Germany. After representing Ireland at the Vatican for several years, Charles Bewley was transferred to Berlin in July 1933. He had long coveted this post, but was denied in his first attempt to secure it in 1929, because the Cumann na nGaedheal government doubted whether he could remain impartial in the light of his pro-German sentiments.[38] Only when Fianna Fáil assumed power in 1932 was he able to secure an appointment in Berlin, this despite the fact that Robert Briscoe, whom he had insulted in the Tauenzien Palast, was a Fianna Fáil TD. Evidently, Bewley had impressed de Valera during a meeting in Rome several months earlier.[39]

Given his German bias, as well as his predilection for the authoritarian, modernising aspects of Mussolini's fascist regime, Bewley naturally empathised with various features of Nazi ideology. The longer his stay in Berlin lasted, the more apparent these embryonic sympathies became. Indeed, many of the threads of his 'incipient fascism' were in place by 1933, according to one observer.[40] These predilections, combined with the long duration of his tenure, exposed him to the hazards of gradual Nazification.

On Thursday, 31 August 1933, Bewley fulfilled his life's ambition when he presented his credentials to President Hindenburg. Thinking that such a reference would be favourably accepted, yet clearly parting from departmental policy, he 'rather freely' translated part of the text prepared by the Department of External

---

35 See, for example, Richard Griffiths, *Fellow Travellers of the Right: British Enthusiasts for Nazi Germany* (London, 1980), chapter 1. **36** NAI DFA 34/125, McCauley to Walshe, 15 March 1933. **37** Ibid., 11 May 1933. **38** John P. Duggan, *Neutral Ireland and the Third Reich* (Dublin, 1989), p. 28. **39** Ibid., p. 27. See also Dermot Keogh, *Ireland and Europe, 1919–1989: A Diplomatic and Political History* (Cork, 1989), pp 55–7, 100–2. **40** Duggan, *Neutral Ireland*, pp 28–34.

Affairs to refer positively to the 'national rebirth of Germany'. President Hindenburg duly noted Bewley's congratulatory remarks.[41] Bewley also attended the Nazi Party's annual rallies at Nuremberg, unlike the diplomatic representatives of most of the democratic western states, including the USA, Britain and France, all of whom generally shied away from purely political events.[42] The conventional separation of party and state in democracies, however, was blurred in the Third Reich, because through the process of Gleichschaltung the party and the state had become synonymous, a trend fostered by the 'Law to Ensure the Unity of Party and State', which was passed on 1 December 1933.[43] Diplomatic attendance at the Nuremberg rallies, therefore, was a decision that had to be taken separately by each foreign government. In the Irish case, it appears that official instructions had not been forthcoming, and Bewley made up his own mind. He did not even request departmental permission, in contrast to William Warnock, who succeeded him in 1939.[44] Indeed, in 1933 he urged Dublin to forward his credentials so he would 'be in a position to accept the invitation' from the Führer to attend the rally, which he was 'anxious' to do.[45] Nevertheless, as questionable as Bewley's enthusiasm now seems, it is important to note that in 1934 the full repercussions of the Nazis' policies for the German state were not yet clear.

Although Bewley was a diplomat representing a small European state, high Nazi officials attempted to win over his sympathy for their cause. Bewley welcomed this attention; in fact, he 'thrived in the labyrinthine implications of dinner party intrigue under the Nazi regime'.[46] Consequently, he was able to provide unflattering insights into the personalities of Robert Ley (a Nazi labour leader) and Alfred Rosenberg (a Nazi theorist and ideologue).[47] On the other hand, Bewley was on such close terms with Hermann Göring, 'the Second Man in the Third Reich', that he later wrote an apologetic biography of him, aided by privileged access to private documents and recollections provided by Göring's widow, Emmy, and her family. Bewley himself recalled in his book that 'as minister to Berlin ... he had the opportunity of knowing personally all the prominent figures of the Third Reich as well as many of the former ruling class under the Monarchy, and was on friendly terms with the Göring family'.[48]

Such intimacy with leading Nazi figures distorted Bewley's analysis of German politics. The ambivalence of his reporting of certain ominous develop-

---

41 NAI DFA 217/28, Bewley to Walshe, 4 September 1933. **42** See Bewley's annual reports in NAI DFA 19/50 and 19/50/A. Neville Henderson, however, reversed previous British policy and attended the rallies after he became British Ambassador to Germany. **43** D.G. Williamson, *The Third Reich* (Harlow, 1982), p. 21. **44** NAI DFA 235/65, Warnock to Walshe, 19 August 1939. **45** NAI DFA 217/28, Bewley to Walshe, 17 August 1933. **46** W.J. McCormack, 'Camp Literature', in Bewley, *Memoirs*, p. 291. **47** Bewley, *Memoirs*, pp 145–53. See also NAI DFA 19/50, Bewley to Walshe, 23 January, 26 February 1934. **48** Charles Bewley, *Hermann Göring and the Third Reich* (New York, 1962), p. x.

ments became progressively evident. One topic of particular concern to Dublin was the treatment of the Catholic Church and religious minorities. In January 1934 Bewley highlighted the Nazification of the Lutheran Church,[49] but he optimistically saw little in the NSDAP programme harmful to Catholics, except the Sterilisation Law. Like most other observers, Bewley erroneously argued that having von Papen – a Catholic – as Vice Chancellor was a 'guarantee' that 'Catholic interests' were protected. He noted, however, that Catholic clergy previously involved in the Centre Party had maintained their opposition to National Socialism as well as their political activism and thus had breached the 1933 Concordat – the Nazi–Vatican agreement whereby the Church promised to remain loyal to the new regime and to stay out of politics in exchange for religious freedom. Specifically, some clergy had violated stipulations preventing them from discouraging contributions to Winterhilfe (the Nazi's social welfare scheme), 'spreading rumours' about National Socialist atrocities and possessing communist literature. Still, Bewley asserted, 'It would, I think, be entirely incorrect to suggest, as has been done, that there is any sort or kind of persecution of Catholics'. German Catholics, he believed, were grateful towards the Nazis for the 'miracle' of 'the purification of the stage, literature and the general life of the German cities'. And the 'suppression of Freemasonry' was another benefit.[50]

One month later, however, Bewley revised his initial optimism. He now believed that anti-Catholicism was growing among 'influential members' of the Nazi Party. Catholic youth organisations were to be dissolved and incorporated into the Hitlerjugend (Hitler Youth). He admitted that while 'in a communist or even strongly socialist Germany it is certain that there would have been a persecution of religion, one cannot help feeling that the misgivings of the Holy See are to a great extent justified'.[51] He foresaw difficulties ahead. The incorporation of the group Catholic Youth into the Hitlerjugend could not be achieved in the same way that the Catholic Youth in Italy was absorbed into the Ballilla. After all, Italy was a Catholic state, but the majority of Germany's population were non-Catholics.[52] By May 1934 he believed that 'something in the nature of a *Kulturkampf* against the Catholic Church' was possible as a result of the steady deterioration in relations between Nazism and the Church.[53] Throughout the following year, 1935, Bewley reported that the persecution of the Catholic Church was intensifying.[54]

Nevertheless, Bewley largely accepted the sacrifice of the German Catholics because it was outweighed by Nazism's virulent anti-communism. As he later recalled in his autobiography:

49 NAI DFA 19/50, Bewley to Walshe, 23 January 1934. **50** Ibid. **51** Ibid., Bewley to Walshe, 26 February 1934. **52** Ibid., 9 April 1934. **53** Ibid., 11 May 1934. **54** See NAI DFA 19/50/A, Bewley to Walshe, 25 April 1935, 2 May 1935, 11 June 1935, 19 July 1935, 26 July 1935, 19 November 1935, 27 November 1935.

For myself, I needed no argument to convince me that National Socialism, whatever might be its defects, should be upheld by the western powers as the strongest, perhaps the only, force which could prevent the spread of the Communist Empire over half Europe – and subsequent events have more than sufficiently confirmed my view.[55]

His anti-communist mindset, accentuated after 1935 by the Abyssinian crisis and the Spanish Civil War, dominated his reporting on European affairs. As he stated in 1936, 'I do not think that it is possible to form a reasonable view of events and policy in Central Europe at the present time without taking into account the (at least potential) menace of Moscow and Prague.'[56] He effectively believed that in comparison to communism, Nazism was the lesser evil.

Overall, Bewley maintained that the 'troubles of the Catholic Church in Germany' were caused by the ecclesiastical authorities themselves.[57] The Church, in his view, had allied itself with left-wing parties against the NSDAP during the Weimar period. This coalition, joined by the SPD, then legislated for amoral, unChristian, unCatholic measures such as divorce, contraception and sexual licence. The Nazis finally ended these 'abuses' when they came to power. Bewley asserted that Catholics, especially some of the clergy, were indiscreet and unnecessarily provocative following the Nazi takeover, and their actions played 'into the hands of the anti-Catholic elements' in the government.[58] In April 1934 he reminded Joseph Walshe:

> I am not, of course, attempting to palliate or excuse in any way the conduct of the present regime towards the Church: it has undoubtedly broken the Concordat both in the letter and the spirit, and is taking every possible step to discredit the Church in the eyes of the German people. But I also believe that matters would never have come to their present state, and that Hitler himself would probably not have given a free hand to the anti-Christian wing of the Party, if the same policy had been pursued in Germany as in Italy by the Episcopate.[59]

Still, Bewley increasingly adopted the Nazi regime's explanations and views and became truculent in the face of any criticism of the regime, even if it appeared in Irish broadsheets such as the *Irish Times* and *Irish Press*.

Following the 'Night of the Long Knives' on 30 June 1934, when Hitler revealed the true nature of his naked, arbitrary power by murdering in cold blood his rival Ernst Röhm, the leader of the Sturmabteilung (SA), and nearly 200 other political opponents, Bewley's apologetics reached a new low. He

---

55 Bewley, *Memoirs*, p. 125. **56** NAI DFA 19/50/A, Bewley to Walshe, 15 July 1936. **57** Ibid., 24 August 1936. **58** NAI DFA 19/50, Bewley to Walshe, 9 April 1934. **59** Ibid.

accepted Hitler's methods as justified. He denounced Röhm's 'proclivities' (his homosexual tendencies), contrasting them with the laudable 'puritanical and ascetic personality of Hitler', and he fell for the Nazi explanation that 'a foreign power' was involved in an imminent 'second revolution'.[60] It was only after 1935, however, that Bewley became a transparent admirer of the Nazi regime and vociferously criticised his own government's foreign policy. These complaints were a reaction to de Valera's support for the Soviet Union's membership of the League of Nations, his backing of League sanctions against Mussolini's Italy for invading Abyssinia and Irish adherence to the Anglo–French non-intervention policy in the Spanish Civil War. Irish foreign policy at the League of Nations upheld the rights of small nations, condemned aggression, counselled for peaceful international arbitration and moved steadily towards neutrality after 1936.[61] Bewley interpreted de Valera's stance as unduly deferential to Britain, anti-Catholic, a denial of the justified rights of Italy and even an indirect aid to communism.[62] He said that Irish policy at Geneva had 'a most unfortunate result on our international reputation': French, Germans and Italians now regarded Ireland simply as an extension of Britain, blindly adhering to the metropolitan power's wishes.[63]

The most infamous indication of Bewley's extremism in the later 1930s was his report on the 'Night of the Broken Glass' (Kristallnacht). On the evening of 9–10 November 1938 at least 100 Jews were murdered and practically all the synagogues in Germany and about 7,000 Jewish shops were destroyed. Josef Goebbels, the Nazi Minister for Propaganda, used the assassination of the legation secretary in the German embassy in Paris as a pretext to launch the pogrom.[64] Soon afterwards External Affairs demanded a report from Bewley. The dispatch Walshe received one month later was clearly inadequate and echoed radical Nazism's crude racist justifications for anti-Semitic acts.[65] Incredulously, Bewley stated that he was unaware of any cases of 'deliberate cruelty on the part of the [German] government ... towards the Jews'.[66] By this time not only was Bewley's behaviour attracting negative attention in Dublin, but so were the domestic policies of the Third Reich. Furthermore, Berlin's destabilising revisionist foreign policy had affected the peace of the continent. In this situation it was unwise to permit Bewley to remain in Berlin – he was

---

60 Ibid., Bewley to Walshe, 2 July, 16 July 1934 61 Michael Kennedy, *Ireland and the League of Nations, 1919–1946: International Relations, Diplomacy and Politics* (Dublin, 1996), *passim*. 62 O'Driscoll, 'Irish–German Diplomatic Relations', chapter 6. 63 NAI DFA 19/50/A, Bewley to Walshe, 18 May 1936. 64 Helmut Krausnick and Martin Broszat, *Anatomy of the SS State* (London, 1982), pp 57–8. See also Karl D. Bracher, *The German Dictatorship: The Origins, Structure and Consequences of National Socialism* (London, 1985), p. 456. 65 For a detailed account, see Keogh, *Ireland and Europe*, pp 100–2; Keogh, *Jews in Twentieth-Century Ireland*, pp 132–6. 66 NAI DFA 202/63, Bewley to Walshe, 9 December 1938.

neither a faithful executor of official policy nor a trustworthy chronicler of German developments – and External Affairs recalled him to Dublin.

DUBLIN'S INTERESTS AND PERCEPTIONS

In comparison to Bewley, Eamon de Valera was considerably more even-handed in his assessment of the Third Reich. Neither he nor Joseph Walshe relied on Bewley's judgements of Nazism after 1936. Other Irish diplomats posted on the continent were a more valuable source of information. Similarly, de Valera never forgot his first encounter with Hitler's regime, which was ominous. In 1933 the German newspaper *Deutsh-Wochenschau* had portrayed him as a half-caste Jew.[67] It made similar deprecatory remarks about the character of Irish republicanism, linking it to a world-wide Jewish conspiracy and drawing attention to the Jewishness of Robert Briscoe. Not surprisingly, Bernhard von Bülow, the Staatsekretar of the German Foreign Office, received an official Irish protest from Bewley.[68]

These early Irish apprehensions were substantiated by the dismissal of Dr Georg von Dehn from his position as German ambassador at Bucharest in 1934. His removal stemmed from his actions as the first German minister to the Irish Free State. Despite his Protestant faith, Dehn cultivated Irish Catholic circles in deference to the beliefs of the Free State's denizens.[69] As one of his final acts in Dublin before taking up a new post in Bucharest, he paid a farewell courtesy call to the Papal Nuncio, Paschal Robinson, during which he was photographed kissing the Nuncio's ring. After this photo was published Dehn was recalled from Bucharest and forcibly retired from the German diplomatic service.[70] The German Foreign Office construed Dehn's behaviour as inappropriate at a time of strained German–Vatican relations and claimed that it 'amounted to public criticism of the policy of the German Government', especially since, as a Protestant, he had no need to kiss the Papal Nuncio's ring.[71]

This cavalier treatment of the former German minister to Ireland and, by implication, the Catholic Church and the Free State upset the Irish government. De Valera regretted that Dehn was fired for appearing 'to go too far in observing the local customs' of Ireland out of a desire 'to do his country's work more efficiently'.[72] This incident demonstrated to the Irish Government the practical effects of Nazi religious policies. Dehn's dismissal was motivated by anti-Cath-

---

67 NAI DFA, Berlin Letterbook (1932–3), Hearne to McCauley, 29 July 1933. 68 Horst Dickl, *Die Deutsche Aussenpolitik und die Irische Frage von 1932 bis 1944* (Wiesbaden, 1983), p. 33. 69 NAI DFA EA 231/4B, Binchy to Walshe, 21 August 1930. 70 Duggan, *Neutral Ireland*, pp 22–3. 71 NAI DFA 18/10, Bewley to Walshe, 19 February 1935. 72 Ibid., Bewley to Walshe, 26 February 1935.

olic and anti-religious Nazi prejudices. As the totalitarian rule of Adolf Hitler developed, de Valera and the Department of External Affairs, in line with Catholic world opinion, increasingly disapproved of his domestic policies, even though the regime served as a bastion against Soviet Communism.

RESPONSES TO NAZI DOMESTIC POLICIES

Irish concern about the suppression of the Catholic Church acted as the motive for limiting Irish–German cultural exchanges from the mid-1930s onwards, the very time, incidentally, that Bewley was drawing closer to the Nazi regime. In June 1935 Joseph Walshe instructed Bewley to discourage requests from German university professors to deliver lectures in the Free State – 'in view of the general trend of things in Germany, especially the attitude of the state towards Christianity'.[73] Two years later Walshe informed Bewley that Eamon de Valera would not permit 'the official supply of information on Irish affairs to the German press until such time as the religious question in Germany becomes less acute'.[74]

In 1939 de Valera displayed even further disapproval. On 10 March Helmut Clissmann, the representative in Ireland of the Deutscher Akademischer Austauschdienst (DAAD), a German academic exchange organization, suggested an alteration in an existing German prize scheme for Irish secondary schools. Normally, the DAAD awarded picture and book prizes to Irish students to encourage the study of German. Now, the DAAD, in association with the German Foreign Office, indicated that it was willing to grant an annual travelling scholarship to the student gaining the highest marks in German on the Leaving Certificate Examination that would enable him or her to spend four weeks in Germany, of which one or two weeks would be spent in a state youth camp.[75] De Valera did not oppose the study of foreign languages among Irish students. He could not recommend the acceptance of the German proposal, however, because 'in the present position of the Catholic Church in Germany, the Government should not take the responsibility of sponsoring a scheme for sending Catholic children to German youth camps'.[76] The Nazification of German youth was also widely criticised in public circles in Ireland. The president of the Irish National Teachers' Organisation remarked in April 1939 that the youth movement's philosophy was 'Snap the child from his mother's arms and give him a gun'.[77] The *Irish Press* deplored efforts to erode the influence of the family and religion as well as the cultivation of militarism in totalitarian societies.[78]

---

[73] NAI DFA Berlin Letterbook (1934–5), Walshe to Bewley, 26 April 1935. [74] NAI DFA Berlin Letterbook (1936–7), Walshe to Bewley, 30 June 1937. [75] NAI DFA 238/59, Clissmann to Secretary of the Department of Education, 10 March 1939. [76] Ibid., Walshe to Secretary of the Department of Education, 2 May 1939. [77] *Irish Press*, 13 April 1939. [78] Ibid.

Although Ireland's primary concern lay with the position of the Catholic Church in Germany, there were other intimations of public unease with the Nazi regime. Soon after it assumed power, for instance, demonstrations gathered at the German embassy in Dublin to protest against the Nazi's persecution of the Jews.[79] Evidence of official disquiet further revealed itself in April 1934 when Georg von Dehn, the German minister in Dublin, asked the Department of Justice to supply him with 'the names and addresses of the Marxist and Jewish organisations and, if possible, of the anti-communist, fascist, national socialist and anti-Semitic corporations in the Irish Free State'.[80] Although the Nazis never attempted to manipulate domestic anti-communism and anti-Semitism in Ireland on a large scale, this chilling request illustrates their subversive methods. The Department of Justice recognised the Germans' intentions and left the enquiry unanswered. D.J. Browne, a Justice official, commented that 'Hitler is apparently not satisfied with driving the Jews out of Germany. He wants to keep his eye on them in all parts of the world'.[81] On 23 May 1934 Dr Schlemann, chargé d'affaires in the German embassy, renewed the request,[82] but one week later Seán Murphy, an assistant secretary in the Department of External Affairs, turned him down.[83] No state would communicate such delicate and confidential information relevant to its own security to a foreign government.

The anti-Jewish policies of the Nazis were subjected to further Irish reproof following Kristallnacht in November 1938. Although latent anti-Semitism existed in Ireland, Nazi persecution of the Jews was generally perceived as unacceptable. Both the *Irish Press* and the *Irish Times* unreservedly condemned Kristallnacht. They rejected spurious Nazi protestations that the pogrom was a spontaneous outburst of righteous indignation following the murder of a German diplomat in Paris. Instead, they insisted that the Nazis had excited Germans with their vitriolic anti-Semitic propaganda and then organised the resultant violence. According to the *Irish Times*, the Third Reich no longer ranked as a 'civilised country'.[84] The *Irish Press* alleged that Aryanism was 'the laughing stock of the scientific world', with no basis in fact.[85] In sum, these attitudes were more indicative of the opinions of informed Irish people than the distorted report on Kristallnacht that Charles Bewley had forwarded to Dublin.

IRISH APPEASEMENT?

Eamon de Valera disapproved of Nazi domestic policies, but as an Irish nationalist he sympathised with Germany's foreign policy aims. His discrete attitude

---

79 Elsasser, *Germany*, p. 49. **80** NAI DFA 17/197, von Dehn to Browne, 25 April 1934. **81** Ibid., Browne to Roche, 2 May 1934. **82** Ibid. **83** Ibid., Schlemann to Roche, 23 May 1934; minute by Murphy, 30 May 1934. **84** *Irish Times* 12 November 1938. **85** Ibid., 17 November 1938.

was, to some extent, a derivative of his views about the League of Nations and *Hibernia Irredenta*. De Valera considered that the League had potential as a peacemaker between nations, but its Covenant required revision to deal with the evolving international system. It was not flexible enough to incorporate new states nor to address the issue of repressed nationalities. He was also conscious of the League's origins as a guarantor of the Treaty of Versailles, a settlement that he thought was unduly harsh towards Germany.[86] Moreover, Irish representatives – including de Valera – had been snubbed when they pleaded the case for statehood before the Versailles Conference.[87] And like Versailles, the Anglo–Irish Treaty of 1921 had been imposed under the threat of violence. Therefore, just as de Valera revised and undermined the Anglo–Irish Treaty during the 1930s, he accepted Germany's attempt to secure its legitimate rights stripped away in 1919.

The Irish Government thus supported the appeasement of German territorial ambitions in the 1930s. It believed that such a policy was morally correct, that it was a redress of injustices committed against Germany, just as the Anglo–Irish Treaty of 1938 was a recognition of legitimate Irish national claims. Also significant was the underlying belief that if Britain recognised Germany's right to remilitarise the Rhineland, unite with Austria and reoccupy the Sudetenland, then it might also be persuaded to concede the Irish Free State's claim to Northern Ireland.[88] Accordingly, although Hitler's methods and his treatment of Austrian Catholics were unsettling, External Affairs 'formally acknowledged' Germany's official notification of the Anschluss in June 1938.[89]

Ireland maintained its policy of appeasement throughout the Munich crisis of September 1938. A palpable fear of a European-wide war pervaded Irish diplomacy, and Joseph Walshe was very pessimistic about the prospects for peace.[90] De Valera and J.W. Dulanty, the Irish High Commissioner in London, encouraged Neville Chamberlain to pacify Hitler.[91] As de Valera declared in an address broadcast from Geneva to the USA at the height of the crisis:

> The war of sheer aggression ... is not the war that we need to fear the most. The most dangerous war is that which has its origin in just claims denied or in a clash if opposing rights – and not merely opposing interests – when each side can see no reason in justice why it should yield its claim to the other. If, by conceding the claims of justice or by reasonable compromise in the spirit of fair play, we take steps to avoid the latter

---

86 Eamon de Valera, *Peace and War: Speeches by Mr de Valera on International Affairs* (Dublin, 1944), pp 5–14.   **87** See Dermot Keogh, 'Origins of Irish Diplomacy in Europe, 1919–1921', *Etudes Irlandais*, no. 7, Nouvelle Serie (December, 1982), pp 145–64.   **88** Dickel, *Deutsche*, p. 33.   **89** NAI DFA 207/10, Rynne to Leydon, 4 June 1938.   **90** Keogh, *Ireland and Europe*, p. 99.   **91** Deirdre McMahon, 'Ireland, the Dominions and the Munich Crisis', *Irish Studies in International Affairs*, vol. 1, no. 1 (1979), pp 30–7.

kind of war, we can face the possibility of the other kind with relative equanimity.[92]

De Valera's policy was to concede Hitler's just national claims, and if he then presented illegitimate demands or a *fait accompli* his true character would be revealed. As he stated, 'To allow fears for the future to intervene and make us halt in rendering justice in the present is not to be wise, but to be foolish.'[93] He sent letters of encouragement to Chamberlain during the latter's continental search for a solution to the Sudetenland crisis.[94] On 15 September Walshe assured Edouard Hempel, the German Minister in Dublin, 'that the Irish Government understood the necessity of obtaining full rights of self-determination for the Sudeten Germans'.[95] As the situation worsened De Valera, in his position as President of the League of Nations Assembly, considered appealing directly to Hitler and Mussolini to preserve the peace if Chamberlain failed on his mission to Berchtesgaden.[96] In London, meanwhile, Dulanty urged the British Government to find a peaceful solution to the crisis.[97]

On 3 November, several weeks after the Munich Agreement had temporarily resolved tensions in Europe, the Irish Government issued an official statement announcing the renewal of the Irish–German trade agreement; the communiqué noted that the 'German Reich' included the Sudetenland and Austria.[98] Ireland thus extended *de jure* recognition to these recent German territorial acquisitions.[99] To Irish officialdom, the Munich deal, the remilistarisation of the Rhineland and the Anschluss were thus 'a rectification of injustices' identical to the Anglo–Irish Agreement of April 1938 that ended the 'economic war' and led to the handing back of the Treaty Ports.[100] On another level, the Sudentenland crisis reinforced de Valera's emerging preference for a policy of neutrality, and the transfer of the Treaty ports made this goal realisable. The maintenance of partition, however, meant that Irish neutrality would be precarious at best if Britain and Germany were opponents in a major conflagration. In early September 1938, before the solution to the Sudetenland issue, de Valera had unsuccessfully drawn a tenuous parallel between Irish partition and the Sudetenland question. He suggested to Thomas Inskip, the British Minister for Coordination of Defence, that if Britain granted Hitler's demands on the

---

92 De Valera, *Peace and War*, p. 72. **93** Ibid., p. 73. **94** Deirdre McMahon, *Republicans and Imperialists: Anglo–Irish Relations in the 1930s* (New Haven, 1984), p. 198; Kennedy, *Ireland and the League of Nations*, pp 234–7. **95** *Documents in German Foreign Policy*, Series D, vol. 2, Doc. 483, Hempel to Foreign Ministry, 15 September 1938, pp 781–2. **96** Ibid., Series D, vol. 4, Doc. 483, Hempel to Foreign Ministry, 2 January 1939, p. 357. **97** McMahon, 'Ireland', p. 31. **98** NAI DFA 232/1, 'Statement Issued by the Government Information Bureau', 3 November 1938. **99** NAI DFA 205/161, Boland to Walshe, 12 December 1944. **100** Earl of Longford and Thomas P. O'Neill, *Eamon de Valera* (London, 1974), p. 324.

Sudetenland then Britain should end Irish partition or redraw the border to include the areas with a majority nationalist population, since Ireland had more rights to Ulster than Germany to the Sudetenland.[101]

Conversely, following Hitler's forced entry into Prague on 15 March 1939, the Irish government denied that Germany had a legitimate claim to the rump Czechoslovakia. It did not extend *de jure* recognition to the new German Protectorate of Moravia and Bohemia nor to the state of Slovakia.[102] According to de Valera's logic, Hitler's just demands had been met, but his treatment of Czechoslovakia revealed his underlying aggressive intentions. In fact, his declarations of peace were no longer reliable, and de Valera agreed with Chamberlain that it was impossible to negotiate with Hitler. Further, he now 'feared that we should find it impossible to stop Hitler's further advance in Eastern Europe ...'[103]

For his part, Charles Bewley defended the takeover of the rump Czechoslovakia. He overlooked both the fact that Germany's claims to it were untenable and that Hitler had coerced Josep Tiso, the Slovak leader, and Dr Emil Hacha, the President of Czechoslovakia. Bewley's criticism of the French and British governments for their 'cowardice' and 'military weakness' unmasked his disdain for democracy. As he concluded: 'The events of the last few days will go very far to convince the remaining countries of [Central] and Eastern Europe that democracy as a political system can only lead to weakness and eventually disaster.'[104] During April and May, Bewley's analysis of the emerging Nazi–Polish clash over the German-inhabited autonomous city of Danzig was that 'the German government will probably take no step for some months in the belief that time will work more effectively on the morale of their opponents'. He reported that the common view in Berlin was 'that as time passes England and France will become even less desirous of fighting for a Polish Danzig'.[105] As events transpired, however, this opinion proved to be false.

By this time, Bewley's opinions carried little weight in Dublin, because his relationship with the Department of External Affairs had drastically deteriorated. Bewley had alienated de Valera, Joseph Walshe and most of the Irish diplomats serving on the continent. Moreover, maintaining a brazenly pro-German and anti-English diplomat in Berlin would compromise the evolution of de Valera's new policy of neutrality – his response to the war now looming in Europe. Consequently, de Valera recalled Bewley to Dublin. Reacting to this reduction in rank and status, Bewley resigned from the Irish diplomatic service.[106] William Warnock, representative of a new class of professional Irish diplomat, took up Bewley's post in Berlin just as World War II began.

---

101 Robert Fisk, *In Time of War: Ireland, Ulster and the Price of Neutrality, 1939–45* (London, 1985), pp 66–8. **102** See NAI DFA 205/161. **103** PRO FO 800/310, Chamberlain note, 27 March 1939. **104** NAI DFA 19/50/A, Bewley to Walshe, 15 March 1939. **105** Ibid., Bewley to Walshe, 9 May 1939. **106** Bewley, *Memoirs*, p. 177.

CONCLUSION

The stark contrast in the calibre of Irish diplomats posted to Germany before 1939 highlights the shortage of qualified candidates available during the early development of the Irish foreign service. It now seems incomprehensible, for example, that Charles Bewley's anti-Semitic outburst in 1922 was downplayed at the time or that eleven years later the Fianna Fáil government appointed him minister to Germany. It is true that the first two years of Bewley's posting in Nazi Germany were uncontroversial, although hints of naiveté and undue appreciation of the Nazi regime's early domestic accomplishments surfaced in his dispatches (a trait that was also common to Leo McCauley's reports). But even after the more ominous nature of Nazism had become evident Bewley showed no inclination to revise his perspective. At home he acquired a reputation for being a difficult personality who often acted unprofessionally and without official sanction. He was reluctant to defend aspects of Ireland's diplomacy that he thought created obstacles to Irish–German relations, such as its stance at the League of Nations. Therefore, after 1935 he became increasingly disconnected from the mainstream of an Irish foreign policy steadily dissociating itself from Nazism.

Some commentators, however, while sharing this negative assessment of Bewley, advocate the case for revising the existing historical explanation of his performance in Berlin after 1933. Michael Kennedy, for instance, while condemning Bewley's anti-Semitism and predilection towards Nazi ideologies, argues that most accounts of Bewley's diplomatic career gloss over his complexity. Instead, he proposes a 'dynamic radicalisation' interpretation of Bewley's personality.[107] The Hitlerian environment gradually Nazified him. In other words, Kennedy suggests that other authors adopt a one-dimensional, even deterministic, interpretation of Bewley's career, assessing it retrospectively in view of his anti-Semitic outburst during Kristallnacht in 1938 and his explosive disagreements with Dublin at the end of his posting. Kennedy believes, therefore, that many authors see Bewley's actions and behaviour in 1938 as inevitable, as the definitive Bewley, and neglect the normal processes of character formation and the impact of German events. Kennedy's proposition leads to a debate that mirrors the historiographical arguments between the intentionalist and structuralist schools of thought about Hitler, that is, did Hitler *intend* to exterminate the Jews and start a European war to gain *Lebensraum* from the outset in 1933 or did the Holocaust and World War II arise out of piecemeal events, *ad hoc* political evolution and accidents that unfolded over a long period of time? In the same way, was Bewley's anti-Semitism, anglophobia and his critique of Irish for-

---

[107] See Michael Kennedy, 'Our Men in Berlin: Some thoughts on Irish Diplomats in Germany, 1929–1939', *Irish Studies in International Affairs*, vol. 10 (1999).

eign policy inevitable or did they develop gradually? In other words, was Bewley the same in 1933 as he was in 1938 or did he become a pro-Nazi admirer in the intervening period?

This approach has value, but it is a simplification of the existing debate on Bewley. For instance, there is an admission by most authors that Bewley 'went native' in Berlin. This implies that these authors recognise that Bewley experienced a process of conversion. Kennedy is correct in seeing 1936 as the turning point in Bewley's transformation from a largely benign observer of German developments into a biased admirer and defender of the Nazi regime. Thus the key question when it comes to interpreting Bewley's transparent transmutation is: was it simply the events of 1935–6 that changed his attitudes or was he already showing signs of susceptibility to the new German regime? Kennedy opts for the former causative interpretation, but there is a strong case for combining these two approaches. Bewley's reports of the Nazi state before 1936, while on the whole satisfactory and accurate, on close reading frequently display a degree of ambivalence about the regime that strongly suggest that his resistance to fascist ideology was ambiguous. His change needs to be considered from the long-term perspective of his evolution as a diplomat during the entire inter-war period. His personal beliefs and mentality also require contextualisation. Bewley was not alone in his vulnerabilities and predilections. His critique of Irish foreign policy during the Abyssinian crisis and the Spanish Civil War mirrored significant domestic Irish discontent with de Valera's foreign policies. The popularity of Paddy Belton's Irish Christian Front is evidence of this phenomenon. Even the secretary of Foreign Affairs, Joseph Walshe, expressed sympathy for authoritarianism, anti-Semitism and Italian fascism, a characteristic that mirrored the confusion produced by the upheavals of the inter-war period. Whatever interpretative approach is adopted, Bewley is not an unusual individual in the 1930s, but a complex diplomat demanding careful historical analysis.[108]

* * *

For his part, Eamon de Valera was disgusted by the Nazis' domestic policies, but this aversion did not extend to the Third Reich's revisionist foreign policy until 1939. De Valera was an appeaser; he recognised a parallel between the German aspirations for a Grossdeutschland and Irish irredentism. Hence, until the establishment of puppet regimes in the rump Czechoslovakia in March 1939 de Valera's foreign policy discriminated between the excesses of Hitler's domestic rule and his revisionist foreign policy. Thereafter, Hitler's regime proved to be

---

[108] For a further discussion of these issues, see Duggan, *Neutral Ireland*, pp 27–30, 65; Keogh, *Ireland and Europe*, pp 28–9, 46–7, 54–7, 100–2; W.J. McCormack, 'Afterword: Camp Literature', in Bewley, *Memoirs*, pp 283–96; O'Driscoll, 'Irish–German Diplomatic Relations', chapters 4, 5, 6; Keogh, *Jews in Twentieth-Century Ireland*, pp 99–103, 110–11, 129–32.

reprehensible in both its internal and external dimensions. During World War II, de Valera pursued a policy of neutrality, because he deemed it to be in Ireland's national interests. It was not, however, a display of common cause with Germany. On the contrary, Irish authorities secretly colluded with Allied authorities throughout the war, most notably in the sensitive area of intelligence. It was a 'benevolent neutrality' tilted towards Britain and the United States.

Feeling uncomfortable at home, Charles Bewley returned to Axis Europe, where he is widely suspected of collaborating with Axis intelligence and propaganda organisations during the conflict. Daniel Binchy, who earlier had taken up his academic interests at Oxford University, was seconded to the press section of the British Foreign Office when the war broke out. He was appointed to the Italian section, because the 'Foreign Office felt that he was too biased to be asked to report on the Germans'.[109] Ironically, the first two Irish Ministers to Berlin were on opposite sides during World War II. De Valera, meanwhile, tried to maintain a 'middle way', thus symbolising the typical moral and national experiences of many Irish people during World War II.

---

109 Duggan, *Neutral Ireland*, p. 34.

Ireland, Vichy and Post-liberation France, 1938–50

Robert Patterson[1]

INTRODUCTION

Recognising the potential usefulness of propaganda and international public opinion as political weapons, the Irish provisional government made Paris a centre of 'diplomatic' activity during the War of Independence, which lasted from 1919 to 1921. Strong historical ties between Ireland and France also made it a natural site for the establishment of a nascent mission. Coincidentally, the two central characters who played the leading roles in the conduct of Irish relations with France during the Second World War, Joseph Walshe, the secretary of the Department of External Affairs, and Seán Murphy, the Irish minister to France, were both stationed in Paris during these years.

Following the signing of the Anglo–Irish Treaty of 1921, the Irish Free State set about formalising its diplomatic apparatus. It was some years, however, before the Irish foreign service was placed on a relatively sure footing.[2] Throughout much of the 1920s the Department of External Affairs operated under the threat of absorption by the Department of the President. It was not until the appointment of Patrick McGilligan as Minister for External Affairs and Joseph Walshe as permanent secretary in 1927 that there was an opportunity to expand. Attention then turned to Paris once again. A small consular presence had been maintained there during the 1920s, and it was upgraded to a legation in October 1929. The opening of a French legation in Dublin followed in July 1930. Throughout the 1930s relations between Ireland and France were conducted on a very friendly basis, with few areas of dispute. Towards the end of the decade Seán Murphy was appointed as the third Irish minister to France.[3] He had joined the Irish foreign service in 1919. After working not only with Joseph Walshe, but also Seán T. O'Kelly and Michael MacWhite, in making Paris the focus of Irish diplomacy on the continent during the War of Inde-

[1] The views expressed in this essay are the author's alone; he is writing here in a personal capacity. [2] A full account of the establishment of the Irish diplomatic service can be found in Dermot Keogh, *Ireland and Europe, 1919–1989* (Cork and Dublin, 1990). [3] He succeeded Art O'Briain, who had succeeded Count O'Kelly de Gallagh in 1935.

pendence, he represented the Free State there, taking over from O'Kelly following the latter's dismissal over his anti-Treaty stance in 1922. In 1925 Murphy was recalled to Dublin, where he worked as assistant secretary in the Department of External Affairs until his assignment to Paris as minister in 1938.[4] It was a fortuitous appointment in the context of the difficulties which were to confront the Irish legation during World War II.

The Second World War was a particularly difficult period for the relatively infant Irish foreign service. Yet Irish representatives in France coped admirably in tense and uneasy times. The staff of the legation had to contend with many difficult situations both in Paris and at headquarters in Dublin. These problems ranged from the upheaval in France in the aftermath of defeat in the summer of 1940 and the day-to-day problems of operating a legation in wartime to, most importantly, maintaining as far as possible positive relations between Ireland and France.

It was not always easy to sustain amicable relations between the two nations. In the early stages of the Vichy regime the Irish legation, and Murphy in particular, had to spend much time and effort counteracting the pro-Pétainist inclinations of Joseph Walshe. In this respect, the policy dispute between Walshe and Murphy, and the eventual acceptance of the latter's viewpoint, is of major importance, particularly when set in the context of Irish attitudes towards the Vichy regime and its consequences for French attitudes towards Ireland in the post-war period.

The newly installed Vichy government also maintained a legation in Dublin throughout the entirety of its existence. Its presence caused serious difficulties for the Irish government, not least as the war progressed and French loyalties became increasingly divided between Vichy and the Comité Française de la Libération Nationale (CFLN). The liberation of France and the fall of the Vichy regime was also highly problematic for the Department of External Affairs, as it fought a battle of principle with the provisional government of Charles de Gaulle for the recognition of its minister and its right to have remained neutral. That Ireland was successful in this necessary diplomatic tussle will be seen to have brought its own problems, since it delayed the resumption of normal, friendly relations in the post-war period.

THE 'PHONEY' WAR AND THE EVACUATION OF PARIS

The outbreak of war in September 1939 and the rapid defeat of Poland did not appear to impinge greatly on the work of the Irish legation in Paris nor did it seem, according to Murphy, to have impacted greatly on daily life in the French

4 Keogh, *Ireland and Europe*, pp 8, 21, 26.

capital. The minister reported that 'the atmosphere is very normal except for the fact that the city is rather empty and that at night practically all street lighting is extinguished. There is as yet little evidence of extensive military activity in the city'.[5] Much of the legation's time was taken up reporting on the German 'peace terms' and the Allied reaction to those terms. This was to change in the summer of 1940 with the outbreak of war in the west.

The scale and speed of the French defeat in the summer of 1940 was a massive shock which led to the paralysis of French governmental institutions. The extent to which these institutions had broken down can be seen in an extensive report that Seán Murphy sent to Dublin on 18 June from Ascain, a temporary refuge during the legation's evacuation from Paris. The report serves as an excellent account of the problems faced by the staff during their ordeal.[6] It indicated that the French government had made contingency plans in the event of a forced withdrawal from Paris and had intended to place a residence 'at the disposal of the heads of mission so that they might be able to continue to fulfil their functions with the aid of a reduced staff'.[7] The evacuation of the Irish consulate had taken place on 11 June following consultation with the papal nuncio, Monsignor Valerio Valeri, and the American Ambassador, William Bullitt. It had been decided that no Irish diplomats would remain in Paris, owing to the limited nature of Irish interests there and to the fact that no member of staff would have any standing with the French government. However, Count O'Kelly de Gallagh, formerly Irish minister in Paris from 1932 to 1935, would later return to Paris to deal with consular work.

The evacuation was a distinctly uncomfortable one, taking place as it did while millions of refugees were fleeing from the fighting in the North. The city of Tours was in a complete state of chaos and, in the eyes of Murphy, likely to worsen further. It was decided to move further south, as far as Bordeaux. But Bordeaux proved to be equally chaotic, so it was decided to move further south again to Ascain, which the legation staff reached on 15 June. The party remained there for three weeks before relocating to La Bourboule. The staff reached Vichy soon after this.[8] It was not, however, until

---

[5] NAI DFA PE 19/34A, Murphy to External Affairs, 4 September 1939. [6] NAI DFA 246/118, report by Murphy to External Affairs, 18 June 1940. This report has been extensively drawn on to provide a complete description of the evacuation of the Irish legation from Paris. [7] Ibid. The French Government had, indeed, placed a chateau at the disposal of the Irish legation near Tours. When Murphy visited the residence on 29 May, however, he found that the proprietor had made certain changes so as to render it unsuitable. In addition, the chateau was later rendered completely unusable as the owner had moved his entire family onto the premises. In any case, the extent of the French defeat meant that the relocation of the French government in Tours became academic. [8] NAI DFA 219/69. The exact date is unclear; however, a report by Frederick Boland indicates that the legation was in place by 16 July: NAI DFA 219/24, Boland to secretary, Department of Finance, 16 July 1940.

late October that the Hotel Gallia, the permanent residence of the Irish legation in Vichy, was occupied.⁹

IRISH ATTITUDES TO THE VICHY REGIME

The change in government in France induced no alteration in Ireland's foreign policy, which was based upon relations with states, rather than governments. It is, nonetheless, interesting, considering the fact that the new French government differed so greatly from its predecessor, to examine how the Pétain government was viewed in Ireland.

One of Marshal Pétain's first actions was to announce the initiation of a new *révolution national*, which, he hoped, would enable France to rise again out of defeat. It appeared that this campaign would give a new prominent and respected place to religion in France. Consequently, it was perhaps only natural that the seemingly Catholic and clerical nature of the *révolution national* should be supported in Ireland by staunchly Catholic publications such as the *Standard*. One article, in particular, is worthy of extensive quotation for its unstinting praise:

> the French government intends effecting a progressive but radical improvement in the souls of the nation herself. They consider that during the last twenty years, or possibly since the beginning of the twentieth century, French people have forgotten too many of the moral principles which had been the foundation of their rise to fame. Religion had been deemed useless and even misleading by the Third Republic; secret societies had increased in number and power; recently the different classes of society had practically lost that magnificent understanding of the value of work, which had contributed in a high degree to the prosperity of French industry and agriculture and for which the French were renowned abroad. Consequently, the French government has undertaken to restore religion to its essential place in the state, to reform education and teaching, to give more prominence to physical education in school-life, to suppress alcoholism and to educate the younger generation to a proper understanding of their responsibilities. The whole social and political structure is to be purged of the unhealthy atmosphere of the last decades. *'Travail, Patrie, Famille'* becomes the new motto of France.

Marshal Pétain would appear to have undertaken a programme of regeneration which takes into account the spiritual needs of man. This development must naturally be exclaimed by Catholics throughout the

---

9 NAI DFA 219/69, telegram received by External Affairs, 29 October 1940.

world, and Ireland, in particular, tenders her best wishes to the provider of these reforms.[10]

It was not just the Catholic publications which offered support to the new French regime. The *Irish Times,* in an editorial in August 1940, paid tribute to Pétain's patriotism and courage in facing up to a very difficult task.[11] The *Irish Press* also praised the Marshal quite highly, believing that he 'will do whatever he considers is his duty to France'.[12]

It did not, of course, necessarily follow that the sentiments expressed above were reflected in the official government attitude to the new French regime. The question of what that attitude should be became a thorny one and resulted in a serious policy dispute between Seán Murphy and Joseph Walshe. The outcome was to have some far-reaching effects on the manner in which war-time policy towards France was conducted.

THE POLICY DISPUTE BETWEEN MURPHY AND WALSHE

The apparently Catholic nature of the *révolution national* appears to have attracted the interest of Walshe, whose pro-Catholic sympathies are well-documented. The attitude of the Vatican to this development was of considerable interest to him. On 20 July 1940 he requested the views of the Holy See through the Irish minister there, T.J. Kiernan. But his interest in the Catholic nature of the regime was already clear from a memorandum he had prepared for the Taoiseach and Minister for External Affairs, Eamon de Valera. This document, written just after de Gaulle's Appel du 18 Juin, placed great emphasis on the new leadership of France being 'distinguished French Catholics held in the highest esteem'.[13] For his part, Kiernan, in his reply to Walshe, noted that there was cautious support in the Vatican for the new French government, because of Pétain's character and the nature of his programme. This attitude was tempered, though, by the possible impermanence of the programme and by the totalitarian nature of the regime.[14] Walshe, however, did not wait for Kiernan's reply before he wrote to Murphy expressing his exaggerated belief that the Vatican was showing the 'greatest sympathy' towards the Pétain government.[15]

---

10 *Ministère des Affaires Étrangères Série: Guerre, 1939–1945, Vichy-Europe* (MAE G V-E), vol. 298, quotation from *The Standard*, 17 September 1940; de Laforcade, Dublin, Bordereau d'envoi, no. 205, 24 September 1940. 11 MAE G V–E, vol. 297, leader from the *Irish Times*, 14 August 1940; de Laforcade, Dublin, télégramme no. 188, 14 August 1940. 12 MAE G V–E, vol. 298, *Irish Press*, 16 November 1940; de Laforcade, Dublin, Bordereau d'envoi, no. 163, 16 November 1940. 13 NAI DFA SF A 2 /1, Walshe memorandum, June 1940. 14 NAI DFA SF P 12/1, telegram from Vatican legation to Walshe, 24 July 1940. 15 NAI DFA PE 19/34, telegram from Walshe to Murphy, 23 July 1940.

The thrust of Murphy's reports during this period, however, was disagreement with his superior's assessment of the situation. Murphy first sounded a warning on 8 July. He noted a lack of realism in French circles. He believed that there was a 'distinct possibility of the French government and public cherishing illusions as to France's future, both from drawing inexact historical parallels and attributing the French defeat wholly or partially to wrong motives'.[16] He also sounded a warning regarding the illusory sense of the power and authority of the new regime:

> It is difficult to see how, in the event of final victory, Germany will not impose conditions on France, and provide for their observance, which will keep France harmless. Official utterances do not, however, seem to betray a consciousness of this likelihood and speak of the future of France as if it is something which depends exclusively on the French people and government, untrammelled by any outside interference.

This warning was repeated less than a week later when Murphy expressed the view that 'one cannot help feeling that neither the government nor the people fully appreciate the serious situation of France', a feeling endorsed by other diplomats with whom Murphy had spoken.[17]

Although the minister was merely counselling caution, Murphy received in reply what was effectively a reprimand from Walshe, whose support for the new regime is clear from his telegram to Paris. The secretary claimed that the 'sympathy of the whole country is with Pétain [and] our destiny henceforth will be cast with that of the continental Catholic nations. As you are no doubt aware, [the] Vatican [is] showing [the] greatest sympathy towards [the] new regime in France'.[18] Walshe instructed Murphy to keep in close contact with the papal nuncio, 'who is more likely to know [the] real views of [the] French right than other diplomats', and requested him to 'please always give [the] source of your information'.

Murphy was undoubtedly annoyed by Walshe's telegram. Given that the latter believed himself to be better informed about French politics than the minister whose task it was to inform him, it was likely that matters would come to a head between the two. Four months later they did just that. On 18 November 1940 Murphy reported on the prevailing situation in France. The subject of this report is of less interest than the attitude which Murphy took towards Walshe. Opening his report with a reference to the talks between Pétain and Hitler at Montoire, the minister claimed that since he 'knew from [the] wireless that you were aware of these meetings, [he] considered it was [a] needless expense to tele-

---

16 Ibid., report from Murphy, 8 July 1940.   **17** Ibid., telegram from Vichy to External Affairs, 14 July 1940.   **18** Ibid., telegram from Walshe to Murphy, 23 July 1940 [no. 98].

graph when I was unable to add anything to what you already knew'.[19] His frustration with Walshe comes much more to the fore later in the report:

> I would have sent telegraphic reports of my impressions of the situation here were it not for the fact that I understood from your telegram that you only wanted reports which could be supported by some authoritative source and that you were generally better informed on situation from elsewhere than I could inform you, which is correct.

Walshe's reply can be described as terse at best. In a curt telegram he requested the papal nuncio's view of the situation and asked a number of specific questions in relation to Pétain, Laval and French collaboration with Germany.[20] Murphy's reply was two-fold. On 1 December he sent a report in which he carefully responded to all the questions put to him, presenting them as the papal nuncio's viewpoint.[21] He followed up with a second dispatch in which he gave his personal view of the situation in France, a report which should have removed any doubts about the dangers of adopting a position of active support for the Vichy regime. However, he opened with a vigorous defence of his professional integrity:

> I gather from your telegrams nos. 98 and 391 that you have formed a definite opinion on the situation with which the views expressed in my reports are not in complete harmony. I have always endeavoured to give you the facts of the situation as I see it objectively and without prejudice, and it is somewhat disheartening to receive telegrams of the kind to which I have referred which seem to suggest that I am drawing on my imagination. Whatever be your other sources of information, I think my reports are entitled to be taken on their face value until they are at least shown to be incorrect.[22]

Murphy's outburst must have caused some consternation in Dublin. There appears to be no record of any discussions that Walshe may have had with de Valera on the issue, but there are certain indicators that such discussions took place. For instance, Con Cremin, secretary to the Irish legation at Vichy, reported a feeling of tension at headquarters when he travelled to Dublin for debriefing.[23]

Whatever discussions took place, it seems clear that Walshe drew back from his earlier criticism. He sent a telegram to Murphy on 7 January 1941 in which he said that:

---

19 NAI DFA SF P 12/1, report from Murphy to Walshe, 18 November 1940. **20** NAI DFA PE 48/18, telegram from Walshe to Murphy, 25 November 1940 [no. 391]. **21** NAI DFA SF P 12/1, telegram from Murphy to Walshe, 1 December 1940. **22** Ibid., report from Murphy to Walshe, 7 December 1940. **23** Dermot Keogh, 'Ireland, de Gaulle and World War II', in Pierre Joannon (ed.), *De Gaulle and Ireland* (Dublin, 1991), p. 26.

no criticism [was] intended in our telegrams 98 and 391. You have evidently misunderstood our desire to know [the] Vatican attitude. It is, of course, of the utmost importance to know Vatican views at all stages of [the] situation, especially owing to [the] character of [the] Pétain government. The questions in my telegram 391 were put for the purpose of obtaining more detailed information on the matter treated by you and were not intended as criticism of the objectivity of your reports. Questions may often be necessary in order to elucidate certain points.[24]

Murphy, in reply, accepted the apology, but drove home his point. He realised that:

questions may be necessary for various reasons. It was not the fact, it was the way in which the questions were put which led me to misunderstand the position. I am in constant contact with [the] nuncio. His views on the situation here may not necessarily be those of the Vatican. Further, the views that the nuncio expresses to me may not be exactly those he gives to Vatican. [I] will send reports whenever [there are] matters of interest to report.[25]

Murphy had risked a potentially strong reprimand from his superiors for the manner in which he had defended his position. The resultant softening of the pro-Pétain line in Iveagh House, possibly because of de Valera's intervention, will be seen to have been important, not least in how relations with France were conducted in the immediate post-liberation period. Six weeks later Murphy continued to counsel against cultivating too close a link with the Vichy government. He warned that the:

révolution nationale does not go very deep. The Marshal is very sincere in his intentions and ideas, but, unfortunately, the application of these ideas is not very widespread. There have been considerable changes in the personnel of the government and municipal administrations, but with very few exceptions, the faults of the old administration persist; instead of the stability which was hoped for and promised, there have been more changes of government than under the old regime.[26]

Murphy also had harsh words for Pétain, stating that although he was 'universally respected and admired', he was also 'vain, self-opinionated and stub-

---

24 NAI DFA PE 48/18, telegram from Walshe to Murphy, 7 January 1941. **25** Ibid., telegram from Murphy to Walshe, 13 January 1941. **26** NAI DFA SF P 12/1, Murphy to Walshe, 1 March 1941.

born'. Nonetheless, Murphy was not unaware that Walshe continued to harbour a certain respect for Pétain;[27] consequently, many of his later reports are couched in terms calculated to be more palatable to the secretary, with regular references to the papal nuncio.

THE IRISH LEGATION AND THE JEWISH QUESTION

The regime which Pétain led holds a unique position in that 'the men, women and children sent to die in Germany from Vichy-controlled areas were the only Jews to be deported from a European territory that was not occupied by the Germans'.[28] In the light of the open anti-Semitism of the regime it is, therefore, important to examine the attitude taken by the Irish legation towards the 'Jewish question'.

Murphy sounded an early warning in the first weeks of the Pétain regime. He asserted that the repeal of a law permitting the taking of legal proceedings in response to slander or insults of a 'racial or religious character' could give rise to an anti-Semitic campaign, and that the 'latent tendency towards anti-Semitism' in France would be 'clearly enhanced'.[29] Murphy's reports on the issue became rather infrequent after this point and, rather surprisingly, he did not specifically comment on La Grande Rafle, a major operation carried out by the French police on 16 and 17 July 1942 in which as many as 9,000 Jews were rounded up. The minister, however, did report one month later. He stated that public opinion in the occupied zone was revolted by the 'very severe measures taken against the Jews and the internment of large numbers of women and children in concentration camps under appalling conditions'.[30] He expressed the fears of Jews living in the Free Zone that the same measures taken in the Occupied Zone would be applied to them and felt that Pétain would eventually give way to the Germans on this issue. These fears were well-founded. A further report in October 1942 describes how Jews of foreign origin who had come to France after 1933 were being arrested and handed over to the German authorities. (Interestingly, in this dispatch, Murphy states that once the Jews were arrested 'no one knows what becomes of them', but that 'it is certain that the Jews in the Free Zone are having a very bad time'.)[31] The legation's annual report for 1942 also confirms that the

---

27 NAI DFA SF A 2, Walshe to de Valera, 9 October 1944. Even by October 1944 Walshe was still displaying his personal respect for Pétain. When the French envoy to Ireland asked Walshe what the idea of the Irish Government would be to a request for asylum from Pétain, Walshe replied that on a 'personal and unofficial' level he felt that Ireland would welcome him as a 'distinguished soldier'. **28** Paul Webster, *Pétain's Crime* (London, 1992), p. 3. **29** NAI DFA PE 19/34A, Murphy to External Affairs, 29 August 1940. **30** NAI DFA 219/1D, report from Murphy to Walshe, 18 August 1942. **31** Ibid., report from Murphy to Walshe, 24 October

regulations put in place by the French government 'put the Jew ... on a plane which tended more and more to approximate to German ideas on this question'.[32] The legation's annual report for 1943 is equally explicit about the difficulties faced by the Jews in France, although on this occasion the minister placed more responsibility on the German, rather than the French, authorities.[33]

As useful as it is to examine the legation's attitude to the overall 'Jewish question', it is perhaps more important to examine its role in more specific cases. Indicators suggest that the legation was quite limited in what it could achieve. Iveagh House raised the question of granting temporary visas to Jews wishing to leave German territory in October 1943, but understood that whatever the position about granting these visas, exit permits for those wishing to travel were impossible to obtain from the German authorities. Murphy confirmed that this was the case.[34] These restrictions were further highlighted in December 1943 when an English Jewish organisation (possibly the Agudas Israel World Organisation) suggested to the Department of External Affairs that the possession of a visa granted by a neutral state could provide effective protection against deportation and urged the Irish government to provide visas as a humanitarian gesture. Replying to a query about this proposal from the department, Murphy was most discouraging, although he later clarified the position.[35] At the beginning of 1943 the German government had informed the governments of Spain, Portugal, Sweden, Denmark and Switzerland that their Jewish nationals had to be repatriated before the end of October 1943; after that point Jews of those nationalities would cease to have any standing in the eyes of the occupying forces. On a more positive note, the French foreign ministry had indicated to Murphy that, subject to the agreement of the German authorities, it might be possible to allow a certain number of Jews to obtain exit visas for Ireland.[36] This appears to have given the Irish authorities an impetus to act. Murphy was notified that there were 200 Polish Jewish families at the French city of Vittel which the Irish government was willing to take if the agreement of the German authorities could be obtained.[37] Murphy approached the French authorities, who told him that the Germans were no longer accepting French intervention with regard to foreign Jews and that he should approach the Germans directly.[38] Con Cremin, then Irish envoy in Berlin, contacted the German authorities, but had no success. The Jewish families remained in Vittel.[39]

1942. **32** NAI DFA PE 113/9, annual reports of the legation, 1942. **33** Ibid., annual reports of the legation, 1943. **34** NAI DFA PE 49/20 (1), telegrams from External Affairs to Murphy and Murphy to External Affairs, 25, 27 August 1943. **35** Ibid., telegrams from External Affairs to Murphy and Murphy to External Affairs, 1, 3 December 1943. **36** Ibid., legation to Dublin, 14 December 1943. **37** Ibid., telegram from External Affairs to Murphy, n.d. **38** Ibid., telegram from legation to External Affairs, 28 December 1943. **39** Dermot Keogh, *Jews in Twentieth-Century Ireland: Refugees, Anti-semitism and the Holocaust* (Cork, 1998), pp 179–80.

The legation was approached by a number of individuals during the war. Sophie Philipson requested information about her husband, Serge, the manager of a factory in Galway. She wished to know if he had become a naturalised Irish citizen, which might afford her some protection against deportation.[40] The legation requested permission (which was subsequently granted by the Department of Justice) for the Philipson family to go to Ireland.[41] The family remained too long in France, however, and most members, alas, were caught and deported. The legation did attempt to assist in the care of Mrs Philipson's daughter, Rachel. The child's guardian, Aline Rilly, sought advice from the legation on how best the child could be protected, since she herself feared deportation. It was felt that there was no hope of the child being allowed to leave France to join her father; accordingly, it was decided to leave the child in the care of friends of Aline Rilly and to devise some means by which the legation could keep track of the child.[42] It appears that Rachel was the only member of the Philipson family in France to survive the war.[43]

Yet this was not the only case the legation was involved in. Seán Murphy received a touching letter from a Jacques Darblay in April 1944, thanking him for his efforts on his behalf (while the letter does not go into details, it implies that Rachel Philipson was not the only child the legation was keeping track of).[44] The legation also intervened in the case of Fay Abusch at the request of Robert Briscoe, the Fianna Fáil TD. Briscoe sought the legation's help in securing an exit visa for Abusch, whose sister was a personal friend of the deputy. Con Cremin did a large amount of work to secure the visa, which was eventually granted in October 1942.[45] However, complications arose. Abusch had difficulty securing a Portuguese transit visa, and the legation was unable to assist her.[46] A far more serious matter was the introduction of a new regulation requiring the holders of French passports who wished to leave France, such as Fay Abusch, to obtain a special authorisation sanctioned only by the minister or the secretary-general of the Ministry of the Interior.[47] This problem seems to have been insurmountable for the legation, and concern turned to ensuring the financial security of Fay Abusch.[48] The documentation on the case ends at this point.

---

40 NAI DFA 49/20 (1), telegrams from legation to External Affairs and External Affairs to legation, 28 December 1943, 26 February 1944. It emerged that Mr Philipson was not a naturalised Irish citizen and had never made an application to become one. **41** Ibid., telegram from External Affairs to legation, 27 March 1944. **42** Ibid., internal legation memo for minister, 28 February 1944. **43** Ibid., Letter to Marcel Goldberg, 28 April 1945; Keogh, *Jews in Twentieth Century Ireland*, p. 162. **44** NAI DFA 49/20 (1), letter from Jacques Darblay to Murphy, 14 April 1944. **45** Ibid., telegrams from Robert Briscoe to legation and legation to External Affairs, 10, 26 September 1942; handwritten notes by Cremin, 1, 3, 12, 21 October 1942. **46** Ibid., Abusch to Irish legation, 14 November 1942; legation to External Affairs, 16 November 1942. **47** Ibid., Cremin note, 25 November 1942. **48** Ibid., Irish legation to

THE FRENCH LEGATION IN DUBLIN

The situation for the staff of the French legation in Dublin was no less difficult, due both to the sharply divided loyalties within the legation and the policies pursued by a neutral Irish government. De Gaulle's Appel du 18 Juin involved a decision for all of the French people. Choices were made in favour of Pétain, Admiral Darlan and, of course, de Gaulle. Although these decisions were not made immediately, it was a situation which had to be faced at some point by all members of the legation staff. A confidential memorandum prepared by G2, the Irish intelligence service, in October 1943 gives an excellent indication of the divisions within the legation at that time.[49] The minister, M.F.X. de Laforcade, tacitly supported Pétain at an early stage, although this sentiment did not last. He was on very friendly terms with the British and American representatives in Dublin and his social contacts included British, American and Gaullist supporters, but never Axis sympathisers. Although the minister did not officially declare in favour of de Gaulle until September 1943, this was explained by his desire to prevent collaborationist elements from taking over the legation in Dublin and in the interests of maintaining the most positive relations possible between Ireland and France. De Laforcade's deputy, Benjamin Frederic Cauvet-Duhamel, was considered to be more cautious. However, he was on very friendly terms with his superior and moved in the same social circles. In fact, out of his own similar fear that collaborationist elements would otherwise take over the legation, he took over as chargé d'affaires after de Laforcade rallied to de Gaulle.

Those whom De Laforcade and Cauvet-Duhamel feared and disliked most were the military personnel of the legation. The minister feared that the naval attaché, H.E. Albertas, had been sent to Dublin to spy on his activities. The G2 memorandum indicated that Albertas was pro-Vichy and anti-British. His secretary, Marcel Kergoat, was thought to be similarly minded.

The commercial attaché, Eugène Lestocquoy, who had already spent some years in Dublin, attempted to stay aloof from the divisive nature of French legation politics. But he was a complex figure. On a personal level, he was considered by G2 to be pro-British and included among his friendships Messrs Rochat and Saffroy, the first members of the legation staff to rally to de Gaulle. Yet Lestocquoy was also a particular favourite of Joseph Walshe, who described him as the 'most logical and honourable member of the French officials'.[50] This may have had something to do with Walshe's concurrence with Lestocquoy's view that de Gaulle was a subversive force in French politics.

Abusch, 13 January 1943. **49** NAI DFA SF P 75, memorandum prepared by G2, 25 October 1943. This report has been extensively drawn on. **50** NAI DFA SF A 2, report from Walshe, 5 November 1943.

The tensions which had been latent in the French legation were seriously exacerbated following the Anglo–American landings in North Africa in November 1942. On 26 November de Laforcade received a telegram from Admiral Darlan (who, with American support, had set himself up in as the leader of the French opposition to Vichy), requesting the minister's backing for his newly-installed regime in Algiers. De Laforcade's loyalty to Vichy, never strong, wavered. He asked Walshe what the Irish government's likely reaction would be if he rallied officially to Algiers. He also suggested that the Irish government move its representation from Vichy to Algiers. The latter suggestion was immediately rejected by Walshe, although he did say that if Pétain resigned, and if governing became impossible under the Germans, then the Irish government would withdraw its representatives from Vichy. But he did not go so far as to say that Ireland's legation would move to Algiers. Regarding support for Darlan, Walshe urged caution, stating that he would prefer if the Irish government was not forced into a difficult position through the actions of the French legation, and requested de Laforcade to delay any decision until the position had become clearer and the Irish legation in Vichy had been consulted.[51]

De Laforcade still had to reply in some form to Darlan's telegram, and his statement had to be carefully drafted if he was to remain on friendly terms with all sides. He accepted a formula drafted by Walshe which enabled him to avoid alienating either Vichy or Algiers:

> Representing France in a neutral country which has always maintained relations with the government at Vichy, and which is inspired by a great esteem and deep affection for our country, I advise absolute prudence towards it. The Irish government, taking into account the situation in the [French] Empire, does not believe itself able to change its attitude without much more precise information than that available until now. Between times, I am convinced that a patient attitude towards a country which could be for us a strong supporter in the future is the policy to be pursued. For the Irish, the relations between the [French] Empire and the Metropole are far from clear.[52]

De Laforcade's urging of a change in Irish policy was at least partially dictated by his reasoning that the Allies were certain to win the war. Nonetheless, the Irish government continued to pursue a cautious line. This stance did not change when the minister rallied officially to de Gaulle in September 1943.[53] De Laforcade was then informed by Vichy on 3 November that he had been relieved

---

51 NAI DFA SF P 75, Walshe memorandum, 27 November 1942. 52 Ibid., Walshe memorandum (translation from the French), 28 November 1942. 53 MAE G V–E, *Irlande*, vol. 370, télégramme à l'arrivée, le 23 Septembre 1943.

as minister and that Cauvet-Duhamel would act as chargé d'affaires. De Laforcade, however, was allowed to retain all his diplomatic immunities and was later recognised as the official delegate of the CFLN. In this respect, the Irish government did not act in a manner dissimilar to other neutral nations.[54]

Although Irish policy towards the French resumed its normally cautious track, it could not avoid some elements of controversy. The attempt to maintain friendly relations with all shades of the political spectrum could have fallen into complete disarray had a suggestion by Walshe to Murphy in September 1943 – that he approach the French Foreign Ministry to suggest that de Laforcade be allowed to simultaneously represent Vichy and Algiers – been accepted.[55] This plan was striking in its naiveté. Murphy, to his credit, counselled strongly against the move, saying that it 'would be disastrous'.[56] The proposal appears to have been quietly dropped.

Further controversy arose when a Free French (CFLN) delegate, Roger Lalouette, received something of a 'dressing down' from Irish officials on his arrival in Dublin in June 1944, primarily because Iveagh House had not been informed of his appointment and, perhaps worse, because he was carrying a passport bearing a British diplomatic visa. Lalouette was instructed to maintain a low profile while in Dublin and was warned that any changes in his situation were to take place gradually and in accordance with political changes on the continent.[57] He later caused further difficulties for the Department of External Affairs. David Gray, the American representative in Dublin, received an anonymous letter which claimed that Lalouette had come to Ireland against the wishes of the provisional government and that he was pro-Vichy.[58] Frederick Boland, assistant secretary at the Department of External Affairs, was not inclined to believe the charges, although he did telephone Sir John Maffey, the British representative, to initiate a security investigation. Although Maffey initially refused to grant the request (he remarked somewhat caustically that even if Lalouette were pro-Vichy it should make little difference to an Irish government which already tolerated a German legation),[59] he later relented. As it turned out, the anonymous charges did not stand up to scrutiny, but were related to an internal

---

54 NAI DFA 205/124, *passim*. The Irish legation at Berne informed Iveagh House that the Swiss government did not officially recognise the CFLN, but dealt with them on a *de facto* basis: telegram from Berne, 8 September 1943. Madrid replied that Spain recognised the CFLN on a *de facto* basis and had granted its representatives diplomatic privileges as a matter of courtesy: legation to External Affairs, 6 September 1943. Lisbon indicated that the CFLN had been recognised semi-officially: legation to External Affairs, 15 October 1943. **55** NAI DFA 48/18bis, Walshe to Murphy, 13, 17 September 1943. **56** Ibid., Murphy to External Affairs, 20 September 1943. **57** NAI DFA SF A 2, memorandum from Walshe to de Valera, 22 June 1944. **58** NAI DFA SF A 61, telephone conversation between Gray and Boland, 22 July 1944. **59** Ibid., telephone conversation between Maffey and Archer, 22 July 1944.

French dispute. Maffey was inclined to place the blame for the incident on David Gray, because of his impetuosity in involving the Department of External Affairs so unnecessarily.[60] Nevertheless, in the context of the 'American Note' (a request in 1944 from the American government, supported by the British, demanding that Axis representatives in Dublin be removed, because of Allied fears of security leaks before the Normandy landings) and allegations that Dublin was a 'hotbed of intrigue', the possibility of a Vichy 'spy' could not have been welcome to the Irish government.

THE LIBERATION OF PARIS AND THE RECOGNITION OF THE FRENCH AND IRISH MINISTERS

In contrast to General de Gaulle's triumphant procession down the Champs Elysees on 26 August 1944, de Laforcade was quietly and without ceremony informed three days later by Walshe that his title of minister plenipotentiary had been restored to him and that de Gaulle's provisional government had been recognised as the legitimate French government.[61] The question of the status of Seán Murphy was not, however, resolved quite so quickly. This issue proved to be a serious obstacle to the maintenance of friendly relations between Ireland and France in the autumn of 1944. The dispute arose from the new French government's unwillingness to accept as representatives to the new regime envoys who had been accredited to the Vichy government. The Irish government did not accept this position and was not willing to comply with it.

The Irish authorities were quite surprised that the dispute arose at all. The final weeks of the Pétain government, and the early weeks of the provisional government, were marked by extreme communications difficulties. It was impossible to communicate with the Irish legation in France, except through the medium of other Irish diplomatic posts, and even then only to a very limited extent. Walshe seems to have succeeded in getting a message to Murphy on 27 August,[62] which repeated an earlier cable advising him to be guided primarily by the general attitude of other diplomats (especially that of the papal nuncio). Saying that his personal safety was paramount, Walshe granted Murphy complete discretion as to whether he should stay in France or move elsewhere.[63] It was not, however, until 5 September that Dublin received a message from Murphy, and this related only to his and his family's well-being.[64] The month of September passed with communications from France proving all but impossible. It must, therefore, have been more than a little disturbing for Walshe to read a

60 Ibid.   61 NAI DFA SF P 97, 29 August 1944.   62 Ibid., telegram from Berne to External Affairs, 27 August, 1944.   63 Ibid., telegram from External Affairs to Berne, 16 August 1944.   64 Ibid., telegram from Berne to Dublin, 5 September 1944.

Reuters report stating that the new provisional government was refusing to recognise the credentials of diplomats of neutral countries who had been accredited to Vichy.[65]

Walshe, though, should not necessarily have been surprised at this development. De Laforcade had hinted at this possibility when speaking with him on 29 August. On this occasion Walshe had strongly defended the Irish position and had rejected the principle that the provisional government's stance would apply to Ireland, regarding it as interference with Ireland's legitimate right to pursue a policy of neutrality and a slight on the professionalism of Murphy.[66] Despite this strong defence, however, Walshe should have been more prepared, particularly as he did not believe that de Laforcade was held in high esteem in Paris.[67] Surprised or not, he was not unduly worried. Although he threatened to withdraw recognition from de Laforcade, which had been 'granted on the hypothesis that there would be no question of an equal recognition of [Murphy's] position on the other side' being withheld, he maintained that he was 'reasonably certain' that recognition would be granted and that 'the French government would not contemplate doing anything which in our particular case would be regarded as unfriendly'.[68]

He was quickly disabused of this notion by a telegram from Denis McDonald, the new legation secretary, which noted that '[Murphy] was very coldly received by [the] secretary-general, who stated that they wanted no heads of mission who served in Vichy. The same attitude was adopted towards [the papal] nuncio and other colleagues. [The] nuncio [was] extremely annoyed'.[69] Walshe reacted quickly. He protested very strongly to the French ambassador in London and threatened to withdraw recognition from the French legation in Dublin if an apology and complete acceptance of Murphy as the Irish representative were not forthcoming.[70] Given the strong mood of the provisional government against the Vichy regime and anything connected with it, it is unlikely that Walshe's protest would have succeeded had the matter not come to the attention of de Gaulle. Although it is unclear how this came about, speculation centres on the good relationship between Frederick Boland and Hervé Alphand, son of Charles Alphand, the first French minister to Ireland and director-general of economic affairs in the Quai d'Orsay. Following de Gaulle's intervention, Walshe reported to Murphy on 10 October that the 'misunderstanding [had] ended. You are fully recognised as minister by [the] new government'.[71]

---

65 Ibid., Harold King, special correspondent, Reuters, 27 September 1944. **66** Ibid., Walshe report, 29 August 1944. **67** Ibid., Walshe to Murphy, via Berne, 9 October 1944. Walshe opined that 'Minister here should long ago have made all this known to his Government, but we fear they regard him as useless and may not read his telegrams'. **68** Ibid., Walshe to Murphy, 30 September 1944. **69** Ibid., Berne to Dublin, 4 October 1944. **70** Ibid., Walshe to Murphy, via Berne, 9 October 1944. **71** Keogh, *Ireland and Europe*, p. 187.

Yet the matter was not completely resolved. Press reports announcing the reestablishment of the Irish legation on 25 October had prompted a Dáil question from James Larkin, a Labour TD, seeking the reason for the delay. The background note for de Valera's information cautioned against giving away any more details than were absolutely necessary and warned that the 'whole matter is still bristling with difficulties'.[72] The issue seemed close to a resolution by 17 November. One outstanding item was the question of an audience with de Gaulle. Given that the French decision to allow only Ireland, of all the neutral nations, to move its representative from Vichy to Paris, and that this decision had caused difficulties with the other neutrals, the provisional government was unwilling to grant Murphy a personal meeting with de Gaulle, since this might exacerbate the situation. A compromise was reached whereby Murphy would take his long overdue leave and would be granted an audience on his return.[73] The long-awaited meeting took place on 24 March 1945 in an atmosphere described as cordial. The tensions which had marked Irish–French relations the previous autumn had dissipated, and the general appeared to have a high opinion of Murphy. De Gaulle also expressed his personal admiration for the manner in which de Valera had kept Ireland neutral. The guard was also turned out in Murphy's honour, adding an official touch to what was essentially a 'private' audience.[74]

THE POST-LIBERATION RELATIONSHIP

Despite the cordiality of the meeting between Murphy and de Gaulle, it would be a mistake to assume that relations between Ireland and France immediately resumed their earlier friendly tack. It took some time for this to happen. De Laforcade informed Iveagh House in December 1944 that he had reached the statutory retirement age and that the French government had decided to replace him. His successor was Jean Rivière, who had several qualities calculated to appeal to the Irish authorities. He was Catholic and counted among his relatives several leading clerics, including the bishop of Monaco and the late Archbishop of Aix-en-Provence. He had also served at the French embassy in the Vatican.[75] Despite these characteristics, though, Iveagh House officials considered him the poorest French representative since diplomatic relations had been established between the two countries.

Although the cordiality of the Murphy–de Gaulle meeting was reprised in Rivière's courtesy call on de Valera,[76] some ill-feeling was generated almost from

---

72 NAI DFA SF P 97, memorandum from Walshe, 9 November 1944. **73** Ibid., Murphy to Walshe, 17 November 1944. **74** Ibid., report from Murphy to Walshe, 26 March 1945. **75** NAI DFA 318/2, cv of Jean Rivière. **76** Joseph Carroll, 'A French View of Irish Neutrality', in

the beginning of his posting in Ireland. The tone and content of the Letters of Credence presented by the French diplomat were considered objectionable by officials in the Department of External Affairs, because of their exaggerated references to the British sovereign.[77] It is not inconceivable that the documents were intended as a deliberate slight to Ireland on the part of the Quai d'Orsay. De Gaulle may have expressed his admiration for Irish neutrality, but this view was not shared by the French foreign ministry. Hostility towards Ireland was manifested in a number of ways. Murphy was constantly reminded that his presence was no more than tolerated in the French capital and that he was allowed to remain there only with great reluctance on the part of the French authorities.[78]

It was the firm belief of Irish officials that many of the problems encountered with Rivière in Dublin were the result of instructions that the minister was receiving from his headquarters.[79] A primary example may be what was viewed as an overreaction on his part to an incident in Dublin at the war's end, when, along with the British and American missions, the windows of a French restaurant, *Jammet's*, were broken. It has been suggested that the attack was motivated more by anglophobia than francophobia, the restaurant having strong Ascendancy links.[80] An official protest was lodged with the Department of External Affairs. The restaurant owner, Louis Jammet, was described as 'le chef moral de la colonie Française de Dublin et l'initiateur du mouvement de la resistance Française en Irlande pendant la guerre', and Rivière expressed his fear that the Irish government's policy of neutrality had extended to being anti-French.[81] Although both the British and American representatives received official apologies from the Irish government for the attacks on their diplomatic premises, there is no record that such an apology was extended to the French minister (this may have been due to the fact that such an apology would not have been automatic, as the restaurant was not French diplomatic property). The French protest was considered superfluous, and Rivière's *démarche* was thought to have made a 'bad impression' in Iveagh House.[82]

Walshe was more forthright about Rivière. He considered that 'his egregious *faux-pas* in relation to the Jammet affair revealed an immaturity of judgement and outlook which raises considerable doubts about his future'.[83] More seriously, given that Ireland was unpopular among the Allied states because of its war-time

Etudes Irlandaises, vol. 14, no. 2 (December 1989), p. 160. **77** NAI DFA 318/27, memorandum prepared in Department of External Affairs, 12 February 1947. By contrast, the letters of credence presented by Rivière's successor, Count Ostroróg, were very sparing in their references to the British sovereign. **78** Dermot Keogh, 'Ireland, de Gaulle and World War II', p. 51. **79** NAI DFA 318/27, External Affairs to Murphy, 24 September 1946. **80** Joseph Carroll, *Ireland in the War Years* (Newton Abbott, 1975), p. 161. **81** Carroll, 'A French View of Irish Neutrality', p. 160. **82** NAI DFA 318/2, report by Murphy, 9 December 1946. **83** NAI DFA SF P 12/1, Walshe to Murphy, 7 June 1945.

neutrality (particularly following de Valera's expressions of condolence after Hitler's death), Walshe was of the impression that a number of heads of mission were playing 'fast and loose with our sentiments'. He included the French minister in this group and suggested that Murphy 'talk to somebody like the former, friendly Catholic Minister for Foreign Affairs and indicate to him by a few apt parallels how much harm can be done to good relations by entrusting French interests here to people who put the attractions of snobbery and flattery before their country's interests'. In this respect, Irish officials were dismayed by the pro-British, or Ascendancy, attitude of the French minister. Those whom Rivière entertained were considered by Walshe to be the 'most anti-Irish and the most collaborationist elements in the Ascendancy class'.

Fortunately, Rivière did not remain long in Dublin. Such was the dissatisfaction with his performance, coupled with the fear that he may have been acting on instructions, that Irish officials made an informal approach to the Quai d'Orsay. Murphy made the director of Europe, M. Coulet, aware of the department's unhappiness with Rivière in a meeting in December 1946.[84] This was reinforced even more strongly in a similar meeting with Coulet the following month, when Murphy said that the Irish authorities would not tolerate a repeat of Rivière's earlier performance.[85] The Irish views appear to have been taken into account. Indicative were the Letters of Credence presented by Count Ostroróg, Rivière's successor, which were very sparing in their references to the British Crown.[86] The Irish authorities could, perhaps, look forward to a resumption of the normal, friendly relations between Ireland and France that had obtained previously.

If Irish officials were unhappy with the performance of the French minister in Dublin, and were concerned at the state of relations between Ireland and France, it should be said, perhaps, that they, too, carried some of the blame for this situation. Murphy remained as Irish minister to Paris until March 1950, when he was appointed Irish ambassador to Ottawa. Given that there was considerable hostility to him because of his accreditation to Vichy, this was far too long a period. Although one must always be conscious of the fact that the Irish foreign service was very small at that time, and that there were not many experienced personnel within the Department of External Affairs, relations between Ireland and France might have been better served had Murphy been recalled soon after the Irish authorities had succeeded in making their political point that Ireland had a perfect right to maintain a policy of neutrality during the war. By retaining Murphy in Paris, however, the Irish authorities left him in a difficult position with his hosts, a fact that he was constantly reminded of.

84 NAI DFA 318/2, report by Murphy, 9 December 1946. **85** Ibid., report from Murphy to Boland, 6 January 1947. **86** NAI DFA 318/27, memorandum prepared in the Department of External Affairs, 12 February 1947.

CONCLUSION

The difficulties between Ireland and France eased with the passage of time. Relations between the two countries took a new, positive turn in 1950 when it was decided to upgrade relations to ambassadorial level. Perhaps the clearest indication of how the wounds had healed was the ready acceptance by the French authorities of Con Cremin as Ireland's first ambassador in Paris: Cremin, after all, had acted as secretary to the Irish legation in Vichy up to 1943. President Seán T. O'Kelly also paid a state visit to France in 1950, the first trip abroad by an Irish President since the Republic had been declared. There was some symbolic significance given that the president was returning to the city where he had earlier represented the clandestine Irish foreign service. The embassy's annual report for 1950 noted that O'Kelly's visit 'was very successful, as he was received with great friendliness by the officials and by the press'.[87]

The relationship between Ireland and France during World War II was tense and uneasy. Ireland was fortunate to have had a diplomat of the quality of Murphy stationed in France at that time. He managed to maintain a cautious policy towards the Vichy regime, curbing the enthusiasm of Walshe for that government. Despite this, the immediate post-war relationship continued to be somewhat difficult. The new French government did not easily forget Ireland's neutral policy during the war, and a degree of hostility remained for some time. However, old wounds healed, and by the time Con Cremin became Ireland's first ambassador to Paris relations between the two countries had resumed their hitherto friendly course.

---

87 NAI DFA PE 113/9, annual report, 1950.

'Benevolent Helpfulness'? Ireland and the International Reaction to Jewish Refugees, 1933–9

Katrina Goldstone

INTRODUCTION

It is generally agreed that the attitude of our delegation should be one of benevolent helpfulness, except in the case of any attempt being made to impose a quota on Ireland.[1]

These were the instructions emanating from the Department of External Affairs in July 1938 regarding the position to be taken in relation to Jews fleeing the Third Reich by Francis T. Cremins, Ireland's permanent delegate to the League of Nations, at the Evian Conference, which was due to open within days. This statement encapsulates the contradictions and different influences at work in the development of Ireland's policy towards Jewish refugees during the 1930s. The position which eventually emerged was essentially restrictive, leaning towards the pragmatism of quotas, rather than towards the ideal of 'benevolent helpfulness'. This theme surfaced in a minute that Frederick Boland, assistant secretary of External Affairs, forwarded to J.J. McElligott, secretary of the Department of Finance, in 1944 – a document, interestingly enough, in which Boland also argued for a more cooperative post-war attitude:

In view of the fact that, unlike other neutral countries such as Sweden and Switzerland, Ireland has not made, or been in a position to make, any effective contribution to the solution of the serious international problem of refugees, the Minister for External Affairs is anxious that this country should not withhold its cooperation from the International Committee on Refugees in the discharge of the tasks entrusted it.[2]

This chapter thus examines the evolution of Irish policy towards the Jews of Europe in the years preceding World War II. It assesses its development in the context of wider historical events and the attitudes of other states, especially the

[1] NAI DFA 243/1055, 2 July 1938. [2] Ibid., Boland to McElligott, 28 May 1944.

influence of British policy dictates. Like most of the countries faced with the Jewish refugee crisis, Ireland's administration adopted a restrictive stance. This chapter, therefore, focuses on the decisions taken by Irish officialdom. It also examines some of the ideas which fed this policy, principally, that it was preferable to limit the number of Jews entering Ireland.

In a broader context, the desire to restrict Jewish immigration was common amongst government officials in Britain, the United States, Canada and South Africa throughout the inter-war period.[3] Since the 1920s, for instance, America had employed a system of immigration quotas, with ethnic preferences accorded to those who spoke English. The British and Canadian governments were less overt in their screening along racial or religious lines. But they did limit immigration at key periods by using administrative practices as an adjunct to legislation, and, in the main, these policies were unofficial and unspoken, as was the case in Ireland. In essence, the idea of restriction was neither new nor remarkable.[4] During the economically depressed 1930s, in particular, the notion of limiting immigration seemed eminently practical to many of the bureaucrats formulating policy.[5] The fact that restriction was predicated on what today would be regarded as discriminatory practices seems rarely to have entered into their appraisals. In Ireland's case, the nation's high rate of emigration meant that its officials had little or no experience of the country as a destination for immigrants.[6] Thus the policy that evolved was modelled heavily on British establishment thinking and also measured through the prism of Anglo–Irish relations.

Nonetheless, the pivotal idea underpinning Ireland's stance was that large numbers of Jews were undesirable, mainly because officials assumed they were difficult to assimilate and they provoked outbursts of anti-Semitism. This view stemmed from the belief – widespread and rooted in the nineteenth century – that homogeneity was one of the prime guarantees of political stability. To many

---

3 See, for example, David Cesarani, 'An Alien Concept? The Continuity of Anti-Alienism in British Society before 1940', in David Cesarani and Tony Kushner (eds), *The Internment of Aliens in Twentieth-Century Britain* (London, 1993); Irving Abella and Harold Troper (eds), *None is Too Many: Canada and the Jews of Europe, 1933–1948* (New York, 1983).   **4** Albert Lindeman, *The Jew Accused* (Cambridge, 1993), p. 23.   **5** For general reading on the development of immigration policy in Ireland, see Dermot Keogh, *Jews in Twentieth Century Ireland: Refugees, Anti-Semitism and the Holocaust* (Cork, 1998); in Britain, see Bernard Wasserstein, *Britain and the Jews of Europe, 1939–45* (Oxford, 1979), Louise London, 'Jewish Refugees, Anglo-Jewry and British Government Policy, 1930–40', in Cesarani and Kushner, *The Making of Anglo-Jewry*; A.J. Sherman, *Island Refuge: Britain and Refugees from the Third Reich, 1933–39*, second edition (London, 1994); Michael Marrus, *The Unwanted: European Refugees in the Twentieth Century* (Oxford, 1985).   **6** For the background to Ireland in the 1930s, see Terence Brown, *Ireland: A Social and Cultural History 1922–79* (London, 1981); Dermot Keogh, *Twentieth Century Ireland: Nation and State* (Dublin, 1995); J.J. Lee, *Ireland 1912–1985: Politics and Society* (Cambridge, 1989).

of the European political elite anti-Semitism constituted a social evil, mainly because it presented a threat to law and order. Still, British politicians did amend their restrictive stance in the months before the outbreak of World War II and finally admitted large numbers of Jews proportionate to the country's population. This was partly due to the strength of public opinion in the aftermath of Kristallnacht in November 1938 and the involvement of the Anglo–Jewish elite, who had pledged total financial support for the refugees and had lobbied strongly on their behalf after the pogrom.[7] The role of Irish Jewry has yet to be fully investigated in this context. Certainly, the cooperation of the Anglo–Jewish elite, and its controversial role in shaping policy and helping determine who was suitable as a refugee, is one area where there appears to be a sharp divergence between what happened in England and what took place in Ireland.

The response of Irish diplomats and politicians to the Jewish refugee crisis has recently been described by Professor Dermot Keogh.[8] However, Professor Keogh has not fully identified the significant influence of British policy on the development of Irish attitudes nor has he acknowledged the ideology of restrictive immigration, which was influenced by Social Darwinism. In other words, many governments of the day believed there were groups of immigrants, or 'aliens', that were less desirable and less easy to assimilate than others, and Jews fell into that category. Therefore, the received negative image of the Jew influenced, in part, the direction of policy. The economic depression of the 1930s was also a significant factor in determining the restrictive stance adopted by many European countries, including Ireland, but it alone does not account for the limitations imposed upon Jewish refugees.

At the same time, it will be argued that Ireland, like Britain, did not have a clearly defined refugee policy, but, in fact, altered the strict tenets of aliens policy to fit the circumstances of Jews fleeing Germany. That is to say, aliens policy was clumsily applied to refugee cases without full cognisance being given to the desperation of the situation. Indeed, until the passage of the Aliens Act in 1935 Ireland's policy was based on the British Restriction of Aliens and Amendments Bill (1914), legislation passed in the frenetic atmosphere of war, spy scares and xenophobia. After the outbreak of World War II and the adoption of neutrality Irish attitudes became stricter still, but then relaxed somewhat after 1943 – too late, however, to be of significance to most Jews still left on the continent. Ireland, nevertheless, came to be viewed as a potential haven by some

---

7 Geoffrey Alderman, *Modern British Jewry* (Oxford, 1992), pp 277–80; Tony Kushner, 'Beyond the Pale? British Reaction to Nazi Anti-Semitism', in Tony Kushner and Kenneth Lunn (eds), *The Politics of Marginality: Race, the Radical Right and Minorities in Twentieth-Century Britain* (London 1990), p. 148. **8** Dermot Keogh, *Jews in Twentieth Century Ireland: Refugees, Anti-Semitism and the Holocaust* (Cork, 1998).

refugees. This was partially because Eamon de Valera, the Minister for External Affairs as well as Taoiseach, and other Irish diplomats had garnered a reputation for sympathy towards minorities.[9] In addition, once the war started Britain was no longer a feasible destination for many Jews, since they could not leave Germany for a country at war with the Fatherland.

This chapter utilises numerous visa application documents and related archival sources, plus Irish diplomatic *démarches* at the League of Nations, to chart the evolution of Ireland's Jewish refugee policy. It focuses on the inter-departmental debates which, at times, prevented a coherent and consistent policy from being implemented. It also takes account of the fact that the humanitarian principles which are central to refugee matters today were not fully thought out in the 1930s, when economic circumstances forced harsh pragmatism on many governments. Nevertheless, one cannot ignore that in private memos, and behind closed doors, bureaucrats and politicians were more likely to pronounce that it was the 'Jewishness' of the refugees that made them less desirable, a fact that leads to the conclusion that covert anti-Semitism in the 1930s was far more common, particularly amongst Irish civil servants, that has been accepted.

IRELAND, THE LEAGUE OF NATIONS AND THE REFUGEE CRISIS

Within months of Hitler becoming chancellor in January 1933, Ireland's envoy to Berlin, Leo T. McCauley, started reporting on the 'Jewish question'. His dispatch of 11 May devoted a section to his interpretation of the situation. McCauley began:

> The government has been faithful to the anti-Semitic portion of the Nazi programme. It has endeavoured to oust the Jews from public offices, the press, theatre, the academies of art, the professions and business. The official actions of the government are sufficiently severe. They aim at depriving Jews in official life, the professions, etc., of their means of livelihood.[10]

McCauley went on to describe the terms of the recently introduced Re-Establishment of the Civil Service Law (April 1933), which first racialised Jews and set in train the process of placing them apart from German citizens. He then outlined its immediate impact on public life:

---

9 NAI DFA 26/73, annual review, *Saorstát's* Work in the League of Nations; NAI DFA 24/11, Council Minority Committee minutes, *passim*. By March 1932 Seán Lester, Ireland's permanent delegate to the League of Nations, had served on 8 Council Minority Committees. See also, *Jewish Chronicle*, 8 May 1964. **10** NAI DFA 34/125 McCauley to Walshe, 11 May 1933.

the general effect of the government's measures against the Jews has been to deprive Germany of the services of many men distinguished in the sciences [and] in medicine, and otherwise to reduce many ordinary, inconspicuous people to poverty and despair. The press has reported a remarkable number of suicides amongst such people.

McCauley concluded that 'to some extent the Jews brought this trouble on themselves', because of their ostentatious displays of wealth. It is unclear whether McCauley was repeating his own prejudices here or was interpreting public opinion as he read it in Germany. One month earlier he had sent a report to External Affairs officials detailing the first signs of a Jewish exodus. He informed them of the increase in visa applications to Ireland and commented that he had discouraged such persons, 'as they are really only refugees'.[11] McCauley added: 'it assumes that this line of action would be in accordance with the department's policy'. Again, it is not clear whether this statement was an example of McCauley acting on his own initiative or whether he was carrying out direct instructions from Dublin, but it does indicate that some form of nascent policy, no matter how tenuous, had been formulated at this point.

* * *

It was not just in Berlin that Irish diplomats were becoming aware of a burgeoning refugee problem. In Geneva, the heart of the international community, both Seán Lester, Ireland's permanent delegate to the League of Nations, and Eamon de Valera were lobbied to make intercessions on behalf of the Jewish minority in the Third Reich. Seán Lester, subsequently, became involved in international attempts to censure the German government's treatment of Jews. In May 1933 he acted as *rapporteur* for minority questions to Council of the League of Nations and was required to adjudicate on what became known as 'the Bernheim petition'.

Franz Bernheim, a German Jew living in Upper Silesia, brought a case to the League Council in relation to the position of the Jewish minority there. As a result of the Re-Establishment of the Civil Service Law Bernheim had lost his job as an employee of Deutsches Familien-Kanthaus in Gleiwitz. His protest was based on the assumption that the dismissal was unfair and a violation of the Geneva Convention governing Upper Silesia. Bernheim and other Jews, however, wanted to use his case to focus international attention on Nazi racial policies.[12]

Sean Lester constituted a committee of jurists, including Max Huber, the president of the International Red Cross Committee, to investigate the Bernheim case. Bernheim's petition protested against 'certain legislative and administrative orders enacted in Germany and affecting the position of persons of non-

---

11 Ibid., McCauley to Walshe, 10 April 1933.   12 Marrus, *The Unwanted*, p. 160.

Aryan descent'.¹³ Bernheim wished to test the legality of these anti-Semitic decrees under international law. In his report on the matter Lester observed:

> It is a fair generalisation that these laws and orders involve restrictions in various forms which would apply only to persons belonging to the Jewish population. The petition refers, without mentioning any actual cases, to the boycott of Jewish shops, lawyers and doctors, etc., and the failure of the authorities and officials to protect the Jewish population, who, it is alleged, have been officially outlawed.¹⁴

It was generally agreed at the League that Lester's handling of the affair was judicious. It earned him an honourable reputation as regards delicate minority questions and, in part, contributed to his appointment as League of Nations High Commissioner of Danzig.¹⁵ For his part, Anthony Eden, British Minister for League of Nations Affairs and Lord Privy Seal, 'knew that all his colleagues would join with the German representative in expressing their obligation to the *rapporteur* for the outcome of the earnest endeavours which he had so frequently to make of late and in which he had always been successful'.¹⁶ Lester himself was pleased with the way in which he and the Irish diplomatic team had handled a tricky situation. He wrote to Joseph Walshe, the secretary of the Department of External Affairs, indicating that Ireland's international standing and her reputation 'for independence and courage' had been enhanced by the outcome of the affair.¹⁷ Lester's role also elicited a number of letters from German Jews and from Jewish charities in America, Britain and France, and his record alerted those lobbying on behalf of Jewish refugees that Irish diplomats and politicians might be enlisted to the cause.

* * *

By 1936 the vexed question of the legal status of Jewish refugees from Germany was occupying even more time at the League of Nations. The Office of the High Commissioner for Refugees (Jewish and Other) Coming from Germany had been established in 1933, and the Council appointed James McDonald to head it. In early 1936 a new High Commissioner for Refugees, Sir Neill Malcolm, replaced McDonald. There was a need to clarify the status of German Jewish refugees as regards passports and citizenship, because the Nuremberg Laws of

---

13 *League of Nations Official Journal, 1933* (Geneva), vol. 14, no. 7 (Part I), p. 845. **14** Ibid. **15** See Stephen Barcroft, 'The International Civil Servant: The League of Nations Career of Seán Lester', unpublished Ph.D. thesis, Trinity College Dublin, 1972. **16** *League of Nations Official Journal, 1933* (Geneva), vol. 14, no. 7 (Part I), p. 848. For a less favourable view of Lester's role as an intermediary, see Marrus, *The Unwanted*, p. 160. **17** NAI DFA 24/28, Lester to Walshe, 30 May 1933.

September 1935 had robbed Jews of their full rights as citizens and reduced many of them to the position of 'statelessness'. In July 1936 Sir Neil Malcolm convened an inter-governmental conference in Geneva to assess the situation. Beforehand, Francis T. Cremins, the new Irish permanent delegate to the League, circulated memoranda to the relevant Irish government departments: Justice, Industry and Commerce and External Affairs. The Minister of Justice, P.J. Ruttledge, whose own attitude reflected the general view of his department, asserted that 'the permanent delegate at Geneva ... should resist any efforts to impose additional obligations on the Saorstát in relation to such refugees'.[18] The External Affairs ethos was more liberal and tended to take the influence of international opinion into consideration (the outlook of the Department of Industry and Commerce is discussed below). There was also some lobbying from the Irish League of Nations Society requesting the liberalisation of aliens laws to take account of the special circumstances of the refugees.[19]

A provisional text of the Convention of the Status of Refugees Coming from Germany was signed by only 6 of the 15 governments who attended the conference. Ireland sent no representative – because, as Cremins noted, it clashed with a visit by de Valera to Geneva – nor did the government sign the convention. As a result, further lobbying was undertaken by Lord Duncannon from the Office of the High Commissioner for Refugees, who paid an unofficial visit to Joseph Walshe in October 1936. Summing up the outcome of the meeting, Michael Rynne, assistant legal adviser in the Department of External Affairs, observed: 'We did not commit the department to anything definite in conversation with Lord Duncannon, although [we were] fairly sympathetic to his point of view that the Jews of Germany required assistance once expelled.'[20]

Meanwhile, the well known Jewish Dáil deputy, Robert Briscoe, had been engaged in informal lobbying of his own from the early 1930s. In May 1936 he forwarded to the Department of the President documents on 'The Treatment of Jews and Non-Aryans by the German Government' together with an appeal for Irish government support from Melvin Fagen of the American Jewish Congress. Fagen requested a number of meetings with de Valera, but was not granted one.

THE FORMULATION OF GOVERNMENT POLICY

Throughout the 1930s the refugee issue provoked dissension between the three government departments processing the entry and employment of aliens, and their working relationship became quite complicated. The result was often a three-handed reel between Industry and Commerce, External Affairs and Just-

[18] NAI DFA 243/67, Roche to Walshe.   [19] Ibid., Lavery to de Valera, 26 November 1936.
[20] Ibid., External Affairs memorandum, 15 December 1937.

ice. Policymaking could be fluid, and constant consultation was needed by the personnel of all three departments to thrash out decisions on the admission of aliens. The process was a constant weighing up of the advantages and disadvantages of each alien's application.

The peculiar ethos of each department strongly dictated the way in which decisions were made. Thus the judgement of Department of Justice officials was influenced by whether or not they believed a candidate was a threat, or potential threat, to security. External Affairs, as we have seen, was sensitive to Ireland's reputation abroad, although it did not, by any means, rubber stamp every application. The Department of Industry and Commerce, which, under the aegis of Seán Lemass, was promoting an industrialisation drive, did look positively upon aliens who could provide employment, share technical skills or fill a position no Irish national could. But a May 1937 memorandum outlined its principle objection to a wholesale liberalisation of the guidelines governing the entry of aliens into Ireland: 'Owing to the number of persons unemployed in this country, it is desired that there should be no relaxation of the existing arrangements for the control of aliens entering the Saorstát for employment. It is not proposed to promote legislation for the purpose of altering this position.'[21]

Aliens wishing to relocate to Ireland were first interviewed and vetted by Irish diplomats abroad. (In locations where no Irish officials were present, a British diplomat stood in.) It was of paramount importance that Irish officials establish the *bona fides* of intending visitors, with much emphasis being placed on the 'good character' of each applicant. The main criteria were that the applicant be financially solvent, free from infectious diseases, not a lunatic and not likely to jeopardise national security. The political views of the person were also taken into consideration: anything vaguely socialist was considered suspicious. After ascertaining the alien's suitability Irish officials forwarded the applicant's documentation, with their own comments, to Dublin. Copies were passed on to both Industry and Commerce – for the granting of a work permit, if necessary – and to Justice – for the ultimate seal of approval. Justice officials could refuse entry even if the other two departments had approved an application. It is also evident that the personal idiosyncrasies of officials affected the outcome, a tendency most starkly illustrated by the example of Charles Bewley, the Irish minister in Berlin.

Much emphasis was placed on British intelligence about aliens, a tradition dating back to the foundation of the state, when the Irish and British governments agreed that it was mutually advantageous to know who was travelling between the two countries.[22] Irish officials were constantly provided with up-

---

21 Ibid., Industry and Commerce memorandum, 22 May 1937. **22** Eunan O'Halpin, 'Intelligence and National Security in Ireland, 1922–1945', in *Intelligence and National Security*, vol. 5, no. 1 (1990), *passim*; NAI DFA 72/2, letters of 2 August 1930 and 5 June 1931.

dates of the British Black List or the Suspect Index. In the processing of aliens Irish officials regularly consulted their British counterparts, whether in the Home Office, Dominions Office or at the British Passport Control Office. It is evident from early-1930s visa files that the consultation could be informal or formal, taking the form of a telephone call or an official written communication.[23]

The case of Mr Abraham Bayer, a Jew from Frankfurt who applied for entry into Ireland in 1933, provoked a spat between the Departments of Justice and Industry and Commerce and highlights the differences which could arise between civil servants influenced by different departmental cultures. Ironically, the stereotype of the Jew as a shrewd businessman seems to have been the inspiration of a decision to waive normal regulations in this instance. A July 1933 Industry and Commerce minute stated that 'owing to the present situation in Germany, it is quite possible that we could have some new industries here started by Jews whose businesses are now closed down and this one [Bayer] may be a case in point'.[24]

Department of Justice officials, however, had received information from the British Home Office that Bayer (described as 'German, presumably of Jewish race. Compelled by present conditions to leave that country') had been refused permission to start a business in England and had also been involved in an altercation with a British immigration officer. J.E. Duff, a senior civil servant in the Department of Justice, inferred that Industry and Commerce had not been vigorous enough in its vetting of aliens. Nor were his colleagues impressed by the warm recommendation offered on behalf of Bayer by J.W. Dulanty, Ireland's High Commissioner in London. Consequently, in a memorandum dated 6 February 1934 the Department of Justice reiterated that it possessed the ultimate veto on the admission of aliens into Ireland, even if the employment branch of Industry and Commerce had already granted a work permit.[25] This document thus signals a shift in Justice's attitude. Although the notion of restrictive immigration had been an unofficial element in aliens policy, there is little evidence that it was rigidly enforced prior to the mid-1930s. But this memorandum, which expresses concern 'regarding the number of aliens, Jews and Italians chiefly, who are finding their way to this country', denotes a significant change.

* * *

23 See, for example, NAI DFA 2/127, NAI DFA 2/555, NAI DFA 2/652. **24** NAI DIC TID 1207/300, 13 July 1933. **25** Ibid., Department of Justice report, 6 February 1934. A later clash between Justice and Industry and Commerce occurred in the case of Herman Heinemann. Justice refused a visa, but Industry and Commerce officials wanted Heinemann to join Roscrea Meat Products. Justice subsequently reversed its decision: NAI DFA 202/366, 6 January 1939.

Efforts to instigate schemes for German–Jewish entrepreneurs to set up businesses in Ireland were made by two different Jewish organisations in 1936 and 1939. In June 1936 the Council for German Jewry in London submitted a memorandum to J.W. Dulanty, which he duly forwarded to External Affairs headquarters. Outlining the success of German Jews in setting up thriving businesses in England and Holland, the document proposed that 'there might be openings for the establishment by a relatively small number of new enterprises in the Irish Free State for the manufacture of articles not at present manufactured there or only manufactured on a limited scale'. Stephen Roche, secretary of the Department of Justice, signalled the general hostility of his department to the proposal and explained its origins in a minute to External Affairs: 'the Minister for External Affairs will be aware that there have, of recent years, been numerous protests regarding the number of alien Jews who have established themselves in this country and the Minister [of Justice] would not look with favour on any policy that might tend to increase that number'.[26]

Roche's minute is thus an indication of the hardline stance Justice officials now espoused on the Jewish refugee issue. The exact source of the 'numerous protests' in question is unclear. Objections by Irish businessmen and politicians to what was called 'alien penetration' of Irish industry did occur throughout the 1930s, and Jews were sometimes specified as aliens, but the target more often was the 'rapacious' English business concern.[27] It is clear, though, that a number of industries were set up by émigré manufacturers, who, in turn, employed a small number of refugees. The key figure in this initiative was Marcus Witzthum, a Polish Jew who became a naturalised Irish citizen and who was friendly with Robert Briscoe, the well-known Jewish Dáil deputy. With the cooperation of Fianna Fáil Senator John McEllin he established a ladies' hat factory in Galway, a sister factory in Castlebar and was involved in a third factory, Hirsch Ribbons, in Longford.[28] The Irish Leather Goods company in Dublin was another of these enterprises which were either founded or staffed partially by Jewish refugees.

Even though Witzthum's hat factories in Galway and Castlebar offered employment to many in the deprived west of Ireland, an opposition campaign was mounted in the region.[29] This may explain why more Jewish entrepreneurs were not allowed into Ireland. On the other hand, in a June 1938 letter that J.E. Duff forwarded to Joseph Walshe it is clear that this stance was not absolute. A Mrs Bennington-Cooper had enquired about the regulations guiding Jewish immigration and Duff encouraged Walshe to inform her that 'persons who are

---

26 NAI DFA 2/994, Roche to External Affairs, 14 August 1936. **27** *Irish Industry*, vol. 5, no. 1 (1937), p. 20; Naida Reports (1936), pp 12–16. **28** *Connaught Telegraph*, 29 April 1939; interview with Hans Lowy and Jenny Kenny, granddaughter of Emil Hirsch (1996). **29** *Connacht Sentinel*, 24 January 1939, 7 February 1939; interview with Mrs John McEllin (1996).

in a position to establish useful industries may be admitted if the Minister of Industry and Commerce is prepared to recommend their admission'.[30]

In 1938 another initiative to secure refuge in Ireland for Jewish émigré industrialists was undertaken by the English rabbi Solomon Schonfeld. In conjunction with Irish Jewish leaders, Schonfeld met de Valera on 15 November 1938 and encouraged him to accept more Jewish businessmen into Ireland. De Valera's initial response was lukewarm, but potentially favourable. By the end of June 1939, though, Schonfeld had not elicited a positive response to any of the applications he had forwarded to the Department of Justice. In a somewhat disgruntled tone he wrote to the department that 'Mr De Valera intimated to me at our interview that it was a policy of your government not to exclude experts who could introduce industries to Ireland. So far the Minister of Justice does not seem to coincide with the principle laid down by Mr De Valera'.[31] Scant documentary evidence survives of Eamon de Valera's direct role as Minister of External Affairs in shaping early official attitudes towards Jewish refugees. Here, however, we have a concrete example of a policy clash, with de Valera having given indications of a more liberal line, but the Department of Justice stance eventually holding sway. Nonetheless, despite the lack of cooperation from Justice, Schonfeld persisted in his requests and continued to propose further schemes. These met with little success, for eventually war-time conditions altered policy tenets once again.[32]

THE ANSCHLUSS AND THE EVIAN CONFERENCE

Before 1938 the Irish government had not been inundated by requests for asylum from Jewish refugees. Germany's annexation of Austria in March 1938 – the Anschluss – altered this situation, however. The Nazis raised the number of Austrian citizens classified as 'German non-Aryans' to 126,000, and, out of sheer desperation, the refugees began to cast their net ever wider, to ever more unlikely destinations. In response, President Franklin D. Roosevelt called for an international conference to address this severe crisis, and it convened in July 1938 at the chic French spa resort of Evian-les-Bains.[33]

Ireland was not originally included in the list of more than 30 governments invited to Evian. The Department of External Affairs, though, determined that

---

30 NAI DFA 202/105, Duff to Walshe, 19 December 1938. For similar exemptions in England, see Louise London, 'Jewish Refugees, Anglo-Jewry and British Government Policy, 1930–40', pp 171–2. **31** NAI DFA 202/157, Schonfeld to Department of Justice, 29 June 1939. **32** Schonfeld, by the way, was a controversial figure with a reputation for using varied means to help refugees. I am grateful to Tony Kushner for this observation. **33** Marrus, *The Unwanted*, p. 166.

it was essential for Ireland to attend and, as a result of making representations through the Washington legation, sent three delegates to France: J.E. Duff from Justice, W.J. Maguire from Industry and Commerce and Francis T. Cremins, Ireland's permanent delegate in Geneva.[34] During preparatory meetings for the conference, Eamon de Valera evinced some sympathy for the restrictive stance of the Department of Justice. In a letter to Joseph Walshe, Stephen Roche referred to de Valera's view that 'in common with other small countries similarly placed ... it would be impossible for us to allow any immigration into this country'.[35] But the confusion that still existed in the formulation of policy at this point is evident from a letter Roche sent to Walshe on 5 October 1938, which refers to a conversation he had with de Valera the previous month, during which 'the Taoiseach indicated that he wished that a sympathetic policy should be adopted towards Austrians and Germans who desire to settle here'.[36]

It is apparent, however, that the decision to limit the admission of Jewish refugees into Ireland had been made prior to Evian, and there is little evidence to suggest that it was substantially altered after the conference. For instance, in the middle of June External Affairs had sent several dispatches to Paris regarding entry conditions for refugees. Seán Murphy, wrote to Art O'Brien in Paris confirming the regulations he was to follow. It is worth quoting extensively from Murphy's letter, which sets out the conditions for visas:

> I am to inform you that the main purpose for the establishment of the visa is to control the entry into Ireland of persons who, for political, racial or religious reasons, may wish to take refuge in this country. Special care will, accordingly, be necessary in dealing with visa applications of those who express the intention of going to Ireland for some temporary purpose, but whose real object is to remain there indefinitely. Visas may be granted to ... persons provided (1) that the legation is fully satisfied as to the *bona fides* of the applicant and (2) that the applicant is not of Jewish or partly Jewish origin or has no non-Aryan affiliations.[37]

Murphy also enumerated some of the new rules for visas, including the proviso that holders of German and Austrian passports were to obtain a direct entry visa

---

34 NAI DFA 243/1055, External Affairs memorandum, 28 May 1944. For details on the Evian Conference, see Marrus, *The Unwanted*, pp 170–1. **35** NAI DFA 102/438, Roche to Walshe, 29 August 1938. **36** NAI DFA 104/453, Roche to Walshe, 5 October 1938. **37** NAI DFA PE P2/11, 9 June 1938; NAI DFA PE P2/102. In Britain visas had been introduced as a vetting procedure for German nationals in March 1938 at the suggestion of Jewish communal leaders: see Alderman, *Modern British Jewry*, p 278. **38** Louise London, 'Jewish Refugees, Anglo–Jewry and British Government Policy, 1930–40', p. 165.

for Ireland. The visa system at this point thus became, as it did in England, a way of sifting normal applications from potential refugee applications.³⁸

Within a month of Murphy's directive phrases referring to the religion of visa applicants in Paris started to occur more frequently. The visa application cards filled in by potential refugees carried no designation for religion, but Seán Murphy and Con Cremin, first secretary in the Paris legation, applied their own informal vetting procedure. Phrases such as 'this man, from his appearance and name, may be of [the] Jewish race' or 'more than likely of Jewish origin' appear in communications from Paris to Dublin. In August 1938 the procedure was alluded to in more specific terms by Cremin in a report to External Affairs about one applicant, a Dr Guttman. He wrote:

> I would say from his appearance (and from his name) that Dr Guttman is a Jew. In view of the instructions we have received from the department to the effect that Jewish refugees from Germany will be excluded from Ireland, I informed him that I considered that there is very little chance, if any, that he will be granted a visa for Ireland.³⁹

One can interpret these comments in a number of ways. Since the crux of aliens policy – the ability to deport visitors – had been undermined by German domestic policy, which had made Jews stateless and refused to readmit them to Germany once they had left, it was vital for one official to alert another as to what might prohibit applicants from entry into Ireland. Concurrently, given the serious consequences for those who were refused admission there seems to have been no systematic attempt to ascertain whether or not someone could return to Germany. Anyone who was vaguely suspected of being a Jew appears to have run the risk of being refused a visa.⁴⁰ A certain degree of confusion reigned, not only with regard to the procedure concerning German and Austrian passport holders, but also with regard to regulations in general. By the end of 1938, though, refugee policy was starting to be administered in a much more systematic fashion, due mostly to collaboration between the Irish government and a number of charitable organisations.

THE IRISH COORDINATING COMMITTEE

Before 1938 a number of Irish charities and philanthropists were working to alleviate the plight of Jewish refugees. Since 1933 the Society of Friends, in particu-

---

39 NAI DFA PE P2/102, Cremin to External Affairs, 17 August 1938. **40** See the cases of Gerhard Friedrich, Albert Laske, Dr Guttman, Mr and Mrs Kraus, Helen Klotz and Siegfried Waechter: DFA PE P2/102. **41** See Anthony Read and David Fisher, *Kristallnacht:*

lar, had been aware of the humanitarian problem developing because of Nazi policy. In November 1938, just two weeks before Kristallnacht,[41] the Irish Coordinating Committee for Refugees was formed. Professor Theobald Dillon of University College Dublin was its secretary and prime mover. Its main function was to pool the resources of all the various bodies involved in refugee work in Ireland. Amongst the sub-committees united by the main body were the Society of Friends Germany Emergency Committee, the Church of Ireland Jews' Society (a conversionist organisation), the Jewish Standing Committee for Refugees and the Irish Committee for Austrian Relief. A deputation from the Coordinating Committee liased with the Department of Justice, and a format was devised to facilitate the Committee's objectives without compromising the government's policy. The Committee was influential in shaping the overall approach to refugees, but, ultimately, it was subordinate to the approval of Department of Justice mandarins, who still controlled the quotas of refugees admitted into Ireland.

The ground rules for quotas were discussed at a meeting between Dillon and Justice officials on 8 November 1938, and less than a week later the basic outlines of an agreement were drafted. The document, entitled 'Refugees', stipulated that most of the refugees would be admitted on a temporary basis only, and that the Coordinating Committee would be responsible for arranging their transit to other destinations. It also specified the categories of refugees to be admitted and their actual numbers, which, at this initial stage, were kept to a minimum.[42] The first group consisted of 'fifty persons who already have some training in agricultural work in the Kagram group (a charity project run by Quakers in Austria and Germany)'; group two comprised 'adult refugees who will be maintained by well-to-do Irish citizens'; and group three included 'children who come for the purposes of education'. These original categories were confirmed by 24 November, and admission was granted to fifty persons under scheme one, twenty 'non-Aryan Christians' under scheme two and twenty 'non-Aryan Christian children' under scheme three.

The document, however, confirmed that these 'proposals relate only to Christians with Jewish blood. The Coordinating Committee are of the opinion that this country should confine its efforts to such persons, as there are adequate funds subscribed by the Jewish communities in other countries to deal with the case of professing Jews'. This was an extraordinary distinction to make, one that set Ireland's response apart from that of its closest neighbour. British functionaries did not make such a clear-cut differentiation between 'non-Aryan Christians' and professing Jews. The former term is, indeed, a ridiculous one, as it employs spurious racial categories. Still, in its publicity and its statements to the press,

Unleashing the Holocaust (London, 1989); Walter Pehle (ed.), *November 1938: From Kristallnacht to Genocide* (Berg, 1991). **42** NAI DFA 243/9, 24 November 1938.

the Irish Coordinating Committee emphasised the Christianity of the refugees coming to Ireland.

Officials from both Justice and External Affairs used the Committee to deflect enquiries about entry into Ireland. A standard reply was developed in response to queries from both those who were willing to sponsor refugees and those wanting to come to Ireland. According to Irish civil servants, the only way to enter Ireland was to be on the Coordinating Committee's quota list. By 1939 External Affairs officials were informing questioners that their only route into Ireland was via the Committee, and that its quota lists were full.[43] The Committee, of course, constantly pleaded with the Department of Justice to increase the monthly quota, but its requests, for the most part, were denied.[44]

For the government departments concerned with processing refugees, the Coordinating Committee was both a boon and a potential excuse not to take more refugees. In Britain civil servants dealing with refugees after the Anschluss were afraid of being overwhelmed and their collaboration with several refugees organisations eased this burden.[45] The Irish Committee performed a similar function.

* * *

At a practical level, there was the problem of who would fund the refugees. In Britain the leaders of Anglo–Jewry had given a guarantee in 1933 that no Jewish refugee would become a charge on the state. This promise was made, however, before the magnitude of the refugee problem became apparent. After 1938 the Jewish community in Britain had severe problems keeping this guarantee. The British government, though, relaxed its restrictions, partly due to public pressure, and admitted 11,000 refugees in the nine months prior to the outbreak of World War II.[46]

This policy revision did not occur in Ireland. One of the Irish Coordinating Committee's documents highlights the potential hosts in Ireland: 'numerous applications have been received from genuine and well-meaning people in the country for the permission for refugees to settle here'.[47] The natural caution of

---

43 DFA 202/20, December 1938; DFA 202/32, February 1939. **44** Interview with Stella Webb, Irish Coordinating Committee (1991); NAI DT S/11007A, memorandum, 28 February 1953. **45** Louise London, 'Jewish Refugees, Anglo–Jewry and British Government Policy, 1930–40', p. 169. **46** There are still disputes over the exact statistics for those admitted. Alderman states that between the end of 1938 and September 1939, 25,000 refugees entered Britain, almost as many as were allowed in between 1933–8, while Tony Kushner puts the figure at 60,000 in all before 1939: Alderman, *Modern British Jewry*, p. 280; Tony Kushner, 'Anti-Semitism in Britain', in Tony Kushner and Kenneth Lunn (eds), *Traditions of Intolerance: Historical Perspectives on Fascism and Race Discourse* (Manchester, 1989), p. 180. **47** See NAI DFA 102/513; NAI DFA 102/488; NAI DFA 202/155; NAI DFA 202/189; NAI DFA 202/317; NAI DFA 202/691; NAI DFA 202/120, Duff to Walshe, 8 December 1938.

the bureaucrat, though, meant that such altruism was viewed with distrust and regarded as likely to lead to breaches of security. Thus for the civil servants involved, the Committee's vetting satisfied the bureaucratic tendency to caution and pragmatism, while also reducing each department's workload. Indeed, in early December 1938 J.E. Duff reiterated, in a minute to Joseph Walshe, a key provision of the original agreement between the government and the Committee stipulating that refugee applications would be considered only via Committee channels.[48] Duff trotted out a variation on the theme in another letter to Walshe some weeks later: 'Jewish refugees will be allowed to settle in this country only if their presence can be regarded as an advantage to this country. Accordingly, each case will be decided on its merit.'[49] Nevertheless, considering the swiftness with which some refusals were returned by Justice – in some cases in less than a week – it is difficult to view this as anything more than bureaucratic hypocrisy.[50] Duff added that 'as regards admission of refugees for temporary periods, the only persons who are so admitted are a limited number of persons whose applications are supported by the Irish Coordinating Committee'.[51]

In March 1939 Robert Ditchburn, a member of the Committee and a professor of science who had become interested in the problem because of the number of prominent Jewish scientists affected by Nazi policies, forwarded a summary of its work to the Department of Justice.[52] He referred to the fact that the Committee had requested a separate quota for Jewish refugees (as opposed to 'non-Aryan Christians'), but that it had been refused. It is difficult to conceive that many Irish officials took little or no account of the fact that the bulk of refugees from Germany were Jews who had been forced out by Nazi racial policies. However, Ditchburn recorded that the fundraising activities of the Committee had harvested £3,000, and just prior to his death Pope Pius XI had donated £1,000 to the St Vincent de Paul Society to be allocated to refugees. Committee members had also devoted a good deal of energy to facilitating the speedy migration of the refugees to other destinations. Ditchburn attached a memorandum on this subject to his general report. It specified that some refugees had already received permits to enter Brazil and New Zealand, and less successful approaches had been made to the Australian government.

In his reply to Ditchburn, dated 9 March, J.E. Duff reiterated that the Committee must be certain of the 'good character' of any prospective refugees. He also referred to the primary role of the Irish minister in Berlin, Charles Bewley, in approving the granting of visas. This comment was somewhat mis-

48 NAI DFA 202/120, Duff to Walshe 8 December 1938. **49** Ibid., Duff to Walshe 19 December 1938. **50** See, for example, NAI DFA 202/693; NAI DFA 202/685; NAI DFA 202/25; NAI DFA 202/28; NAI DFA 202/41; NAI/DFA 202/42. **51** NAI DFA 202/120, Duff to Walshe,19 December 1938. **52** NAI DFA 243/9, Ditchburn to Justice, 7 March 1939.

leading, because Justice officials actually possessed the ultimate sanction, not External Affairs. What's more, the reference to Bewley highlights one of the more controversial aspects of Ireland's refugee policy. It has been pointed out in studies of other nations that the personalities and prejudices – or lack thereof – of officials in key positions were crucial in the administration of policy.[53] The fact that Captain Foley of the British Passport Office gave out visas without stringently applying the rules, for example, saved many lives, and his courage was acknowledged during the Nuremberg trials.[54]

Charles Bewley did not fall into the same heroic category. His reports to Dublin throughout 1938 summarising German attitudes to Jewish immigration were flagrantly and virulently anti-Semitic. Yet for a crucial period he played an instrumental part in the vetting procedure of applicants eventually considered by the Coordinating Committee. He narrowly avoided hanging at the end of World War II due to his dubious wartime association with the Nazi government, and his passport shows he travelled frequently to Germany throughout the conflict. In Ireland Professor Dillon wrote personally to Joseph Walshe in February 1939, asserting that Bewley was becoming 'more unreasonable than ever'. Two months later J.E. Duff notified Walshe about the Committee's complaints with regard to the serious delays in issuing visas.[55] It is difficult to establish precisely Bewley's role in obstructing or delaying visas. Nonetheless, he was open in his distrust and disdain for Jewish refugees.

By the late 1930s the whole business of obtaining visas for refugees was fraught with difficulty, particularly if they were stateless. For Jewish refugees the process was even more problematic. If families could not arrange to emigrate together, they might try to obtain a place on the immigrant quota list for America. However, there was often a waiting period of two to four years. In the interim many refugees tried to gain temporary residence in any country until they were granted American permits. Some of the applications to Ireland were of this type. Uncertainty about their destinations, and the fact that their circumstances could change from hour to hour, did not convince bureaucrats of the sincerity of refugee statements. Bewley made much in his correspondence of the fact that many applicants were unsure of their destinations or even lied about their circumstances. In reference to one case he stated: 'I presume that the department will require genuine enquiries to be made in [the] future so as at least to ensure that an influx of convicted criminals does not take place.'[56]

---

53 Irving Abella and Harold Troper, *None is Too Many: Canada and the Jews of Europe, 1933–1948* (New York, 1982), p. 7; Sherman, *Island Refuge*, p. 7. **54** *Irish Independent*, 26 April 1961, p. 3. **55** NAI DFA 202/114, Dillon to Walshe, 25 February 1939; NAI DFA 243/9, Duff to Walshe, 6 April 1939. **56** NAI DFA 202/63, 9 December 1938; see also ibid., 30 January 1939

THE OUTBREAK OF WAR

The advent of war and Ireland's subsequent policy of neutrality altered official attitudes to Jewish refugees. Indeed, the upsurge in anti-Semitism in Ireland during the war years, and the emergence of groups, albeit marginal, with anti-Semitic agendas had a direct effect on security concerns, which had already been heightened by the jittery atmosphere of the Emergency. As we have seen, Irish officialdom's perception of Jews tended to be negative. Thus the rise of isolated, yet vocal, groups with an anti-Semitic message simply confirmed what many bureaucrats already believed: too many Jews were a potential threat to public order.

After the outbreak of World War II in September 1939 Ireland embraced neutrality, as did Sweden, Switzerland, Portugal and Turkey. Eamon de Valera proclaimed this policy on 2 September 1939, the day before England declared war on Germany, and notice was officially served on belligerents through diplomatic channels.[57] For the purposes of this chapter it is not intended to dispute the facts of Irish neutrality, only to examine its implications for refugee policy. The war footing imposed even stricter restrictions on the admission of aliens. Military Intelligence (G2) personnel now took their place in the vetting of alien applications. Thus aliens attempting to reach Ireland were subjected to the glare of G2 officials as well as the usual scrutiny of those from Industry and Commerce, External Affairs and Justice. At the same time, neutrality had an ironic, unintended consequence: German Jews, or those in German-occupied territory, were not allowed to emigrate to a country at war with Germany, which ruled out Britain as a destination, but increased the number of refugees seeking asylum in Ireland.[58]

In purely practical terms, the involvement of yet another department in the fraught business of visas and entry requirements meant that the already tortuous procedure was slowed down even further. And there were other implications for refugees. Liam Archer and Dan Bryan of G2 were both vehemently opposed to the admission of aliens, particularly those of former Austrian or German nationality: they viewed them as representing a threat to the fragility of neutrality.[59] The decision not to admit persons of former Austrian or German nationality,

---

57 Keogh, *Twentieth-Century Ireland*, p. 110. General works on neutrality include Joseph T. Carroll, *Ireland In the War Years* (Newton Abbot, 1975); Robert Fisk, *In Time of War: Ireland, Ulster and the Price of Neutrality, 1939–45* (London, 1983); J.P. Duggan, *Neutral Ireland and the Third Reich* (Dublin, 1985). **58** NAI DFA 202/758, Seán Nunan to External Affairs, 8 February 1940. **59** Eunan O'Halpin, 'Army, Politics and Society in Independent Ireland, 1923–45', in T.G. Fraser and Keith Jeffrey (eds), *Men, Women and War: Historical Studies XVIII* (Dublin, 1993), p. 169. Dan Bryan took over from Liam Archer as Director of G2 in June 1941 and remained resolutely opposed to liberalising aliens policy in the post-war era.

and in particular refugees, had initially been taken at an inter-departmental conference in October 1939. As well as posing a threat to neutrality – because to admit them implied criticism of Germany's domestic policy – what legitimised the decision for Irish policymakers was the refugees' status – or lack of it, since most were stateless. In addition, the decision coincided with the British line and was supposedly backed by public opinion. Freddie Boland stressed this in a minute sent in early 1940 to Seán Nunan, first secretary in the office of the High Commissioner in London:

> As you no doubt know, we made a special effort after the outbreak of war to reduce the number of people of German and Austrian nationality residing here, and it was felt that even though the persons concerned might apply for admission in the guise of refugees, it was desirable to keep the numbers of such persons coming here in [the] future down to a minimum. We feel that the British authorities concerned would strongly sympathise with this point, and, of course, it is vigorously supported by a considerable section of public opinion here.[60]

Boland's phrase 'in guise of refugees' captures the type of bureaucratic suspicion that prevailed at the time. Officials, particularly those with a security remit, were conditioned by years of viewing aliens as problematic transmigrants. Now they were being asked to apply humanitarian principles to a raggle taggle of humanity with little to recommend it by bureaucratic standards. Indeed, the general line of policy, which was being strictly adhered to, was encapsulated in another minute Freddie Boland had sent to Sean Nunan in October 1939. The Irish Coordinating Committee, according to Boland, was 'the principal body concerned with the admission and care of refugees', and to admit any refugees outside of this channel would undermine the agreement between the Department of Justice and the Committee and, in essence, discourage its work.[61]

CONCLUSION

As we have seen, the evolution and execution of Jewish refugee policy across Europe throughout the 1930s was a complex process. It was conditioned by the workings of aliens legislation and official attitudes towards aliens, sentiments which were essentially negative, particularly towards Jews. British policy on aliens had developed out of a perceived need in the nineteenth century to set

60 NAI DFA 202/720, Boland to Nunan, 12 January 1940.   61 NAI DFA 243/9, Boland to Nunan, 14 October 1939.

boundaries for the admission of foreigners. Irish policymakers looked to the British model for guidance. At the same time, British officials needed to police Irish administrators for their own nation's security. As we have seen, a tradition of informal Anglo–Irish collaboration over the admission of foreigners had existed since 1922. And like their British counterparts, Irish officials actually applied the principles and dictates of aliens legislation to Jewish refugees, rather clumsily moulding aliens policy to fit the circumstances of people fleeing a regime where they were the victims of both political repression and religious discrimination.

After 1938 policy was dictated by international events. It is clear that Irish responses to them were in step with the mood of the times, and that Irish official thinking stemmed from British establishment precedent. However, while British policy had generally been restrictive, British officials did liberalise it in the aftermath of Kristallnacht.[62] For their part, Irish civil servants did not give any serious thought to developing a specific refugee policy until 1938, when dynamics in the international arena – the Evian conference – and at home – the prospect of an increase in refugee applications – forced them to confront the issue.

We do not know how many Jewish refugees applied to come to Ireland, although it is definitely in the hundreds, if not thousands. Only a small percentage of applicants were actually admitted. A post-war policy review stated that:

> In the nine years, 1939–47, that a combined [Coordinating] Committee functioned, representing Catholics, members of the Church of Ireland, Society of Friends, Jews, etc., refugees were admitted through its auspices, and the number included forty-two on behalf of the Jewish sub-committee, sixty-five for the Catholics, twenty-four for the Church of Ireland and nine for the Society of Friends. All the time the Coordinating Committee was functioning, the Jewish sub-committee was continuing to press the claims of the Orthodox Jews as preeminent.[63]

The memorandum also noted that these approaches were made on a number of occasions, and that each time the applications were refused. Thus the Irish response was, in general, niggardly. Indeed, while it is important to examine Ireland's reaction to the refugee crisis in the light of the broader historical context, and the policy examples provided by other countries, especially Britain,

---

62 Sherman, *Island Refuge*, p. 7. 63 NAI DT S 11007/A, draft memorandum, Department of Justice, 28 February 1953. Figures in the Schonfeld papers put it at 60 between the years 1933–48: Anglo–Jewish Archive, Southampton University, Schonfeld Papers, Section F 302(ii), Olga Eppel to Solomon Schonfeld, 24 May 1948.

one cannot ignore a persistent theme about this episode in Irish history: immigrants were not welcome, refugees were not welcome, but Jewish immigrants and Jewish refugees were less welcome than others. For behind closed doors Irish policymakers, like their counterparts in Canada, South Africa, Britain and Australia, all referred to the fact that 'too many Jews would create anti-Semitism'.[64]

64 Abella and Troper, *None is Too Many*, p. 5; *Irish Independent*, 14 April 1937; Wasserstein, *Britain and the Jews of Europe*, p. 115.

'The Virtual Minimum': Ireland's Decision for *De Facto* Recognition of Israel, 1947–9

Paula Wylie

INTRODUCTION

In its broadest definition in international law, diplomatic recognition is 'the acceptance by a state of any fact or situation occurring in its relations with other states'.[1] Recognition in foreign policy, however, is often a political act of the state granting recognition to a particular body in a particular capacity, usually a community with the attributes of a sovereign state. The Montevideo Convention of 1933 codified the requirements for statehood: 'The state as a person of international law should possess the following qualifications: a permanent population; a defined territory; a government; and a capacity to enter into relations with other states.'[2] While a government considers whether these conditions have been met by an aspiring state, *de facto* recognition is extended. *De jure* recognition follows once the four criteria are in place. The text *Oppenheim's International Law* suggests, though, that in practice the usage of the terms *de facto* and *de jure* are 'convenient but elliptical'.[3] For 'even where the requirements of statehood are satisfied', many states still opt for *de facto*, not *de jure*, recognition.[4] The resulting policy, generally referred to as 'non-recognition', implies that no formal diplomatic relations will occur between the two states until *de jure* recognition is granted.

In this context, after the new state of Israel declared its independence on 14 May 1948 it immediately sought diplomatic recognition from countries around the world, including Ireland. The Irish government hesitated, however. Its approach to Israel's request was clearly encapsulated in a Department of External Affairs memorandum recommending that Ireland grant 'the virtual minimum of recognition' towards the new state that it was 'possible to concede'.[5] This policy required the government to recognise the state of Israel and its government *de*

---

[1] Robert Jennings and Arthur Watts (eds), *Oppenheim's International Law* (Harlow, 1992; ninth edition), p. 127. [2] Convention on the Rights and Duties of States, 26 December 1933.
[3] Jennings and Watts, *Oppenheim's International Law*, p. 156. [4] Ibid., p. 183. [5] NAI DFA 305/81/I, memorandum, Rynne to Boland, 10 February 1949.

facto, but not *de jure*, which implied an acceptance of the situation on the ground, but without any commitment to exchange diplomatic representatives or establish formal relations. Ireland's long-term policy of *de facto* recognition was, in effect, non-recognition. It persisted until 1963, when, in a streamlined effort to establish a more consistent international position, Ireland recognised Israel *de jure*.

Several factors distinguish Ireland's policy towards Israel. First, *de facto* recognition was maintained from 1949 to 1963 by a small number of Irish government officials, whose justifications for the policy, although not anti-Semitic, stemmed from normative reasoning which viewed Israel as *anti-Christian*. Second, non-recognition endured as a policy in deference to the diplomatic wishes of the Holy See, in spite of the opportunity for independent initiatives towards Israel. Third, even considering the ambiguities that arise when international recognition law is translated into foreign policy practice, Ireland's position was politically untenable. As the years passed, many officials within various government departments, but especially External Affairs, knew that the policy was unsound, yet were reluctant to change it. On the surface, the rationale for *de facto*, rather than *de jure*, recognition is easily explainable: Ireland insisted on guarantees from the Israeli government for protection of the Holy Places in and near Jerusalem. Upon examination of the diplomatic recognition files, however, the Holy Places thesis becomes transparent and another argument emerges: the refusal to recognise Israel *de jure* from 1948 to 1963 reflected a desire to delay Israeli diplomatic representation in Dublin, which was politically motivated by a fear of rising 'Jewish influence' in Ireland.

THE BIRTH OF THE ISRAELI STATE

No example of state creation in the twentieth century is more emotionally charged than the case of Israel. Chaim Weizmann's statement to the Peel Commission in 1936 – 'Have we the right to live?' – highlighted the plight of European Jews trying to emigrate to Palestine before World War II.[6] Although Theodor Herzel and others demanded a Jewish state during the first World Zionist Congress in 1897, the imperative gained critical mass only after 1945 as a means of assuaging the collective guilt of Western civilisation for the atrocities of the Holocaust. During the years 1945 to 1947, the majority of the remaining Jewish population in Europe migrated to Palestine, the United States or to other countries. The indigenous population of these countries often feared the influx of Jews. Likewise, in Ireland hostile attitudes towards Jews were prevalent, but hushed, during the post-war period.[7]

6 Quoted in Conor Cruise O'Brien, *The Siege: The Saga of Israel and Zionism* (New York, 1986), p. 196.   **7** See Dermot Keogh, *Jews in Twentieth-Century Ireland: Refugees, Anti-*

Between 1920 and 1936 almost 165,000 Jews were admitted into the British-controlled mandate of Palestine.[8] Many of these new settlers took up residence in a vicinity outside the walled city of Jerusalem called the New City (or West Jerusalem). Their presence was a persistent threat to the Arab-controlled Old City (East Jerusalem) and riots often erupted between Arabs and Jews. The British attempted to preserve the *status quo* through policies often interpreted as pro-Arab by the new Jewish immigrants. In 1937 the Peel Commission, after hearing evidence predominantly provided by Jews in Palestine,[9] concluded that the problem between the Arabs and Jews in Jerusalem, and in other parts of Palestine, was intractable. The 'practicable' solution was a partitioned state.[10] To no one's surprise, the indigenous Arabs did not accept partition as suggested in the Peel Report and denounced the concept of a 'national home' for the Jews.

After 1945, while the Arabs were feeling the sharp betrayal of the British government, the international Christian community latched onto the concept of a Jerusalem and Palestine dominated by neither Arab nor Jew. Muslims were concerned about protection of the Old City, not only for the Holy Places of Islam contained therein, but also for the retention of the political power which they held there. The concern of the United States and Britain, while each had a similar interest in the protection of Jerusalem, was to strengthen the two states resulting from a partition settlement and to stabilise the Middle East.

ATTITUDES FORESHADOWING A POLICY

In the beginning of the Palestine crisis the Irish government's attention focused on guarding against the implications that rising Jewish nationalism in Palestine might have for Irish citizens at home. In October 1946 Joseph P. Walshe, former secretary of the Department of External Affairs in Dublin and the newly appointed ambassador to the Holy See, sent the following letter to Frederick H. Boland, his successor in Iveagh House:

> My dear Secretary,
> It is always interesting to know the reactions of our people when they travel abroad and to see how these reactions affect their attitude towards Ireland. In recent weeks, as you know, I have met a large number of Irish priests and nuns visiting Rome for the purpose of their orders, in most cases to elect a new superior general. All of them, without exception, spoke in terms of the highest praise of the Taoiseach and the government

Semitism and the Holocaust (Cork, 1998). **8** Richard H. Pfaff, 'Jerusalem', in John Norton Moore (ed.), *The Arab–Israeli Conflict* (Princeton, 1989), p. 255. **9** O'Brien, *The Siege*, p. 224. **10** Ibid., p. 226.

and of the manner in which difficulties were being surmounted and real progress achieved. Indeed, if the religious orders are a good indication of the mind of the Church in Ireland, the government has its complete confidence.

Speaking of the difficulties facing the government, [the visiting clergy and religious] were unanimous in thinking that something ought to be done to prevent the jews [sic] buying property and starting or acquiring businesses in Ireland. There was a general conviction that the jewish influence is, in the last analysis, anti-Christian and anti-national and, consequently, detrimental to the revival of an Irish cultural and religious civilisation. Some of them say that jewish materialism encourages communism (not an unusual view here). They were also generally perturbed by the influx of British subjects who are purchasing Irish property.

These comments were made with the full recognition that there was a real problem which had to be solved somehow and not in any way through lack of loyalty or sympathy. I am sure the Taoiseach [Eamon de Valera] would wish me to pass on these views of Irish men and women holding the highest positions in their respective orders. Although my natural reaction to sympathetic critics is to ask them to formulate a precise plan, I could not but be struck by the fact that, in their view, our only serious problem was the jewish infiltration. It is one of the problems in all other Western European countries, where it is very much graver than in Ireland, but all these countries have infinitely graver tasks before them.[11]

The letter was received in Dublin one week later and marked 'copy for Taoiseach', most likely by one of Boland's assistants. Walshe assumed that Boland would 'pass on' the views of the visiting clergy to Eamon de Valera; instead, a further notation on the letter read: 'copy not sent to Taoiseach on recommendation by secretary'. Walshe's fear of 'jewish infiltration' was thus contained by Boland's better judgement. Clearly, Walshe's concern was not the growing emigration of European Jews to Palestine, but rather the influx of Jewish refugees into Ireland. As will be seen, Walshe was influential in setting policy towards Israel in 1948.

Although official policy allowed for the immigration of 10,000 refugees into Ireland beginning in early 1946, other attitudes towards Jewish refugees within the Irish government echoed Walshe's concerns.[12] The wording of a draft memorandum from the Department of Justice was doctored from the blatant 'restrict the immigration of Jews' to the more subdued 'the immigration of Jews is gener-

---

11 NAI DFA 313/6, letter, Walshe to Boland, 17 October 1946. 12 Keogh, *Jews in Twentieth-Century Ireland*, p. 206.

ally discouraged'.¹³ Eamon de Valera's 'liberal and generous'¹⁴ immigration policy was not well-received by all departments within the government, which may explain Boland's tactful handling of Walshe's letter.

IRELAND AND THE ESTABLISHMENT OF ISRAEL, 1947–8

Just over one year later the issue was no longer the immigration of Jews into Ireland, but the establishment of a Jewish state. In November 1947 the United Nations General Assembly passed a resolution partitioning Palestine and providing for a national home for the Jewish people.¹⁵ By December reports were sent to Iveagh House from the Irish representatives in Ottawa and Washington concerning the non-viability of the proposed solution.¹⁶ The difficulties inherent in a forced territorial settlement between the Jews and the Arabs in Palestine were compared to Ireland's own partition dilemma.

The awkwardness of Ireland's ultimate position concerning Israel (refusing to recognise Israel as a state *de jure* until long after it was legitimately established) stems from the ironic absence of a sympathetic echo supporting self-determination – either for the Jews or the displaced Palestinians. But if the drafters of Irish foreign policy failed to notice the similarities inherent in the diasporas of both nations, as well as the effects of imposed partition upon the Palestinian Arabs, neither the Jews nor the displaced Palestinians were oblivious to the parallels.¹⁷ Yitzak Shamir recalled in his memoirs that he chose 'Michael' as his *nom de guerre* in the underground organisation Lehi (the force formed by Abraham Stern in 1940 and also known as the 'Stern Gang'), because he 'was stirred in some special manner by what [he] had read about Michael Collins, the Irish leader'.¹⁸ Chaim Herzog, who spent much of his childhood in Dublin, remembered that his father 'was an open partisan of the Irish cause' and that the Herzog name 'is still associated with those who fought for liberty'.¹⁹

The parallels in rhetoric were apparent. But in the atmosphere of 1946 to 1949 the drafters of Irish foreign policy could not contemplate taking an independent position. Ireland, after all, had no voice in the United Nations, since it did not become a member until 1955. The Irish thus were not direct participants in solving the international puzzle of Palestine. They did, however, receive intelligence reports throughout 1947 which were placed into a file entitled 'The

---

13 Ibid., p. 203.   **14** Ibid., p. 206.   **15** General Assembly Resolution 181 (II).   **16** NAI DFA 305/62/1, *passim*.   **17** Although widely used by Irish historians in reference to the flight of emigrants from Ireland, it should be remembered that the word diaspora is of Greek origin, describing the Jews who were exiled after the Babylonian captivity. The basis of the concept is Biblical and found in Deuteronomy 28:25.   **18** Yitzak Shamir, *Summing Up: A Memoir* (London, 1994), p. 8.   **19** Chaim Herzog, *Living History: A Memoir* (New York, 1996), p. 12.

UNO and Palestine', which forms the core working file concerning the diplomatic recognition of Israel.[20] Dáil records reveal one reference to the Palestine question in 1947, which is found under the topic 'Jewish Immigration to Palestine'. The debate showed the limited extent to which Ireland had a stake in the problem, namely, the supposed embarrassment caused by the TD Robert Briscoe, who was accused by the ever-virulent Oliver Flanagan of advocating a homeland for Jewish refugees.[21] Eamon de Valera dismissed the allegation that Briscoe had personally been involved in negotiations between the United States and Britain concerning the immigration of 100,000 Jews to Palestine in 1946. For de Valera, however, the issue of Jews in Palestine had strong emotional connotations due to his personal relationship with Briscoe and the former Chief Rabbi of Ireland, Isaac Herzog. Chaim Herzog, the latter's son, described the relationship of the three men in his memoir:

> My father was an open partisan of the Irish cause ... After the establishment of the Irish Free State, when Eamon de Valera was in the opposition, he would come to visit, usually with Robert Briscoe, and unburden his heart to my father. He obviously never forgot these sessions, because in 1950, after the state of Israel was established, de Valera was one of the first foreign statesmen to visit. He dined with [David] Ben-Gurion and Bobby Briscoe at my parents' home in Jerusalem.[22]

In the years immediately following World War II de Valera did not concentrate on Palestine. The majority of the archival material concerns the Jewish refugee situation in Europe and its implications for Ireland. Dermot Keogh, whose research has examined the interplay of the Departments of Justice and External Affairs in refugee policy, concluded that de Valera's government 'failed to respond generously' to the post-war problem of refugees.[23] In fact, when Rabbi Herzog requested assistance from de Valera after the war the responses wired to Herzog suggested 'doing everything possible', while the reality was 'no action is fine'.[24] The position of the Irish government towards refugees foreshadowed its lack of responsiveness towards a national home for the Jews. The rhetoric masked an attitude of fear and uncertainty towards Jews within Ireland and an unwillingness to enter into any diplomatic relationship with Jews in Palestine.

---

20 Ireland refused to participate in the American initiative concerning the North Atlantic Treaty Organisation (NATO) and also severed all colonial ties with Britain in 1949 by declaring Ireland a republic, repealing the External Relations Act and leaving the Commonwealth. **20** NAI DFA 305/62/1. **21** *Dáil Deb.*, 104, 1473, 27 February 1947. Flanagan's anti-Semitic remarks are described at length in Dermot Keogh, *Jews in Twentieth-Century Ireland*, pp 172–3 and 187. **22** Chaim Herzog, *Living History*, p. 12. **23** Dermot Keogh, *Jews in Twentieth-Century Ireland*, p. 224. **24** Ibid., p. 191.

To complicate matters, in February 1948, three months before the end of the British mandate, Eamon de Valera's government fell. Fianna Fáil was replaced by an eclectic grouping of five parties called the first Inter-Party government, which was led by the new Taoiseach, John A. Costello. The implications of the change in government for the Department of External Affairs were significant. For the first time since Patrick McGilligan's tenure as Minister of External Affairs ended in 1932 someone other than Eamon de Valera was in control of Irish foreign policy. He was replaced by the leader of the Clann na Poblachta Party, Séan MacBride, who approached the difficulties in Palestine with ambivalence.

* * *

In the months leading to the establishment of Israel in May 1948 the task of implementing the partition plan became extremely difficult. The commission sent to implement and supervise partition could not begin operations in Palestine for two reasons. First, Britain would not transfer authority until the official end of the mandate on 14 May; second, the partition decision was a catalyst for what the commission identified as virtual civil war in Palestine.[25] Critical to the partition issue was the status of Jerusalem. The United Nations resolution called for the internationalisation of Jerusalem and the protection of the Holy Places, in other words, a *corpus separatum* under the supervision of the Trusteeship Council of the UN. The initial response of the international Christian community to the developing crisis in Palestine, led by the Vatican and including Ireland, was to insure the safety of the Holy Places in the region.[26] Chaim Weizmann, elected the first President of Israel in 1948, described the confusion associated with the term Holy Places, remarking that 'although the Vatican had never formulated any claims in Palestine, it had a recognised interest in the Holy Places. But then practically all of Palestine could be regarded as a Holy Place'.[27]

The UN resolution created considerable uncertainties for most states. When the British flag was lowered on 14 May 1948 and David Ben-Gurion announced the independence of the state of Israel later that same day, the United States was the first nation to recognise Israel *de facto*.[28] Several states followed with *de facto* recognition, including the Soviet Union three days later. Poland, Czechoslovakia, Uruguay and Nicaragua were among the other forerunners in recognis-

---

25 Richard H. Pfaff, *Jerusalem: Keystone of an Arab–Israeli Settlement* (Washington, 1969), p. 23. **26** The Holy Places include the Basilica of the Holy Sepulchre, Bethany, Cenacle, Church of St Anne, Church of St James the Great, Church of St Mark, Tomb of the Virgin, House of Caiphas and Prison of Christ, Sanctuary of the Ascension, Pool of Bethesda, Birthplace of John the Baptist, Basiclica of the Nativity, Milk Grotto, Shepherd's Field and the Nine Stations of the Cross, collectively known as *Via Dolorosa*. **27** Chaim Weizmann, *Trial and Error: The Autobiography of Chaim Weizmann* (London, 1948), p. 240. **28** In international law, the American *de facto* recognition is cited as *precipitate*, as it was granted on

ing Israel. Czechoslovakia, which participated in gun-running for the Israelis, announced *de jure* recognition on 19 May. The Catholic countries of South America, including Venezuela, Paraguay and El Salvador, granted *de facto* recognition in the first few months after Israel's declaration of independence. Canada granted *de facto* recognition in December 1948. The Western European states, especially those with Catholic populations, were much slower to address the issue. Britain, due to its sensitive relations with the Arab states, faced a particularly difficult challenge and withheld *de facto* recognition until January 1949.

On 28 May 1948 Ireland received a telegram sent the previous day from Moshe Shertok, the Foreign Secretary of the provisional government in Israel, asking that 'Eire may grant official recognition to [the] state of Israel and its provisional government'.[29] On 4 June the Irish government discussed the cable's content's. In a memorandum circulated to his cabinet colleagues the day before, Seán MacBride proposed 'that no action be taken on the telegram apart from the appropriate acknowledgement', meaning that only confirmation of its receipt should be forwarded to Israel.[30] The cabinet duly approved MacBride's recommendation.[31] Throughout the summer neither the Department of External Affairs nor the Taoiseach's office reconsidered the issue of Israel. However, significant intelligence gathering continued.

* * *

William Warnock, a seasoned diplomat who had been stationed in Germany during World War II, reported on the Israeli situation from his post as chargé d'affaires in Stockholm. On 29 May 1948 the UN Security Council had adopted a resolution calling for a four-week truce between the warring Arabs and Israelis and appointing a mediator to oversee the maintenance of the cease-fire as well as to make recommendations for a permanent solution. Count Folke Bernadotte, a well-respected Swedish diplomat, was appointed to the post. Warnock wrote to Dublin that 'Bernadotte considers [that] his chance of success is about one percent'.[32] The Security Council resolution also called for a cessation of all military shipments to the area.[33] The Israeli army took advantage of the lull in the fighting, which lasted from 11 June to 9 July, 'to replenish [its] equipment with weapons procured from diverse sources around the world'.[34] In Iveagh House there was confusion as to whether or not the Security Council resolution applied to Ireland, since it was not a member of the United Nations. While the truce was in effect, a member of the United States legation in Dublin, Edward McLaughlin, visited the

---

the same day independence was declared: Jennings and Watts, *Oppenheim's International Law*, p. 144. **29** NAI DT S 14330, telegram, 27 May 1948. **30** Ibid., memorandum for the government, 3 June 1948. **31** NAI DT CAB 5/18, 4 June 1948. **32** NAI DFA 305/62/1, letter, Warnock to Boland, 27 May 1948. **33** Ibid., Security Council Resolution 187 (5–2). **34** George W. Ball and Douglas B. Ball, *The Passionate Attachment* (New York, 1992), p. 26.

department on 17 June to determine whether or not Ireland was complying with the arms embargo.[35] McLaughlin's primary interest was to monitor illegal flights travelling through Irish airports. External Affairs replied that it had received no official communiqué from the UN, but the government would, nevertheless, abide by the terms of the Security Council Resolution.[36]

Less than a month later McLaughlin became specifically interested in flights from Miami to Israel.[37] His memorandum to External Affairs reported that three B-17 Flying Fortresses had left Miami without proper clearance and were believed to be intended for use as bombers or for the transport of munitions within the Middle East. Reports in the *New York Times* traced the bombers up the eastern coast of the United States, after which they disappeared.[38] By the evening of 15 July they had bombed Cairo on their way to Israel.

In McLaughlin's haste to find the Flying Fortresses he missed transactions taking place right before his eyes. In the summer of 1948 Aer Lingus was eager to sell several spare Vickers Vikings.[39] In the midst of a second UN truce, which lasted from 18 July to 15 October 1948, two of the planes were sold to an 'Egyptian air company'. On 30 August Con Cremin, an assistant secretary in Iveagh House, recorded his uneasiness with the transaction:

> On Friday afternoon 20 August Mr Devlin telephoned from [the London embassy] to say that ... he had approached the British authorities for permission for two Vikings, which were being ferried to Egypt to be taken over by an Egyptian air company which had bought them, to land in Tripoli and Libya, but that he had been told that such permission would not be granted ... as Britain, in common with other members of the United Nations, was bound by a resolution of the United Nations which imposed an embargo on the transport of arms and equipment, including civil aircraft, to the Arab states and Palestine ... On Saturday morning 21 August Mr. Shanagher [from Industry and Commerce] telephoned to say that Aer Lingus and the Department of Industry and Commerce were rather worried about the news from London as the proposal [by Egypt] to buy the aircraft was the only reasonable [offer] received.[40]

The next few lines of Cremin's note illustrate Ireland's ability to exploit ambiguities in international law during this period, a pattern repeated throughout its policy of non-recognition of Israel:

---

35 NAI DFA 305/62/1, internal memorandum, 17 June 1948. **36** Ibid., internal memorandum, Rynne to Boland, 8 July 1948. **37** Ibid., memorandum from the American legation, 13 July 1948. **38** These reports are confirmed in David Ben-Gurion, *Israel: A Personal History* (New York, 1971), p. 218. **39** See the Aer Lingus history at www.aerlingus.ie. **40** NAI DFA 305/62/1, note, Cremin, 30 August 1948.

> [Mr. Shanagher] wondered whether, in the circumstances, there would be any objection to sending the planes via Spain and Italy, neither of which is a member of the UN. I informed him that I had, in the meantime, ascertained that we had received communication of the UN resolution concerned and that the government had contemplated observing it, but that no definite action had been taken …

In the final action, Séan MacBride approved the departure of the planes to Egypt, 'provided there was no suggestion that the government had approved their course'. Freddie Boland advised 'that it was essential to avoid any publicity whatever'. The files do not show whether the planes were diverted through Spain or Italy.

Cremin's note concerning the dispensation of the planes is significant in several ways. First, it shows a lack of coordination between the Departments of External Affairs and Industry and Commerce and Aer Lingus. Second, during this period Israel was scrambling for arms and equipment, but the airplanes were sold clandestinely to Egypt. Third, Cremin's note was written one week after the diversion of the planes had occurred. It is possible that he was contemplating whether to make the entry in the files at all. Fourth, although Iveagh House had assured Edward McLaughlin that Ireland would comply with the terms of the truce, Cremin noted that 'the government had contemplated observing it, but that no definite action had been taken'. Finally, it is evident that McLaughlin did not know of the Aer Lingus transaction. On 28 August he sent a memorandum to the Department of External Affairs requesting the Irish government's help in surveillance and inspection of cargo and personnel in 'clandestine air operations of American planes by American citizens between points outside the United States'.[41] McLaughlin was still trying to solve the puzzle of the Flying Fortresses while the Vikings had flown out of Dublin.

RECOGNITION: 'DE FACTO' OR 'DE JURE'?

By September 1948 Israel's government was stable and its position as a sovereign state was in less doubt. Count Bernadotte had worked throughout the summer on a plan for Jerusalem and the Holy Places and submitted a report to the UN on 16 September. His plan included a new partitioning of Palestine and the repatriation of 360,000 Arabs. It was very unpopular with the Lehi, however. Coming only four months after Israeli independence, the underground forces saw it as a certain threat and assassinated Bernadotte on 17 September.[42]

---

41 Ibid., memorandum, McLaughlin to External Affairs, 26 August 1948. 42 Yitzak Shamir, *Summing Up*, p. 75.

Although Ben-Gurion's provisional government detained members of Lehi and disbanded the Irgun, another underground organisation, the murder provoked considerable outrage against Israel within the international community.

Bernadotte's assassination certainly did not make it any easier for other states to recognise Israel. The number of states doing so had continued to rise throughout 1948, but Britain, France, the Netherlands, Denmark, Norway, Sweden, Switzerland, Italy, Spain, Greece and many Central and South American countries still hesitated. At the same time, Britain and other European countries knew that a decision on recognition was required in order to stabilise relations with both the Arabs and Israelis. The Vatican, meanwhile, maintained its uncompromising position: no recognition of Israel until it guaranteed the internationalisation of Jerusalem and the protection of, and free access to, the Holy Places throughout Palestine.

For Ireland the issues of Israeli statehood, protection of the Holy Places, the status of Jerusalem and diplomatic recognition remained unresolved. It could have chosen any tack concerning Israel, including the Arab position that the partitioning of Palestine was illegitimate. Partition rhetoric was abundant in Séan MacBride's department in 1948–9. Conversely, Irish foreign policy could have capitalised on the diaspora argument and championed a national homeland for the Jews. Instead, Ireland chose the position of the Holy See as a basis for its policy towards Israel. Not only did the Holy Places argument win prestige for Ireland from the Holy See, but placing such a condition on recognition meant that Ireland would not be entering into diplomatic relations with Israel in the immediate future. One may even argue that the unspoken aim of the policy was to prohibit 'Jewish infiltration' into Ireland.

Until January 1949 the Department of External Affairs had played a waiting game with the Israeli issue. Then Joseph Walshe began to wrestle with his own demons. Towards the end of the month, with Britain's *de facto* recognition of Israel imminent, he began a series of letters to Freddie Boland. On 20 January he advised against joining a proposed Catholic-nations *démarche* on Jerusalem, since the Vatican Secretary of State, Monsignor Tardini, had told him that Ireland 'would be more influential on its own'.[43] Walshe was convinced that by working in this singular capacity Ireland could exert pressure on other states to follow the 'thesis' of the Vatican on internationalisation and he provided Boland with a list of rationalisations to prove his point:

> Our position *vis-à-vis* America and Australia enables us to exercise persuasive influence on the two governments to accept the thesis of the Holy See that Jerusalem should be ruled internationally and Catholic nations given an important place on the ruling body ... [which] would not nec-

---

43 NAI DFA 305/62/1, letter, Walshe to Boland, 20 January 1949.

essarily be composed exclusively of [United Nations] members. Indeed, I gather ... that the [Holy See] would like to see us on it and probably Spain ...

He felt compelled to remind Boland that the crux of the problem for the Holy See was 'at the very least they regard [Israel] as anti-Roman Catholic', thus echoing the irresponsible comments he made in his 1946 letter to Freddie Boland. Walshe also commented on what steps he felt should be taken to reconcile Ireland's position towards Israel:

> I see from the Jewish press that some of the [Israeli government] ministries [have] already been transferred to Jerusalem from Tel Aviv, and there does [not] seem to be any doubt that it is [the] intention of the Jews, while the going is good, to establish the capital in the Holy City at the first possible opportunity ... It seems the prospect of an international regime is getting darker every hour, and it may be better for the Holy See to take half a loaf. Certainly there is little prospect of securing the adhesion of the American and British governments for an international regime. The powerful Jewish propaganda has become too strong for both of them, and they couldn't stand up to the accusation of trying to deprive the Jews of their ancient capital ... One has the feeling that we have to [go] slowly just now rather than walk into a morass, with or without bad company.

On 22 January Walshe sent Iveagh House another letter. The urgency for Walshe, and the sense of haste in his letters, stemmed from his notion that the Department of External Affairs should not follow Britain's lead without prior counsel from the Vatican. Walshe suggested that the 'form of the British declaration will provide us with some guide ... whether Jerusalem is being regarded by the [Americans] and [British] as an integral part of the [Israeli] state'.[44] Following Britain's formal announcement, Walshe promised to 'ascertain from the Vatican and inform you by cable what their attitude would be in face of the taking over of the whole of Palestine, including Jerusalem, by the Jews'.

* * *

Meanwhile, on 27 January Freddie Boland received Count Ostroróg, the French ambassador. The French envoy explained that his government faced a real challenge in Palestine – trying to maintain functional relationships with the

---

44 Ibid., letter, Walshe to Boland, 22 January 1949.

Palestinian Arabs while protecting the French Catholic religious and educational establishments in Israel – and so had, like the British, decided to grant *de facto* recognition to Israel. The Count mentioned that the French viewed the United Nations as 'the appropriate body to assume the responsibility' of internationalising Jerusalem.[45] When Ostrorόg asked Boland what Ireland planned to do, he replied that the matter was 'under consideration', but, for Ireland, 'the question was now less one of substance than of timing'. Boland's methodical approach to the issue was in sharp contrast to the over-zealousness of Walshe. On 28 January he sent Walshe a report of the meeting with Ostrorόg.[46] That same day Britain granted *de facto* recognition to Israel.

Interestingly, the internationalisation of Jerusalem and the Holy Places was not presented to the Irish public as a rationale for non-recognition of Israel. The Irish newspapers reported on the appointment of a new Chief Rabbi of Ireland, Immanuel Jakobovits, with headlines such as 'Recognition of Israel: Irish Attitude Surprises Rabbi' and 'Chief Rabbi Hopes Eire Will Recognise Israel'.[47] The rationale which Jakobovits had assumed drove the government's policy played well with the Irish public: 'I expect the reason [for not granting recognition towards Israel] is that Ireland, being a partitioned country, is rather slow to recognise a state that is based on partition'.[48] Jakobovits' assertion, however, was inaccurate: Ireland's policy towards Israel still hung on the internationalisation of Jerusalem.

In the meantime, on 5 February Walshe wrote to Boland offering a new, bizarre justification for the continuing non-recognition of Israel:

> On the question of doctrine, you know that the Arabs have always believed and advocated the immaculate conception of our Lady, whereas the Jews have always adopted the most insulting attitude towards this doctrine. That is one of the strongest reasons why the Holy See hates to have any truck with the Jews.[49]

Walshe again asked Boland to reconcile any decision on Israel with the wishes the Holy See, and said that if Ireland did grant *de facto* recognition to Israel it should be conditional on 'the rights of Catholics to approach the Holy Places and to celebrate the Sacred Mysteries'.

* * *

As Walshe put pressure on Boland to make a decision compatible with the Vatican's policy, Boland did research on his own. He asked Michael Rynne, the

---

45 NAI DFA 305/81/I, note, Boland, 27 January 1949. **46** Ibid., letter, Boland to Walshe, 28 January 1949. **47** NAI DT S 14330, various reports from the *Irish Times*, *Irish Independent* and *Irish Press*, 1 February 1949. **48** Ibid., *Irish Independent*, 1 February 1949. **49** NAI DFA 305/62/1, letter, Walshe to Boland, 5 February 1949.

Department of External Affairs' legal adviser, for his opinion. Rynne reasoned that *de facto* recognition was 'the virtual minimum' and that the idea of 'conditional recognition' would be 'improper' under international law.[50] He suggested that if Ireland 'were to attach ... a condition about the preservation of the Holy Places we should ... be going too far below the minimum prescribed by commonsense and normal practice'. What's more:

> Commonsense indicates that since *de facto* recognition is recognition of a state of fact, no extra conditions or proviso would ever be relevant in the context. A condition, or string, to the government's recognition ought therefore not to be announced in the actual instrument whereby its recognition is accorded to the Israeli Government.

Rynne also advised that if questions should arise in the Oireachtas concerning the Holy Places, reference should be made to the Israeli government's promise 'to safeguard the sanctity and inviolability of the shrines and Holy Places' given in Shertok's original telegram in May 1948. To bolster the governments' position, Rynne suggested that an official press release should explain 'why full recognition of Israel is not yet being granted'.

Rynne addressed one final issue that turned the problem of recognition on its head. He stated that it was 'not easy to defend mere *de facto* recognition of the Israeli government at this advanced stage'. He was convinced that it Britain were to later grant *de jure* recognition Ireland would be 'bound' to withdraw or complete its own recognition. If the Irish government were not prepared to either provide *de jure* recognition at some later date or withdraw recognition altogether, then the 'onus [would] immediately rest upon [the Department of External Affairs] to show why we are going thus far, but no further just now'. Rynne was aware that only *de jure* recognition would eliminate considerable legal difficulties in the future. A citizen of a non-recognised state would have no standing in Irish courts. And Irish citizens doing business with Israel would encounter considerable risk in establishing trade relationships with a non-recognised state, since they would not have access to Irish courts.[51]

Boland concurred with Rynne's commonsense conclusions. After considering the legal adviser's submission he sent his own memorandum to Séan MacBride on 11 February proposing that the Irish government:

> decide to recognise *de facto* the state of Israel. It is suggested that the decision should be announced by the Taoiseach tomorrow night at the

50 NAI DFA 305/81/I, memorandum, Rynne to Boland, 10 February 1949. 51 In contract law this difficulty is averted by declaring a court of jurisdiction in the original contract (i.e., Israel).

dinner for the new Chief Rabbi of Ireland [Jacobovits], and that a telegram should be despatched to Mr. Shertok, the Israeli Foreign Minister, tomorrow.[52]

Boland explained that recognition should be limited to *de facto* status, even though the United States had announced *de jure* recognition of Israel on 31 January, since France and Britain had 'not yet accorded' full recognition due to the internationalisation issue. He reasoned that 'as public opinion here would probably expect this country to be not less zealous in endeavouring to secure proper provision for the future of the Holy Places', granting *de jure* recognition 'might possibly invite attack and criticism'. The cabinet met on 11 February 1949 and granted *de facto* recognition to the state of Israel.[53] The decision was announced to the public the following day.[54]

* * *

Joseph Walshe had hoped that any form of recognition towards Israel would be delayed as long as possible. He was thus concerned when he received a telegram from Iveagh House stating that *de facto* recognition had been accorded. In a letter dated 24 February he asked Freddie Boland for an explanation, emphatically urging that the government withhold *de jure* recognition 'until the guarantees are defined and are accepted by the HOLY SEE [*sic*]'.[55] His primary concern was the possible loss of prestige in the Vatican. He was convinced that Ireland should continue to support the internationalisation issue and would gain prestige only if *de jure* recognition were delayed. In his familiar tone of rationalisation, he assured Boland that the question of the Holy Places has 'in it all the elements which make it an ideal case for championing by our Minister'.

Boland had also sent a letter to Walshe on 24 February. He explained that 'everything that could be reasonably done' was carried out before the decision was made, including requesting assurances on the protection of the Holy Places from the Israeli government through diplomatic channels in London and Washington'.[56] To placate Walshe's vanity, Boland suggested that Ireland could 'exert an indirect pressure by withholding the *de jure* recognition which the Israeli Foreign Minister [had] already solicited'. Interestingly, the files suggest that Walshe began to lose interest in the issue once the *de facto* decision was made. By the end of September 1949 he had dropped the initiative entirely.

---

52 NAI DFA 305/81/I, memorandum, Boland to MacBride, 11 February 1949. **53** NAI DT S 14330, cabinet minutes, 11 February 1949. **54** NAI DFA 305/81/I, press release, 12 February 1949. **55** NAI DFA 305/82/I, letter, Walshe to Boland, 24 February 1949. **56** Ibid., letter, Boland to Walshe, 24 February 1949.

PRESERVING THE 'STATUS QUO' TOWARDS ISRAEL

Throughout the 1950s the question of *de jure* recognition was raised occasionally within the Department of External Affairs. As early as April 1950 the files reveal that Séan MacBride questioned the legality of Ireland's position and instructed Walshe 'to explain to the Vatican that we [propose] to accord *de jure* recognition in the very near future'.[57] The response from the Vatican was not surprising, as Walshe was told that 'the Holy See could not regard our change of policy with anything but disapproval'.[58] MacBride dropped the issue in 1950.

Although the Israelis adjusted to the Irish position, the continuing policy affected Ireland's relations with other states in the Middle East. When Egypt and Britain recognised the independence of the Sudan in January 1956, Ireland (now a member of the United Nations) was asked for formal, *de jure* recognition of Israel. Eoin MacWhite, first secretary in the Department of External Affairs, provided a lucid argument for 'giving up the ghost' and recognising Israel *de jure:*

> Our membership of the UN gives us added reason for a reconsideration of our recognition policy in regard to the UN member states which we do not recognise … In most of these cases we are very much 'the odd man out' in not recognising these new states and our attitude is not what might be expected from a country which won its freedom the hard way not so very long ago … If you agree that the time is ripe for a general clearing of outstanding recognition matters on which there are good grounds for changing our present attitude … I will have up to date memoranda prepared on each case so that we can decide what we will put to the government.[59]

MacWhite's idea developed into a diplomatic circular sent to all Irish missions in an effort to clear up recognition issues. The list elevated some states from *de facto* status to *de jure*, including Cambodia, Jordan, South Korea, Laos, Libya, Morocco, Sudan, Tunisia and South Vietnam.[60] The circular also provided an explanation on recognition policy towards troubled areas, including China (the two-government problem), Germany (the two-state issue), Poland (government-in-exile problem) and the USSR (annexation of the Baltic states issue). Communist-controlled Eastern European states were also accorded *de jure* status. Ironically, there was no mention of Israel in the circular.

In response, through a hastily-written and colourful letter, the former legal adviser, Michael Rynne (now serving as ambassador in Madrid) expressed his

---

57 NAI DFA 305/62/I, internal memorandum, Question of the *de jure* Recognition of the State of Israel, 11 September 1951. **58** Ibid. **59** NAI DFA 305/149/I, memorandum, MacWhite to Murphy, 16 January 1956. **60** Ibid., circular, no. 6/56, November 1956.

surprise at the omission of Israel: 'Incidentally, I presume our attitude to Israel remains unchanged, despite its membership of the United Nations?'[61] Rynne knew the decision for *de facto* recognition was untenable when it was made in 1949. Seven years later his sarcastic remark bespoke the intransigence of Ireland's policy towards Israel.

* * *

The impetus in 1962 which caused a change in policy towards Israel emanated from an unusual source. In July of that year Con Cremin considered the possibility of Ireland entering into a trading relationship with South Vietnam. The South Vietnamese government, however, had not received any notice that the Irish government had recognised their country *de jure* and insisted that the Irish government provide evidence of recognition. In the course of a discussion in Iveagh House about South Vietnam, the question of Israel arose:

> After a short discussion … the Minister [Frank Aiken] came to the conclusion that it might be best in all circumstances if we were to accord *de jure* recognition, [which] would almost certainly be followed by a request to us to accept an Israeli mission. The Minister would prefer if such a move could be postponed for some years, but feels that this matter can be dealt with independently of the grant of *de jure* recognition.[62]

What was unstated for so many years finally found its voice in Frank Aiken's explanation of why *de jure* recognition was delayed for so long: if Ireland were to recognise Israel *de jure*, a diplomatic mission in Ireland would be the next request from Israel.

Con Cremin, by now secretary of the Department of External Affairs, was pragmatic in addressing this issue in a circular sent to Irish missions abroad. His first argument justifying the *de jure* recognition of Israel was that trade would be enhanced. Second, Ireland would no longer be the diplomatic 'odd man out' owing to its policy of non-recognition. Third, Cremin argued that 'it seems unlikely that the situation in relation to the Holy Places will change and even more unlikely that our failing to accord *de jure* recognition will bring about a change'.[63]

Aiken agreed with Cremin's logic, and in May 1963 his arguments were presented to the government in the form of a memorandum on recognition policies in general. The resulting circular to the diplomatic missions abroad provided the following explanation regarding Israel:

---

61 Ibid., letter, Rynne to Murphy, 27 November 1956.   62 Ibid., note, Cremin, 10 July 1962
63 Ibid., circular, no. 2/63.

Israel was not granted *de jure* recognition because of the dispute over the future of the Holy Places. On this question we have taken the same view as that of the Holy See that Jerusalem and the surrounding area should be placed under the international supervision with international guarantees on the lines proposed by the United Nations in 1948 and 1950. [We] approached the Vatican authorities in the matter and [were] informed that there would be no objection to the granting of full recognition to Israel, but that the Holy See would be pleased if due care were taken by the government not to recognise Jerusalem as the capital of Israel. There is little likelihood either that the position regarding the Holy Places will change in the near future or that failure on our part to recognise Israel would help to bring change.[64]

Israel's Foreign Minister, Golda Meir, was to be informed without publicity of the matter. The *New York Times* reported Ireland's *de jure* recognition of Israel in January 1964, just after Pope John XXIII's historic visit to Israel and the Holy Places.

CONCLUSION

Ireland's policy of non-recognition towards Israel was sustained by the Department External Affairs from 1949 to 1963 as a unilateral foreign policy. To date, historians have accepted the thesis that Ireland refused *de jure* recognition to protest Israel's lack of regard for the Holy Places in and around Jerusalem. The archival materials from the Department of Foreign Affairs and the Taoiseach's Department, though, suggest that the policy was also motivated by the desire to delay a request for the establishment of normal diplomatic relations, including the diplomatic presence of Israel in Dublin. In the final analysis, non-recognition is the prerogative of the sovereign state initiating it, although non-recognition does not change certain facts on the international plane nor does it effect 'the continued existence of the state itself'.[65] In handling some issues of diplomacy in the twentieth century, Ireland has often moved within the grey areas of international law. Relatively few legal consequences result from unilateral behaviour in our state system. As one international legal scholar of recognition has noted, 'where ideological and political motives influence the decision whether or not to recognise a state, a government or a territorial situation, abuse is quite possible. History and state practice provide examples of such abuse'.[66] In the case of Israel, Ireland provides another historical example.

64 Ibid., internal memorandum, 22 May 1963. **65** Jennings and Watts, *Oppenheim's International Law*, p. 198. **67** Quoted in Burns Weston, Richard Falk and Anthony D'Amato (eds), *International Law and World Order* (St Paul, 1990, second edition), pp 845–6.

A Larger and Noisier Southern Ireland: Ireland and the Evolution of Dominion Status in India, Burma and the Commonwealth, 1942-9

Deirdre McMahon[1]

This chapter is dedicated to the memory of Nicholas Mansergh.

DOMINION STATUS: THE ALL-PURPOSE SOLUTION?

The fate of Dominion status as applied to Ireland in 1921 had many lessons for British statesmen and officials, particularly its suitability for countries which were not 'natural' Dominions. In Ireland Dominion status laboured under crushing handicaps: as a concept it was still in the process of evolution; the Irish had never asked for it; it came too late; it was imposed; and it was accompanied by partition and civil war. In 1929, eight years after Ireland, Dominion status became the declared goal of British policy in India. Would it suffer the same fate as in Ireland? This article looks at the way in which Irish precedents influenced British policy makers, negatively and positively, as Indian independence crawled slowly into sight.

It is worth noting the overlapping connections between those responsible for policymaking in Ireland and India up to and after the Second World War. Of the signatories of the 1921 Irish Treaty, Austen Chamberlain and Lord Birkenhead served as Secretaries of State for India, while Winston Churchill led die-hard Tory opposition to the Government of India Act in the early 1930s. L.S. Amery was the first Dominions Secretary (1925–9) and later served as Secretary of State for India (1940–5). He had been one of ablest intellectual opponents of Irish Home Rule and was a brother-in-law of Hamar Greenwood, Chief Secretary for Ireland from 1920 to 1922. Lord Rugby (Sir John Maffey), the first United Kingdom representative to Ireland in 1939, had been private secretary to the Indian Viceroy, Lord Chelmsford, during the period 1916 to 1920. His successor in Dublin, Sir Gilbert Laithwaite, had also held this position from 1937 to 1943 under the Viceroy, Lord Linlithgow.

[1] My thanks to the Oriental and India Office Collections, British Library; the Hartley Library, University of Southampton; Public Record Office, London; National Library of Ireland; Academic Research Committee, Mary Immaculate College. Permision to quote from the Mountbatten Papers is acknowledged to the Trustees of the Broadlands Archives

In the decades after 1921 British ministers and officials tended to forget that Dominion status was conceded very reluctantly to Ireland. There was even more reluctance in the case of India. Lord Birkenhead, who became Secretary of State for India in 1924, told the Viceroy, Lord Reading, that it was 'frankly inconceivable that India will ever be fit for Dominion self-government'.[2] There was more progress when Ramsay MacDonald's second Labour administration came to power in 1929 and announced that Dominion status was the aim of British policy in India. But this sparked off a die-hard revolt among a section of the British Conservative Party led by Birkenhead and Churchill which aroused intense suspicion among Indian nationalists, who rightly feared that the evolution of Indian independence would be at the mercy of British party politics, as had happened in Ireland.

Ireland was the cloud that loomed over the Indian debate in the early 1930s as the National government attempted to push its new Government of India Bill through parliament. The Conservative Party was 'terrified of a repetition of the Irish negotiations', wrote Samuel Hoare, the Secretary of State for India.[3] Conservative apprehensions appeared to be fulfilled when Eamon de Valera, the voice of unappeased Irish nationalism, came to power in 1932 and began his assault on the 1921 Treaty. Die-hard Tories were even more alarmed when prominent Congress politicians such as Subhas Chandra Bose and V.J. Patel subsequently visited de Valera in Dublin.[4] De Valera's accession marked the beginning of the six-year dispute known as the Economic War, which forced the British government to make a fundamental reassessment of the Commonwealth. During the 1921 Treaty negotiations, de Valera had formulated the concept of external association, by which Ireland would be associated with, but not be a member of, the British Empire for certain purposes. It was a bold and imaginative idea, but was before its time in 1921 when it was rejected out of hand by the British negotiators. But when de Valera returned to power in 1932 he resurrected external association as the basis of his programme to reshape Anglo–Irish relations. The implications of these developments for India caused deep anxiety among British ministers.

In June 1936 the British cabinet was considering the lengthy proposals which the new Dominions Secretary, Malcolm MacDonald, had submitted as an outline settlement of the dispute with de Valera. One of MacDonald's suggestions was a statement by the British government that the Irish were free to secede from the Commonwealth if they wished. In a minute for the Secretary of State for India, Lord Zetland, an official at the India Office objected that 'a statement in these terms will inevitably evoke the response from India – "when shall we reach the

---

2 Anthony Read and David Fisher, *The Proudest Day: India's Long Road to Independence* (London, 1998), p. 205. **3** John Barnes and David Nicholson (eds), *The Empire at Bay: The Leo Amery Diaries, 1929–45* (London, 1988) p. 95. **4** Deirdre McMahon, *Republicans and Imperialists: Anglo–Irish Relations in the 1930s* (New Haven and London, 1984), p. 184.

position in which a similar answer could be given to the question of our seceding?"' The statement was not proceeded with.⁵ At the end of that year, during the Abdication crisis, de Valera passed the External Relations Act, which recognised the King as the symbol of the cooperation of Commonwealth states and confirmed certain of his functions in external affairs. In 1937 de Valera's new constitution was passed, a constitution that was republican in all but name. After consultations with the other Dominions in June 1937 the British government stated that the new constitution would not affect the Irish position in the Commonwealth. This statement had the merit of papering over the immediate cracks in the Commonwealth fabric, but by avoiding awkward questions it simply postponed the day of reckoning. As Indian independence approached in the 1940s British ministers found themselves floundering once more in the constitutional quagmire they thought they had escaped in 1937. What lessons had been learned from Ireland in the intervening decade, not just by the British, but by the Indians?

* * *

The 1935 Government of India Act increased the powers of the provincial governments, widened the franchise in preparation for elections in 1937 and provided for a federation between the states of British India and the Princely States. The administration of Burma was also separated from that of India. Despite its reservations about the act, Congress contested the provincial elections held in 1937 and triumphed, winning a majority of the vote in nine of the eleven provinces of British India. The act appeared to be working well until the outbreak of the Second World War, when the Viceroy, Linlithgow, declared war on behalf of India without consulting any Indian political leaders. Congress was incensed and contrasted the Indian position with the other Dominions, especially Ireland, which had stayed neutral. In a speech at the Bombay Orient Club on 10 January 1940 Linlithgow declared that the British government's aim was to grant India full Dominion status 'of the Statute of Westminster variety'. This provoked predictable expressions of wrath from Tory die-hard MPs who cited Ireland as an awful precedent.⁶

Debates about Dominion status seemed irrelevant when on 20 March the Congress party meeting at Ramagarh declared that 'nothing short of complete independence can be accepted by the people of India. Indian freedom cannot exist within the orbit of Imperialism, and Dominion status or any other status within the Imperial structure is wholly inapplicable to India'.⁷ However, Con-

---

5 British Library, Oriental and India Office Collections, India Office Records [hereafter BL OIOC IOR], L/PO/6/69, minute by Dawson, India Office, c.10 June 1936. 6 BL OIOC IOR L/P&J/8/504, correspondence between Zetland, Sir Alfred Knox and Sir Henry Page Croft, January–February 1940. 7 'Resolution adopted by Indian National Congress at the Ramagarh Session, 20 March 1940', in Nicholas Mansergh (ed.), *Documents and Speeches on*

gress' right to speak for India on this question was challenged two days later when the Muslim League passed the Lahore Resolution, which called for a separate Muslim state of Pakistan. With the possibility of partition now looming, parallels with Ireland were reinforced and it was no coincidence that in the speech which preceded the resolution the Muslim League leader, Mohammed Ali Jinnah, made a pointed reference to Ireland:

> To yoke together two such nations under a single state, one as a numerical minority and the other as a majority, must lead to growing discontent and the final destruction of any fabric that may be built up for the government of such a state. History has presented to us many examples, such as the Union of Great Britain and Ireland, of Czechoslovakia and Poland.

It is interesting that Jinnah chose this parallel and not the more obvious one of Northern and Southern Ireland. He was later to state that he did not regard Muslims as a minority: they were 'as much a "nation" as the Czecho–Slavs [sic] or the Irish were a nation' and as much entitled to a separate homeland.[8] Jinnah, unlike the Ulster Unionists, was careful not to define what he meant by Pakistan. His opponents in Congress, like Sinn Féin in 1921–2, believed that a moth-eaten Pakistan, a disparate collection of Muslim states, was unviable.

CHURCHILL AND INDIA

Churchill's accession to power in May 1940 was a watershed for Indian affairs. He appointed a new Secretary of State for India, L.S. Amery, who had served as Colonial Secretary and Dominions Secretary in the 1920s. It was an odd appointment for Churchill to make as they had argued violently over India in the 1930s. Amery did not believe that responsible government could ever ultimately stop short of Dominion status and argued that it was wiser to concede the demand for self-government than to keep the safety valve screwed down. But Amery loathed the Congress leaders, especially Nehru, in whom he perceived disagreeable comparisons with de Valera. Nehru, he wrote in 1942, was 'a man who has spun himself into a cocoon of his own perversion of history and diatribes against the British which blind him to all real facts. The type is not

---

British Commonwealth Affairs, 1931–52: Volume II (Oxford, 1953), pp 606–7. **8** 'Presidential Address of M.A. Jinnah to All-India Muslim League, 22 March 1940', Syed Sharifudden Pirzada (ed.), *Foundations of Pakistan: All-India Muslim League Documents, 1906–1947: Volume II* (Karachi, 1970), p. 338; *India: The Transfer of Power* (London, HMSO, 1970–83) [hereafter TOP] *Volume III*, report of talk with Jinnah, November 1942, p. 268. Jinnah had been very critical of British policy during the Anglo–Irish War: see Pirzada (ed.), *Foundations of Pakistan: Volume I* (Karachi, 1969), speech to Muslim League 7 September 1920, p. 543.

unfamiliar among nationalist intellectuals in other countries – de Valera for instance, though he evidently has some executive ability'.[9]

India, as Amery realised, was one of the major issues of the war, but one on which he received little cooperation from Churchill, whose views on India had, if anything, become even more reactionary. Churchill understood nothing about recent developments in the Commonwealth, a term which he scorned in favour of 'Empire'. In August 1940 a new policy statement was drafted in which Dominion status was again declared to be the goal of British policy in India, but there was no mention of the date or method of introduction. Indians were also invited to join the Viceroy's executive council and war advisory committee. The most controversial aspect of the statement was that Muslims were guaranteed that there would be no transfer of power if the authority of any system of government was denied 'by large and powerful elements in India's national life'.[10] This statement gave the Muslim League a virtual veto over any constitutional advance and reinforced the parallels with Ireland, as Amery recognised. The breakup of India 'on Ulster and Eire lines', he wrote to Linlithgow on 16 September, would be 'a most disastrous solution'. However, he later came to believe that partition might not be such a catastrophe and calculated that Indian divisions could allow British influence to remain predominant.[11] Not surprisingly, Congress rejected the August offer and Amery and Linlithgow concluded that there was nothing more to be done with the Congress leadership. Gandhi was opposed to participation in the war, while the Forward bloc in the party, led by Subhas Chandra Bose, launched a civil disobedience campaign.

There was also unrest in Burma. The Burmese leader, U Saw, strongly pressed Amery for an immediate declaration of post-war Dominion status for Burma. Amery temporised, observing that 'all progress in the Empire had been step-by-step and not by statements in advance and that the most we can do was to make it clear that there would be the fullest discussion immediately after the war'. U Saw was 'very disappointed',[12] and in January 1942 he was arrested for communicating with the Japanese. Although Amery doubted whether the failure to get a declaration about Dominion status had much to do with U Saw's defection, more perceptive critics thought otherwise.

THE CRIPPS MISSION

What were British intentions in India? As W.R. Louis observed, 'to a significant segment of the American public, the history of Ireland was hardly reassuring'.[13]

9 TOP II, Amery to Linlithgow, 25 July 1942, p. 455. **10** Gowher Rizvi, *Linlithgow and India: A Study of British Policy and Political Impasse in India* (London, 1978), p. 158. **11** Wm. Roger Louis, *In the Name of God Go! Leo Amery and the British Empire in the Age of Churchill* (London, 1992), pp 137, 141. **12** *Amery Diaries,* pp 739–41. **13** Wm. Roger Louis, *Imperialism*

It was in an effort to allay American unease that the Lord Privy Seal, the Labour MP Sir Stafford Cripps, was sent to India in the spring of 1942 to try and reach a settlement with Congress. The Labour members of the British government had become increasingly anxious about the deadlock in India. In preparation for the Cripps mission Amery prepared a draft statement of policy which declared that India would have full Dominion status, 'including freedom to remain in, or separate itself from, partnership with the British Commonwealth'. But this aroused warning bells at the India Office, where Sir David Monteath professed himself:

> alarmed by the probable effect of saying in terms that India may leave the Empire when she likes ... I see no harm in stating the meaning of Dominion status in terms of the Balfour Declaration: the intelligentsia know it already and know its implication of the 'right to secede'. The uneducated don't but won't be alarmed by 'equal in status', 'in no respect subordinate', etc., etc. But to say in terms to the masses that it means the end of the British Raj is asking for trouble which we are in no condition to face. And it is the masses, not the intelligentsia, who matter.[14]

The statement finally approved by the cabinet's India committee on 7 March made no reference to any freedom to secede, but borrowed heavily from the 1926 Balfour Declaration. The aim of British policy was a new Indian union which would be a Dominion 'associated with the United Kingdom and the other Dominions by a common allegiance to the Crown, but equal to them in every respect, in no way subordinate in any aspect of its domestic or external affairs'. At the end of the war, following new provincial elections, a constituent assembly would be elected in which the Indian states would take part. But the crucial proviso to this was that any province of British India had the right to opt out if it was not prepared to accept the new constitution. The British government would then be prepared to draft new constitutions with any non-acceding provinces which would give them the same status as the new Indian union.[15] Linlithgow was so unhappy with this statement that he threatened to resign, but Churchill managed to soothe him with the assurance that the purpose of the Cripps mission was to assuage the Americans and if, as seemed likely, the Indians rejected it 'our sincerity will be proved to the world'.[16]

To other observers, however, the most objectionable aspect of the British proposals was that they seemed an active encouragement of partition. Smuts

at Bay, 1941–45: The United States and the Decolonisation of the British Empire (Oxford, 1977), p. 11. **14** PRO CAB 91/1, India Committee, 27 February 1942; ibid., note by Monteath 1 March 1942. **15** *The Lord Privy Seal's Mission*, Cmd. 6350: quoted in Mansergh, *Documents and Speeches*, pp 616–17. **16** TOP 1, Churchill to Linlithgow, 10 March 1942, pp 394–5.

cabled Churchill on 5 March warning him against using 'Irish tactics of partition'. In a letter to the Canadian Prime Minister, Mackenzie King, Churchill argued that the question to be solved was 'not between the British Government and India, but between different sects or nations in India itself ... Moslems ... declare they will insist upon Pakistan, that is, a sort of Ulster in the North'. Amery also used Ireland as a justification:

> Nobody is going to work a constitution which has been imposed upon them against their will ... The British constitution was pretty nearly wrecked by the Irish. If we had to force a majority constitution upon India I have no doubt the Moslems would probably wreck it in the Parliamentary sense, if they did not wreck it in the military sense long before ...[17]

The purpose of the Cripps mission, as Patrick French has written, was to promise Indian politicians 'jam tomorrow in exchange for cooperation today'.[18] In this there was a more potent Irish parallel, since this had been the very purpose of Malcolm MacDonald's secret missions to de Valera on behalf of the British government in the early summer of 1940, when he offered Irish unity in exchange for immediate entry into the war. One of de Valera's reasons for refusing this offer was his belief that once the wartime emergency was over the offer of unity would be reneged upon. It was a view shared by Gandhi, who famously called the Cripps offer a post-dated cheque on a failing bank. Their scepticism about Churchill's sincerity was borne out by his later contemptuous comment on the Cripps offer that 'we made [it] when in a hole and can disavow it because it was not accepted at the time'.[19]

* * *

As predicted, the Cripps mission failed. Churchill and Linlithgow had made little secret of their hope that it would fail, while the Congress leaders, aware that British power in Southeast Asia was reeling after the catastrophic defeats in Burma, Malaya and Singapore, hoped that the balance of power might tilt even more in their direction as the war continued. It did, but the impasse between Congress and London also greatly strengthened the position of the Muslim League.[20] According to Amery, Cripps believed that Nehru went against a settlement because he could not carry a majority of the Congress executive, but the former discounted this reasoning, claiming that 'I have heard that kind of story before from the Irish'.[21] Within months of the Cripps mission Congress em-

---

[17] TOP 1, Smuts to Churchill, 5 March 1942, p. 327; Churchill to King, 18 March 1942, p. 440; Ministry of Information press conference, 7 April 1942, p. 677. [18] Patrick French, *Liberty or Death: India's Journey to Independence and Division* (London, 1998) p. 146. [19] *Amery Diaries*, p. 1040. [20] French, *Liberty or Death*, pp 146–7

barked on the Quit India movement, which culminated in the arrest of the party's leaders in August 1942. Amery and Linlithgow were anxious to arrest Gandhi, and even deport him, undeterred by the likelihood that he would go on hungerstrike. 'If he insists on committing suicide', Amery wrote in exasperation, 'surely he might as well do it in seclusion and India be informed of the fact afterwards? I would certainly not tolerate the kind of day-to-day bulletins which were issued about the wretched Lord Mayor of Cork years ago'.[22] In the event, Gandhi was confined not to prison, but to the rather more comfortable surroundings of the Aga Khan's summer palace at Poona. It is striking that prominent critics of the government's crackdown cited Ireland in their statements. British policy in Ireland, Egypt, Burma and Malaya had failed, they asserted, because there was no 'organic relationship between the state and the people'. If Britain was to succeed in India 'she must enlist popular will and enthusiasm'.[23]

The government's initial confidence that it had spiked Congress and the Quit India movement quickly faded. Frantic attempts to find links between Congress and the Germans – a 'German Plot' – were unsuccessful (and must have given some wry amusement to de Valera, who was jailed after similar efforts with Sinn Fein in 1918). Linlithgow began to think that Quit India was 'by far the most serious rebellion since that of 1857',[24] while Churchill fulminated against Indians in general: 'I hate Indians. They are a beastly people with a beastly religion'.[25] The paralysis in policy was also affecting Burma. In March 1943 Amery had a difficult discussion with two of his officials at the India Office about the date on which Burma was to be given complete self-government, but he found officials trying to 'hedge' on the seven-year period agreed with the Governor of Burma, Reginald Dorman-Smith. They were 'afraid of committing ourselves to a definite date in an indefinite future'. Amery thought that 'there is everything to be said for a fixed date … not only from the point of view of the outside world but even from that of the Burmans … I am all for encouraging the sentiment of self-government now and letting them feel their own feet and the façade of independent status'. Churchill's reaction was predictable: 'entirely unreasonable and, indeed, silly', wrote Amery.[26]

WAVELL, DE VALERA AND BOSE

In the summer of 1943 the government appointed Field-Marshal Sir Archibald Wavell, the Commander-in-Chief in India, to succeed Linlithgow as Viceroy.

---

21 *Amery Diaries*, p. 814.   **22** TOP II, Amery to Linlithgow, 3 August 1942, p. 550. The reference was to Terence MacSwiney's death on hungerstrike at Brixton Prison in October 1920. **23** TOP II, 8 August, 9 September 1942, pp 627, 937.   **24** Rizvi, *Linlithgow and India*, p. 220. **25** *Amery Diaries*, p. 832.   **26** Ibid., pp 876, 881.

The week before his departure Linlithgow told an Indian journalist that India 'could not hope to become free for another fifty years', since the country was so new to parliamentary institutions and would require the presence of British officials for some time to come to ensure that these institutions worked successfully.[27] In contrast Wavell, as Patrick French noted, was 'no crusty old militarist … [but] a progressive, creative and fearless realist' who was determined to advance Indian independence.[28] As his diary testified, he was appalled by Churchill's views on India and their relations, never easy, soon deteriorated: '[Winston] has still at heart his cavalry subaltern's idea of India, just as his military tactics are inclined to date from the Boer War … [He] hates India and everything to do with it'.[29]

When Wavell reached India he found a major famine in Bengal. Churchill was unresponsive to Wavell's pleas for more supplies, commenting that famine or no famine Indians would continue to breed 'like rabbits'.[30] De Valera sent £100,000 towards famine relief, a gesture which prompted the suspicious query from Amery as to whether the money was being sent to the proper fund and not to sources under Congress' control. Wavell replied that the money had been sent from the Irish Red Cross direct to the Indian Red Cross and was being used for the purchase of woollen blankets.[31] One of the reasons for Amery's suspicion was that the BBC Monitoring Service had picked up broadcast messages from Subhas Chandra Bose to Ireland in November and December 1943. Bose had met de Valera in Dublin in the 1930s and in 1941 he had gone to Germany in the hope of enlisting German support against the British in India. After two frustrating years in Germany he decided that the Japanese were more likely allies and he managed to reach Tokyo by June 1943. He took command of the Indian National Army, which consisted of captured Indian soldiers who were offered their freedom if they fought on the Japanese side. He was also styled 'the Head of the provisional government of Free India'. Bose broadcast his thanks to de Valera for his donation towards famine relief, and some days later the Japanese Telegraph Service was reporting Bose as:

> heartily reciprocating the message of felicitations from the Irish Republic … Of all freedom movements we Indians have studied closely and from which we have received inspiration, there is perhaps none that can equal the Irish struggle for independence. The Irish nation has had the same oppressors and exploiters as ourselves. It has had the same experience of ruthlessness, brutality and hypocrisy as we have had.

27 Read and Fisher, *The Proudest Day*, pp 334–5. **28** French, *Liberty or Death*, p. 172. **29** Penderel Moon (ed.), *Wavell: The Viceroy's Journal* (Oxford, 1973), pp 3–4, 12–13. **30** Louis, *Amery*, p. 173. **31** TOP IV, Amery to Wavell, 19 November 1943; Wavell to Amery 9 December 1943; pp 486, 532.

A subsequent monitored broadcast referred to the fact that Ireland had 'sent a congratulatory message to the Indian provisional government'.

In a further message Bose claimed to have been inspired by the 1916 provisional government:

> The other day the question of recognising our provisional government was raised in the Irish Parliament. I read with the deepest interest the proceedings of that debate. I know for a fact that the sympathy of the entire nation is with us in the struggle against the common foe and, having had the privilege of knowing President de Valera and his Cabinet Ministers personally, I am fully aware that in their attitude toward India there is no difference whatsoever between the Government and the people of Eire ... Even now one does not know if the Anglo–Americans will not swoop down on Eire and occupy it ... I am sure that Eire would have been occupied by our enemies long ago but for the fact that the rulers at Whitehall have not yet forgotten the determined and courageous fight which the Irish nation put up during the last World War and after.

The communications between de Valera and Bose were much more innocuous than these broadcasts implied. When the Japanese consul in Dublin informed de Valera of the establishment of the Indian provisional government, his communication had simply been acknowledged by the secretary of the Irish Department of External Affairs, hardly the felicitations and congratulations referred to in Bose's broadcasts.[32]

One of Wavell's first moves as Viceroy was to suggest a round table conference of the main Indian political leaders, including Gandhi. Churchill declared that this would happen 'only over his dead body'.[33] But Wavell argued that the British government could not by-pass Congress and the Muslim League: 'Even if Gandhi and Jinnah disappeared tomorrow ... I can see no prospect of our having more reasonable people to deal with. We have had to negotiate with similar rebels before, e.g., De Valera and Zaghlul'.[34] But there was little recognition

---

32 PRO DO 35/2059, monitored broadcasts, 30 November, 2 December 1943, 28 March 1944. The communications between de Valera and Bose surfaced after the war at the end of 1945, when three officers of the Indian National Army were put on trial in Delhi for 'waging war against the King'. One of the accused asked for copies of the telegrams exchanged between de Valera and Bose, though for what reason was not clear. Aware of the delicate nature of the subject, the Dominions Office asked the UK Representative in Dublin, Sir John Maffey, to raise the matter with the Department of External Affairs. The Department informed Maffey that the only documents they had on file were the communication from the Japanese consul, dated 17 November 1943, and Walshe's acknowledgement of this. This Dominions Office file was only released in 1994   33 *Wavell Journal*, p. 23.   34 TOP V, Wavell to Churchill, 24 October 1944, p. 131.

by the British cabinet that circumstances had changed since 1942. The Lord Chancellor (Lord Simon) 'regretted loose talk about Dominion status by people who ought to have thought out carefully what Dominion status means before they gave currency to such an expression in connection with India'.[35]

'THE PROBLEM OF AN ANGLO–INDIAN TREATY'

In an effort to press the cabinet Amery presented a memorandum to the India Committee on 1 February 1945 which looked at the shape of a future treaty with India once it was decided to transfer power. There was a lengthy appendix written by an unidentified official at the India Office, 'The Problem of an Anglo–Indian Treaty', which examined the precedents for such a treaty, specifically the 1921 Anglo–Irish Treaty.[36] In the twenty-three years since the signing of that instrument, this was the most comprehensive post-mortem ever undertaken by the British government and it was carried out in the context of what to do about India. It was noted that nearly every article of the 1921 Treaty was relevant to an Indian treaty. But it had to be acknowledged that 'the subsequent history of the relations between Great Britain and Southern Ireland has not been a very happy one. [The Treaty's] ratification was carried by a majority of 64 to 57, and the party opposed to it, Fianna Fáil, continued to work for its practical nullification'. Articles 1–3, defining the Free State's constitutional status, had been substantially modified since 1922 with the passing of the Balfour Declaration and the Statute of Westminster. But 'the plan of basing the relations with the British government on the analogy of Canada never really worked and step by step the relations have in effect been converted into those between two entirely independent states'. The stipulation that any article of the Free State constitution repugnant to the Treaty was invalid had also caused serious problems:

> The objection to the principle appears to have been founded on the theory that Ireland had never ceased to be a sovereign state. It is to be hoped that such a theory will not be so passionately held in regard to India, and in this view it seems proper that the doctrine of repugnancy should be in some form or other recognised and maintained for whatever period the treaty or treaties remain valid.[37]

As for the oath of allegiance, this had been the main target for attack and was 'finally abolished in 1933 by unilateral action'. The Irish experience showed that

---

35 PRO CAB 91/4, I (45) 5, note by Lord Chancellor, 3 January 1945.   **36** TOP V, India Committee, memorandum by Secretary of State, 1 February 1945, Appendix 1.   **37** The repugnancy clause was not in the Treaty, *per se*, but in the Irish Free State Constitution.

'to enshrine that allegiance in a set form of oath has its dangers. There are many of the present Indian leaders and of their followers quite as ready as some Irishmen to regard such an oath as "an empty formula having no binding significance in conscience or in law"' (a quotation from de Valera's description of the oath in 1932).

As for the defence clauses (articles 6 and 7), the document was surprisingly sanguine about Irish neutrality, whatever about Churchill's fulminations:

> Possibly a 'not unfriendly' Eire added to the power of the Navy, and the existence of Northern Ireland as a land and air base helped to deter Hitler from a descent on that country. At least the decision [to return the ports in 1938] tended to remove an old obstacle to good relations between Great Britain and the United States.[38]

Article 10, which dealt with civil servants and the police, had generally worked well and 'was in accordance with the spirit of the Treaty. Whether it would have been so, but for the fact that this article had largely exhausted its function before the Fianna Fáil party obtained power in 1932, is another question'. In a somewhat contentious assertion, it was argued that the protection of minorities against religious discrimination mentioned in articles 15 and 16 'appears to have been, on the whole, respected in both areas, perhaps because reprisals are easy'. The document's conclusion is worth quoting:

> It is unlikely that any of the signatories to the Treaty expected that that document would be the effective instrument for governing the relations between Great Britain and Ireland for a very long period of time. But some, if not most, doubtless hoped for its main provisions a greater 'expectation of life' than events accorded to them.
>
> Their anticipations were falsified chiefly by the survival and ultimate predominance of a party unwilling to forget the past or to abandon the political theory that the state of Eire rests, not on agreement between two political entities previously in union, but on the natural right of a nation to self-government. That party was, moreover, ready to carry its hostility to the Treaty to the point of armed opposition to those of their countrymen who had accepted it. Although it is to be devoutly hoped that the settlement between Great Britain and India will not be preceded by a

---

38 In a subsequent discussion of the defence issue the permanent under-secretary at the India Office, Sir David Monteath, commented: 'The surrender of the bases in Eire facilitated that country's adoption of a foreign policy (neutrality) different from that of HMG. Contrariwise, the adoption of that policy w[ou]ld have caused the surrender of the bases'. TOP V, c. 12 March 1945, p. 677.

civil war, it is impossible to rule out the likelihood of a strong body of opinion in India intensely critical of the terms of a treaty confirming the settlement.

It is, further, unhappily true that it is easy to keep national sentiment alive and indeed to intensify its bitter components by tendentious historical teaching administered to the younger generation. The history of South Africa and of Eire, to say nothing of that of the United States, sufficiently illustrate that danger.

LABOUR IN POWER

The crushing electoral defeat of the Conservatives in July 1945 helped to sideline the imperial die-hards within the party, although they remained a vocal and influential minority. The more hard-headed pragmatists among the leadership were determined that they would not be stranded again on the wrong side of history. But defeat or no defeat, Churchill still retained all the charisma and prestige of his wartime leadership, and the new Labour government could not afford to ignore his views, however unpalatable. In any event, the new administration displayed considerable caution towards imperial affairs as their Burmese policy demonstrated. The White Paper on Burma was published in May 1945, and in reply to a query from the Supreme Allied Commander in Southeast Asia (Mountbatten), the governor of Burma, Sir Reginald Dorman-Smith, stated that when Burma became a fully self-governing unit of the Commonwealth it would have equal status with the other Dominions and with Britain. This status 'carries with it the right to secede. There is no, repeat no, intention of which I am aware to compel Burma to remain in the Commonwealth against her will'.[39] At a meeting held at the headquarters of the Southeast Asia Command in Ceylon, the commander-in-chief, General Slim, argued that the White Paper had failed to allay Burmese suspicions of bad faith on the part of the British. The Burmese believed that Dominion status would not be granted until the British had re-established political and economic control over the country. What was needed was a firm statement on a date for Dominion status by the government. Dorman-Smith agreed strongly, but the new Secretary of State for India and Burma, Lord Pethick-Lawrence, counselled caution: 'We are most reluctant to add any fuel to the flames by using at the moment ... the term "Dominion status" in connection with Burma or elsewhere ... we have got to be a bit careful in our phrasing.'[40]

But time was running out in both Burma and India, as those on the ground realised. The machinery of the Raj was slowly grinding to a halt. In March 1946

39 *Burma: The Struggle for Independence, 1944–48* (HMSO, 1983–4)[hereafter BSI] *Volume I*, Dorman-Smith to Mountbatten, 27 May 1945, p. 287. **40** Ibid., meeting, 5 September 1945, p. 433; Pethick-Lawrence to Dorman-Smith, 26 October 1945, p. 521.

the government sent another Cripps mission to India consisting of Cripps and two cabinet colleagues, Pethick-Lawrence and A.V. Alexander (First Lord of the Admiralty). But it was as unsuccessful as its predecessor. Wavell was scathing about Pethick-Lawrence's 'deference' and 'sloppy benevolence' towards Gandhi. 'G[andhi] is a remarkable old man, certainly, and the most formidable of three opponents who have detached portions of the British Empire in recent years: Zaghlul and de Valera being the other two. But he is a very tough politician and not a saint'.[41]

The sticking points of the 1946 mission were the right to nominate Muslim members to the proposed constituent assembly and the autonomy of the proposed groupings of Muslim states which were coterminous with Jinnah's demand for Pakistan. However, Jinnah also believed that the cabinet delegation, and especially Cripps, were openly biased towards Congress. During the three month negotiations the delegation had decided not to stress Indian membership of the Commonwealth for, as they informed Attlee by telegram, 'the less we appear to insist upon it the more likely it is to happen ... We do not want to hammer it in. Reference to the past benefits of the British connection are, we fear in the present atmosphere, a red rag to a bull'.[42] The Chiefs of Staff did not think the cabinet was aware of the military repercussions if India stayed out of the Commonwealth and emphasised this forcefully.[43] This led the Chiefs of Staff to place more emphasis on India staying in the Commonwealth. Pethick-Lawrence told Wavell that it was now 'out of the question to concede complete independence in the interim period'.[44] A similar ambivalence was demonstrated regarding Burma. In a memo for the India and Burma committee, Pethick-Lawrence noted that the government had for some time avoided using the term Dominion status in relation to Burma and had, instead, been referring to 'full self-government within the British Commonwealth' since the middle of 1945:

> We have to consider possible reactions on Ceylon. I would recommend we should in general continue to avoid the term 'Dominion status'. The Governor [of Burma] in conversation can make it clear that 'full self-government within the British Commonwealth' is still our objective and that is, of course, Dominion status.[45]

MEMBERSHIP OF THE 'CLUB'

For six months over the winter and early spring of 1946–7 there was an intense debate between the Dominions Office, the India and Burma Offices, the For-

---

41 *Wavell Journal*, p. 236.   **42** PRO CAB 127/278, cabinet delegation to prime minister, 15 May 1946.   **43** TOP VIII, Chiefs of Staff Committee, 30 August 1946, pp 348–51.   **44** PRO CAB 127/278, Secretary of State to Viceroy, 26 July 1946.   **45** BSI 1, Cabinet India and Burma Committee, memorandum by Secretary of State, 29 August 1946, p. 972.

Ireland and Dominion Status in India, Burma and the Commonwealth 169

eign Office and the Colonial Office over the merits of whether India and Burma should stay in the Commonwealth. The Dominions Office, as its historian Joe Garner observed, had taken little interest in India (surprisingly in view of the fact that Dominion status had been the declared goal of British policy since 1929) and relations with the India Office were tenuous.[46] The gulf between the two departments was revealed in this debate to which the Dominions Office brought two decades of bruising experience in Anglo–Irish relations. Ireland loomed large in the minds of British officials. At the beginning of October 1946 a senior India Office official, F.F. Turnbull, drafted what he called a *'ballon d'essai'* for Sir Eric Machtig, permanent secretary of the Dominions Office. Commenting on this draft, a colleague at the India Office observed bluntly that:

> it will conduce to realism if you avoid discussing ... the reasons why it would be nice if India were prepared to come in and behave exactly like the four [sic] Dominions. She will not and cannot ... I see no reason to suppose that India (which is essentially different from the Dominions in history, geographical position, culture, population, economic development, etc.) will accept, or be naturally fitted to carry out, any of the broad unwritten obligations of membership. She will cooperate, if at all, on the same basis as any foreign country and subject to the same kind of limitations – that is, we could not expect more from her than was set out in treaties, or than for the moment appeared to fit in with her particular view of her interests.[47]

Another official, E.P. Donaldson, was even more forthright:

> We regard membership of the 'club' as a privilege to be prized and shared only by people who (a) 'play the game' in our illogical, empirical, easy-going British way; (b) don't need rules to tell us when a thing is 'fair' or 'unfair'; and (c) value loyalty for its own sake. Judged by these tests we are far from sure that these clever but inscrutable Orientals sufficiently satisfy our standards or share our ideals to qualify them for election.[48]

Donaldson raised what was to become a crucial issue: Commonwealth membership was conditional on common allegiance to the Crown. But this concept, he noted, was repugnant to Indian political leaders, 'who see in the Crown not a link between free peoples, but a symbol of domination by one part of the Commonwealth over the rest ... Even Eire recognises the Sovereign for some

---

46 Joe Garner, *The Commonwealth Office, 1925–68* (London, 1978), pp 143, 175. **47** BL OIOC IOR L/P&J/10/122, Donaldson to Turnbull, 14 October 1946. **48** Ibid., undated minute by Donaldson.

purposes and might be induced to draw closer if the difficulty could be eliminated'.

Sir Gilbert Laithwaite, permanent secretary of the Burma Office, agreed that India did not have the same natural link with Empire as the white Dominions, but pointed out that this was also true of Burma and Ceylon, where 'conquest, largely forced upon us by the necessity of keeping order in defence of an original commercial connection, has been the source of the association'. However, the point had been reached when these states wanted to make their own mistakes in their own way. 'The example of Southern Ireland is very relevant (though Southern Ireland is a very small problem, and that country so economically tied up with us that in practice she has to move largely in our orbit)'. Laithwaite, like Donaldson, thought that allegiance was critical:

> The Crown, though a most intangible link, is the real and sole link between the units of the Commonwealth. Even in the case of Southern Ireland, which has ties of blood much closer with us than India, the nominal link of the Crown has been retained. I think it might strike a very severe blow at the roots of Empire association were we to weaken at all on this issue. I am sure it would not necessarily go well with the Dominions; and one would expect a pretty critical reaction here ...[49]

Sir David Monteath, the permanent secretary at the India Office, concluded that it was doubtful whether India:

> is worth having in the Empire. If she was outside we could squeeze her much more ruthlessly and hence reduce the occasions on which we get the worst of the bargain ... On the other hand there are many people in India who regret the severing of the British connection and who, when the Indian politicians have come a real cropper, may increase greatly in influence.[50]

This kind of wishful thinking had been expressed many times in relation to Ireland, but Monteath seems to have been unaware of it.

* * *

Outside the India Office views were more divided. Machtig of the Dominions Office argued that India should stay in. Its departure would weaken the Commonwealth and would be seen as proof that equality of status and real independence were incompatible with Commonwealth membership. He ack-

---

49 Ibid., minute by Laithwaite, 10 October 1946. Laithwaite had been born in Dublin, where his father was employed by the Post Office. **50** Ibid., Monteath to Turnbull, 7 October 1946.

nowledged that Ireland was 'an unfortunate precedent' both in terms of cooperation and allegiance to the Crown, but reminded Monteath that these matters had been discussed in 1937 after the passing of de Valera's constitution and that the conclusion then had been that Ireland remained in the Commonwealth. These arguments also held good for India, although he conceded that it would be infinitely preferable if there was genuine acceptance of the Crown.[51] Monteath was unimpressed, noting that Machtig's letter contained 'a good many "ifs"'. However, the Foreign Office agreed with Machtig. Indian departure from the Commonwealth would be 'a blow to British authority and prestige and as a diminution in the political, military and economic strength of the Commonwealth as a whole'. In any event:

> we should not wish to repeat the relationship between the United Kingdom and Ireland. The conditions which have rendered workable what appeared originally to be an intolerable situation in the case of Ireland are not present in the case of India, i.e., common language, geographical proximity, interdependence of markets, use of Irish labour in the United Kingdom, and above all the growing Irish fear of isolation in an unsympathetic if not hostile world.[52]

The only support for the India Office came from the Colonial Office. 'The whole basis of the Commonwealth is ... that of a willing partnership founded in unwritten understandings'; a reluctant member would be 'more of a liability than an asset'. There was also the thorny question of colonial policy over which India would be bound to disagree with the rest of the Commonwealth. However, the Colonial Office stressed that any new formulation of Commonwealth membership should not be based on colour. There was a precedent for a treaty relationship in Ireland, but the Commonwealth Office was emphatic that this should not be taken 'as a precedent for all "non-white" territories'.[53]

DOMINION STATUS AND INDIAN INDEPENDENCE

In January 1947 Nehru made a speech to the new constituent assembly (which the Muslim League boycotted) which cited the example of Ireland as a republic in the Commonwealth. But apart from the fact that it was nowhere stated in the Irish constitution that the country was a republic, just what did this mean? Sir William Croft, legal adviser to the India Office, had already concluded that any relationship which enabled India to remain in the Commonwealth as an

---

51 Ibid., Machtig to Monteath, 22 November 1946.   52 Ibid., Sargent to Monteath, 7 December 1946.   53 Ibid., Gater to Monteath, 6 December 1946.

independent republic 'would be indistinguishable from the relationship between Eire and ourselves'. But as he noted in some puzzlement, 'what there is of substance in the Eire relationship is rather a mystery. But perhaps the mystery is due to the fact that we are looking to find something where there is really nothing'.⁵⁴ Other India Office officials expressed exasperation with the 'blandly obvious' points being made by the Dominions Office. Of course, the best solution would be for India to remain a cooperative member of the Commonwealth, 'but the whole point is that we are assuming for very good reasons that that will not happen. The Dominions Office do not come down on either side of the fence'.⁵⁵

* * *

At the beginning of 1947 there were significant developments in India: Wavell was replaced as Viceroy by Lord Mountbatten, the former Supreme Allied Commander in Southeast Asia; within another month Pethick-Lawrence was replaced as Secretary of State by Lord Listowel. The path of the new Viceroy was to be eased substantially by the decision of the Congress party on 8 March 1947 to accept partition as the price of retaining a strong central administration for independent India. However, Congress, like Sinn Féin with Ulster in 1921–2, continued to believe that Pakistan would be too weak to survive.

Mountbatten went to India with instructions to transfer power by June 1948, and so the question of whether India should or could remain in the Commonwealth rapidly moved out of the realms of inter-departmental debate. The Muslim League leaders, Jinnah and Liaquat Ali Khan, were determined that after partition, whatever about India, Pakistan would stay in the Commonwealth, a prospect which Mountbatten privately considered 'most disastrous'.⁵⁶ Mountbatten was well aware of the feeling in London about India's continued membership of the Commonwealth, but was determined to secure it if at all possible. He discussed Dominion status with Nehru on 8 April, but the latter was lukewarm and declared that 'under no conceivable circumstances is India going to remain in the Commonwealth, whatever the consequences. Any attempt to remain in the Commonwealth will sweep away those who propose it and might bring about major trouble in India'.⁵⁷

Nehru's opposition, however, was not shared by other Congress leaders. They were attracted by the proposal put forward by V.P. Menon, Mountbatten's Reforms Commissioner, who had established close links with Congress. Menon proposed that power be transferred to two central governments in India and

---

54 Ibid., note by Croft, 13 January 1947. 55 Ibid., minute by Turnbull for Croft and Monteath, 10 January 1947. 56 University of Southampton, Mountbatten Papers [hereafter MP] MB1/D130/8, extract from Viceroy's staff meeting, 26 April 1947. 57 Read and Fisher, *The Proudest Day*, p. 437.

Pakistan on the basis of Dominion status. Instead of waiting for the constituent assembly to devise a new constitution (a process which might take years), power could be handed over at once to the two new governments, which could operate for as long as they wanted under the terms of the 1935 Government of India Act. On 8 May Mountbatten telegraphed his chief of staff, General Ismay, to tell him that Nehru was willing to accept Dominion status at least until the new constitution was drafted. Mountbatten was delighted: 'This is the greatest opportunity ever offered to the Empire and we must not let administrative and other difficulties stand in the way'.[58] But as he told his staff meeting two days later, the attitude of the Congress leaders had been anything but enthusiastic. Nehru had expressed his desire to have the closest possible relations with Britain, but he was not sure what form those relations would take. He 'did not intend to talk about "Dominion status" openly because of the many suspicions. He wanted to prepare the ground ...' He also raised the thorny issue of secession, insisting that under any form of Dominion status India 'would always have the power to leave the Commonwealth when she wished'.[59]

The Congress decision drastically accelerated the transfer of power which was now set for 15 August 1947, ten months earlier than originally planned. But the unexpected acceptance of Dominion status also caused consternation in London. Following discussions with Ismay, Sir Norman Brook, the cabinet secretary, proposed a high-level enquiry into the possibility of a looser form of Commonwealth membership. As he told Attlee:

> We ought to be giving serious and urgent consideration to the possibility of finding some form of association other than the existing 'Dominion status' in which independent states can maintain the British connection. This is not merely a question for India alone. Eire is already in an anomalous position, as an independent republic within the Commonwealth. South Africa was chafing at Dominion status before the war and may do so again ... We may fail in the attempt to find a new basis which would hold the whole of our existing group together; but it seems to be wrong to allow the opportunity to go by default.[60]

The Dominions Office cited Ireland as a negative precedent for any major changes. The 1937 constitution had been accepted by the British government and the Commonwealth in the hope that the substance of the Commonwealth

---

58 MP MB1/D130/13, Viceroy to Secretary of State (for Ismay), 8 May 1947. **59** MP MB1/D130/19, extract from Viceroy's 11th misc. meeting, 10 May 1947. **60** MP MB1/D130/20, Ismay to Mountbatten, 10 May 1947; PRO CAB 1/45, Documents on the Commonwealth Relationship, vol. 1: India, A1, minute by Brook for Attlee, 12 May 1947. In 1949 Brook compiled two very useful volumes of documents on Commonwealth relations, 1947–9, the first of which dealt with India and the second with Ireland.

relationship would remain, but 'this hope was disappointed by Eire's attitude of neutrality in the war. Since then Eire has not been brought back into the general system of consultation and remains apart from the Commonwealth system'. However, 'Eire's general attitude is that of a Western European country and likely, therefore, to support western civilisation, for which the countries of the British Commonwealth stand, which justifies the treatment of Eire as being in some sense a country of the British Commonwealth'. The Dominion Office also argued that the other Dominions would take 'the strongest exception' to any explicit statement on the right to secede from the Commonwealth, although its evidence for this assertion was somewhat vague.[61]

* * *

Mountbatten, who had been summoned back to London for discussions, strongly disagreed with the Dominions Office's view of secession. He argued that there would have to be a statement on the freedom to secede if the bulk of the Congress party was to accept Dominion status and urged that the right to secede should be mentioned in the bill transferring power. But after representations from the Dominions Secretary, the India and Burma committee agreed that secession should not be mentioned in the legislation.[62] However, on his return to Delhi Mountbatten told a press conference on 4 June that:

> the British Commonwealth of Nations is a completely free association of peoples. Each state is completely independent. There is no sort of power that I know of to force them to stay in if they want to go out. The whole essence of independence is that you must have complete freedom to do what you like … The only connecting link is the King.

Mounbatten, as Ismay diplomatically explained to Monteath at the India Office, felt that there was a lot of misunderstanding about Dominion status which had to be dispelled.[63] In London Attlee decided to set up a committee of ministers, assisted by officials and outside experts, which would examine whether an independent republic could be a member of the Commonwealth: 'there was general agreement that it would be necessary to insist that membership of the Commonwealth should imply recognition of the Crown, at least to the extent at present accorded by the Eire Government, i.e., in the sphere of external relations'.[64] The Irish External Relations Act was to become an increasingly important fig leaf in the months ahead.

61 PRO CAB 1/45, A3, note by Dominions Office, 'The Structure of the British Commonwealth', May 1947; MP MB1/D131/3, extract from India and Burma Committee, 22 May 1947.   **62** PRO CAB 134/343, IB (47) 25th, 26th, 27th meetings, 19, 20, 22 May 1947.   **63** TOP XI, press conference, 4 June 1947, pp 115–122; Ismay to Monteath, 9 June 1947, p. 221.   **64** PRO CAB 1/45, A4, minutes of meeting of ministers, 9 June 1947.

BURMA LEAVES THE COMMONWEALTH

With Dominion status and partition accepted in India, Burma now moved centre stage. Here the long British vacillation on Dominion status was to have profound consequences. As with India, half-digested Irish precedents were in ministerial minds. In preparation for a discussion on a Burmese constituent assembly, a note on the framing of the Irish Free State constitution in 1922 was submitted to the India and Burma Committee. In this it was stated that the provisional government's final draft constitution:

> was taken to London for consultation with the British Government, though the latter publicly stated that the Irish were under no obligation to do so. Negotiations took place between the respective Law Officers to ensure that the draft constitution was, so far as possible, in conformity with the Articles of Agreement [the Treaty] at certain controversial points, and the finally agreed draft was published on 15 [sic] June 1922.[65]

Nothing in this blandly innocuous account indicates that the tense negotiations on the draft constitution led directly to the Irish Civil War in June 1922, hardly an auspicious precedent for the Burmese.

However, to the dismay of ministers and officials in London, Burmese leaders were far more interested in the present Irish position in the Commonwealth. U Tin Tut, who was a member of the Governor's executive council, favoured 'some form of association like Eire's'. Listowel, the new Secretary of State, told the Governor, Sir Hubert Rance, that there would be 'grave difficulties' if U Tin Tut and others wished to follow the Irish example and that in any event the Irish situation had 'special features'. Listowel followed this up with a long note (bearing the marks of Monteath's authorship) stressing that a republican constitution not making adequate provision for the Crown 'is not, repeat not, despite precedent of Eire (which UK and Dominions are most unlikely to wish to see repeated), compatible with membership of Commonwealth'. If the Burmese were hoping that they could negotiate some form of external membership of the Commonwealth they should be told that this was 'a wholly novel conception of the Commonwealth connection' which could not be adopted without the agreement of the other Dominions. The disadvantages of leaving the Commonwealth should be emphasised to the Burmese and they should not be encouraged to believe that they could rejoin later. Rance told Listowel on 5 June that the Burmese were still talking about Ireland and about a Commonwealth of sovereign states. Listowel replied that the 1937 Irish constitution referred to a sovereign independent state, not to a republic, and that if the Burmese were not con-

---

[65] PRO CAB 134/344, IB (47) 6, note by Secretary of State for Burma, 7 January 1947.

tent to give Dominion status a fair trial then they should leave the Commonwealth immediately.⁶⁶

On 9 June the Burmese leader, Aung San, informed Rance that at the first session of the constituent assembly on 13 June he would move a resolution that Burma become a sovereign, independent republic. Rance suggested (in line with Listowel's comment on the Irish constitution) that he should substitute state for republic, but Aung San stated that his party was determined on complete independence. Acceptance of Dominion status would split his party and drive its left-wing elements into the arms of the communists. The cabinet's India Committee was unimpressed with this news and agreed that there could be no question of granting Dominion status to Burma merely as a device for expediting the transfer of power. If power was transferred on this basis and Burma left the Commonwealth in a few weeks, 'the whole conception of Dominion status would have been brought into contempt'.⁶⁷ Since Congress had adopted Dominion status precisely as a device for expediting the transfer of power, this attitude was somewhat hypocritical.

At the end of June a Burmese delegation arrived in London. One of its leaders, Thakin Nu, President of the constituent assembly, proposed to Listowel that Burma be an independent republic outside the Commonwealth. He also suggested that the British government summon an imperial conference which would include colonial territories moving towards Dominion status. This conference would decide how sovereign, independent states outside the Commonwealth might be brought into a special relationship with the Commonwealth as members of a loose 'federation'. This relationship would not involve any recognition of the Crown. Listowel deemed these proposals not 'practicable'. But his parliamentary secretary, Arthur Henderson, disagreed. Since the future structures of the Commonwealth were being discussed, why shouldn't the Burmese proposals be considered? But he was overruled by the rest of the India and Burma Committee. Attlee even suggested that a minister of cabinet rank should go to Burma 'with a view to dispelling the ignorance and misapprehension which clearly existed about the nature of Dominion status'.⁶⁸ Since his government had consistently refused to spell out the implications of Dominion status, despite pleas from Dorman-Smith, Slim, Mountbatten, Rance and others going back to 1942, the ignorance and misapprehension lay elsewhere than in Burma.

---

66 BSI II, Rees-Williams to Pethick-Lawrence, 15 April 1947, p. 482; Listowel to Rance, 21 May 1947, p. 528; Listowel to Rance, 24 May 1947, p. 531; Listowel to Rance, 4 June 1947, pp 558–59; PRO CAB 134/345 IB (47) 92, note by Listowel, 31 May 1947; BSI II Rance to Listowel, 5 June 1947, p. 564; Listowel to Rance, 7 June 1947, p. 567. **67** PRO CAB 134/343, IB (47) 30th meeting, 9 June 1947. **68** Ibid., IB (47) 33rd, 34th meetings, 23, 24 June 1947.

***

The cabinet's hidebound view of Dominion status was causing considerable frustration among British representatives in Asia, not only Mountbatten, but Rance in Burma, Lord Killearn, the special commissioner for Southeast Asia and Malcolm MacDonald, who was British Representative in Singapore. They were all very conscious of the seismic political shifts which had accelerated throughout Asia in the wake of the war. MacDonald wrote a long and forceful letter to the Colonial Secretary, Arthur Creech-Jones, on 26 June. As Dominions Secretary from 1935 to 1938, MacDonald had been largely responsible for terminating the six-year Economic War with de Valera (with whom he established friendly relations) and for the conclusion of the 1938 Anglo–Irish agreements. He had also been the moving force behind the decision of the British government to accept de Valera's constitution in 1937. That constitution, he told Creech-Jones, could be a starting point in any debate about the future evolution of the Commonwealth:

> One reason why I advised Cabinet to adopt that line [in 1937] was that it seemed likely that when the time came for India, Burma and other 'non-White' countries in the Empire to attain Dominion status, some at least of them would adopt a similar attitude to the Southern Irish towards the British Crown … I agree that the Irish Constitution is in many ways unsatisfactory. Nor has the Irish experiment been as successful as we hoped at the time that it would be. In particular, it did not result in Ireland joining us as a fighting comrade in the war. Nevertheless, in many other ways Eire has been a cooperative member of the Commonwealth, and she is likely to become more and more so as time goes on. Sometimes the mills of God grind slowly … If we could get a settlement on something like the Irish model, the position of His Majesty will be very much stronger than it otherwise would be. The alternative is a gradual withdrawal of various peoples from the Empire, and a consequent diminution of his sovereignty.[69]

MacDonald's telegram was discussed by the India Committee on 1 July. It was, ministers agreed, 'important and thoughtful', but they thought it neglected the political consequences of India's decision to accept Dominion status. If power could be transferred successfully on this basis then it would effectively counteract the adverse impression created by the Burmese departure from the Commonwealth. There was no justification for any change in the existing Commonwealth association beyond that needed to accommodate the Irish.[70]

69 BSI II, MacDonald to Creech-Jones, 26 June 1947, pp 615–18. **70** PRO CAB 134/343, IB (47) 38th meeting, 1 July 1947.

MacDonald, Mountbatten, Killearn and Rance were informed of the committee's views.

Their frustration was understandable, but the Labour government was at the time engaged on the delicate and hazardous task of steering the Indian Independence Bill through parliament in time for the transfer of power on 15 August. Considering the long debate about whether or not Ireland was still in the Commonwealth, it is noteworthy that de Valera, as a Dominion leader, was consulted about the Bill and, specifically, about the change in the King's title as Emperor of India; his acquiescence in the change, without any qualification, was deemed 'satisfactory' by the Dominions Secretary.[71] But far more important to Labour ministers was the parliamentary cooperation of the Conservative opposition, whose leader, Churchill, viewed the whole proceedings with glowering disapproval. Government ministers were well aware that Churchill regarded Malcolm MacDonald as 'rat-poison' because of his handling of the 1938 Anglo–Irish agreements which had returned the Irish ports on the eve of war.[72] On the very day the India Committee discussed MacDonald's telegram Churchill had written to Attlee objecting to the title of the bill: 'Dominion status is not the same as independence, although it may be freely used to establish independence. It is not true that a community is independent when its ministers have in fact taken the Oath of Allegiance to the King'.[73] Fortunately for Attlee, Churchill's views were not shared by other Conservative leaders, who ensured that the bill safely passed all its stages in time for independence on 15 August.

* * *

Ireland was mentioned several times during the debates, and as independence approached it was also in the minds of political leaders and officials in India. On 24 July, in a conversation with Ismay, Jinnah 'went off into a long yarn about the constitutional position of Eire. He said India and Pakistan would have the same constitutional status as Eire, i.e., unlike the other Dominions they would be able to secede without an Act of Parliament. He was, therefore, in favour of the Eire model'. Ismay was dismayed, and knowing of Jinnah's concern for post-independence military relations, asked him whether he really wanted Anglo–Pakistan relations to be on the same basis as Anglo–Irish relations: 'We did not help Eire with officers, or supply them with the latest equipment; nor did we admit them to our Staff Colleges. In fact, they enjoyed none of the benefits of a Dominion'.[74] With just three weeks to go until independence, this interview sparked off, on Mountbatten's instructions, a hasty reexamination of the position of India and Pakistan in the Commonwealth vis-à-vis Ireland. Mount-

---

[71] TOP XI, Addison to Attlee, 3 July 1947, p. 862. [72] David Dilks (ed.), *The Diaries of Sir Alexander Cadogan* (London, 1971), p. 341. [73] TOP XI, Churchill to Attlee, 1 July 1947, pp 812–13. [74] TOP XII, interview between Ismay and Jinnah, 24 July 1947, p. 324.

batten's constitutional adviser, W.H. Morris-Jones, was particularly concerned about allegiance to the Crown, an issue which had dogged Anglo–Irish relations for over two decades and which ministers and officials in London still deemed vital to India's continued membership of the Commonwealth. Morris-Jones regarded this position as untenable ever since the acceptance of de Valera's constitution in 1937. The government's 1937 statement:

> may be regarded as what it undoubtedly was at the time, *viz.*, a formula which put a brave face on an embarrassing situation. It may, on the other hand, be taken as the first recognition of the Commonwealth ... To translate the matter into terms of India, 'a looser association within the Commonwealth' may be sought not by trying ... to recover the bond of common allegiance to the Crown, but by recognising that even this is no longer necessary as a basis.

Morris-Jones cited de Valera's statement to the Dáil in July 1945 in which he stated that Ireland was an independent republic; but he also percipiently noted that de Valera did not say that Ireland was *not* in the Commonwealth, an indication that de Valera thought Commonwealth membership might still have some potential advantages for Ireland. In the light of this statement, and India's rapidly approaching inclusion in the Commonwealth, the British government had now to devise an association 'which is based simply on mutual advantages'.[75]

In September 1947, a month after Indian independence, the committee of officials appointed in May by Sir Norman Brook submitted its report on Commonwealth relations which demonstrated once again the gap between London perspectives and those of officials on the ground in India and elsewhere in Asia. The Commonwealth system, the committee concluded, drew its strength from the community of sentiment and interest between the different members and the Crown was the symbol of this. It was the 'only formal link' and, as such, the Commonwealth could not include republics which did not recognise the King in either their internal or external affairs. A dilution of the role of the Crown on the Irish model would only provoke resentment among older members of the Commonwealth and might also result in foreign countries refusing to recognise the rights and privileges of Commonwealth membership. Burma was of immediate concern, but the committee did not consider that Burma's retention in the Commonwealth justified any major changes in the role of the Crown, although Burma's decision could well influence Ceylon and Malaya.[76] Later that month the Burmese constituent assembly approved the first clause of the draft constitution, which declared that Burma was a sovereign,

---

[75] MP MB1/D132/7, paper by Morris-Jones, 5 August 1947. [76] PRO CAB 1/45, A5, first report of committee of officials, 15 September 1947.

independent republic. This effectively signalled Burma's departure from the Commonwealth.

After the passing of Indian independence, the British government knew it had a temporary breathing space while the new Indian constitution was being drafted. Mountbatten, who stayed on until June 1948 as Governor General of India, was determined that India would stay in the Commonwealth, but the whole debate was soon to be galvanised by events in Ireland.

'THE IMPLICATIONS OF EIRE'S RELATIONSHIP WITH THE BRITISH COMMONWEALTH'

In November 1947 the historian Nicholas Mansergh gave a lecture at the Royal Institute for International Affairs (where he held the Bailey Chair in British Commonwealth Relations) on 'The Implications of Eire's Relationship with the British Commonwealth of Nations'. The lecture was attended by several Labour ministers. Mansergh came from an Anglo–Irish Tipperary family, many of whom had served the British Empire as soldiers, sailors and administrators. But unlike many of his class, Mansergh watched the evolution of the new Irish state after 1922 with sympathy and understanding and he developed a particular respect for de Valera. During the war, he had worked in the Empire section of the Ministry of Information and in 1947 he had recently attended the first Inter-Asian Conference in New Delhi which gave him a valuable insight into the attitudes of newly independent states in Asia. He was uniquely qualified to understand the implications of the troubled Irish relationship with the Commonwealth and how they might affect India:

> The problem that now confronts British statesmanship is the same in essentials as that which confronted it in Ireland a quarter of a century ago. The problem, broadly stated, is that of associating a people with a cultural tradition of its own and an intensely national outlook with a group of states whose existence depends upon the reconciliation of individual interests with those of the community as a whole ... Recent experience of Anglo–Irish relations is likely to provide a source from which many lessons may be learnt. Of that, those who determine the destinies of India, of Pakistan, of Burma and of the other countries in Southeast Asia, are well aware.[77]

There were fundamental questions, Mansergh argued, which successive British governments had consistently evaded. Was Dominion status the right solution in 1921? Could Dominions be made artificially? Had the wisdom of the

[77] The lecture was published in *International Affairs*. It is reprinted in Diana Mansergh (ed.), *Nationalism and Independence: Selected Irish Papers by Nicholas Mansergh* (Cork, 1997), pp 148–68.

solution been justified by the sequel? Mansergh considered the decision to accept de Valera's constitution in 1937 as a prime example of this evasion and, worse, of a 'disturbing rigidity of outlook', with the British government attempting to paper over political inconsistency with verbal consistency.

For Mansergh, external association, as presented by de Valera and the Irish delegates in 1921, 'is likely to provide a more satisfactory basis for common action in external affairs between two countries, who share a wide community of interest but different political concepts, than Dominion status, based as it is on unwritten conventions'. External association was not a colourless compromise, but 'the positive answer to a certain set of circumstances'. It also had the merit of allowing for growth. The most vital lesson to be learned from the Irish experience was 'the supreme importance of reconciling constitutional forms with political and psychological realities', and it was precisely because external association was the solution contemplated by Irish republicans in 1921 that it was a good starting point for the new nation-states in Asia. Dominion status depended for its working on a whole set of ideas and common associations containing nice implications only readily understood by people with similar backgrounds and training. What did it mean to the peoples of the East? 'The Indian mind, which in common with the Irish and the French inclines towards precision, would welcome [it] more if at least the foundations on which this new relationship may be built could be more closely defined'. It was believed in Burma, as in every other Asian country, that Dominion status meant subordination, and 'no amount of explanation will remove the conviction that somehow or other Dominion status implies something less than full sovereignty'. One advantage of external association, Mansergh concluded, was that no one in Asia or in any other continent 'has ever supposed that the actions of Mr de Valera are in any way controlled by the British government, or that any subordinate status would ever be acceptable to him. The integrity of his nationalism is above suspicion'. Mansergh's lecture, which was published in *International Affairs,* was read with great interest by the British Representative in Dublin, Lord Rugby. 'I have always felt', he wrote to Mansergh, 'that Dominion status was quite unsuited to Eire ... To me the External Relations Act seems to be an ideal solution, but I realise that is not everybody's view'.[78]

* * *

The foregoing analysis was certainly not the view of the new Irish government which took office in February 1948, just three months after Mansergh's lecture. The new Taoiseach, John A. Costello, was a trenchant critic of the External

---

78 PRO DO 130/93, Rugby to Mansergh, 10 March 1948. Rugby's view of the act appears to have changed considerably. In January he had told Machtig he would not be sorry to see 'this strange device' removed: ibid., Rugby to Machtig, 27 January 1948.

Relations Act, as was the Minister for External Affairs, Seán MacBride. While it was true that de Valera had been contemplating repeal of the act after the war, he had taken no action, because he was watching what was happening in India with keen interest. Indeed, the Indian government had sent a delegation to Dublin at the end of 1947 to consult de Valera about their future constitutional status. The secretary of the Department of External Affairs, F.H. Boland, recalled in 1952 that de Valera had strongly impressed upon them the desirability of some form of external association. De Valera himself later told Mansergh that if he had remained in office he would have happily accepted the solution eventually worked out for India; in fact, he 'would have striven for it'.[79] Rugby perceptively observed that the new government's attitude to the External Relations Act was largely conditioned by their hostility to de Valera. 'If Dev had not invented it ... the attack might not have developed. All this was very personal'.[80] For the British government, the prospect of renewed constitutional controversy with the Irish, at the very moment when India's relations with the Commonwealth had to be resolved, caused considerable anxiety. However, the new government took no immediate action.

DE VALERA'S VISIT TO INDIA

Mountbatten's conversations with Indian leaders indicated that Irish parallels were being closely considered. Mountbatten discussed the matter with the Indian government's constitutional adviser, Sir B.N. Rau, and asked him for copies of the Lloyd George–de Valera correspondence in 1921. He stressed to Rau the importance of avoiding the word republic; Rau confirmed that so far there was no reference to a republic in the draft constitution.[81] Mountbatten emphasised that there was no apparent alternative to retaining the Crown as the link between Commonwealth members, though he thought there would be no objections to India electing its own head of state. Once these modifications were made to the Commonwealth structure, Mountbatten declared in an expansive mood, not only might Burma reapply for membership, but the Irish position might be placed on a more regular basis, 'resulting, perhaps, in that island becoming unified once more'. Rau gave Mountbatten an account of his recent conversations with de Valera and 'particularly described how Mr de Valera had succeeded in winning the agreement of his colleagues to the continued link of Ireland with the Crown under the heading of "External Association"'.

79 *Nationalism and Independence*, conversations with Boland and de Valera in 1952, pp 185–6, 188–90. **80** PRO DO 130/93, Rugby to Mansergh, 10 March 1948. **81** MP MB1/D132/13, 14, record of interviews with K.M. Panikkar, Sir B.N. Rau and Sir Maurice Gwyer, 16, 22 January 1948.

Mountbatten's conference secretary, Erskine Crum, noted after this interview that it was now transparently clear that allegiance to the Crown was the real stumbling block. 'Should we not face up to the fact that it is highly improbable that India, and out of the question that Burma, will agree to remain in (or return to) the Commonwealth so long as allegiance to the Crown remains a prerequisite for this?'[82] On 23 February Rau informed Mounbatten that the dreaded word 'republic' had now been inserted into the draft constitution. It was evident to Mountbatten that there was nothing more to be gained by harping on about allegiance; he told the Commonwealth Relations Office (as the Dominions Office had been rechristened) that a republic could be accommodated within the Commonwealth and, citing the 1937 Irish constitution, declared that the time had now come for a new conception of Commonwealth association not based on allegiance to the Crown.[83]

* * *

But this was still a step too far for the government in London. On 11 March Attlee wrote to Nehru, describing the Commonwealth as a 'unique experiment', a 'close association with complete freedom … and a remarkable degree of flexibility owing to the absence of any constitution'. As proof of this Attlee cited Ireland:

> The course of Irish history resulted in the establishment within the Commonwealth of a republic which is, however, linked to the other states by the Crown. It is, as so many things British are, illogical, but it works. Even during the war the ambassadors [*sic*] of Eire to countries with which we were at war received their authority from the Crown …

But allegiance was fundamental: 'The common allegiance to the Crown is the link within which all kinds of association for mutual advantage are possible; without it they are more difficult to establish. If one seeks to go beyond this and to draft any form of constitutional relationship one finds oneself in very great difficulties'.[84]

Nehru's reply to Attlee was graceful, but uncompromising:

> I am more interested in real friendship and cooperation between these countries than merely in a formal link … Right at the beginning of its

---

82 MP MB1/D132/16, note by Crum, 6 February 1948.   **83** MP MB1/D132/24, *aide-mémoire* by Mountbatten, 25 February 1948.   **84** PRO PREM 8/820, Attlee to Nehru, 11 March 1948. Irish diplomatic representatives did not have ambassadorial status until 1949. Attlee also seems to have been unaware that no new Irish ministers were appointed to Axis states during in the war, precisely to avoid the necessity of accreditation by the King. Their duties were carried out by chargés d'affaires instead.

> existence the constituent assembly laid down certain objectives. It stated that the constitution was going to be an independent sovereign republic ... I entirely agree with you that words have an inherent force and power of their own. Behind the words, of course, there lies a complex of thoughts and memories, both conscious and subconscious, which exert a powerful influence on the minds of the people.[85]

Shortly after this letter, in the course of a lengthy anti-partition tour, de Valera paid a brief visit to Delhi, in the course of which he met Nehru twice and had several meetings with Mountbatten, who was his host. At the press conference he gave on 15 June de Valera described the Irish relationship with the Commonwealth as external association which in no way affected the country's status as a sovereign, independent republic. The only link with the Crown was the accreditation of diplomatic papers. External association was thus a convenience, designed in part to meet the feelings of those in Ireland who wished to maintain ties with Britain. However, de Valera was considerably more positive about the Commonwealth in another part of the press conference when he discussed international cooperation:

> Wars could only be prevented by coordination between different nations. Since a world-wide association of nations was not immediately workable, they could try to advance the goal by smaller organisations ... By being associated with the Commonwealth Eire was thus cooperating in an effort towards international amity.

In his report on the press conference the British high commissioner in Delhi noted that while de Valera was 'frank and unreserved in his opinions', he 'made it clear that he was suggesting no analogies nor did he want to express views which might be taken as suggestions for India. They in Eire had to face certain problems and they had solved them according to their own needs'. The *Bombay Chronicle* found de Valera's statements 'delightfully vague' and declared that by staying in the Commonwealth Ireland was aspiring to the achievement of 'the lotus in the mud pond, which lives and thrives through the mud and yet remains untouched and unspoiled by it'.[86]

THE REPEAL OF THE EXTERNAL RELATIONS ACT

These events did nothing to advance the debate on India and the Commonwealth which dragged on throughout the summer. In an attempt to break the

---

85 Ibid., 8/820, Nehru to Attlee, 18 April 1948.   **86** PRO DO 35/3930, Shone to the Commonwealth Relations Office, 17 June, 9 July 1948.

stalemate Attlee sent the cabinet secretary, Sir Norman Brook, on a mission to Ottawa, Canberra and Wellington. In each capital Brook found that ministers and officials wanted India and the other Asian states to stay in the Commonwealth, despite the differences of background and history. They also told Brook that if the Indians accepted some form of recognition of the Crown then a republican constitution could be accommodated in the Commonwealth. With regard to Ireland, the Canadian Prime Minister, Mackenzie King, was 'very sceptical', as Brook noted, about the possible repeal of the External Relations Act, as he thought that such a move would disrupt Costello's government and set back the campaign against partition. Brook wrote that King, the Australian and New Zealand Prime Ministers (J.B. Chifley and Peter Fraser) were agreed that if the act was repealed Ireland could no longer be regarded as a member of the Commonwealth. But in the light of later events it was significant that King believed that even if the act was repealed, Ireland could still be associated with the Commonwealth, something which might also apply to India and Pakistan.[87]

In Dublin Rugby was keeping the Commonwealth Relations Office in touch with the debate over the External Relations Act. After the initial flurry when the new government took office, the issue had subsided, but Rugby was sure it had not gone away. On 16 August he wrote to Sir Eric Machtig saying that he expected the repeal of the act when the Dáil reassembled in November.[88] Following a press report on 5 September MacBride assured Rugby on the morning of 7 September that while the Irish government intended to repeal the act 'no definite time had been fixed for this step'.[89] By the following morning the news of Costello's statement in Canada announcing the repeal of the act *and* secession from the Commonwealth greeted astonished ministers and officials in Dublin. If, as Costello was wont to claim in later years, the decision had been agreed by the cabinet, this reflects even more unfavourably on his government, since the archives do not reveal that there was any preparation for such a momentous step which was bound to have serious implications for Irish trade and for the thousands of Irish people living in Britain. One of his senior ministers, Richard Mulcahy, commented that Costello 'must have been drinking some heady wine in Canada'.[90] By announcing secession from the Commonwealth, in addition to the repeal of the act, Costello had certainly burned

---

87 PRO CAB 1/45, B13, report by secretary of cabinet, 14 September 1948.   **88** PRO DO 130/93, Rugby to Machtig, 9, 16 August 1948.   **89** Ibid., Rugby to Machtig, 7 September 1948.   **90** Risteard Mulcahy, *Richard Mulcahy, 1886–1971: A Family Memoir* (Dublin, 1999), p. 250. When Nicholas Mansergh spoke to Costello in 1952, the latter denied that his announcement had been provoked by the alleged slights of the Governor-General of Canada, Lord Alexander. However, from the way he spoke about the matter Mansergh was pretty sure this was the reason: *Nationalism and Independence*, p. 187.

his boats. After a conversation with Costello in 1952 Nicholas Mansergh observed with some understatement that the link between secession and repeal 'would not seem to have been carefully considered'.

Since Ireland's departure from the Commonwealth has been treated by a number of scholars,[91] it is not proposed here to go into the details except as they concern India, an aspect which has not been discussed. As we have seen, the repeal of the External Relations Act had been expected by the British government, but there was deep resentment at the cavalier manner of its announcement by Costello, and this was aggravated by the complications it would cause in the delicate negotiations about India. Rugby favoured Irish attendance at the forthcoming meeting of Commonwealth Prime Ministers, but this was forthrightly rejected by the British cabinet.[92] The ramifications of the Irish departure from the Commonwealth seemed hideous. In the vexed area of trade preferences, temporary trade preferences had been given to Burma, but if Ireland became a foreign country similar concessions could not be hidden. On this point both the Foreign Office and the Board of Trade were clear in view of the problems which would arise in the case of most-favoured-nation status in British commercial treaties.[93] The Lord Chancellor, Lord Jowitt, warned ministers not to assume that the only alternative was to treat Ireland as a foreign country; every form of new status should be explored, and he reminded them that whatever decision was reached would affect India. However, after consultation with the Solicitor General, the Foreign Office, the Home Office and the Commonwealth Office Jowitt concluded that Ireland would have to be treated as a foreign country after the repeal of the External Relations Act.[94] Still, Brook's tour of the Dominions in August had given warning signs that Dominion ministers would not be stampeded into any precipitate action against the Irish, and this was borne out when British, Irish and Dominion ministers met at Chequers on 17 October. There was clear a consensus among Dominion ministers that some form of Irish connection with the Commonwealth must be maintained.[95]

* * *

---

[91] Ian McCabe, *A Diplomatic History of Ireland* (Dublin, 1991); F.J. McEvoy, 'Canada, Ireland, and the Commonwealth: The Declaration of the Irish Republic, 1948–49', *Irish Historical Studies*, vol. 24 (1985); John O'Brien, 'Australia and the Repeal of the External Relations Act', in Colm Kiernan (ed.), *Australia and Ireland, 1788–1945* (Dublin, 1986), pp 252–66.   [92] PRO CAB 1/46 (Documents on the Commonwealth Relationship, vol. 2), A2, cabinet memorandum CP (48) 220 by Noel-Baker, 9 September 1948; A3, cabinet conclusions, 10 September 1948.   [93] Ibid., A4, note by Brook, appendix 1, 5 October 1948.   [94] PRO CAB 1/46, A4, committee on Commonwealth PMs meeting, 5 October 1948; PRO CAB 1/46, A7, committee on Commonwealth relations, minute by Jowitt, 9 October 1948.
[95] PRO CAB 1/46, A10, cabinet memorandum CP (48) 258, 17 October 1948.

But where did this leave India? On 23 October the Commonwealth Secretary, Philip Noel-Baker, wrote to Mounbatten, who had left India in June, but who, behind the scenes, was still a powerful influence on British policy towards India. Nehru was in London, and Noel-Baker and other British ministers had discussions with him, but Ireland had been an unwelcome complication. 'They [the Irish] want to continue some kind of reciprocal citizenship and trade preference, but they also want to be *out* of the Commonwealth. That makes it much harder to maintain that India is *in* the Commonwealth, if the only link is that of reciprocal rights of citizenship'.[96] What was needed was some form of declaration by India that it was a member of the Commonwealth. The form of this putative declaration was revealed two days later when Sir Gilbert Laithwaite met Sir B.N. Rau and suggested an affirmation of Commonwealth membership 'in principle not unlike what had happened in Eire over the External Relations Act'.[97] It was a measure of the British government's desperation that over the next few months the act was increasingly employed as potential fig-leaf for India. Indeed, Attlee even expressed the hope that the Irish might rejoin the Commonwealth if a suitable basis was found.[98] Churchill, still glowering on the opposition benches, was scornful. The glorious names of Empire, Dominion and British, he declared, were being suppressed in order to pander to Nehru and Costello.[99]

Further talks with Irish and Commonwealth leaders were scheduled for Paris in the middle of November, but by 12 November British ministers were no further advanced. Jowitt and the Attorney-General told the cabinet that there was 'no device by which they could hope to satisfy an international court that a country which was not a member of the Commonwealth was not a foreign state'. While there were now fundamental differences between the Irish and Indian attitudes to the Commonwealth, there remained the basic problem of how international law would recognise Commonwealth states which no longer owed allegiance to the King.[100] At the Paris talks these fears were dismissed by Commonwealth ministers, who doubted whether any such legal challenge could or would be mounted. While expressing irritation at the manner of the repeal of the External Relations Act, they were anxious to find some form of special association for Ireland and the Commonwealth and minimise the consequences of repeal. MacBride stressed that his government wanted the closest possible relations with Britain and the other Commonwealth states and described the act as 'a flimsy, dishonest and, indeed, derisory instrument which could not be defended on its merits'. (These sentiments must have disconcerted Laithwaite, who was present at this meeting, as it was just three weeks since he had sug-

96 MP MB1/F40, Noel-Baker to Mountbatten, 23 October 1948. **97** PRO CAB 127/115, note by Laithwaite, 25 October 1948. **98** PRO CAB 1/45, cabinet memorandum CP(48)244 by Attlee, 26 October 1948. **99** *House of Commons Debates*, 457, 242–51, 28 October 1948. **100** PRO CAB 1/46, A16, cabinet conclusions, 12 November 1948.

gested the act as a possible model to Rau.)[101] By the end of the Paris talks it was decided that a reciprocal exchange of trade and citizenship rights was the best solution. British ministers were unhappy with this, but as Noel-Baker and Jowitt told the British cabinet, they had no choice but to go along with the rest of the Commonwealth, which regarded the British stress on the consequences of repeal as a form of retaliation. What if India demanded the same treatment, other ministers asked. Might not this lead to the two-tier system they had been anxious to avoid? Noel-Baker and Jowitt demurred. MacBride told Rugby that British ministers were exaggerating the legal difficulties and that they were really more afraid of Churchill.[102]

* * *

By the New Year the debate within the British cabinet showed no sign of resolution, but with elections due in Canada, Australia and New Zealand, and with the enactment of the new Indian constitution expected in July, a decision would have to be taken within the next few months. Supporters of Indian membership argued that since political expediency had dictated the compromise with Ireland, there was no reason why a similar compromise could not be worked out with India; for opponents, allegiance was still the sticking point. Ministers were impressed with the comment by F.H. Boland, the secretary of the Irish Department of External Affairs, that in practice very few foreign countries would pay any attention to the constitutional niceties of the British Commonwealth.[103]

In March Attlee sent Listowel, Gordon-Walker and Brook as his personal emissaries to discuss India with the other Commonwealth states. In the documents prepared for the emissaries (none of which were to be shown to the Indians), it was stated that the basic question was whether a republic owing no allegiance could be accommodated within the Commonwealth. The immediate aim was to keep India in the Commonwealth, but if the question was answered it might meet the views of republican states such as Ireland and Burma which had left the Commonwealth and might even lead to them returning. Attlee proposed recasting the Balfour Declaration so that members of the Commonwealth could be defined as (1) independent sovereign states which owe or have owed allegiance to the Crown; (2) equal in status and in no way subordinate one to

---

[101] Ibid., A18, cabinet conclusions, 13 November 1948; A20, cabinet memorandum CP (48) 272 by Lord Chancellor and Commonwealth Secretary, 17 November 1948. In Evatt's opinion the repeal of the act was due mainly to domestic political considerations in Ireland and to the Irish government's desire to 'take the gunman out of politics'. When Rugby read the report of these talks, he wrote 'Rubbish' beside this comment: PRO DO 130/93. [102] Ibid., A21, cabinet conclusions, 18 November 1948; DO 130/93, Rugby to Machtig, 19 November 1948. [103] PRO CAB 1/45, C32, cabinet committee on Commonwealth relations, 4 March 1949.

another in any aspect of their domestic or external affairs; (3) not foreign in relation to each other; (4) freely associated as members of the Commonwealth united with one another, some by allegiance to the Crown and all by their acceptance of the principle of consultation on all matters of common concern and by the rights of common citizenship. Attlee anticipated that the Irish precedent would be raised, but instructed the emissaries to stress the disadvantages the Irish now faced by losing Commonwealth membership and to dispel the impression that they had got 'something for nothing'.[104]

The Canadian Prime Minister, Mackenzie King, told Brook that the peoples of the Commonwealth must be free to choose their own constitutions; if not the Soviets would claim that they did not enjoy real freedom. King also argued that instruments like the Statute of Westminster simply reflected changes which already happened and the evolution of the Commonwealth could not be crystallised in any set form: 'definitions were dangerous', he concluded. Listowel met a similar response in Australia. Chifley, the Prime Minister, 'did not think that a republican form of government ... mattered so long as the real basis of mutual confidence and consultation remained'. In New Zealand Fraser was more reluctant, although Listowel attributed this to the imminent elections and to Fraser's fear that the issue would be exploited by the opposition. He wanted any statement on India to be postponed until after the elections. In South Africa Malan favoured a treaty relationship with India. In view of the strained relations between his government and India over the treatment of Indians in South Africa (apartheid had been introduced the previous year), it was not surprising to find Malan expressing the opinion that 'he could see no matters on which the governments of the Union and India could cooperate except joint opposition to the advance of communism'. Smuts also poured cold water on Indian membership of the Commonwealth, stressing that the paramount consideration was 'the maintenance of the strong cohesive character of the old Dominions association'. In Pakistan Prime Minister Liaquat stated that it would be impossible for Pakistan to retain its link with the Crown if India became a republic, a view echoed by the Cingalese Prime Minister, Senanayake.[105]

Before the all-important talks with the Indian government Gordon-Walker asked for guidance on a vital point. 'Would we or would we not regard something on the lines of the Eire External Relations Act as constituting a satisfactory and defensible Crown link?' This telegram provoked an interesting reaction in London. Noel-Baker drafted a reply which urged Gordon-Walker to 'encourage any suggestion by Nehru of a solution on the lines of the Eire External Relations Act', although he did not think this likely. However, the draft sent to Gordon-

---

104 PRO CAB 1/45, D34, cabinet memorandum, CP(49) 58 by Attlee, 14 March 1949. 105 Ibid., D35, telegram from Brook, 18 March 1949; telegrams from Listowel, 15, 21, 24 March 1949; telegrams from Liesching (South Africa), 13, 14 March 1949; telegrams from Gordon-

Walker omitted the reference to the Irish act.[106] When he met Nehru on 28 March the latter asked about the Irish position. Gordon-Walker explained about the exchange of trade and citizenship preferences, but emphasised that the Irish were not entitled to any exchange of information or consultation nor could Irish representatives attend Commonwealth meetings: 'I spent some time on this point', Gordon-Walker reported to London, 'and I hope I convinced him that the Irish relationship was not for India'. Nehru, however, did suggest that India might perhaps recognise the King as the symbol or head of Commonwealth unity, a direct borrowing from de Valera's concept of external association. In another less cordial conversation with Copelswami Ayyanger, one of Nehru's closest colleagues, Ayyanger asked Gordon-Walker 'why were we being stiffer with India than with Ireland'. The Governor-General told him that in Indian eyes 'the Crown was associated with alien rule from which they had won their liberty'. V.P. Menon 'several times mentioned the Irish analogy as being completely false and of no use to India', from which Gordon-Walker deduced that 'someone or other out here (possibly even Nehru) is playing with the idea'.[107]

INDIAN ACCESSION, IRISH SECESSION

After digesting these reports back in London the cabinet committee on Commonwealth relations finally threw in the towel and agreed on 8 April that the best alternative would be that India recognise the King as head of the Commonwealth and as the symbol of the free association of Commonwealth peoples.[108] Events moved swiftly after this. On 18 April Ireland left the Commonwealth and became the Republic of Ireland. Nine days later, at the Commonwealth Prime Ministers' Conference in London, India affirmed its desire to remain in the Commonwealth and to accept the King as the 'symbol of the free association of its independent member nations'. On 3 May the British government published its Ireland Bill which revealed a bitter sting in the tail in the shape of the clause stipulating that in no event would Northern Ireland or any part of it cease to be part of the United Kingdom 'without the consent of the Parliament of Northern Ireland'. Rugby, who had retired the previous month, expressed his dismay to his successor in Dublin, Gilbert Laithwaite. The guarantee was 'useless, needless, provocative!' but he still blamed Costello 'for so recklessly breaking up a delicate piece of machinery and poisoning an atmosphere which was rapidly becoming healthy'.[109]

Walker, 12, 14, 21, 22 March 1949. **106** Ibid., D35, Gordon-Walker to CRO, 20 March 1949; D36, draft by Noel-Baker, 23 March 1949; Attlee to Gordon-Walker, 25 March 1949. **107** Ibid., D39, Gordon-Walker to CRO, 31 March, 1 April 1949. **108** Ibid., D42, cabinet committee on Commonwealth relations, 8 April 1949. **109** BL OIOC, Laithwaite Papers Mss

In September 1949 the Labour MP A.L. Ungoed-Thomas met de Valera in Strasbourg and reported their conversation to the Commonwealth Relations Office. De Valera 'emphasised that he had always been most careful to state that he did not wish to leave the Commonwealth so long as it was understood that no allegiance to the Crown of England was involved. The Indian Commonwealth solution would have exactly met his position, and he was clearly angry at Mr Costello's action'. British ministers and officials were very encouraged by these comments, and Laithwaite told Gordon-Walker that if Southern Ireland was prepared:

> not only to come back into the Commonwealth on the same basis as India, but in addition to accept allegiance to the King, then it might no doubt be possible to devise some system under which, subject to adequate guarantees to the North and to the agreement of the Northern Ireland Parliament, there could be an all-Ireland parliamentary body. But I question very much whether, even if Southern Ireland came back into the Commonwealth on the Indian basis, the North would be prepared to whittle away its relation to the King or be satisfied with [his] position merely as 'Head of the Commonwealth'.[110]

But what had been done could not be undone, as de Valera regretfully explained when he returned to power in 1951. External association, he told Nicholas Mansergh, was 'the idea that failed'.[111] Mansergh did not agree and in several major studies on the Commonwealth was in no doubt that in 1949 external association, that stillborn alternative to the 1921 Treaty, had at last found its time.

Eur F138/85, Rugby to Laithwaite, 25 May 1949. After initially good impressions, Laithwaite came to share Rugby's opinion of Costello and MacBride, about whom he wrote trenchantly in reports to the CRO. His view of de Valera became correspondingly warmer. **110** PRO DO 35/3941, memorandum by Ungoed-Thomas of conversation with de Valera and Frank Aiken, 5 September 1949; minute by Laithwaite, 2 November 1949. **111** *Nationalism and Independence*, pp 185, 188–90.

Anti-partitionism, Irish America and Anglo–American Relations, 1945–51

Troy Davis

INTRODUCTION

In the wake of World War II a potential obstacle to post-war Anglo–American collaboration was Irish nationalist agitation against the partition of Ireland.[1] Such nationalist activism had helped militate against close Anglo–American relations in the past, most recently in the aftermath of World War I. Following that conflict, large numbers of Irish Americans had rallied behind the republican cause in Ireland's War of Independence of 1919–21. Those same Irish Americans had also worked with the larger isolationist movement in the United States to thwart aspects of Woodrow Wilson's pro-British internationalist foreign policy, ultimately keeping America out of the League of Nations.[2]

Some American and British officials feared that history would repeat itself after World War II and that anti-partitionist Irish Americans, encouraged by the Dublin government, would strive to wreck the Anglo–American alliance that played such a key role in the post-war strategies of both Britain and the United States. The individual most alarmed by that prospect was David Gray, the American minister to Ireland from 1941 to 1947. Gray, therefore, spent much of his time during the war, and immediately thereafter, seeking to discredit the Irish government in American eyes. In this campaign the minister focused on the supposedly harmful effects of Ireland's wartime neutrality. Gray was supported in his efforts by Sir John Maffey, the British representative in Dublin, who shared the American's concerns.[3] It is reasonable, however, to ask whether

---

[1] The broader context of the material discussed below is covered in Troy D. Davis, *Dublin's American Policy: Irish–American Diplomatic Relations, 1945–1952* (Washington, 1998), pp 58–94. [2] For the Irish American impact on American foreign policy following World War I, see Francis M. Carroll, *American Opinion and the Irish Question, 1910–23* (Dublin, 1978) and Alan J. Ward, *Ireland and Anglo–American Relations, 1899–1921* (London, 1969). [3] Davis, *Dublin's American Policy*, pp 16–39; T. Ryle Dwyer, *Irish Neutrality and the USA, 1939–47* (Dublin, 1977), pp 162–68. Dwyer's *Strained Relations: Ireland at Peace and the USA at War, 1941–45* (Dublin, 1988) also provides an insightful look at Gray's generally invidious impact

Anti-partitionism, Irish America and Anglo–American Relations 193

such fears of Irish agitation in America were justified. Was there any realistic possibility that Irish nationalists, and their supporters in the United States, could have had the pernicious influence on Anglo–American affairs that such diplomats as Gray and Maffey foresaw? Likewise, was the minister's estimation of Irish influence in America anachronistic – geared more towards the realities of the 1920s than the 1940s?

THE BRITISH FOREIGN OFFICE AND THE IRISH FACTOR

To answer this question, it is helpful to consider what most officials in the British Foreign Office thought about the alleged Irish threat to Anglo–American relations and post-war stability.[4] Though the Foreign Office might naturally be expected to take a critical view of the anti-partitionists and their arguments, its evaluation of the potential Irish nationalist impact on American opinion and policy would, in all likelihood, be realistic as well. The United Kingdom was, after all, somewhat dependent on good relations with the United States as World War II came to an end. That conflict had ensured the demise of the British Empire and had left Britain itself physically damaged, with serious economic problems. American aid and goodwill were thus essential to British recovery. With so much depending on close cooperation between the Americans and themselves, therefore, British policymakers were keenly aware of possible obstacles to such cooperation. Thus if Irish protests over the boundary between Ireland and Northern Ireland had represented a real threat to Anglo–American solidarity, United Kingdom authorities would presumably have been attentive to the danger.

In this connection, Foreign Office files on matters affecting Anglo–American relations in the last days of World War II and in the immediate post-war period are enlightening. With regard to the possible impact of the partition question on American policy towards Britain, the files are most notable for their overall silence on the subject. The policymakers within the Foreign Office were simply not worried, for the most part, about the Irish and their compatriots in America having an adverse effect on Britain's standing in the United States. When Irish grievances are mentioned, they are generally rejected as a serious source of anti-British feeling. Even in British embassy treatments of 'hyphenated groups' in the United States, which twenty-five years earlier were dominated by

---

on US policy towards Ireland during and immediately after World War II. **4** Until 1949 Ireland was still formally a member of the British Commonwealth. During and immediately after World War II, therefore, Maffey was answerable to the Dominions Office (later the Commonwealth Relations Office) and, consequently, did not have the full benefit of the Foreign Office's insights into the political climate in the United States.

news about the Irish American community, ethnic Irishmen are dismissed as a factor – when they are mentioned at all. Instead, Jews, Italians, Poles, and Blacks are the groups considered most important.[5]

As events developed in the immediate post-war period this Foreign Office evaluation of the perils of Irish agitation in America proved to be accurate. There was some anti-partition activity in the United States between the end of the war and early 1948, but it was of a tentative and ineffectual nature, consisting largely of petitions from such groups as the American Association for the Recognition of the Irish Republic and the American League for an Undivided Ireland. These petitions generally called for official American promotion of Irish unification and were addressed to either the State Department or the White House. They invariably received the State Department's standard reply to such requests for involvement in the partition question: while it appreciated receiving the petitioners' views on the matter, the State Department took the position that the altering of political boundaries between Ireland and Northern Ireland was not a matter in which the United States government might properly or usefully intervene.[6]

THE ANTI-PARTITION MOVEMENT IN AMERICA

At this point – that is, before 1948 – these activities in the United States did not generally receive active support from the Irish government, then under the leadership of Eamon de Valera and the Fianna Fáil Party. This government was aiming most of its anti-partition rhetoric at Irish audiences; what support the American activities did get in Ireland usually came from more extreme nationalist sources, such as those associated with the Irish Anti-Partition League, an organisation inaugurated by Northern nationalists near the end of 1945 without de Valera's blessing.[7]

In the first half of 1948, however, developments in Irish domestic politics would lead to an official anti-partition campaign in the United States. The specific development which triggered this turn of events was the outcome of the Irish general election of February 1948. In that contest, Fianna Fáil was driven from office for the first time in sixteen years, and de Valera traded the job of Taoiseach for that of leader of the opposition; the new government was a coali-

---

5 PRO FO 371/44555–9, 44605–8, 44614–15, 44635. **6** See, for example, National Archives and Records Administration, College Park, Maryland [hereafter NARA], State Department Decimal File [hereafter DF], 841D.00, Reilly, American Association for the Recognition of the Irish Republic, to Byrnes, Secretary of State, 8 August 1945; Hiss, State Department, to Reilly, 18 September 1945. **7** John Bowman, *De Valera and the Ulster Question* (Oxford, 1982), p. 258.

tion of five parties whose common denominator was their determination to oust de Valera from power.

The new Taoiseach was Fine Gael deputy John A. Costello, while de Valera's successor as Minister for External Affairs was Seán MacBride, whose new Clann na Poblachta party hoped to displace Fianna Fáil as the champion of constitutionally minded Irish republicans. The political chemistry of this change in government rekindled the partition question as a live issue in Irish politics. There were two major reasons for this: first, the coalition government was determined to open up the issue, mistakenly believing that the Labour government in London would be receptive to nationalist arguments; and second, Fianna Fáil, with its leadership of the anti-partition forces in question, responded to the challenge by calling for an end to the border more insistently than it had done in years. In the words of Maffey (now Lord Rugby), 'each party must now outdo its rivals in a passionate crusade for Irish unity'.[8]

This competition among the parties to 'outdo' one another in their opposition to partition soon led de Valera to attempt to raise the issue to an international plane, particularly in the United States. However, throughout an American tour in early 1948 his rhetoric was designed primarily for Irish consumption. As one United States diplomat put it in a report to Secretary of State George Marshall, de Valera was first and foremost a politician, and Irish nationalist propaganda abroad was merely 'the best way to practice his trade' at that time.[9]

As de Valera's tour progressed, the Foreign Office's belief that American interest in Ireland was on the decline seemed to be borne out, and it became increasingly clear that the campaign was having no lasting political effect. Certainly, Anglo–American relations were not hurt in any serious way. Thus in commenting on the tour to the Commonwealth Relations Office, Rugby wrote that while he would never suggest that an Irishman could forget history, it appeared that in the United States Irish Americans were 'slightly less frenzied' than they had been in the past.[10]

De Valera's tour was by no means the only Irish propaganda mission to America during the anti-partition activity that simmered in Ireland throughout the coalition government's three years in office. The dynamics of Irish politics during the period ensured that members of the government would emulate de Valera's example in order to prove their own nationalist credentials. Thus both Costello and MacBride made trips to the United States while in power and, in each case, they delivered the anti-partitionist message in speeches and press conferences. None of these expeditions, however, received as much attention from British diplomats and officials as de Valera's trip did nor did any of them lead

---

8 Ibid., pp 267–9.   **9** Ibid., p. 274.   **10** PRO DO 35/3928, Secret Dispatch, Rugby to Machtig, 30 March 1948.

the Foreign Office to reconsider its conviction that American interest in Irish issues was dying.[11]

BRITISH LOBBYING IN THE UNITED STATES

The Foreign Office's belief that the British had little to fear from the Irish American community in regard to partition finally led the United Kingdom to try its own hand at overt propaganda in the United States, mainly as an experiment in countering the ineffectual, yet bothersome, activities of Irish and Irish American anti-partitionists. This British initiative took the form of a visit to America by the Northern Ireland Prime Minister, Sir Basil Brooke, in the spring of 1950.

The story behind the British decision to let Sir Basil go to the United States to present the Ulster unionist case for partition provides an instructive look at the evolution of Britain's strategy for fighting the Irish government's manoeuvres in America. Immediately after World War II the Foreign Office's standing advice to the Northern Ireland government on the best way to meet occasional outbreaks of anti-partition rhetoric in the United States was 'to let sleeping dogs lie'. That, for example, was the Office's counsel to Brooke in June 1946, when the Northern Ireland premier proposed that a Six Counties spokesman be sent to the United States to publicise the facts that Northern Ireland and Ireland were separate political entities and that Northern Ireland had not been a party to Irish neutrality in World War II. Foreign Office functionaries explained to the Prime Minister that such an official visit would probably do more harm than good, since it might revive the quiescent Irish American community's interest in partition. Thus the British embassy in Washington met Brooke's suggestion with the judgement that it was 'sheer wishful thinking on the part of the Northern Ireland government to imagine that they would do their cause in the United States any good by accentuating the political fact of partition'.[12] In the face of these objections Brooke's proposed American campaign dissolved.

Almost exactly three years after its veto of the Northern leader's original suggestion of a unionist campaign in the United States, however, the Foreign Office encouraged a similar public relations effort in America, this time by Sir Basil Brooke himself. In June 1949 Brooke reported to the British Home Secretary

---

11 See, for example, PRO FO 371/74190, Broad, Foreign Office, to Allen, Washington embassy, 12 May 1949; confidential dispatch, chancery of Washington embassy to Foreign Office, 6 June 1949; North American department of Foreign Office to chancery, 17 June 1949.
12 PRO FO 371/51741, Evans, British consul-general in New York, to Butler, Foreign Office, 22 June 1946; Butler to Evans, 31 July 1946; chancery to North American department, 23 September 1946.

that the Ulster Irish Society of New York had invited him to be its guest of honour at the Society's annual banquet the following spring. Brooke and his colleagues in the Northern Ireland cabinet were enthusiastic about the premier's opportunity to speak before the Society, and Brooke felt that he should accept the invitation. Since a visit by Brooke to the United States might affect Anglo–American relations, the Home Office asked for the Foreign Office's views on the proposed visit before the Home Secretary approved the undertaking. The Foreign Office's response to this proposed visit to America was in marked contrast to its discouragement of Sir Basil's suggestion of 1946. This time the North American department of the Office reported to Sir Oliver Franks, the British ambassador in Washington, that as a result of 'noisy' anti-partition propaganda in the United States the Northern Ireland case had largely gone by default. The department, therefore, believed that Brooke should be encouraged to accept the Ulster Irish Society's invitation and, if possible, to speak at other American venues as well. Franks, again in contrast to the Washington embassy's position three years earlier, agreed with this recommendation, as did Foreign Minister Ernest Bevin on 5 July.[13]

Obviously, the Foreign Office's response to Brooke's invitation to speak in New York represents a dramatic departure from its attitude towards the Prime Minister's earlier suggestion that Ulster's position be publicised in the United States. It would probably be a mistake, however, to interpret this new Foreign Office position as evidence that informed British officials were now seriously concerned about the possibility that anti-partitionism might succeed in disrupting Anglo–American relations. Rather, a more likely explanation of the new strategy seems to be that the British saw Brooke's visit as a test of anti-partitionism's true strength in the United States.

As the Washington embassy explained in a report to the North American department near the end of 1949, embassy staffers still held their previous opinion that the Irish, and their American friends, had failed to gather any significant momentum behind their cause. They believed, however, that Sir Basil's appearances in the United States would serve to clarify the situation. Brooke's presence

13 PRO FO 371/74190, Basil Brooke to Home Secretary, 23 June 1949; Nunn, Home Office, to Kinna, Foreign Office, 1 July 1949; Broad, Foreign Office, to Franks, 5 July 1949; memorandum, Beaumont, Foreign Office, to Bevin, 5 July 1949; Kinna to Nunn, 7 July 1949. Brooke's decision to visit the United States may have been prompted by a December 1948 suggestion from William Smale, the American consul in Belfast, that 'some suitably qualified' unionist representative from the North make such a visit. Brooke responded to Smale's suggestion enthusiastically and said that he himself might make the trip. The consul then advised the premier that Sir Frank Evans would undoubtedly be able to find a college or university willing to confer an honorary degree on Sir Basil, thus keeping the visit private and unofficial: NARA, 800 post files, Dublin legation (unclassified), Record Group 59, dispatch, Smale to State Department, 3 December 1948.

in America, the embassy reported, was certain to serve as a focal point for the American anti-partition campaign, and it would remain to be seen whether the noise and excitement his visit would bring to the surface could be 'mobilised into an effective movement'.[14] The fact that the embassy itself encouraged the visit suggests that its staffers did not believe that any such movement could be created.

SIR BASIL BROOKE IN AMERICA

Once again, British confidence was justified by events, as the unionist leader's program proceeded with little controversy. Although there was some Irish American protest against the Prime Minister's presence in the United States (especially in New York, where Mayor William O'Dwyer declared, during a St Patrick's Day speech, that Brooke would be welcomed at City Hall only over his dead body), such demonstrations were not widespread. Anti-partitionist protests against Brooke's arrival on American soil were disorganised, and only a handful of pickets were at Idlewild Airport in New York when he touched down on 6 April 1950. No demonstrators at all awaited him when he landed in Washington, where his tour officially began.[15]

During his stay in Washington, on 6–11 April, Sir Basil met with Secretary of State Dean Acheson, Pentagon officials and a number of friendly congressmen and senators, many of whom expressed embarrassment at Mayor O'Dwyer's St Patrick's Day remarks. He also addressed a meeting of the National Press Club.[16] Following these events in the capital, Sir Basil travelled to New York for a week-long visit, which the British Information Service (BIS) agent there characterised for his superiors as an 'outstanding success'. At a BIS luncheon for journalists at the Harvard Club the Prime Minister explained the historical position of Ulster under the Ireland Act of 1920 and the Boundary Agreement of 1925. Afterwards, Bill Chaplin of the National Broadcasting Company asked Sir Basil to deliver a radio address over his network the following Sunday, and that broadcast was later arranged. At the Ulster Irish Society banquet that had brought the Northern Ireland leader to America in the first place, Brooke received a standing ovation after making conciliatory comments about the Republic.[17]

Following his departure from New York, Brooke spent four days in Philadelphia, where he presented a number of addresses before proceeding to Chicago. Surprisingly, it was in Chicago that Brooke received what was proba-

---

14 PRO FO 371/74191, confidential letter, chancery to North American department, 15 December 1949. **15** PRO FO 371/81648, confidential letter, Franks to Bevin, 2 June 1950. **16** Ibid. **17** PRO FO 371/81648, confidential political report, Ormerod, New York office, BIS, to controller, BIS, 21 April 1950. Documents in PRO FO 371/74190 and 74191 make it clear that the journalists at the Harvard Club luncheon were all carefully selected by the BIS.

bly his warmest welcome of the entire American visit. He was, for example, formally received at City Hall by the Irish American mayor, Martin H. Kennelly, and greeted by a friendly editorial in the normally anti-British *Chicago Tribune*, which condemned the bad manners of 'professional Irishmen' like Mayor O'Dwyer. Remarkably, Sir Basil was not the target of any picketing at all in Chicago, and after a final weekend as guests of Illinois Governor Adlai Stevenson, the Prime Minister and his wife left the United States for further touring in Canada.[18]

The British were pleased with the premier's American performance. Ambassador Franks' report to Bevin on the visit expressed the British evaluation quite succinctly:

> Considered in retrospect, I think that the Prime Minister's visit shows a clear balance on the plus side and has proved a most interesting experiment in testing out, and in showing the shallowness of, the Irish movement in the United States today ... In my opinion, the fact that he should have been able to carry out a successful visit to such cities as New York and Chicago, without meeting with any significant opposition, is ample evidence that the Irish movement in this country is now moribund.[19]

Despite Franks' predictable emphasis here on the success of the visit, the ambassador's reading of Brooke's stay in America seems to be accurate. Foreign Office officials, long inclined to believe that the Irish American community represented no real threat to British interests in the United States, now had what appeared to be unusually compelling evidence that their judgement was correct. Nor was the lesson of Sir Basil's trip of only passing interest to these officials. One Foreign Office observer cited the tour over eight months later as an indication that Irish American influence was on the wane.[20] By October 1951 the Foreign Office was dismissing anti-partitionism in America as an issue widely regarded as a 'bore or a joke'.[21]

IRISH AMERICA AND THE DECLINE OF ANTI-PARTITIONISM

It seems clear, then, that the Irish anti-partition campaign of 1948–51 failed to garner any substantial support in the United States. Hence, wartime and post-

---

18 PRO FO 371/81648, confidential letter, Franks to Bevin, 2 June 1950.   **19** Ibid.   **20** PRO FO 371/90939, unsigned marginal notation, Hadow, UK consul-general, Los Angeles, to chancery, 2 February 1951.   **21** PRO DO 35/3922, notes of inter-departmental meeting at the Home Office, 24 October 1951. R. Cecil, who attended the meeting, was the Foreign Office official who made the above comment.

war fears of such a campaign were largely misplaced; while such British and American diplomats as Lord Rugby and David Gray were correct in predicting that the Irish would launch a propaganda crusade in America against the partition of Ireland, they failed to see that such a campaign had little realistic chance of disrupting the Anglo–American partnership. Irish American interest in the partition question was simply not great enough in the immediate post-war era to sustain the Irish government's attempts to influence American foreign policy and force concessions from the British over Northern Ireland.

The root causes of this lack of interest in partition among Irish Americans appear to lie largely in the American political climate of the period, one of the most striking features of which was the foreign policy consensus that existed in the United States in the immediate post-war era. For most Americans, including those of Irish ancestry, World War II and the events leading up to it had created a sea change in the way they perceived the United States' place in world affairs. Isolationism had, for the most part, been discredited by the events of the inter-war years, as Americans generally saw a connection between the United States government's lack of involvement in international affairs after World War I and the breakdown in order that resulted in World War II. Thus it became a widely accepted tenet of the post-war era that the United States, as the world's strongest nation, could ignore its international responsibilities only at great danger to itself. Consequently, in contrast to the widespread American distrust that kept the United States out of the League of Nations, there was almost universal support for a strong American presence in the United Nations after World War II.[22]

Simultaneous with this rejection of isolationism in the United States was the onset of the Cold War, which reinforced the general American conviction that the United States had to maintain a strong presence in the international arena. To the majority of Americans, the Soviet Union's efforts to secure a buffer zone to its west by controlling the Eastern European, Baltic and Balkan nations appeared similar to Nazi Germany's acts of aggression during the 1930s. Again referring to what they saw as the lessons of the inter-war years, most Americans agreed with their leaders that appeasement of the Soviet Union could not be tolerated and that the United States should take the lead in Western efforts to 'contain' the spread of communism. They thus responded positively to such anti-communist initiatives as the Truman Doctrine, the Marshall Plan and the North Atlantic Treaty Organisation (NATO), the first peacetime alliance in the nation's history.[23]

Given this post-war political climate in the United States, the failure of Irish anti-partition activities in America is not surprising. Much of the anti-partition

---

[22] Melvin Dubofsky, Athan Theoharis and Daniel Smith (eds), *The United States in the Twentieth Century* (Englewood Cliffs, 1978), pp 306–7. [23] Ibid., pp 328–37.

strategy in the United States during the early post-war period was at variance with the basic foreign policy attitudes of the time and was, in fact, reminiscent of the isolationist outlook of the inter-war years, which had included a strong anti-British element. To most Americans during the early Cold War, Britain was not only a recent World War II ally, but also a steadfast supporter of the containment doctrine in both Europe and Asia, where, by the end of 1950, the British military was again cooperating with the United States in Korea. The anti-partitionist tactic of trying to persuade or pressure the American government into changing its British policy to suit the Irish government, therefore, was virtually certain to fail.

* * *

Under these circumstances, Irish Americans who took the post-war anti-partition campaign seriously had few viable foreign policy allies. This situation contrasted sharply with the one that had followed World War I. There was also, however, an even more basic difference between the Irish Americans of the 1940s and 50s and those of a generation earlier. Irish Americans of the post-war period were simply far less interested in Irish affairs than their counterparts of 1919–21 had been. Whereas Irish Americans of the earlier era had so sympathised with the republican movement in Ireland that they had vigorously opposed what they interpreted as President Wilson's pro-British foreign policy, their post-war counterparts in the Irish American community tended to base their foreign policy views more exclusively on their perceptions of American interest.

This change in Irish American foreign policy priorities had a number of causes, both political and social. As several scholars have convincingly argued, the nationalist success in the Irish independence struggle of 1919–21 represented a watershed not only in Irish history, but in the Irish American experience as well. These historians assert that prior to the nationalist victory in 1921 Irish Americans had taken a keen interest in the political affairs of their ancestral home largely for reasons related to their lives in the United States. In the American cities where they had settled, for example, many Irish Americans and their descendants suffered from discrimination and religious bigotry at the hands of nativist Protestants of British descent. Such experiences engendered in the Irish American community a sense of ethnic solidarity, which the community's leaders then used to help forge powerful political machines in such heavily Irish American cities as New York, Philadelphia, Boston and Chicago. Despite this political power, however, many of the American Irish continued to feel that they lacked respectability in the eyes of nativist Americans, and they came to pin their hopes for greater prestige and acceptance in the United States on events in Ireland. Specifically, they became enthusiastic supporters of Irish separatism, reasoning that if the Irish in Ireland won independence, the Irish in America would benefit as a result. No longer would the word 'Irish' connote colonial inferiority and subordination; it would, instead, denote the proud people of a sovereign nation state.[24]

The end of the Irish War of Independence in 1921, and the subsequent creation of the Irish Free State, seemed to most Irish Americans to be the culmination of their fight for respectability in the United States. After 1921 most of the American Irish, though still proud of their ancestry, became less concerned with conditions in Ireland and their primary political focus shifted to the United States itself. In essence, following the achievement of Irish independence, the Irish American community became more fully integrated into American society and was assimilated into the larger American political culture.[25]

CONCLUSION

As the events in this essay have suggested, by the end of World War II the integration process seems to have been largely completed for most Irish Americans, and the Irish American response to the post-war anti-partition campaign indicates that the Irish community in America posed no threat to cooperation between the United States and Britain in the early post-war era. The majority of the community's members did not wish to disrupt the relationship; and even if they had so desired they would have found it almost impossible to do so given the American political climate of the period. It should be equally clear, however, that this interval of relative Irish American apathy concerning events in Ireland was not to be a permanent one. By the time the Troubles in Northern Ireland once again brought the dispute over partition to the fore in the late 1960s, further political and social change in both the United States and Ireland would create a trans-Atlantic environment in which Irish American interest in Irish politics would become reinvigorated, with sometimes decisive consequences.[26]

---

[24] This view of the Irish American community's interest in Irish politics prior to 1921 is offered by several historians. See, for example, Carroll, *American Opinion and the Irish Question*; Ward, *Ireland and Anglo–American Relations*; Lawrence J. McCaffrey, *The Irish Catholic Diaspora in America* (Washington, 1998); Joseph P. O'Grady, *How the Irish Became Americans* (New York, 1973); and Thomas N. Brown, *Irish American Nationalism, 1870–1890* (Philadelphia, 1966). [25] McCaffrey, O'Grady, and Ward are all agreed on the political assimilation of the Irish as it is defined here. See also the editorial entitled 'Police State' in the 29 September 1951 issue of the *Irish Times* for an excellent contemporary analysis of the foreign policy interests of the Irish American community during the early Cold War era. [26] The best, and most complete, treatment of the Irish American community's response to the Troubles is Andrew Wilson, *Irish America and the Ulster Conflict, 1968–1995* (Washington, 1995). See, especially, pp 17–49 for the reemergence of extensive Irish American activism in relation to political events in Northern Ireland.

Integration or Isolation? Ireland and the Invitation to Join the Marshall Plan

Bernadette Whelan

INTRODUCTION

George Marshall's few observations about the Marshall Plan provide a useful starting-point for a study of the central concerns of American policymakers in 1947. In his speech to Harvard graduates, which was delivered on 5 June, Marshall referred to several pressing issues: (a) the dysfunctional capitalist system in Europe; (b) the threatened democratic traditions of European states; (c) the destabilising potential of this situation for America and the free world; (d) the importance of United States leadership of the free world; and (e) the necessity of intensifying and coordinating United States involvement in Europe. But Marshall's views must be examined in their broader context: firstly, a national history of intervention in the wider world; secondly, the apparent threat posed by the Soviet Union to the democratic, capitalist Western Hemisphere in the post-1945 period; finally, the widespread perception present in American political and administrative circles that political, economic and social fissures were weakening Europe.

When Marshall made his speech, the *unrestricted* nature of the invitation to participate in a recovery programme attracted attention throughout Europe. In the State Department George Kennan hoped that the offer would place a severe strain on relations between Moscow and its satellite countries and insisted that the plan be open to allies, former allies, enemies, former enemies and neutrals.[1] Thus the Soviet Union and Eastern European countries were invited, as were Italy and Germany (former enemies) and Ireland and Portugal (both neutral).[2] Kennan's Rooseveltian internationalism, however, was not shared by other American policymakers. Charles Bohlen, William Clayton and Dean Acheson supported an open-ended invitation for a different reason: they believed that once the USSR refused to participate the blame for dividing Europe would then rest squarely on Soviet shoulders. The inclusive American overture may be

---

[1] John Lamberton Harper, *American Visions of Europe: Franklin D. Roosevelt, George F. Kennan and Dean G. Acheson* (Cambridge, 1994), p. 200.

viewed, therefore, as an attempt by the United States to create a bloc of states centred around itself. In addition, each European state was considered valuable in terms of promoting key United States foreign policy interests. This paper is thus concerned with the background to the American decision to invite Ireland to join the Marshall Plan and the Irish reaction to that invitation.

THE POST-WAR CONTEXT

War-time issues still influenced the Irish–American relationship in the post-war period. Irish neutrality, American opposition to it and Allied efforts to offer a thirty-two-county Ireland in return for Irish involvement have all been well documented.[3] After the war Ireland's neutrality still rankled with Washington, yet more crucial was its strategic location, which remained more than a matter of passing interest to American defence and security experts. The United States War Department's Intelligence Review of May 1946 noted that in the world situation then obtaining the political disposition of the Western European countries had never been more significant to American interests.[4] Three years later a CIA report stated that:

> Ireland is potentially a valuable ally because of its strategic location athwart the chief seaways and airways to and from Western Europe. Its terrain and topography lend themselves to rapid construction of airfields which would be invaluable as bases for strategic bomber attacks as far east as the Ural Mountains ... Irish neutrality would probably again be tolerable under conditions of global warfare. However, and assuming these conditions, because hostile forces in Ireland would outflank the main defences of Great Britain, and because it could be used as a base for bombing North America, the denial of Ireland to an enemy is an unavoidable principle of United States security.[5]

Against the background of increasing tensions between the superpowers, the strategic importance of Ireland's geographical location affected American,

---

2 Franco's fascist Spain, also neutral during the war, was not invited to send a representative to the first conference on the Marshall Plan, which opened in Paris on 12 July.   **3** See, for example, T. Ryle Dwyer, *De Valera's Finest Hour, 1933–59* (Dublin, 1982); Robert Fisk, *In Time of War: Ireland, Ulster and the Price of Neutrality, 1939–45* (London, 1983); Seán Cronin, *Washington's Irish Policy, 1916–86: Independence, Partition and Neutrality* (Dublin, 1987).   **4** Harry S. Truman Library [hereafter HSTL], Harry S. Truman Papers [hereafter HSTP], War Department, Naval Aide File, Box 16, Intelligence Review, no. 12, May 1946.   **5** HSTL HSTP, President's Secretary File [hereafter PSF], Box 256, SR 48, CIA Ireland, 1 April 1949.

British and Western European defence planning. Any wish to isolate Ireland in retaliation for its wartime neutrality was counter-balanced by the security need to incorporate the country into some kind of American-sponsored organisation. The Marshall Plan provided just such an opportunity.

Washington received London's support on this policy for three reasons: firstly, security; secondly, a fear that exclusion might refuel the anti-partition lobby, particularly in the United States; and, finally, economic considerations, which will be examined later in this chapter. London's security strategy had traditionally depended on having either direct control of, or a friendly ally on, its western and southern sides to protect its sea and air approaches and ensure the continued flow of badly needed supplies. During the war, these security concerns were tempered by the benevolence of Irish neutrality towards the Allies and possession of the Northern Ireland bases. Although the latter arrangement continued into the post-war period, Ireland's permanent inclusion in a European-based security organisation was a key aim of London's defence strategy; in the absence of that occurring, Ireland's participation in any western bloc was favoured.[6]

Such a course, London hoped, would have a further benefit of normalising Anglo–Irish relations. There were many layers to this relationship, but by 1945 diplomatic discourse was characterised by new levels of cooperation and mutual understanding. Sir John Maffey, the British minister in Dublin, noted in his 1945–6 annual review that for 'the first time in history the British cabinet has been able to conduct a long war without any anxiety about Ireland'.[7] Difficulties lingered, of course, especially over partition and de Valera's visit to the German legation to express his condolences upon Hitler's death. Still, the patriotic slogan 'England's difficulty is Ireland's opportunity' had been moderated to 'England's difficulty is none of Ireland's business'. Maffey believed this was 'something new'. Consequently, at a diplomatic level, at least, moderation prevailed. London supported Irish membership of the United Nations Organisation in the hope that it would extend Irish foreign policy horizons beyond the confines of partition and provide Britain with an ally on the international stage.[8] Irish participation in the European Recovery Programme (ERP) – the official name of the Marshall Plan – was favoured for the same reasons.

Even the sensitive issue of partition formed part of the argument for Irish inclusion. Both London and Washington feared that Irish exclusion would

---

6 For further analysis of this position, see Ian McCabe, *A Diplomatic History of Ireland 1948–49: The Republic, the Commonwealth and NATO* (Dublin, 1991), pp 97–105. **7** PRO FO 371 54722 WX763, John Maffey, Annual Report 1945–6. **8** For further analysis of this episode, see Dermot Keogh, 'Ireland: The Department of Foreign Affairs', in Zara Steiner (ed.) *The Times Survey of Foreign Ministries of the World* (London, 1982), p. 288; Ronan Fanning, 'The Anglo–American Alliance and the Irish Application for Membership in the United Nations', *Irish Studies in International Affairs*, vol. 2, no. 2 (1986).

refuel anti-partition activities in Britain and the United States. De Valera had postponed a planned international propaganda campaign when the war broke out in 1939 and was slow to revive activities at the end of the war because of the decline of interest in ethnic affairs, especially in the United States. Indeed, the 'American Note' (which requested Ireland to expel Axis representatives from the country), de Valera's visit to the German legation in May 1945 and Dublin's refusal to close Axis legations or hand over Axis personnel and property had placed a strain on the relationship with Washington. A public opinion poll conducted in March 1944 during the 'Note' affair indicated that a majority of Americans favoured the imposition of trade sanctions, the use of force and even a declaration of war on Ireland. De Valera's German legation visit revived this anger. According to Ryle Dwyer, de Valera was prepared to wait before relaunching the campaign, but in the meanwhile he encouraged and supported independent anti-partition activity in Northern Ireland, Britain and the United States.[9] The Anti–Partition League of Ireland was established in Britain in 1947, and by the end of 1948 it had 4,000 paid-up members.[10]

London kept a close eye on the Irish American situation. In March 1949 the British embassy in Washington accurately noted: 'Whilst there has, of course always been a measure of sympathy in this country for Ireland, it has been markedly strained by Eire's strict neutrality during the war [and] her refusal of [the] United States' requests for naval and/or air facilities in the anti-submarine campaign.'[11] The State Department concurred. In 1946 John Hickerson, director of the European Affairs section, told David Gray, the American minister in Dublin, that 'We have heard nothing from Congress on this subject in a long time'. Still, Hickerson knew that while de Valera had not resumed the anti-partition campaign in the United States at an official political level,[12] he was 'intensifying his campaign to end partition and reunite Ireland, and seeks to gain support for this objective in the United States'.[13] A February 1947 War Department intelligence report concluded that the revived anti-partition campaign aimed 'to marshal world opinion' against Britain.[14] Officials in London and Washington were more than aware that Irish American interest in ethnic matters may have been diluted during the war, but it had not completely evaporated. Dublin's formal and informal lobby could be reactivated when needed.

---

9 Ryle Dwyer, *De Valera's Finest Hour*, pp 145, 156, 138.   **10** PRO FO 371 120 68045E, British Embassy, Washington, to Commonwealth Relations Office, 26 December 1947.   **11** PRO FO 371 1967 74190, British Embassy, Washington, to Foreign Office, 10 March 1949.   **12** *Foreign Relations of the United States* [hereafter *FRUS*], vol. 5 (1946), Hickerson to Gray, 11 February 1946, p. 113.   **13** National Archives and Records Administration, College Park, Maryland [hereafter NARA], Record Group [hereafter RG] 59, Box 20, Lot 54D 226, Ireland Data Sheet, 18 February 1946.   **14** HSTL HSTP, War Department, Naval Aide File, Box 16, Intelligence Review, no. 52, 13 February 1947, p. 47.

In February 1947, for instance, the Irish government obtained an extra 5,000 tons of grain in addition to the quota agreed by the International Emergency Food Council by lobbying sympathetic Democrats in Congress.[15] That this was not an isolated episode was evident from a comment by Robert L. Oshins, an official in the Office of War Mobilisation and Reconversion, who noted that 'the Irish have been just about the worst offenders against using the regular channels for securing equitable international allocations'.[16]

Later that year, in November, 2,000 delegates from thirty-eight states attended the Irish Race Convention in New York and agreed to establish the American League for an Undivided Ireland 'on behalf of 30 million Irish'.[17] Ryle Dwyer notes that the Convention did not attract much attention from the American newspapers, which, at the time, were more interested in the passage of the Marshall Plan legislation through Congress.[18] But the Irish American lobby had the potential to delay Congressional approval of the Marshall Plan. The American League gathered 300,000 signatures for a petition which included the demand that 'European Recovery funds should be withheld from Great Britain in order that the growing source of irritation be eliminated in Ireland'.[19] Both the existence of the Irish American lobby generally, and specifically when it mobilised around the partition issue, held out the possibility of disrupting the ERP – whatever about the reality of the former achieving its objective. And at minimum, the anti-partition political and public lobby was a source of embarrassment to the administration, particularly to the anglophile elements in the State Department. So, even before the commencement of the Marshall Plan the State Department was given a taste of the Irish approach to ERP matters. Hickerson's advice to Matthew J. Connelly, Truman's Irish American secretary, on the matter of whether or not the League should present its petition to Truman was that 'it has long been the view of this Department that the subject of the boundary which partitions Ireland and Northern Ireland is one for discussions between the Irish and British governments and one in which this country should not intrude'.[20] The State Department intended to stand firm on the partition issue and not allow the ERP be used for national purposes – except United States-designed ones.

Irish America's post-war revival of interest in ethnic matters did not go unnoticed by British officials. In December 1947 British diplomats in Washington described the Irish American element as a 'persistent, formative influence in politically conscious sections of the country'.[21] In such circumstances neither

---

15 HSTL HSTP OF 426, 1947, Box 1273, File WHCF, Ewing to Steelman, 5 February 1947.
16 Ibid., Oshins to Steelman, 22 December 1947. 17 HSTL HSTP OF, Box 823, Folder 218, American League for An Undivided Ireland to Marshall, 12 May 1948. 18 Ryle Dwyer, *De Valera's Finest Hour*, p. 162. 19 HSTL HSTP, American League to Marshall, 12 May 1948.
20 HSTL HSTP OF, Box 823, Folder 218, Hickerson to Connelly, undated, probably 1948.
21 PRO FO 371 120 68045E, British Embassy, Washington, to Commonwealth Relations

London nor Washington could risk omitting Ireland from the ERP, but this did not mean that Washington's annoyance with neutrality and the resurgence of anti-partition activity would not manifest itself in other ways within the programme's framework.[22] Hickerson, who was influential on ERP issues relating to Ireland throughout the period of operation, wrote to Gray in Dublin in January 1945: 'the people of the United States, I believe, will not soon forget that the one time in history when Ireland had an opportunity to do something to assist this country the Irish Government turned a deaf ear'.[23]

AMERICAN INTERESTS

At first glance, Washington had little to worry about with regard to Ireland's anti-communist credentials. Anti-communism had long been a central feature of Irish life. Pope Pius XI's 1931 encyclical, *Quadragesimo Anno*, which condemned communism, atheism and materialism, had heavily influenced the Irish hierarchy's public statements and parish sermons and found a ready audience among a majority Roman Catholic population. A 1946 War Department intelligence report on Ireland noted that the 'fervent Catholicism of the Irish is a bulwark against communist influence',[24] and a 1949 CIA report stated that 'communism has little appeal to the Irish, whose views on political, social and economic matters are conditioned by religious beliefs'.[25] Political parties used 'red scare' tactics to smear the opposition. In 1929 and 1932 Cumann na nGaedheal did so against Fianna Fáil; similarly, in 1943 the National Labour Party smeared the Labour Party. Both right and left of the political spectrum recognised its vote-winning potential.

The Communist Party itself had never made an impact in either local or national elections. But it was active through the work of individuals located

---

Office, 26 December 1947. **22** Washington was not adverse to using Marshall funds to keep European states in line from the very beginning. The US threatened to exclude the Netherlands from Marshall Aid because of the Dutch military offensive against nationalists in the East Indies before December 1948: Petra M.H. Groen, 'Militant Response: The Dutch Use of Military Force and the Decolonisation of the Dutch East Indies, 1945–50' in R.F. Holland (ed.), *Emergencies and Disorder in the European Empires after 1945* (London, 1994), p. 34. **23** NARA RG 59, Box 20, File UK D–5(B), Hickerson to Gray, 1 January 1945. In October 1946 the State Department refused to elevate the American diplomatic presence in Ireland to ambassadorial status on the ground the Irish had been 'about as uncooperative as it was possible to be in the matter of expelling German agents and in taking steps to sequester German funds ... To make a proposal to the Irish Government at this time would be both disadvantageous and humiliating': NARA RG 39, Box 20, File UK D–6, Acheson, 25 October 1946. **24** HSTL HSTP, War Department, Naval Aide File, Box 16, Intelligence Review, no. 12, May 1946. **25** HSTL HSTP PSF, Box 256, CIA Ireland SR–48, 1 April 1949, p. 13.

across the country. The CIA noted about communist accusations levelled at the recently established party, Clann na Poblachta, that 'the Clann has demonstrated no unconstitutional tendencies and has repudiated with apparently justified resentment charges that it harbours communists'. Neither was it perceived that the left-wing political groups posed a threat: the CIA characterised both the Labour Party and the National Labour Party as 'mildly socialistic'.[26] Similarly, the Irish Trade Union Congress (ITUC) and the Congress of Irish Unions (CIU) were considered 'anti-communistic in the broad meaning of that term'.[27] It is worth remembering that since the founding of the state in 1922 nationalism has been at the heart of Irish politics and society, leaving little room for other political ideologies. Public dissatisfaction with the performance of a political party, in or out of government, was expressed through the ballot box during local or national elections. Yet, while there was little chance of Catholic Ireland turning to communism, the prevailing American sensitivity towards communist activity, combined with Washington's view of a deterioration in Irish economic conditions in 1947, strengthened the case for including Ireland in the ERP.

Of special concern were Ireland's economic performance, its relationship with Britain and its ties with Europe. Though Ireland had not been physically involved in the war, its fledgling economy, just recovering from the Economic War of the 1930s, had been seriously disrupted, thus complicating de Valera's war-time attempt to realise his dream of self-sufficiency. The economy was predominantly agricultural. In 1936, 614,000 workers from the total labour force were employed in the agricultural sector, 206,000 in industry and 415,000 in the services area.[28] The economy relied heavily on imported animal feed stuffs, fertilisers, fuel and machinery. Supplies of these items were severely curtailed during the war, and while the volume of gross agricultural output was maintained at pre-war levels, Ireland still suffered a shortage of some foodstuffs since the switch to tillage had adversely affected productivity.

The consequences of the war-time economic dislocation, particularly the shortages of bread, butter, clothing, sugar, tea and tobacco, combined with a wage standstill, resulted in a reduction in living standards. Life was certainly difficult. In comparison with other European countries, however, Ireland's war had not been so harsh – the rate of employment remained at pre-war levels and most food-items were available. Ireland's living standards even attracted attention in

---

26 HSTL HSTP, CIA Ireland, 1 April 1949, p. 11. **27** NARA RG 84, Box 19, file 560.1, American Legation to State Department, 11 August 1949. These political realities, however, were not sufficient to completely convince the State Department that Ireland was safe from the prevailing communist threat. American legation officials in post-war Dublin kept a close eye on all possible avenues of communistic infiltration. **28** Kieran A. Kennedy, Thomas Giblin and Deirdre McHugh, *The Economic Development of Ireland in the Twentieth Century* (London, 1988), table 7.2.

1946 and 1947. The American magazine *Life* published an article indicating that Ireland was self-sufficient in food, even exporting a surplus. This contrasted with the shortages prevailing in most European countries. In the United States, the article stated, the average per capita wheat consumption was half that in Ireland.[29] In February 1947 David Gray was so concerned that this impression might adversely affect Ireland's chances of getting extra grain that in a minute to Washington supporting the country's request he counteracted this image of milk and honey flowing in Ireland:

> there are 324,099 people ... living in tenements with a population density of three or more persons to a room ... the lowest income groups are limited in cooking facilities for the most part to a gas ring with a penny-in-the-slot-meter. This is adequate only for boiling a kettle or frying non-existent bacon. In Dublin there are 130,000 persons dependent upon them. Owing to the stringent shortage of gas coal, gas is strictly rationed and is available only at certain hours of the day ... Lacking the facilities to cook the *pot au feu* or stew of the French peasant, the lowest income groups in Ireland subsist on bread and tea with an occasional bit of fried bacon or fat meat.[30]

Gray feared that the article – combined with the tendency in Irish newspapers to over-emphasise the success of Irish farmers in saving the harvest, the recent Irish gifts of food aid to Europe and the influx of British tourists into Ireland – hid the reality of the difficult situation facing Ireland. But not all officials in the United States administration were convinced by Gray's version: the prevailing view in the Department of Agriculture and the Office of War Mobilisation and Reconversion was that the Irish were better fed than others in Europe. This belief would surface again to influence ERP decisions on Ireland.

But Gray did have a point. Early signs of industrial recovery and improving employment levels were not sufficient to balance out other problems in the economy. Agricultural production fell 13 per cent between 1945 and 1947 because of a reduction in tillage, and unemployment remained high (9.3 per cent), despite a rise in industrial employment. A total of 24,000 persons emigrated in 1945 and 30,000 in 1946. An adverse trade and payments balance also emerged. Due to a trebling in the volume of imports, with little change in the volume of exports, a trade deficit of £92 million had accumulated by 1947.[31] The import-reliant economy found it difficult to prosper in a period of shortage, and Ireland's war-time record of neutrality, combined with the external perception that Ireland had enjoyed a 'comfortable' war, meant that Irish demands for

---

29 *Life*, June, 1946. **30** HSTL HSTP OF 426, Box 1273, 22 January 1947. **31** Kennedy, et al, *Economic Development*, pp 58–9.

scarce supplies from the Allies were not given priority by Washington or by international organisations.³²

By 1947, however, Ireland shared a prevailing European trend: it was increasingly reliant on the dollar area for imports. The United States accounted for 26.5 per cent of imports in 1947, compared with 10.9 per cent in 1938. A mere 0.74 per cent of Irish exports were destined for the United States, a level marginally higher than the 1938 figure of 0.48 per cent. Ireland's dollar deficit was financed by drawing on net invisible earnings comprised of emigrants' remittances and tourist earnings and on accumulated external assets in sterling. Between January and July 1947 the external assets of the Irish commercial banks were reduced by £16 million, leading the Department of Finance to fear that 'our external assets [were being] frittered away on consumer goods'.³³ There is little doubt, then, that an analysis of the Irish situation in early 1947 provided evidence of serious economic problems and social discontent.³⁴ The predominance of agriculture, an underdeveloped industrial base, a reliance on imports, particularly raw materials and capital goods, an export profile which relied substantially on British markets and the absence of comprehensive planning were all clearly symptoms sufficient to convince the United States to include Ireland in the Marshall Plan.

Other considerations besides the plight of the economy influenced Washington's decision. Ireland was regarded as 'an economic satellite of the United Kingdom', because of their close trading and financial ties.³⁵ The close relationship was also confirmed by Ireland's membership of the sterling pool. Thus it is not surprising that Washington viewed Ireland's role in ERP in relation to Britain and Europe. Further, the State Department believed that it was in agriculture, its chief industry and employer, that Ireland could make the 'most effective contribution to the success of the European Recovery Programme'. By increasing production and, therefore, food exports of 'high protein value on which she has traditionally concentrated and which she is particularly suited to produce – meat, eggs and dairy produce' – Ireland could play an important part in meeting 'an urgent demand and reducing the dependence of participating countries (especially Great Britain) on dollar sources of supply'.³⁶ Ireland's contribution to European, particularly British, recovery was 'primarily to provide

---

32 Ronan Fanning, *Independent Ireland* (Dublin, 1983), p. 154. **33** NAI DF F 17/7/47, 21 August 1947. The author wishes to record her gratitude to the Department of Finance for permission to consult its archives. **34** The question of whether the Marshall Plan saved Europe – the thesis posited by Alan Milward and Giorgio Fodor – may also be raised in relation to Ireland and will be explored in a forthcoming work on Ireland's experience of the Marshall Plan by the author. Meanwhile, see Alan Milward, *The Reconstruction of Western Europe* (London, 1984), pp 1–55; Giorgio Fodor, 'Why did Europe Need the Marshall Plan in 1947?', European University Institute Working Paper (Florence, 1984), no. 78, pp 1–41. **35** HSTL HSTP PSF, Box 256, CIA Ireland SR–48, 1 April 1949, p. 19. **36** NARA RG 84, SSR, 1936–49, Box 15, File 700, 20 March 1948.

additional food', thus reducing America's burden. A State Department study on participating countries, prepared in 1947, reached the same conclusion: only a 'relatively small' volume of food was involved, but the exports were 'in the important field of protein foods and fats'.[37] Increased Irish food exports to Britain would thus help alleviate the prevailing crisis situation. Yet without some external assistance Ireland would be unable to meet its own needs or to contribute to British food supplies.

Washington also recognised that Britain's financial problems would be eased by Irish membership in ERP. If Ireland received dollars from the Marshall Plan it could then 'avoid the necessity for making any net draw of gold and dollar reserves from the sterling area pool'.[38] This was a potent factor in 1947, given American concern about Britain's food and finances.

BRITISH SUPPORT

Britain favoured Ireland's inclusion in ERP for the same economic reasons. Most Irish exports went to Britain, and, while not large in terms of Britain's overall trading pattern, almost half of the total consisted of cattle, the remainder being mainly eggs, bacon, ham and butter. British interest in maintaining its neighbour as a supplier of food was evident from the results of a 1946 'fact-finding mission' to Ireland sponsored by the British Minster of Food 'in order to determine how far and [in] what ways Eire's agricultural output could be expanded both in the long – and short – term with mutual advantage to Eire and the UK'.

The study, conducted by two Oxford academics – A.W. Menzies-Kitchin, from the School of Agriculture, and John R. Raeburn, from the Agricultural Economic Research Institute – confirmed that 'Eire's farming is, in general, of a comparatively high standard ... tillage is well farmed ... the livestock are of excellent quality and well managed'.[39] In addition, both countries supported the aim of increasing agricultural output, especially among Irish agrarian free-trade interests who wanted to regain the pre-war share of British markets.[40] The Treasury encapsulated the British position in 1950: 'we can probably feel unreservedly thankful that we have an expanding food source close to hand'.[41] Clearly, ERP assistance would allow Ireland to expand agricultural output.

---

37 US Department of State, *Country Study* (Washington, 1948), Chapter VIII, Part II, p. 139. **38** NARA RG 84, SSR, 1936–49, Box 15, File 700, 20 March 1948. **39** A.W. Menzies-Kitchin, J.R. Raeburn, *Report on Éire Food Production and Export Possibilities* (London, 1947), pp 1–56. **40** Brian Girvin, 'The Political Economy of Failure: Ireland and Post-War Recovery', unpublished paper, p. 10. The author wishes to record her thanks to Dr Girvin for providing her with a copy of the paper. **41** PRO T 236, OF 37/151/01, 22 July 1950.

Not only would ERP provide Ireland with valuable imports, but it would also supply Ireland with the dollars to purchase them, which, in turn, would reduce Ireland's dependence on the sterling pool. Consequently, the onset of the dollar crisis in 1947, which added to the reduction of Ireland's sterling assets held in British bank deposits and security investments, copperfastened British support for Ireland's inclusion. The seriousness of the position is evident from an internal note prepared by Otto Clarke, a senior Treasury official, in January 1948:

> It is of considerable importance to us that Eire should be ready with a very strong case for herself. For if Eire gets insufficient aid the result reacts directly upon ourselves. Indeed it is pretty well the truth to say that it is more important to us that Eire should receive adequate aid than it is for Eire herself.[42]

The case for Ireland's inclusion was strong: its immediate economic difficulties in 1947 were similar to those of most countries in Western Europe; and the United States clearly considered Ireland to be part of Europe. Ireland could assist in relieving some other American headaches, especially British-induced ones. There were also persuasive political, diplomatic and security arguments for inclusion, Still, it was to be seen whether the atavism of partition and, more recently, neutrality would influence Ireland's approach to ERP and Washington's treatment of Ireland. In the short-term Ireland had to decide whether it wanted to be involved.

IRELAND'S RESPONSE

It was against this background that Ireland received an invitation on 4 July 1947 from Norman Archer, the acting British representative in Ireland, and Stanislas Ostroróg, the French minister, to attend a meeting in Paris on 12 July and 'take part in the drawing up of a programme covering both the resources and needs of Europe' for the following four years.[43] The Department of External Affairs, under the guidance of its new secretary, Frederick Boland, was predisposed to new international initiatives. Boland welcomed the opportunity to repair Ireland's international reputation after the damage inflicted by neutrality, de Valera's visit to the German legation, the burning of the British and American flags on VE day and its exclusion from the United Nations in 1946. Also, the Department had finally achieved a strong standing within the administration and, with de Valera's

---

42 PRO T 236, OF 265/13/1, 7 January 1948.   43 NAI DT S 14106/A, External Affairs to the Government, 4 July 1947.

support (as Dermot Keogh points out), it was ready to extend its contacts and horizons.[44] Exclusion from the UN had been a disappointment, but admission had been attempted with American and British support, which eventually led to Irish involvement in the World Health Organisation, the Food and Agriculture Organisation and the UN Conference on Trade and Development. Ireland had also hosted an international aviation conference in 1946 and attended Commonwealth conferences. Ireland did not take up every invitation – the Department of Finance cautioned the government against joining the International Trade Organisation, the General Agreement on Trade and Tariffs and the International Monetary Fund[45] – but, in general, from 1945 onwards Ireland gradually reentered the international mainstream. Consequently, the ERP invitation, which also included membership on the Committee on European Economic Cooperation (CEEC) and later the Organisation for European Economic Cooperation (OEEC), provided an ideal opportunity to expand the country's diplomatic horizons in a multilateral context. ERP participation was also welcomed by External Affairs, because it was 'the first time that Ireland has had an opportunity of cooperating in an international organisation in which the members of the British Commonwealth of Nations were not also participating'.[46]

The European dimension was noted by External Affairs: 'it is the first time that so many nations in Europe have banded themselves together for the purpose of complete economic cooperation'.[47] Also highlighted were American hopes that more permanent relationships would develop, a 'European Customs Union ... [or a] United States of Europe', for example. Still, European unity, *per se*, was not an active matter for Irish government policy in 1947. Hederman suggests that Irish attitudes to Europe and the rest of the world were influenced by four key features. Firstly, there was neutrality, which had officially isolated the country from the outside world from 1939 to 1945. Secondly, there was the ongoing preoccupation with partition, which outweighed all other foreign policy matters. Thirdly, there was emigration, which, on the one hand, isolated Ireland from mainland Europe because it was confined to English-speaking countries, but, on the other hand, ensured close links to emigrant destinations, especially the United States. Finally, while Irish nationalism was underpinned by strong feelings towards Britain and the United States, there were few close relations with any other nation-states.[48] Europe was viewed in a 'warm, nostalgic

---

44 Dermot Keogh, *Ireland and Europe 1919–1989: A Diplomatic and Political History* (Cork, 1989), p. 212. **45** Ronan Fanning, *The Irish Department of Finance, 1922–58* (Dublin, 1978), pp 386–7. **46** NAI DT S 14106/A, External Affairs to the Government, (nd) June 1947. **47** Ibid. **48** Miriam Hederman, 'The Beginning of the Discussion on European Union in Ireland', in Walter Lipgens and Wilfrid Loth (eds), *Documents on the History of European Integration: The Struggle for European Unity by Political Parties and Pressure Groups in Western European Countries, 1945–50* (Berlin, 1988), Series B, vol. 3, pp 763–9.

and idealised' way.⁴⁹ In 1948 Seán MacBride, the Minister for External Affairs, admitted during a Dáil debate on the United States of Europe that Ireland 'should need to think about these plans'.⁵⁰ He was correct: ERP participation would force the government and politicians alike to formulate a position on European cooperation.

In June 1947 the Department of External Affairs did offer a skilful analysis of George Marshall's Harvard speech that outlined American aims, the international reaction to it and matters for future discussion. External Affairs stressed that American motives were economic and political in nature: the achievement of economic recovery and social stability in Europe; the prevention of a slump in American prices; and, following from the Truman Doctrine, the provision of support for, and leadership of, the free world.⁵¹ Thus it was noted that the Marshall Plan was 'in line with President Truman's statements some months ago about the object of aid to Greece and Turkey'. Officials, though, found it 'difficult to see how the USA would give large scale assistance to Eastern European countries under Governments like that in Hungary'. It was clear to them that decisions taken under the ERP would be influenced by political, as much as economic, concerns. Neither this interpretation nor the anti-communist intent of the programme affected External Affairs' support for Ireland's acceptance of the invitation. Recent research has suggested that some Irish diplomats may have had misgivings about the implications of Soviet and American hegemonic aims for Europe and the possibility of its permanent enfeeblement.⁵² Certainly, *Quadragesimo Anno* condemned capitalism as well as communism, but, equally, Irish concerns may be explained by a desire to pursue a neutral line between the two blocs. Regardless, such fears were not potent enough to prevent External Affairs from favouring the acceptance of the invitation.

* * *

The response of the Department of Finance was less positive. Officials regarded the proposals as threatening their special relationship with the British Treasury. Not only was the Irish economy intertwined with Britain's in so many ways, but this closeness was especially evident in the personal ties and friendships which had developed between Finance and Treasury officials. Finance personnel were on first-name terms with their London counterparts, but not with their Irish colleagues in other departments. Ronan Fanning has detailed the evolution and

49 Hederman, 'The Beginning of the Discussion on European Union in Ireland', p. 764. **50** *Dáil Deb.*, 112, 903, 20 July 1948. **51** NAI DT S 14106/A, External Affairs to the Government, (nd) June 1947. **52** Raymond J. Raymond, 'The Marshall Plan and Ireland', in P.J. Drudy (ed.), *The Irish In America: Emigration, Assimilation and Impact* (Cambridge, 1985), p. 300; Desmond Dinan, 'After the "Emergency": Ireland in the Post-war World, 1945–50', *Éire–Ireland*, vol. 24, no. 3 (Fall, 1989), pp 85–103.

strength of this relationship.⁵³ Consequently, the possibility that Ireland's economic future might lie in a European context, thereby disrupting long-standing professional and personal arrangements, was anathema to the department. A second cause for worry was that European involvement would strengthen External Affairs' growing assertiveness in administrative circles.⁵⁴ Finance's fears in this regard were soon realised when External Affairs assumed the leading role in the ERP, directly challenging its control of foreign economic affairs. According to Patrick Lynch, who was in Finance at the time, Boland had already insisted that direct negotiations between British and Irish departments should cease and should instead be conducted through External Affairs.⁵⁵

Of more immediate concern to Finance officials in 1947 were the economic implications of acceptance. J.J. McElligott, secretary of the Department of Finance, believed that Ireland could not expect 'any measure of salvation from the so-called Marshall Plan'.⁵⁶ Instead, ERP funds would deepen, rather than ameliorate, Ireland's problems through increased, heavy and unjustifiable borrowing. Likewise, if free convertibility of sterling existed 'we would have no interest in US aid'. Indeed, Finance wanted to 'avoid the indignity of accepting US aid'. Finance officials feared that greater access to American sources of supplies would result in a growth in imports, which, without an equivalent increase in exports, would hasten the depletion of external reserves. Finance's perennial worry concerning excessive state expenditure also surfaced: 'While it might seem to be a great advantage for the national exchequer to have access to a large volume of funds easily obtained, there were dangers inherent in a facility of this sort which provided a standing temptation to governments to incur expenditure without regard to the economic consequences.' The Department doubted whether acceptance of 'direct aid from the US to overcome … difficulties will be to our ultimate advantage'.

Such misgivings were echoed by the Central Bank: its 1948 Annual Report stated that despite the 'chronic' condition of the Irish balance of payments, 'a loan contract of this kind is a gamble on uncertain future exchange relations of the Irish pound, the pound sterling and the American dollar'.⁵⁷ It argued that ERP assistance should only be accepted as an 'act of necessity', adding that if the funds were spent in any manner other than debt redemption they 'would strengthen inflationary influences'. The two key financial institutions in the state thus opposed participation in the ERP. But, given the dollar crisis and Britain's welcome of the Marshall Plan, they had little choice but to accept Ireland's entry. Their scepticism regarding the entire project, however, would run counter to External Affairs' enthusiasm throughout the entire period.

53 Ronan Fanning, *The Irish Department of Finance, 1922–58* (Dublin 1978), *passim*. 54 See Keogh, *Ireland and Europe, 1919–1989*, pp 197–223. 55 Fanning, *The Irish Department of Finance*, p. 408. 56 NAI DF F 121/10/48, 3 February 1948. 57 *Report of the Central Bank of Ireland for the Year Ended 31/3/1948* (Dublin, 1948).

The Departments of External Affairs and Finance were the main protagonists on the merits of accepting ERP funds, but membership had immediate implications for the work of the Departments of Agriculture and Industry and Commerce. Ireland's invitation indicated that Britain and France viewed the future work of the CEEC proceeding through four technical sub-committees in the areas of food and agriculture, fuel and power, iron and steel, and transport. The main concern of the Department of Agriculture in 1947 was to increase agricultural output and exports, a policy which depended on acquiring 'sufficient supplies of feeding stuffs and fertilisers'.[58] Accordingly, if the department could be said to have a long-term policy, it coincided with Washington's and London's Irish plans: increase and improve agricultural output beyond pre-war levels and direct exports primarily to Britain. As far as the Department of Agriculture and the Fianna Fáil government were concerned, there would be no change from the conclusion reached by the Menzies-Kitchin/Raeburn report: Irish agricultural progress was linked to the British market. Agriculture, therefore, welcomed Marshall aid because it would provide access to much-needed supplies. Its response, though, did not focus on the possibilities of expanding beyond the British market. Nevertheless, for Agriculture and, indeed, for Industry and Commerce, ERP involvement meant that the European dimension of Ireland's foreign trade would have to be faced soon, along with the implications for the productivity and efficiency of the Irish economy.

Each of these departments responded officially to the British invitation between 5 June and 4 July and, excepting Finance's worries, all were in agreement that Ireland had no real alternative but to accept it. Regardless of the consequences for neutrality and sovereignty, the state of the economy in the summer of 1947 was the most influential of all the factors – and realism prevailed. If Britain was accepting assistance Ireland had little choice but to follow suit, a factor which was not lost on Finance officials and one which reveals the limits of Irish economic independence. The cabinet met, discussed and unanimously accepted the formal invitation on 4 July 1947, the same day it had been delivered by Norman Archer. Seán Lemass, Minister for Industry and Commerce, would lead the Irish delegation to the Paris conference, which also included Patrick Smith, Minister for Agriculture, and Frederick Boland.

Ireland did not attach any conditions to its involvement, unlike Switzerland and Italy. The Swiss *provisos* related to protecting its traditional neutral status, ensuring that CEEC economic agreements would not be of a binding character without its agreement and, finally, reserving the right to maintain trade agreements with non-CEEC countries. All were regarded by the Swiss as key issues of national concern. Ireland's neutral status might have permitted the attachments of similar terms to its membership, yet the opportunity was not taken. Italian

---

58 NAI DT S 13965/B, Agriculture to External Affairs, 11 October 1947.

acceptance was accompanied by the condition that the CEEC did not form an anti-Soviet bloc, which might also have caused concern to neutral Ireland. Clearly, the government and External Affairs believed that Irish neutrality would not be jeopardised by involvement in the American-sponsored programme. Safeguarding neutrality was not an obvious problem, but the need for economic assistance was an immediate one.[59]

PUBLIC REACTION

The government quickly decided that Ireland should participate in the Marshall Plan, but to what extent did this decision represent the wishes of the Irish public, particularly those interest groups whose activities would be directly affected. The Irish pattern of Anglo–American external ties (outlined above) was clearly the result of history rather than geography and indicates that the isolationism which was favoured during the war could never fully counteract the depth of feelings towards, and ties with, the rest of the world. However, this should not be interpreted to mean that the public and its political representatives displayed a strong interest in foreign affairs. On the contrary, foreign policy was rarely discussed, with partition being the main exception. This indifference resulted from, among other reasons, Eamon de Valera's secretive approach to policymaking generally.[60]

The public received little information on the Marshall Plan invitation from its political leaders. The government did not release any public statements about the programme until the official acceptance was published in the newspapers on 6 July. On 4 July the Independent Deputy James Dillon had asked Frank Aiken, Minister for Finance, if an invitation to attend the Paris conference had been received; Aiken answered in the negative, but added that one was expected soon.[61] Not until October did the opposition parties again raise the Marshall Plan in the Dáil or Seanad. Richard Mulcahy, the leader of Fine Gael, was one of only three deputies to refer to the topic on 8 October, mainly to inquire about Ireland's contribution to the proposed programme. In a short reply de Valera stated that the estimates were prepared 'from information already available to the Departments', the work was 'too extensive' to discuss at the moment and copies of the report and that of the technical sub-committees would be

---

59 Frederick Boland, in an interview, indicated that Frank Aiken was hostile to participation because it would divide Europe, thus forcing Ireland to abandon neutrality, and it would affect Ireland's access to the sterling pool: HSTL, 'Ireland in the European Recovery Program, 1947–53', Oral History Project, 1978 (conducted by Raymond J. Raymond). **60** T.D. Williams, 'A Study in Neutrality', *Leader*, 31 January 1953. **61** *Dáil Deb.*, 107, 1006–8, 4 July 1947.

placed in the Dáil library.⁶² None of the questions focused on the long-term economic implications of involvement for the domestic economy nor on the political dimensions. Neither did the opposition parties seek a full-scale debate on the topic nor raise it again until the Inter-Party government took office in February 1948. Thus the main opposition parties – Fine Gael, Labour, Clann na Poblachta – did not oppose the government's decision to accept the invitation, although the *Irish People*, the official organ of the Labour Party, warned on 19 July 1947 that 'danger lies in the fact that the USA may expect damaging political and social concessions from the smaller nations in return for material goods'.⁶³ Indeed, except for partition, there was rarely little difference between the attitude of the government and the opposition parties to foreign affairs. On this occasion, the economic argument for acceptance could not be denied, and Clann na Poblachta particularly welcomed the opportunity for Ireland to act independently of Britain.⁶⁴

For those politicians and members of the public interested in foreign affairs, the newspapers were the only other source of information. In the post-war period all three Irish daily newspapers – *Irish Independent*, *Irish Press* and *Irish Times* – relied heavily on international news agencies for information on foreign events. Most of these reports were not prepared for the Irish public and provided little analysis of events from an Irish perspective.⁶⁵ In general, the newspapers welcomed George Marshall's speech and reproduced parts of it, while the news agency reports detailed the behind-the-scenes negotiations between Britain, France, America and the Soviet Union. Following publication of Ireland's acceptance announcement, the limited newspaper analyses focused on some of the domestic implications of the invitation: the end of isolation, the chance to reinforce Irish independence and the economic benefits. The consequences for neutrality or sovereignty were not explored nor were the international political implications *vis-à-vis* the developing Cold War and European integration.

Civil servants who were directly involved, such as T.K. Whitaker and Frederick Boland, recalled a distinct lack of public awareness. This may be explained by a combination of factors: the political consensus on participation; a lack of information; a culture of secrecy in decision-making circles; and the state of the economy. Whitaker remembered that there was 'certainly no interest group activity' about the plan.⁶⁶ Certainly, consultations between the govern-

62 *Dáil Deb.*, 108, 1–4, 8 October 1947. **63** *Irish People*, 19 July 1947: UCDA, Sean MacEntee Papers, P67/548. **64** Peadar Cowan, the Clann na Poblachta TD, was the only politician to publicly oppose Marshall aid because of his belief that it involved a substantial surrender of Ireland's sovereign rights as a nation. **65** For a further review of this topic, see Miriam Hederman, *The Road to Europe: Irish Attitudes, 1948–61* (Dublin 1983), pp 77–92. **66** HSTL, 'Ireland in the European Recovery Program 1947–53'. As the Marshall Plan unfolded,

ment and interest groups on foreign policy decisions were rare. The government's decision-making process on ERP membership, therefore, was no different than its handling of other matters. It is important to note, though, that in the future the Economic Cooperation Administration (the American bureaucracy which administered the Marshall Plan) did encourage interest group cooperation, particularly between business management and trade unions and aming voluntary rural organisations, viewing it as a way of achieving domestic consensus and economic and social stability: the politics of the 'New Deal' would underpin the Marshall planners' attempt to remake the 'old world' in the likeness of the 'new world'. This was not a feature of government practice in Ireland in 1947, but Irish interest groups eventually did comment on the significance of ERP membership for their own organisations.

Early public reaction to the Marshall Plan predictably reflected the conservative, Catholic, anti-communist nature of Irish society. Groups representing rural interests, such as Muintir na Tire, the Agricultural Association of Ireland and the Young Farmers' Club, although distracted by internal divisions, supported involvement because of the intended focus on increased agricultural output. *The Landmark*, the journal of Muintir na Tire, noted that the plan was 'designed to check further Soviet aggression by an orderly restoration of the economic health of Western Europe'.[67]

At this early stage, the implications for Ireland of the underlying free-trade principles and the demands of modernisation inherent to the Marshall Plan did not attract much notice. In 1947 the attention of most workers was, like that of farmers, focused on internal feuds and the state of the economy. The ITUC's and CIU's interest in ERP centred on protecting jobs and wages and improving standards of living generally. Short-term gain was also the central theme of the industrial sector's reaction: the construction industry welcomed America's 'generosity' and hoped the 'unprecedented transfer of capital ... [would] ... be used only for the purposes of economic recovery and stabilisation'.[68] The underdeveloped business sector welcomed the opportunity to obtain goods and capital, but feared the lowering of protectionist legislation and competition, particularly from American goods. Ultimately, the farmers, factory owners, workers and traders could not, in the words of George Duncan, the Trinity College economist, look 'a gift-horse in the mouth', particularly an American one.[69]

---

both local and national newspapers became more interested in ERP. **67** *The Landmark*, December 1947. As details of the CEEC deliberations emerged from Paris – and as ERP evolved – the small communist group in Ireland, through its newspaper, *Review*, began to cover Marshall Plan deliberations regularly. It was described as a 'Wall Street-inspired imperialist plan': *Review*, August 1947, p. 3. **68** *The Irish Builder and Engineer*, May 1948. **69** George A. Duncan, 'Marshall Aid', *Journal of the Statistical and Social Inquiry Society of Ireland*, vol. 18 (1949–50), p. 293.

CONCLUSION

In the immediate post-war years many forces drew Ireland into the Marshall Plan. Firstly, the demands of American and British economic, political, strategic and diplomatic policies necessitated it. Secondly, the needs of the Irish economy, particularly the shortage of dollars in 1947, meant that Ireland had little choice but to participate. Thus it is apparent that Ireland had little or no control over its own destiny on this matter. But its decision to join the Marshall Plan did not mark a break with several existing trends of the post-war era: an expansion of foreign policy horizons; the continued domination of agriculture within the economy; the under-development of industry; and a reliance on British markets as the destination for Irish exports. Finally, the decision-making process reflected the culture of secrecy which characterised de Valera's style of governing.

But the invitation also challenged the Irish government. During the summer of 1947, Irish officials based in Dublin and Paris found themselves operating at a supranational level, often responding to requests from American officials and the CEEC for economic statistics and performance targets for the economy within both national and European contexts. In the political arena the government was at last forced to confront the European issue and reconcile it with traditional foreign policy concerns: the nature and extent of Ireland's commitment to European unity had to be faced. The summer of 1947 signalled the beginning of a greater involvement in European affairs and greater contact with America, particularly on economic issues, than was hitherto the case. Ireland swiftly accepted Marshall aid, even though the programme had not even been fully developed by Washington.[70] It soon became clear, however, that there were strings attached to membership, conditions that would affect Ireland's long-term participation in the programme. Furthermore, it remained to be seen whether ERP assistance would lead Ireland into a period of expansion and growth similar to that experienced by much of Western Europe during the 1950s.

---

70 These themes are explored in greater detail in the following chapter.

The Enthusiastic Response of a Reluctant Supporter: Ireland and the Committee for European Economic Cooperation in the Summer of 1947

Till Geiger

INTRODUCTION

Two competing interpretations of Ireland's involvement in the Marshall Plan are emerging in the growing body of historical literature on this topic.[1] The dominant position, put forward by Brian Girvin and others, argues that the Irish government was a reluctant participant in the process of European reconstruction due to its deep-seated isolationism.[2] Gary Murphy has challenged this view by arguing that Ireland's participation in the Marshall Plan paved the way for the far more outward looking policies adopted in the late 1950s.[3] While Girvin interprets the Irish reluctance about the European Recovery Programme (ERP) as part of a wider rejection of modernisation by Irish policymakers, Murphy argues that the Irish foreign policy-making community embraced European integration in order to open Ireland to outside influences.

These two positions mirror a similar divergence of views between two earlier writers on Ireland's involvement in negotiating the Marshall Plan, Desmond Dinan and Raymond J. Raymond. In an article published in 1989 Dinan emphasised that the reluctance of the Fianna Fáil government to participate in the American-sponsored conference in Paris in the summer of 1947 was in marked contrast to the Inter-Party government's enthusiasm for the Marshall Plan after its election in April 1948.[4] Following a similar line of argument to

---

1 This statement is based on the papers of a recent conference on Ireland and the Marshall Plan organised by the Irish Association of Contemporary European Studies and held in Dublin in January 1999. This paper is an extended version of a contribution to this conference. I am grateful to Michael Kennedy, Hilary Owen, Joseph Skelly and Bernadette Whelan for their comments and suggestions during the writing of this chapter. 2 Brian Girvin, 'Why did Ireland not benefit from the Marshall Plan? A Comparative Approach', in Mary Browne, Till Geiger and Michael Kennedy (eds), *Ireland, Europe and the Marshall Plan* (forthcoming, Dublin, 2000). 3 Gary Murphy, 'Persuading the Americans?: The Irish Administrative and Political Response to Marshall Aid', in Mary Browne, Till Geiger and Michael Kennedy (eds), *Ireland, Europe and the Marshall Plan* (forthcoming, Dublin, 2000). 4 Desmond Dinan, 'After the Emergency: Ireland

Murphy, Raymond argued that the Irish Department of External Affairs positively embraced the Marshall Plan from the beginning.[5]

Bernadette Whelan's contribution to this volume examines the initial Irish response to the American initiative on European recovery and Ireland's inclusion in the Marshall Plan. Her assessment combines strands of both Girvin's and Murphy's analysis by arguing that Ireland's post-war opening to the outside world did not represent a break with established foreign and economic policies, though she concludes that participation in the Marshall Plan posed a challenge to the Irish government. Taking Whelan's finding as its starting point, this chapter reexamines Ireland's participation in the deliberations of the Committee for European Economic Cooperation (CEEC) in the summer of 1947 in order to shed new light on the Irish reaction to the challenge of the Marshall Plan.

* * *

Writings on post-war European integration provide an interesting perspective on the current debate about the Irish response to the Marshall Plan. To some extent, Murphy's interpretation echoes the pioneering study by the Dutch diplomat, Ernst van der Beugel, published in 1966. In his book, van der Beugel argued that the delegates to the Paris conference of the CEEC worked closely together in the summer of 1947 to formulate a European response to the American proposal for a Marshall Plan. During the Paris conference, national representatives transcended, to some extent, their specifically national viewpoints for the greater common good. In this sense, the CEEC deliberations fostered the conviction among officials throughout Europe that further cooperation presented the only solution to Europe's economic problems. Through this experience many officials developed an extended loyalty not just to their national governments, but also to the process of continued European cooperation. Therefore, van der Beugel suggested that at Paris:

> a group of international-minded men was formed on many administrative levels. The officials in the Ministry of Transport or in the Treasury suddenly became part of a European machinery, feeling responsible for a joint venture. It was a primary school for many men who would play a major role on the post-war European scene, with additional loyalties to a broader entity than to their own government. The affinity between these men who worked in Paris day and night during the summer of 1947 formed an indispensable element for future cooperation.[6]

in the Post-War World, 1945–50', *Eire-Ireland*, vol. 24, no. 3 (1989), pp 86–8. **5** Raymond James Raymond, 'The Marshall Plan and Ireland', in P. J. Drury (ed.), *The Irish in America: Emigration, Assimilation and Impact* (Cambridge, 1985), pp 295–328. **6** Ernst H. van der Beugel, *From Marshall Aid to Atlantic Partnership: European Integration as a Concern of American Foreign Policy* (Amsterdam, 1966), p. 72.

Following van der Beugel's line of argument, the CEEC deliberations could be seen as a learning process leading to the formation of a community of policy-makers that would push for further European integration.

In his critique of van der Beugel's position, Alan Milward interprets the quoted passage as implying that this nascent community of civil servants developed a sense of solidarity against their national governments, even if they failed to see the advantages of further cooperation. Arguably, Milward over-interprets van der Beugel's statement to lend weight to his own contention that national governments primarily strove to safeguard their own national interests in the CEEC deliberations. For example, Milward shows how Britain and France sought to control the discussions at the Paris conference through the creation of an executive committee to oversee the deliberations.[7] Milward, however, is right that van der Beugel downplayed the considerable gulf between the American and European governments, because he saw European integration as resulting from the concordance of policy objectives on both sides of the Atlantic.[8]

Nevertheless, the two positions are less incompatible than it may at first seem. For example, the Benelux countries, with support from the Italian government, regarded increased European economic integration as in their immediate national interest. The CEEC deliberations, therefore, provided the opportunity for some countries to pursue their own interests in the revitalisation of intra-European trade. To some extent, this interest in the liberalisation of Western European trade clashed with the domestic reconstruction plans of other CEEC countries, particularly Britain and France. Arguably, these different positions reflected the potential conflict between national economic policy regimes and the market expansion the Americans demanded.[9] The head of the United Nations Economic Commission for Europe (ECE), Gunnar Myrdal, argued that this friction emerged from these conflicting imperatives of restoring national as well as international economic integration in the immediate post-war period.[10] After 1945 many politicians remained apprehensive about surrendering sovereignty over their national economies, because of the recent experience of massive domestic economic problems and the disintegration of the world economy during the inter-war period. While American policymakers believed in market expansion as a panacea for Europe's economic problems, their Western European counterparts argued that the considerable differences in economic development and economic policy regimes between the various CEEC countries ruled out the creation of a single European market.

---

7 Alan S. Milward, *The Reconstruction of Western Europe, 1945–51* (London, 1984), pp 65–6. **8** Milward, *The Reconstruction of Western Europe*, p. 86, fn. 82. **9** Walter Lipgens, *Anfänge der Europäischen Einigungspolitik, 1945–1950* (Stuttgart, 1977), pp 491–510. **10** Gunnar Myrdal, *An International Economy: Problems and Prospects* (London, 1955), pp 17–71.

In the summer of 1947 American foreign policymakers had not quite abandoned the hope of a new international economic order based on the Bretton Woods accords. Still, the Marshall Plan initiative implicitly acknowledged the failure of the International Monetary Fund to achieve an ordered return to a stable international financial system and the slow progress in the negotiations of an agreement on international trade. But American policymakers only reached this conclusion as their thinking about the European Recovery Programme took on a more concrete form during the summer months. At the same time, American planners failed to perceive that the liberalisation of intra-European, let alone international, trade could not be achieved through the creation of a new set of international organisations, but required the restoration of trust between potential trading partners. American economic power had, to some extent, become the major barrier to any international agreement on trade liberalisation in the immediate post-war period, because other governments feared that ending discrimination against imports from the United States would rapidly diminish their meagre dollar reserves and threaten their economic recovery.[11] At the same time, the American Army Department pressed for the revitalisation of the West German economy in order to reduce the cost of feeding their zone of occupation. For officials in the State Department, European and German recovery were intrinsically linked. On this point, American policymakers also underestimated the likely European opposition and ill feeling about the impending announcement of raising the production ceilings for German industry in the American zone of occupation. Policymakers on both sides of the Atlantic thus perceived the economic problem of European reconstruction differently. Conflicts over the form and content of the ERP were inevitable as a consequence.[12]

It would appear that the current Irish historiographical debate is displaying the reverse trend to the discussion now obtaining in the wider literature on the Marshall Plan. While Milward and others have deemphasised the role of the ERP in the process of European integration, Murphy reasserts its importance for the opening up of Irish foreign policy in the 1950s. Milward's analysis, concurrently, shows that other European governments shared the reluctance of the Irish government regarding the American proposals. This chapter compares the Irish response to the Marshall Plan initiative in the summer of 1947 to that of other European governments. It is primarily based on a close reading of Irish records from the Paris conference, but also uses the accounts of Milward, van der Beugel and others as reference points. In contrast to earlier accounts, this

---

11 Hubert Henderson, 'The European Economic Report', *International Affairs,* vol. 24, no. 1 (1948), pp 19–28.   12 Werner Bührer, *Westdeutschland in der OEEC: Eingliederung, Krise, Bewährung 1947–1961* (München, 1997), pp 37–71; Gerd Hardach, *Der Marshall-Plan: Auslandshilfe und Wiederaufbau in Westdeutschland, 1948–1952* (München, 1994), pp 17–56.

chapter focuses on the Irish government's position on the three key issues that dominated the CEEC's deliberations: German recovery, European economic integration and the problem of American power.

SEÁN LEMASS AND IRELAND'S REEMERGENCE ON THE EUROPEAN STAGE

The ambivalence about Ireland's position is reflected in a speech by the Minister for Industry and Commerce, Seán Lemass, to the Conference of European Economic Cooperation in July 1947. Having been sent to Paris by Eamon de Valera, Lemass used his opening statement to lecture the assembled delegates on international trade and Ireland's difficult economic position as a small post-colonial country with a large neighbour:

> We know by theory and experience that we cannot insulate ourselves from the effects of economic decline in other states. This is probably true for all states, but it is unquestionably true for the smaller nations whose power to protect themselves against the repercussions of economic upheavals outside their boundaries is very small, and whose progress must of necessity keep in step with that of their greater neighbours with whom they trade.[13]

Lemass concluded that Europe's economic problems could not be resolved by short-term measures, but required a coordinated plan to ensure full recovery in western Europe. He stated that within such a framework the Irish government would gladly implement all proposals which might augment Ireland's contribution to Western European recovery. Yet he warned that '[a]t best our contribution cannot be a large one. We are a small country which only in the comparatively recent past has won its freedom after a long struggle that delayed our economic development, which indeed is still hampered by the division of our national territory'.[14]

For Lemass, Ireland was still engaged in the process of national development and could only make a limited contribution to Western European recovery. He assumed, nonetheless, the role of seasoned international statesman, praising the Marshall Plan initiative as an opportunity to build a strong European economy, which would provide the basis for long-term peace and stability. Since Irish ministers tended to use any occasion to raise the issue of partition, Lemass' statements about Ireland's divided economy were hardly surprising, but they

---

[13] NAI DFA 305/57/I, European Economic Cooperation Conference, EECC/9, speech by Lemass, 14 July 1947. [14] Ibid.

reflected a deep political conviction that economic nationalism was a precondition to economic development. To Lemass' mind, the underdeveloped and divided state of Ireland's economy justified the government's protectionist policies and prevented the country from playing a more significant role in the efforts to integrate the Western European economy.

* * *

At first glance, Lemass' endorsement of economic nationalism seems to reflect the European trend of strengthening the state's control over the economy. But his statement ignored the fact that Ireland's economy was largely integrated into the British labour, capital and factor markets. The cold weather during the winter 1946–7 had demonstrated the dependence of the Irish economy on imports of British coal. In May 1947 Lemass announced that the government aimed to reduce Ireland's dependence on British re-exporters and prevent a repetition of the 1946–7 fuel crisis by purchasing sixty shiploads of American coal.[15] Likewise, Ireland largely depended on the British market for its exports. But while government ministers demanded unrestricted access for Irish agricultural exports to the British market, they were unwilling to open the Irish market to foreign imports.[16] So in this sense, an end to partition would not achieve national economic integration.

Lemass' obsession with partition reflected a particular Irish concern, because many other European governments at that time were trying to restore national economic integration by overcoming shortages and eradicating widespread blackmarkets. To achieve this objective, most governments accepted that the return to a highly integrated market economy required the existence of strong social solidarity among their citizenry and, therefore, necessitated a widening of social welfare provisions. Much of the reluctance of Western European countries to accept international economic integration reflected the fears that such a step might undermine domestic social welfare reforms.[17] Given the relative social stability of Irish society in this period, ministers in Dublin felt less compelled to adopt the comprehensive social welfare measures of other European countries. Lemass' speech thus reflected more than a degree of apprehension about the American proposals for a united Europe. Its defensive undertones, moreover, suggest that the Irish government had yet to formulate a policy on the American initiative for a European recovery plan.

Press coverage of Lemass' address highlighted its noncommittal tone. In Ireland the leader writers of the *Sunday Independent* criticised Lemass for failing

---

15 'Ireland – In the Economic Crisis', *Roundtable*, vol. 37, no. 147 (1947), pp 276–83; 'Mr. Lemass on Expansionist Foreign Trade Policy and Exclusion of British Trade Intervention – Large Coal Purchase in USA', *Keesing's Contemporary Archive*, vol. 6, 31 May–6 June 1947, 8640/A. **16** On this point, see 'Ireland after Twenty-Five Years', *Roundtable*, vol. 37, no. 146 (1947), pp 160–6. **17** Myrdal, *An International Economy*, pp 59–71.

to plead the case for inclusion of Spain in the ERP.[18] Outside Ireland the speech went largely unnoticed, except for rather critical comments in the Belgian evening paper *Le Soir*. It described Lemass' attitude as anachronistic, given the spirit of good will among the other delegations at the Paris conference:

> The unanimity of the delegates, the absence of obstruction and their desire to limit themselves to the economic field are combined with a sharp susceptibility for their political independence. This was clear when the representative of Eire (*sic*) did not fail in his discourse to pass two remarks which were disagreeable to Great Britain, which the latter bore with phlegm. On the contrary, the gesture of Count Sforza in bowing before the ambassador of Greece and the handshake sealing the reconciliation of two countries which Fascism had made enemies shows that the conference can contribute to the mutual understanding of the peoples.[19]

Lemass' speech during the July meeting of the CEEC in Paris thus inauspiciously launched Ireland's participation in the Marshall Plan.

GETTING DOWN TO WORK: FREDERICK H. BOLAND'S QUIET DIPLOMACY

After the foreign ministers had departed, officials from the various participating countries began preparing Europe's response to the American proposals.[20] The Irish delegation to the CEEC was headed by the secretary of the Department of External Affairs, Frederick Boland. Reporting on the preliminary discussions in late July, he noted several procedural issues that required settling, the emergence of conflicting national positions and the formation of nascent coalitions. On procedural matters Boland informed Dublin that no decision had been reached on whether the final report would be written by the whole CEEC or by the executive committee, which consisted of delegates from France, Italy, Norway, the Netherlands and the United Kingdom. Boland did not state what solution he preferred, even though the option to leave the task to the executive committee would have excluded Irish representatives from taking part in the decision-making.

Boland recounted the intervention of the Dutch representative, Hans Hirschfeld, who argued in favour of German economic revitalisation and the

---

18 'Ireland and the Paris Conference', *Sunday Independent*, 13 July 1947. **19** NAI DFA 305/57/I, letter, Brussels embassy to secretary, 2 August 1947. **20** The following analysis is based on ibid., report by Boland entitled Work of Cooperation Committee, 19 July 1947 [hereafter Work of the Cooperation Committee].

restoration of intra-European trade. Hirschfeld criticised the French position, which, by downplaying the scope for European initiatives, exaggerated the continent's likely dependence on American financial aid. The French delegates, however, vehemently objected to the possibility of a West German industrial revival, because this might lead to the eventual reemergence of a German military threat to French national security. Still, they argued that it would be desirable to expand as rapidly as possible German coal exports, which would assist the economic recovery of the other European countries, and agricultural production, which would reduce the cost to the Allied exchequers of feeding Germany.

The Swedish representative, Dag Hammarskjöld, supported the Dutch call for a clear commitment to the multilateral liberalisation of intra-European trade. He opposed the American demands for a permanent organisation of the CEEC states to administer the distribution of American Marshall aid, because such an organisation would encroach on the work of the United Nations Economic Commission for Europe.[21] Even though Boland did not make this point, the Swedish concern about the future role of ECE mattered less from an Irish perspective, because Ireland had not yet been invited to participate in ECE deliberations as an associate member.[22] Besides the concerns about the potential duplication of efforts to coordinate European economic cooperation, Hammarskjöld objected to a questionnaire proposed by the French delegation as a basis to draw up a European recovery plan. In reply to Hammarskjöld, the head of the British delegation, Oliver Franks, pointed out that the use of the questionnaire would go a long way towards meeting American expectations regarding the European response. This argument struck Boland and most other delegations as eminently reasonable, and they agreed to the questionnaire as a necessary evil.

* * *

In his report Boland observed that the Scandinavian and Benelux countries, as well as Greece and Turkey, tended to act in unison. Ireland, in contrast, seemed outside any such grouping. Arising from this observation, the Department of External Affairs sought to define its role within the CEEC and the wider European community. On the search for potential allies, Iveagh House wrote to its embassies in Berne, Lisbon, Rome and Stockholm requesting reports about the domestic press coverage of the Marshall Plan conference and the likely policy response of the respective national governments.[23] The selection of the

---

[21] The Scandinavian governments had initially insisted that the American initiative should not supplant the United Nations' efforts to co-ordinate European recovery; see Milward, *The Reconstruction of Europe*, p. 81. [22] Ireland was invited to participate after the second session of the ECE in the summer 1947: see Political and Economic Planning, *European Organisations* (London, 1959), p. 21. [23] NAI DFA 305/57/1, telegrams, External Affairs to Stockholm, Lisbon, Berne, Rome, Brussels, 30 July 1947.

four embassies is revealing about External Affair's mental picture of Ireland as part of a group of small, neutral countries (that is, Sweden and Switzerland), but also of Ireland belonging to the circle of underdeveloped Catholic societies (that is, Italy and Portugal). The responses from the various embassies were fairly general, however. Stockholm added nothing to Boland's private conversations with Swedish officials during the CEEC meeting several weeks earlier;[24] the report from Brussels devoted most of its space to the criticism of Lemass' speech in *Le Soir*, which is cited above.[25]

A private conversation Boland had with Dag Hammarskjöld reveals another aspect of Ireland's initial views on European reconstruction. According to Boland, Hammarskjöld told him that Sweden did not want dollar aid, but sought the removal of barriers to intra-European trade and the restoration of exchange convertibility. He argued that the restoration of intra-European trade would allow a return to normal productivity levels in Western Europe. Boland replied that Ireland had similar interests beyond an affinity to the British position, because of its membership of the Commonwealth and the sterling area.[26] Boland's statement is intriguing, because it sets out, and implicitly ranks, Irish objectives in the CEEC negotiations. While Boland accorded an overriding importance to the Anglo–Irish economic relationship due to existing institutional links, he suggested that Ireland's primary interest was the revival of intra-European trade rather than obtaining dollar aid. At one level, this statement suggests that Boland and other Irish policymakers felt that Ireland would benefit more from a revival of multilateral trade in Europe than from dollar aid. In the immediate post-war period, however, almost 90 per cent of Irish exports went to the British market. The Fianna Fáil government thus made restoring Anglo–Irish trade a priority, while blocking Lemass' initiatives to promote economic development.[27] In line with the government's economic objectives, Boland implicitly argued that Ireland did not necessarily need the Marshall Plan. In this sense, his views reflected the absence of a coherent vision for economic development within the Irish government.

The contrast between Lemass' opening statement and Boland's quiet diplomacy is remarkable. In the search for potential allies, Boland projected a less hostile attitude than Lemass on the issues of future economic cooperation and a return to multilateral trade in Europe. For Boland and Iveagh House officials, the CEEC presented an opportunity to return to the international stage after years of self-enforced isolation.[28]

---

24 These private conversations are discussed in more detail below in the text: see ibid., letter, Stockholm embassy to secretary, 25 July 1947; Work of Cooperation Committee.   **25** Ibid., letter, Brussels embassy to secretary, 2 August 1947.   **26** Ibid., Work of Cooperation Committee.   **27** Nearly 90 per cent of Irish exports went to the United Kingdom in this period: see Brian Girvin, 'Ireland and the Marshall Plan: A Cargo Cult in the North Atlantic', in R.T. Griffiths (ed.), *Explorations in OEEC History* (Paris 1997), pp 61–4.   **28** On this point, see also Raymond,

IRISH AND AMERICAN VIEWS ON EUROPEAN RECONSTRUCTION

On the fringes of the initial CEEC meeting, Freddie Boland encountered his first taste of America's 'friendly help' in steering the European cooperation effort in the right direction. Lemass' opening statement expressed at least scepticism, if not outright opposition, to American demands for positive steps towards European economic integration. The assistant to the American ambassador to Paris, Ivan White, stressed the overriding importance of this objective to the Truman administration in a conversation with Boland at the end of July. He underlined the imperative of a common European plan for reconstruction which would provide an analysis of Europe's current economic problems and demonstrate the willingness of Western European countries to work together. In this context, White objected to any further bilateral trade agreements among European countries. He indicated that the Truman administration supported a Benelux customs union and favoured amending the charter of the International Trade Organisation (ITO) to permit the creation of further customs unions. Indeed, the American government expected similar initiatives leading to greater European economic unity to emerge from the Paris conference.

Boland voiced his strong opposition to the American proposals for an intra-European customs union without consulting with government ministers, because he was sure that they would concur with him. Given the weakness of the Irish economy, he insisted that his government would have to retain its protective tariffs to protect its fledgling industries. Since the Irish economy depended heavily on access to the British market, Boland emphatically stated that 'while anything like a customs union was out of the question, [he] could imagine close economic arrangements becoming practicable between [Ireland] and Britain, in particular, specified fields if the difficulty of the unconditional most-favoured-nation clause were out of the way'.[29]

The American and Irish views on the desirability of European economic integration were thus diametrically opposed. At best, Boland could envisage a bilateral trade agreement with Britain to secure preferential market access for Irish exports. Trying to divert American pressure, he pointed out that customs unions were hardly compatible with the broad most-favoured-nation clause contained in the proposed ITO charter. White conceded that the French government had asked similar questions about the American position on customs unions and European economic integration.

White also raised the issue of the future position of West Germany in the European economy. As already pointed out, the Truman administration partly

'Ireland and the Marshall Plan', pp 301–3. **29** NAI DFA 305/57/I, conversation between Irish delegation to CEEC (Boland) and American embassy, Paris (White), 28 July 1947.

launched the Marshall Plan initiative to jump-start the ailing German economy and so revive intra-European trade. France was opposed to such a step, because the revival of the West German economy threatened to undermine the objectives of the French Monnet Plan as well as French national and economic security. White's reference, though, took Boland by surprise, since he had not been given any specific instructions from de Valera regarding Ireland's position *vis-à-vis* Germany's future. Still, he assured the American diplomat that in his personal judgement most Irish citizens believed that Europe's economic problems could not be solved without West Germany's recovery.[30]

* * *

The conversation between White and Boland confirms Ireland's ambivalence about the American initiative, but also reflects another facet of Ireland's involvement in the Marshall Plan. Boland's stance on the customs union issue attests to the Irish reluctance to join an intra-European customs union. He seemed extremely unwilling even to placate the American position by indicating a willingness to study American ideas. His attitude reflected, to a certain extent, the fact that the Irish government did not necessarily require Marshall aid. Yet it is remarkable that Boland had not asked de Valera for instructions regarding the key issues, which had been raised during the CEEC session ten days earlier. Relative inexperience due to its recent isolation in World War II may explain the Irish government's failure to formulate a view on many of the issues concerning European economic cooperation. After all, Ireland had not been involved in any of the earlier attempts at European economic cooperation under the auspices of the United Nations Rehabilitation and Reconstruction Administration and the ECE.

THE PROBLEM OF WEST GERMAN RECONSTRUCTION

In the meantime, the Irish government feverishly prepared its reply to the CEEC questionnaire and its bid for Marshall aid, which were due in early August. Raymond J. Raymond suggests that the detailed Irish replies to the CEEC questions 'reflected Ireland's enthusiastic support for the Marshall Plan'.[31] Indeed, Boland reported proudly to Dublin after the conference reconvened that Ireland had submitted its reply to the technical questionnaire before the deadline. It was praised for its quality, in marked contrast to the replies from Iceland, Portugal and Turkey, which the CEEC returned because they were incomplete. These delays threatened to further undermine the proposed timetable for the completion of the CEEC's final report.[32] The question remains

30 Ibid. **31** Raymond, 'Ireland and the Marshall Plan', p. 305. **32** NAI DFA 305/57/I,

whether this favourable performance is an accurate reflection of the administrative capability of the Irish civil service at this time. Boland's assessment, which is seconded by Raymond, stands in marked contrast to Joe Lee's rather scathing judgement about the government's ability to absorb ideas about economic development during this period.[33]

As Boland reported to Dublin, the assembled CEEC delegates soon realised that they faced a bigger task than the few unsatisfactory replies to the technical questionnaire.[34] It became obvious that other political problems were more likely to derail the examination of the questionnaires even before they got underway. The success of the CEEC hung in the balance as the discussions touched on the *point neuralgique* for the French government: the level of industrial production in West Germany. According to Boland's account, the other participating countries were convinced that European recovery would not be possible without the rehabilitation of the West German economy and, particularly, steel production. At the Paris conference, the French delegation opposed any increase in the permissible level of West German steel production, which had been laid down at Potsdam in the spring of 1946.[35] The delegation argued that since three and one-half tons of Lorraine iron ore were required per ton of Ruhr coal to make steel, it made more economic sense to increase the exports of Ruhr coal rather than increase West German steel production. Moreover, the Monnet Plan would expand French steel production to meet the demand of other CEEC countries and thereby reduce the need for West German steel output.[36]

The other delegations rejected the logic of the French argument, because it failed to solve the West German payments problem. Boland did not elaborate on this point, but noted that Denmark and Sweden hoped that a recovering West German economy would again become an export market for Danish agricultural products and Swedish iron ore.[37] The Benelux countries opposed an

---

European Economic Cooperation Conference, report by Boland, 9 August 1947. **33** Joseph J. Lee, *Ireland, 1912–1985: Politics and Society* (Cambridge, 1989), pp 563–77. **34** The following paragraph summarises Boland's report, European Economic Cooperation Conference, 9 August 1947. **35** The Potsdam Level of Industry Agreement basically restricted German industrial production to 75 per cent of its pre-war level: see Werner Abelshauser, *Wirtschaftsgeschichte der Bundesrepublik Deutschland, 1945–1980* (Frankfurt am Main, 1983), pp 18–19. **36** On this point, see also Frances M.B. Lynch, 'Resolving the Paradox of the Monnet Plan: National and International Planning in French Reconstruction', *Economic History Review*, vol. 37, no. 2 (1984), pp 229–43. **37** In part, the West German payments problem arose from the requirement that West German exports had to be paid for in dollars in order to finance food imports from the dollar area. Without an economic recovery, West Germany could not increase its imports from neighbouring economies, but at the same time West Germany had to be permitted to renew its exports of manufacturing products. In this sense, American planners aimed to restore the traditional trading patterns in western Europe: Christoph

increase in Western Europe's steel production, since it would lead to over-capacity in this sector. The categorical nature of the French opposition delayed the meeting, while Oliver Franks flew to London to consult on a new tripartite agreement on West German industrial production. As the discussion of this problem shifted to London, Boland informed Dublin that he was not optimistic that an early solution to this problem could be found:

> Like other delegates to whom I have spoken, I feel that yesterday's rather dramatic development was tantamount to an open declaration by the French Government of its willingness even to bear the responsibility for a failure of the present conference rather than abandon its fundamental position on the question of the restoration of West Germany's steel industry.[38]

But several days later, and despite his pessimism, Boland informed Con Cremin, the assistant secretary of External Affairs, of the successful conclusion of a new tripartite agreement increasing the permitted level of West German steel production to 10 million tons per annum.[39]

THE CONTENTIOUS CUSTOMS UNION DEBATE

While the assembled delegates waited for the dispute over the level of West German steel production to be resolved between the three occupying powers, the conference became embroiled in the next divisive problem. The French government latched on to the American idea for an intra-European customs union, declaring its willingness to enter such an agreement with any other CEEC country. But only the Italian government expressed a firm interest in the French proposal. Both countries tried to persuade the Benelux countries to join their prospective customs union. The latter hoped that Britain would join such a union to balance it against French domination. Against this background, Oliver Franks told a private dinner party (attended by Boland) that the British government was likely to reject the proposal because it would mean the end to the preferential trading regime between the Commonwealth countries. Franks expressed his view that an outright rejection might affront American foreign

---

Buchheim, *Die Wiedereingliederung Westdeutschlands in die Weltwirtschaft, 1945–1958* (Munich, 1990), pp 171–81.   **38** NAI, DFA 305/57 I, report by European Economic Cooperation Conference, 9 August 1947.   **39** Ibid., note of phone conversation between Boland and Cremin, 14 August 1947. The new tripartite agreement fixed the ceiling of West German steel production at ten and one-half million tons *per annum* and envisaged the internationalisation of the Ruhr: Milward, *The Reconstruction of Europe*, pp 71–6.

policymakers, who favoured a broad European customs union, and so he lobbied other potential opponents of the proposal to support the more nuanced British position.

Franks asked Boland about Ireland's policy. Boland replied that in his personal opinion 'the [Irish] government would almost certainly not be in favour of a customs union with any other country'.[40] Still, Boland asked Dublin for instructions, because it looked like he might have to make a statement on the customs union proposal at a plenary meeting of the CEEC. Given that this issue had already dominated the discussions in July, this request is noteworthy because of its lateness. Not having previously consulted the government, Boland even offered to draft a statement for ministerial approval. At a further meeting Boland reassured Franks that the French and Italian proposals for a European customs union struck most Irish officials as chimerical and dangerous in the short run. Given differences in economic systems, structures, living conditions and labour standards, it would take years to achieve convergence and, therefore, would be inimical to investment and growth. In his report to Dublin Boland stressed the potential significance of backing the British position, because 'the importance of Irish support from the point of view of possible American reactions will be obvious'.[41] Despite the British opposition, the committee of financial experts endorsed the Benelux proposals in amended form a couple of days later. In contrast to Franks' statements, a British Treasury official, David Whaley, told a member of the Irish delegation, Colm Barry, that the British government warmly supported the Benelux plan. The Treasury did fear, though, that under current proposals Marshall aid might be squandered on the expansion of uneconomic industries and lead to the duplication of capacity. Barry speculated that the British government might be attracted to the Benelux approach by the prospect of unlimited American financial support for convertibility. In light of these mixed signals, Boland now urgently requested ministerial instructions on the Benelux plan.[42]

* * *

Officials in the Irish Department of Finance concurred with Boland's views on the matter, but were less dismissive about the desirability of a European customs union. While the Irish position was constrained by its close economic links with Britain, the officials argued that a customs union might be advantageous if such an agreement were to extend the convertibility of sterling. In that case, the Irish government would be able to use its accumulated sterling balances to purchase goods from other Western European countries.[43] This stance by Finance may

---

40 NAI DFA 305/57/I, note of phone conversation between Boland and Cremin, 14 August 1947. **41** Ibid., report by Boland, Conference on European Economic Cooperation, 15 August 1947. **42** Ibid., report by Boland, 17 August 1947. **43** Ibid., memorandum, Redmond

reflect the views of their Treasury colleagues with whom they sought to coordinate the Irish response to the Marshall Plan.[44] Nevertheless, the Irish government decided to join Britain and the Scandinavian governments in opposing the French proposals, but supported the establishment of a working party to study the question of a customs union. Without a note of cynicism, Boland agreed with a report in the *Times* which characterised the British proposal to examine the customs union issue as a delaying tactic, because Britain would never join such a union even if were to lead to the failure of the CEEC conference.[45]

AMERICAN OBJECTIONS TO THE CEEC DRAFT REPORT

As this analysis shows, the Irish government remained ambivalent about the American vision of a new international economic order. As the deliberations of the CEEC were nearing their conclusion, the Irish government considered not signing the draft CEEC report on two occasions, because policymakers felt it impinged on Irish neutrality and national sovereignty.

The initial instance occurred during the discussion of the first draft report in the Cooperation Committee. Irish policymakers objected to the wording of several passages relating to Germany's role in the Second World War. De Valera and Boland could not support calls for large reparations and controls on the West German economy, since Ireland had been neutral during the conflict and they also wished to avoid a repetition of history. During the ensuing debates, the Irish delegation succeeded, in concert with other neutral countries, in toning down the passages in question.[46]

Later, during the final discussion of the draft report, Boland worried that the emerging consensus among the conferees not to form a European customs union and to limit the integration of the German economy into Western Europe's would lead to a showdown with the United States.[47] Boland's reading is interesting, because it reflected only one strand of American thinking, which held that the liberalisation of intra-European trade would lead to a revival of the Western European economies and closer economic integration. The proponents of this view, including William Clayton and other American ambassadors throughout Western Europe, had emphasised in their discussions with the conferees during July and early August that an agreement on these points was essential to ensure the American Congress' acceptance of the Marshall aid proposals. Most foreign

(Department of Finance) to McCauley, 19 August 1947. **44** Ibid., letter, Department of Finance to Department of External Affairs, 12 August 1947. **45** Ibid., report by Boland, Conference on European Economic Cooperation, 15 August 1947. **46** Ibid., message from Boland to Taoiseach, 27 August 1947; memorandum, Taoiseach to Cremin, 27 August 1947; letter, Boland to assistant secretary, Department of External Affairs, 30 August 1947.

policymakers in Washington, however, rejected Clayton's free market convictions and regarded the coordination of national reconstruction plans as a vital component of an integrated strategy for European recovery. For the State Department planners, the draft report amounted to little more than an aggregation of sixteen shopping lists demonstrating no evidence of 'self-help'. Moreover, American policymakers became concerned about the amount of financial aid requested by European governments in the draft report. This absence of a consensus between the State Department and its representatives in Paris contributed to the emergence of a draft report at odds with American objectives.[48]

During initial discussions with the executive committee at the end of August, Clayton and the American delegation stressed that the initial aid request of $29 billion would be politically unacceptable and, therefore, demanded a reduction of the sum to just $15 billion. After this acrimonious meeting Boland reported to Dublin that the British and Italian delegates had been horrified by the tone of the American representatives. Despite being taken aback by the ferocity of the American intervention, most delegates, nonetheless, had become convinced of the extent of the economic crisis in Europe. According to Boland, the general consensus was that European recovery would falter and social revolutions would inevitably result without massive American aid. The European representatives thus realised that they would have to negotiate an agreeable report with the Americans in order not to jeopardise an aid programme on which the welfare of 200 million people depended.[49]

* * *

After George Kennan, the head of the State Department's policy planning staff, and Charles Bonestal, another high-ranking State Department official, joined the American delegation the following day, it set out seven principles that the CEEC report ought to address during a meeting with the executive committee. Oliver Franks then informed the Cooperation Committee of the American demands. Freddie Boland ventured that some of them constituted implicit criticisms of the economic policies pursued by Britain, France and the Scandinavian countries. Nevertheless, he believed that most of the American stipulations would be acceptable to the conferees, except the demand for the creation of a multilateral organisation to review the execution of the recovery plans contained in the report. Such a step might be interpreted as the formation of a Western bloc and, therefore, unacceptable to a number of neutral countries. Boland assessed the likely impact of the American intervention in the following terms:

47 Ibid., report by Boland, 30 August 1947.   **48** On this point, see Michael J. Hogan, *The Marshall Plan: America, Britain and the Reconstruction of Western Europe* (Cambridge, 1987), pp 54–87.   **49** NAI DFA 305/57/I, report by Boland, 30 August 1947.

> So far as we are concerned, the conditions laid down by the American negotiators are not likely to give rise to much difficulty! The people most concerned are the British, the French and the Scandinavians. It is an open secret here that the American administration thinks that the Labour government in Britain is unduly influenced by the attitude of left-wing trade unions in Britain and is not doing as much as they could do to get a higher output from British labour, particularly British coal-miners. The sixth of the seven American points (financial and monetary stability) is aimed against France. The most difficult of the American points, however – and the one to which Mr. Clayton attached most importance – is the last, namely, that this conference should not completely atomise itself as soon as the report has been presented, but that a standing organ of the sixteen governments represented here should remain in being to supervise the progress of European recovery over the next four years and consult with the American government about the administration of whatever aid is eventually extended in accordance with Mr. Marshall's offer.[50]

In contrast to the Swedish and Norwegian delegates, Boland did not think that the formation of an organisation to coordinate Marshall aid would be incompatible with Irish neutrality. As this relaxed attitude emphasised, Irish foreign policymakers perceived themselves as members of a wider 'Western community'. Arguably, the Soviet Union vetoed the Irish application to join the United Nations in 1946, because it feared that Ireland would further strengthen the pro-Western predominance within that institution. Irish foreign policymakers, therefore, were not unduly worried that the Soviet Union would interpret a European Marshall Plan as the creation of a 'Western bloc'.[51]

WORRIES ABOUT AMERICAN HEGEMONY

As the deliberations of the CEEC entered their final stages, Boland became convinced that Ireland should join the customs union study group. His determination is surprising, because no final agreement on the group's terms of reference had been reached. But like the British, Swiss and Danish delegates – and in marked contrast to France and Italy's declared intention to establish one – Boland was anxious to ensure that participation did not imply a commitment to join a future customs union. According to Boland, most CEEC conferees were likely to join this study group, which would be working outside of the CEEC umbrella.

---

50 Ibid., letter, Boland to assistant secretary, 1 September 1947. 51 On this point, see Joseph Morrison Skelly, 'Ireland, the Department of External Affairs, and the United Nations, 1946–55: A New Look', *Irish Studies in International Affairs*, vol. 7 (1996), pp 63–78.

The Danish delegate suggested that it should work closely with the ITO and might even lead to the creation of an organisation governing intra-European trade. It would be important for Ireland to join the group in order to monitor developments and to protect its own national interests. Moreover, membership would open a door to Irish participation in the ongoing multilateral trade negotiations and European economic cooperation under the aegis of the UN. Taking his cue from the Danish delegate, Boland argued, in his report to Dublin, that 'as we are not members of [the] UN or the ECE, the same consideration would apply with even greater force in our case'.[52] De Valera concurred with Boland's decision to join the customs union study group. This step thus marked the beginning of Irish participation in post-war international trade negotiations. Indeed, as Cremin informed de Valera, Ireland was about to be invited to an international trade conference in Havana.[53] And in January 1948 the Irish government decided to accept an invitation to attend the sessions of the ECE as a consultative member.[54]

As his reports show, Boland argued that Ireland should participate more actively in the attempts to reform international economic relations in order to protect its national interests. Given this emphasis, his placid reaction to the American intervention is surprising, because the American policymakers demanded in no uncertain terms a degree of economic integration which involved a significant abrogation of economic sovereignty. Despite the serious disagreements, Boland's reports to Dublin continued to state that a compromise agreeable to both sides would be found. The determined stance of other conferees in resisting some of the American demands may have prompted Boland to downplay the potential for the failure of the Marshall Plan, because he correctly believed that neither side could risk such an outcome. He may not have even apprised Dublin of his own thoughts about the American intervention.

* * *

Still, the Department of External Affairs' file that contains Boland's correspondence to Dublin during the Paris conference also includes an unattributed memorandum, dated 4 September 1947, that may well have been written by him. It argues that the unwarranted interference of the dominant world power threatened Western European recovery and democracy. It also marks the second expression of Irish ambivalence towards an America-inspired new international economic order. In the view of the writer, Western European nations should be allowed to define unhindered their political and economic objectives amidst the current attempt to resolve the economic crisis, because they might otherwise

---

52 NAI DFA 305/57/II: report by Boland, 2 September 1947. **53** Ibid., telegram to secretary, 5 September 1947; brief for the Taoiseach and Minister of External Affairs (de Valera) by Cremin, 5 September 1947. **54** On the invitation to join the ECE, see also ibid., minute, Cremin to assistant secretary, 23 February 1948.

lose faith that a reasonable living standard could be attained under democracy and private initiative. European governments feared that the current discussions would cement American economic dominance, thereby turning them into mere satellites of the United States. To reassure them the Truman administration should offer to cover their dollar deficits and agree to buy as many goods abroad as the United States currently exported. Increased American imports of European goods would provide a basis for a more equitable international settlement than current American foreign policy, which would lead to a prolonged economic conflict between the Western democracies.

If the Truman administration persisted with its attempts to run Western European affairs, the memorandum continued, it would lead to a string of international conferences at which the European governments would busily defend their national interests. These conferences would at best result in a few working parties, but were bound to lead to American disillusionment with European politics. Therefore, the Europeans should seek an honest interchange of views with the American government about future relations between the Western nations. In such talks the European governments should make the Americans understand that they could not sell or be repaid for more than they bought or lent abroad in the long term. And in order to achieve an equitable international settlement, American policymakers would have to answer two questions:

> 1) Are they prepared to buy and lend as much as they sell after 1951, and now enter into a firm commitment to do so, or do they want to acquire economic domination of the world?
> 2) Are they prepared to be satisfied with sole possession of atomic weapons as a safeguard against being attacked and let democratic principles settle all other questions between nations?[55]

This memorandum rejected the attempts of State Department planners to remake Europe the American way. The writer could not contemplate conceding national sovereignty beyond the limited concessions made by the conferees in Paris. In this sense, the agreement on a customs union working group represented the limit of pandering to American demands for most Irish policymakers. While the memorandum implicitly assumes that the dollar gap will remain a

---

55 Ibid., How best America can aid Europe, 4 September 1947. At first sight, it may seem that this memorandum adopted an extreme position, but a report in the *Economist* highlighted the widespread concern among delegates about the cuts in aid proposed by American policymakers. Most delegates thought it highly unlikely that Western European countries would be able to pay for dollar imports out of export earnings at the end of Marshall aid. Therefore, economic aid would not solve Europe's dollar problem and would lead to a long-term dependence on American aid: 'On the Eve of a Paris Report', *Economist*, 6 September 1947, p. 392.

long-term problem, it places the cost of adjustment firmly on the dominant economy, without envisaging a contribution by European countries, including Ireland. At another level, the writer interprets the American search for a creative solution to the economic crisis through a combination of American aid and intra-European economic cooperation as bullying by the world's only nuclear power. The memorandum highlights ambivalence among Irish policymakers about the desirability of Marshall aid under these circumstances.

* * *

On the same day that this document was drafted George Kennan sent a frank report to the State Department acknowledging that the Marshall plan initiative faced the real threat of failure. While not hiding his disappointment, Kennan showed remarkable understanding for the severe economic and political problems which made it difficult for delegates to commit their countries to plan for European recovery. Given these constraints, most delegates had desisted from examining the submissions of other countries in order to prevent the close scrutiny of their own figures. This mentality had led the CEEC to lapse back into the cordiality of pre-war international diplomacy. To resolve the emerging impasse, Kennan suggested that the CEEC should only submit an interim report, which would allow American policymakers to revise the plan for presentation to Congress.[56]

American officials agreed with Kennan's analysis, and the CEEC accepted a subsequent American offer of friendly aid in revising the draft report. During the following week, the Europeans pruned their request for economic aid to $22 billion by proportionally scaling down national figures. The British government, though, successfully blocked American attempts to reopen the examination of national submissions. As a consequence, American officials still remained disappointed with the revised draft report, bemoaning the inadequate screening of national requirements, the haphazard method of reducing national aid requests, the failure to relate national requirements to available supplies and the absence of a spirit of mutual aid. Fearing the collapse of the ERP, the State Department decided to appeal directly to national governments in order to achieve further concessions. On 7 September the Acting Secretary of State, Robert Lovett, instructed American diplomatic missions to inform the foreign ministers of all CEEC governments about the American criticism of the draft CEEC report.[57]

* * *

Following Washington's instructions, the counsellor in the American embassy, Vinton Chapin, met with Eamon de Valera on the afternoon of 9 September to

---

56 *Foreign Relations of the United States, 1947: Volume 3, British Commonwealth, Europe* (Washington, 1972) [hereafter, *FRUS*], pp 397–405. **57** *FRUS*, pp 412–17; Hogan, *The Marshall Plan*, pp 76–82.

apprise him of the State Department's concern over rumours about the scale of European aid requests, which seemed 'inspired more by self-interest than a spirit of mutual help'. While the American government did not intend to coerce any nation, European governments seemed to show no willingness to liberalise intra-European trade by removing quotas and other barriers.[58] Chapin also raised Clayton's suggestion that the completion of the CEEC report should be delayed for ten days in order to allow a reconciliation of the American and European positions. In response, de Valera first emphatically rejected the proposal for a European customs union, which did not feature among the principles set out in the American *démarche:*

> The Taoiseach told Mr. Chapin that, in his opinion, a European customs union, while it might be welcomed by the USA, would be politically impossible, and that, while the states would, of course, be agreeable to go into the question so as to examine the difficulties in the way of such a union, he did not think that the result of their study would lead them to constitute one – to suggest a customs union to European states at this stage would be like suggesting to the United States thirty years ago the abandonment of their tariff policy.[59]

De Valera went on in a more conciliatory vein by suggesting that European foreign ministers should meet two days later, 11 September, as agreed, but discuss the report and resolve any outstanding issues before signing it. He assured Chapin that the Irish government supported 'the view that the final meeting of the conference should be as impressive as possible an occasion for the signing ceremony'.[60]

On the evening after the meeting Cremin called Boland in Paris to advise him of the contents of the American *démarche* and the arrangements for the final session of the conference. Boland could not shed any more light on the American intervention, but recommended that all arrangements for the final meeting should be treated as provisional. In this context, he advised that Lemass rather than de Valera should represent Ireland, since many of the smaller European states, including Austria, Belgium, Denmark, the Netherlands, Norway, Sweden and Switzerland, would not be represented by their foreign ministers. Boland dismissed de Valera's suggestion for direct negotiations among the foreign ministers, because most governments did not want to reopen the discussion of national recovery plans.

At lunchtime the following day (11 September), Boland rang Cremin with the news that the American *démarche* had caused quite a stir at the conference

---

58 NAI DFA 305/57/II, conversation with Mr. Chapin (counsellor of the American embassy), memorandum, Cremin to de Valera, 9 September 1947; brief for Taoiseach, Minister for External Affairs (de Valera) by Cremin on a visit by Chapin, 9 September 1947. **59** Ibid., minute by Cremin on conversation between de Valera and Chapin, 9 September 1947. **60** Ibid.

and had brought matters to a head between the American delegation and the executive committee. Many delegates felt outraged about the high-handed manner of the American intervention and argued for resisting the American demand that the signing of the CEEC report be postponed for a fortnight. The British government led the chorus of those who opposed the further watering down of the European aid requests as a disingenuous representation of their requirements. British policymakers were also concerned that the Dutch and the Scandinavian governments would use the American *démarche* as a pretext for rejecting the Marshall Plan. Most delegates seemed to subscribe to this tough view, because they believed that the Truman administration could not risk the failure of its aid initiative. Boland was adamant that the Executive Committee would hold firm during the day's crisis meetings with the American representatives, leaving the latter no choice but to concede defeat. According to a transcript of a phone conversation with Con Cremin, Freddie Boland stressed that:

> if everybody else were to sign, we should not stand out. He is convinced that aid on the lines indicated in the report is essential if Western Europe is to be saved from a disastrous situation and he is also convinced that, while we might be less immediately affected than other countries, we are bound to suffer if Western European countries generally remain in a bad state. As regards the American *démarche*, he thinks that other countries likely to sign would be liable to suffer more than we would from, so to speak, not acting in accordance with the American suggestion of postponement.[61]

The fear of economic collapse may have swayed the French government into changing its position overnight and thus enabled an uneasy compromise between the two sides during a meeting the next day. As part of this agreement, the Europeans agreed to postpone the final meeting of the conference in order to incorporate some of the American principles into the general segment of the CEEC report. In turn, the Americans consented to accepting a mere declaration of intent by European governments on vital points such as trade liberalisation and the creation of a multilateral organisation to coordinate the distribution of Marshall aid after Congress had approved the European Recovery Bill. Over the coming fortnight the Americans and Europeans revised the draft report in a manner designed to make it more palatable to the American Congress.[62]

As Boland predicted, Irish ministers found little they disagreed with in the CEEC draft report. In his reply, Lemass did not voice any objections to it, but would have preferred a statement that the conferees did not intend to restore the

---

[61] Ibid., memorandum by Cremin on a phone conversation with Boland, 11 September 1947.
[62] Hogan, *The Marshall Plan*, pp 77–87. On French concerns, see also Irwin M. Wall, *The United States and the Making of Postwar France, 1945–1954* (Cambridge, 1991), pp 88–92.

pre-war economic pattern, which reflected the political conditions in the past.[63] Given the lack of controversy, de Valera decided to attend the final session of the conference in person, praising in his speech the American initiative and the sterling work of the CEEC. While not mentioning partition, the speech emphasised that European governments were committed to self-help and were only seeking the minimal assistance required to 'preserve their traditional civilisation'.[64]

CONCLUSION

As this analysis shows, the Irish government responded to the Marshall Plan initiative in a manner similar to other European countries. For Ireland the CEEC provided the opportunity to participate in the negotiations of a post-war international economic order from which they had been excluded by their wartime neutrality. The Marshall Plan allowed Ireland to rejoin the community of Western states to which Irish policymakers felt the country belonged. In marked contrast to other European governments, the Irish government remained unconcerned about the creation of a separate Western bloc reinforcing the division of Europe, because Irish policymakers conceived the Cold War as a struggle between Christianity and the materialist ideology of communism. As van der Beugel suggests, the CEEC deliberations became a real learning process for the Irish delegation, with Boland winning the respect of other delegates. By the end of the conference Boland was asked to chair the customs union study group and join the CEEC delegation to Washington.[65] This personal achievement shows that Irish views were in line with those of the majority of participating countries.

The foregoing analysis supports, to some extent, Gary Murphy's argument that the Department of External Affairs responded enthusiastically to George Marshall's initiative. Nevertheless, the Irish government actually conceded little ground over intra-European trade liberalisation and remained extremely apprehensive about American ideas for a multilateral customs union. As a hesitant supporter of this particular scheme, Ireland pursued a similar policy within the CEEC to that of most other European governments, thus confirming Milward's interpretation of the European response to the Marshall Plan. The most likely explanation of Irish support for the plan remains the fact that it ended Ireland's diplomatic isolation after the end of World War II.

* * *

63 NAI DFA 305/57/II, letter, Williams to Cremin, 17 September 1947. **64** Ibid., statement made by Taoiseach at closing session of European Economic Cooperation Conference, 22 September 1947. **65** Ibid., letter Boland to assistant secretary, Department of External Affairs, 8 September 1947.

At the same time, the Marshall Plan presented an opportunity to overcome Ireland's dollar problem. The fuel crisis in the first quarter of 1947 brought home to ministers the degree to which economic recovery depended on overseas coal and fertiliser imports, which could only be obtained from the United States or Britain. Given its minuscule dollar earnings, Ireland's ability to pay for dollar imports depended on access to the sterling area dollar pool. Therefore, Lemass repeatedly stressed during the summer of 1947 the importance of strengthening Ireland's close economic ties with Britain, while cautiously welcoming Marshall aid and the liberalisation of intra-European trade.

The British convertibility crisis in August 1948 made closer economic cooperation between the two countries almost imperative. For this reason, a high-powered Irish delegation, including de Valera, Lemass, Aiken and Patrick Smith, the Minister for Agriculture, travelled to London in September 1947 to broker a new Anglo–Irish trade accord. Before leaving London to attend the final meeting of the CEEC in Paris, de Valera expressed the hope these negotiations would lead to an improvement in living standards in Britain and Ireland.[66] The two countries reached an informal agreement about bilateral trade in November 1947. As part of this understanding, Britain promised to increase its coal shipments to Ireland in return for Irish agricultural products. More important from a British perspective, the Irish government agreed to reduce its drawings on the sterling area dollar pool and tighten economic controls. Contemporary observers noted that the Anglo–Irish trade agreement marked a significant shift in Irish foreign economic policy, because it represented a departure from the protectionist policies of the 1930s.[67] It is important to remember, however, that most intra-European trade in the immediate postwar period was conducted on the basis of bilateral trade agreements, because such accords maximised the control of governments over their foreign trade and payments. Irish economic foreign policy thus responded to the relative disintegration of the international economy by using the same strategy as other European countries. During discussions between the CEEC delegation and State Department officials in October 1947, Boland spoke for the majority of European policymakers when he defended the use of bilateral agreements as a tool for increasing the supply of essential materials for recovery.[68] At the same time, Boland realised that Ireland would not be permitted to draw on the dollar pool of the sterling area for the duration of the Marshall Plan. Ireland, therefore, would require American financial aid to cover the Irish dollar gap for the foreseeable future.[69]

---

66 'Mr de Valera's Discussions with British Government on Dollar Position and Trade', *Keesing's Contemporary Archive*, vol. 6, 13–20 September 1947, 8828/B. **67** 'Eire faces Dollar Crises', *Economist*, 4 October 1947, pp 567–8. **68** *FRUS*, pp 457–8. **69** NAI DFA 305/57/II, memorandum, Boland to assistant secretary, 29 October 1947.

Speaking to the Dáil in November, de Valera presented the Anglo–Irish trade agreement as an example of the European self-help which the Marshall Plan had called for.[70] Despite his claims, the agreement arguably violated the spirit of the American initiative, because of its discriminatory character. The Irish government's preference for closer economic relations with Britain had clear short-term economic benefits, but the close link with sterling might well have proved detrimental to Ireland's economic prospects in the medium term.[71]

As this chapter shows, historical assessments of the Irish response to the Marshall Plan have overlooked the fact that most European governments only reluctantly supported American ideas on European recovery. The Irish response, therefore, was fairly typical and hardly explains Ireland's eventual failure to benefit from the Marshall Plan. During the CEEC deliberations, Irish policymakers learned that, like the rest of Europe, Ireland required massive American economic aid and would benefit from closer economic cooperation with its large neighbour, the United Kingdom. This emphasis on Anglo–Irish economic relations blinded the Irish government to another potential lesson of the Paris conference. In his account, van der Beugel stressed that in Paris the nascent European policymaking community realised the potential benefits of economic policies being more closely coordinated between the various assembled European countries. This lesson was possibly lost on the Irish government, because of the poor coordination of state intervention in the domestic economy. In contrast to other countries, the Irish government relied on fiscal policy to effect changes in the economy rather than economic planning based on national income analysis as advocated by many Marshall Plan officials and Keynesian economists.[72]

Nevertheless, the analysis here disputes the contention that the Irish response to George Marshall's initiative was deficient during the Paris conference. Like their counterparts in other countries, Irish policymakers had the same opportunity after the CEEC meeting in the summer of 1947 to grasp the potential gains offered by closer economic cooperation in Western Europe. The search for the reasons behind Ireland's failure to exploit the opportunities of the Marshall Plan should concentrate, instead, on the Irish role in the negotiations to liberalise intra-European trade that took place under the umbrella of the Organisation for European Economic Cooperation after its formation in April 1948.

---

[70] 'Agreement on Increased British Coal, Raw Materials and Machinery Supplies to Eire and Larger Food Exports to Britain – Irish Restrictions on Petrol Consumption, Foreign Exchange for Travel, and Commodity Purchases in Hard Currencies', *Keesing's Contemporary Archive*, vol. 6, 15–22 November 1947, 8938/A. [71] On this point, see Cormac Ó Gráda, *A Rocky Road: The Irish Economy since the 1920s* (Manchester, 1997), p. 230. [72] On use of national income analysis for economic planning, see Till Geiger, 'Strumento analitico o modello di crescita? L'influenza americana nell'elaborazione delle statistiche europee sulla crescita economica dopo la seconda guerra mondiale', *Nuova Civiltà delle Macchine* (forthcoming, 1999).

'A Wider Perspective': Ireland's View of Western Europe in the 1950s

Gary Murphy

INTRODUCTION

This chapter focuses on Irish responses to integrationist events in Western Europe during the 1950s and assesses the attitude of various Irish governments to the rapidly changing political and economic landscape in Europe during this decade. The 1950s in Ireland was a fluid political period which saw four changes in government between 1948 and 1957 after an era of Fianna Fáil hegemony which had lasted from 1932 to 1948. It has long been assumed that the culture of isolationism in foreign affairs fostered by Fianna Fáil since 1932 was continued by successive governments up to the time that Seán Lemass' minority Fianna Fáil government applied for entry into the European Economic Community (EEC) in July 1961. This assumption is manifested in the belief that the years between 1945 and 1961 saw a strong sense of public complacency, with elite opinion believing that the depression, war and post-war recovery justified the continuation of isolationist policies which had been in place since before 1932. Ireland's refusal to join the General Agreement on Trade and Tariffs (GATT) in 1948 or the North Atlantic Treaty Organisation (NATO) in 1949 is seen as a further reflection of isolationism, reinforcing the conviction that national solutions were the most appropriate in Ireland's case. This chapter, however, will show that throughout the 1950s Irish policymakers were aware that events in Western Europe would have a major impact on Ireland, with the result that there was a wider perspective to policymaking throughout this decade than is normally assumed to have been the case.

INITIAL STEPS IN THE WESTERN EUROPEAN ARENA

Ireland's initial, tentative steps towards engagement with Europe began with her involvement in the Marshall Plan. While Ireland was initially a somewhat reluctant participant in the Organisation for European Economic Cooperation (OEEC) when it was established in 1948 (the government had to join in order to receive Marshall aid funds), some officials in the Department of External Affairs were arguing that Ireland should play a greater role in Western European matters. At the original Marshall aid discussions, which ran from July to September 1947, Ireland's representative, Frederick Boland, secretary of the Department of External Affairs, made an important speech saying that Ireland would sign the treaty no matter what terms the Fianna Fáil government was able to negotiate. As Boland later commented: 'we didn't look to get anything free out of the thing, but our interest was that Europe should be prosperous, because without a prosperous Europe we couldn't be prosperous ourselves'.[1]

The general Western European importance of this conference is shown by a report that Boland sent from Paris back to Dublin in August 1947, wherein he painted a pretty bleak picture of the economic and political landscape:

> without outside aid of a magnitude that only something like the Marshall Plan can supply, Europe is headed for economic collapse and social revolution within the next two or three years. Even if this outside aid is forthcoming it is more than doubtful whether Western Europe can stand on its own legs after 1952 without reductions in living standards which governments already faced with dangerous internal communist drives can only contemplate with the utmost dismay. It would be difficult to exaggerate the extent to which this realisation of the general position of Western Europe is conditioning the work of this conference.[2]

For Boland, Ireland was intrinsically a part of Western Europe, not simply an isolated outpost on the edge of the continent, and had a role to play in the wider scheme of events.

While Marshall aid can be seen as Ireland's first tentative step into the rarefied atmosphere of the post-war world, the offer to join NATO presented problems of a domestic kind. Ireland's reluctance to become involved in NATO can, in the main, be put down to the continuance of partition. Seán MacBride, Minister for External Affairs in the first Inter-Party government, had campaigned vigorously in the first half of 1948 to persuade the Economic Cooperation Administration, the American organisation set up to administer

---

[1] This comment is from a source entitled *Reminiscence of an Irish Diplomat: Frederick H. Boland, Ambassador to London, Permanent Representative at the United Nations and President of the General Assembly 1960*. It was compiled by Boland's daughter, Mella Boland (Crowley), and is based on a series of extended conversations between the two during the latter stages of his life. Copy in possession of the author. [2] NAI DFA 305/57/1, report from Boland to Taoiseach, 30 August 1947.

Marshall aid, not to acknowledge the partition of Ireland in the allocation of funds. This made little impression on the Americans, but MacBride continued to harbour hopes that the OEEC might emerge as a genuinely supranational organisation and develop as a forum from within which partition could be ended. In fact, on the domestic front MacBride was also coming under increasing pressure from the Fianna Fáil opposition over partition. A question posed to MacBride by a Fianna Fáil backbencher, J.P. Brennan, in March 1948 illustrates the hold that partition had on Irish foreign policy concerns at this time. Brennan asked for a reassurance that at a meeting of the OEEC to be held on 14 March MacBride would not discuss 'any political matter other than economic [issues] until (A) the partition of the country will have been solved to the complete satisfaction of the people of Ireland, and (B) opportunities for freedom of speech will have been conceded to the inhabitants in the territory of Northern Ireland'.3

MacBride, for his part, replied to this demand by deflecting the political ramifications of the acceptance of Marshall aid. He proclaimed that:

> the matters to be discussed at the resumed meeting of the OEEC on March 14 appertain primarily to the economic sphere. In so far as the Deputy's question is intended to elicit the government's attitude to the partition of our country, I should like to add that the government regards the continuance of partition as the most significant obstacle to the political and economic welfare of our people.4

Notwithstanding the partition question, MacBride's use of the word 'primarily' can, in essence, be seen as a tacit admission that there was a link between politics and economics contained within the Marshall Plan and the initial stages of the OEEC. NATO membership, however, would have meant some form of acceptance of the validity of partition, which was something no Irish government was willing to state on the international stage.

In May 1949 the first Inter-Party government signed the Statute of the Council of Europe. While the government played little role in the lead up to the founding of this organisation, the fact that the government signed up is significant, because the Council of Europe did undoubtedly have federal implications. Its aim was to achieve 'a greater unity between its members for the purposes of safeguarding and realising the ideas and principles which are their common heritage and facilitating their economic and social progress', and, as such, the Council of Europe became Western Europe's first post-war political organisation.5

---

3 NAI DFA 305/57/1A. **4** Ibid. **5** Derek Urwin, *A Political History of Western Europe*, 5th ed. (London, 1997), pp 76–7.

Again, the partition question dogged Ireland's role within the Council of Europe. From the outset, MacBride and Eamon de Valera, in opposition for the first time in sixteen years, were committed to raising partition on the international stage, and since members of both the government and the opposition represented Ireland at the Council it seemed the ideal setting in which to do so. For the other members, however, the Irish dispute paled into insignificance alongside the problems of the Saar and Trieste and the threat of Soviet encroachment into Western Europe.[6] In essence, the parameters of Irish foreign policy at this time continued to be defined by the relationship with Britain. This was even more so the case in terms of trade, as Ireland was heavily dependent on the British market. It was the long term futility of such a position that saw Irish policymakers, however tentatively, take steps in the 1950s that would eventually lead to the decision in 1961 to seek membership in the EEC.

Other events in Western Europe in the early 1950s had little impact on Ireland. The creation of the European Coal and Steel Community (ECSC) in 1952 and the Western European Union (WEU) in 1955 passed the country by. Western European discussions between 1950 and 1954 on the development of the so-called Green Pool, an organisation that would be dedicated to the marketing of agricultural products, did, however, impinge on the consciousness of Irish policymakers, since the plan ultimately called for the establishment of a type of European agricultural community. The Department of External Affairs favoured the discussions in the spirit of close economic cooperation between the countries of Western Europe, but the Departments of Finance and Agriculture saw little benefit in the proposals. In fact, both saw extreme dangers for Irish agriculture in the Green Pool negotiations. If Great Britain participated, Ireland's preferential treatment in the British market would be seriously diminished. Moreover, Ireland's negligible share in the European market would be diluted still further. For their part, the British had reservations of their own about the Green Pool, and at a ministerial conference of the OEEC in June 1954 the proposals were forwarded to a new body of the OEEC, the Committee of Ministers of Agriculture, from which they never reappeared.[7] In Dublin, Agriculture and Finance welcomed the effective disappearance of the Green Pool proposal. One official deeply involved in the negotiations at the time, though, noted that although the Green Pool negotiations never got very far, it was recognised within the Irish policymaking community, and within Agriculture in particular, that this proposal marked the beginning of a process

---

6 Miriam Hederman, *The Road to Europe: Irish Attitudes 1948–61* (Dublin, 1983), p. 30. 7 D.J. Maher, *The Tortuous Path: The Course of Ireland's Entry to the EEC, 1948–1973* (Dublin, 1986), pp 44–5. For a detailed analysis of the Green Pool, see Richard T. Griffiths and Brian Girvin (eds), *The Green Pool and the Origins of the Common Agricultural Policy* (London, 1995).

that would see the Irish government having to take a 'wider perspective' to the European integration question, particularly as it impinged on economic policy.[8] While the special relationship with Britain was paramount at this stage, there were officials who realised that an economic future based on the predominance of the British market was likely to be a pretty grim one.

At a political level, however, for the 1951–4 Fianna Fáil government the way to economic prosperity was grounded in the view that Ireland's trade relations with Britain still offered the best possibility of success. Indeed, during the lifetime of this government, Seán MacEntee, the Minister for Finance, continually berated the first Inter-Party government for actually having accepted Marshall aid at all. While the rest of Europe considered the linkage of economics and politics to be fundamental in terms of the Marshall Plan, Fianna Fáil saw it simply in terms of the Inter-Party government actually burdening the Irish taxpayer with extra debt. For MacEntee, it was 'the coalition government alone which is to be condemned for raising an unnecessary loan from the United States ... for squandering the proceeds of that loan and for saddling the people of this country with a heavy external debt which it will take a full generation to discharge'.[9]

This parochial attitude towards Marshall aid was mirrored by Fianna Fáil in terms of Europe. For instance, the British ambassador in Dublin, W.C. Hankinson, noted a conversation with de Valera in May 1952 in which the Taoiseach stated that 'he had scored off Federalists in Europe by pointing out to them that [Ireland] had only recently managed to extract themselves from a much smaller combine'.[10] The rather insular attitude shown by de Valera and MacEntee was not, however, shared by all within Fianna Fáil. Seán Lemass, Minister for Industry and Commerce in the 1951–4 government, was already thinking in terms of ditching the long-held economic policy of protection and was watching events in Western Europe with interest. Dumping protectionism would be a signal that the wider European economic context had implications for Ireland, and Lemass was determined that a Fianna Fáil government would be at the hub of a more positive Irish attitude to Europe.[11]

By 1954, however, Fianna Fáil was out of office again, replaced by a second Inter-Party government which at first glance seemed more homogenous than the anti-Fianna Fáil coalition which had emerged in 1948. With Fine Gael's Liam Cosgrave as Minister for External Affairs in place of the combative Seán MacBride, the Fine Gael-led government adopted a cautious approach to

---

8 Interview with the late J.C. Nagle, 1 September 1994. Mr. Nagle entered the Department of Finance in 1933. He transferred to Agriculture in 1939 and was appointed secretary in July 1959. He died in April 1996. Also, Nagle to the author, 28 February 1995. **9** Letter from MacEntee to the *Irish Press*, 21 August 1953. See also his letters of 12, 15 August on this topic. **10** PRO DO 25/5205, Hankinson to Leisching, 2 January 1952. **11** John Horgan, *Seán Lemass: The Enigmatic Patriot* (Dublin, 1997), pp 164–8, 189–94.

European affairs. Cosgrave was elected chairman of the Council of Ministers of the Council of Europe, but with developments on the continent moving forward apace (as signified by the creation of the ECSC and the WEU), the Council of Europe was, politically, a much reduced body from that which had been set up in 1949. Ultimately, it had failed to live up to the supranational role that it had first imagined for itself. Cosgrave's position as chair, therefore, said much about the Council of Europe. As a body it had simply been taken over by other events on the road to Western European integration. These episodes were watched closely by the second Inter-Party government, but it did little of note in a wider European integrationist context. On a foreign affairs level, Ireland's admission into the United Nations in December 1955 was undoubtedly the high point of Cosgrave's three-year stewardship of the Department of External Affairs.[12]

THINKING SERIOUSLY ABOUT EUROPE

A decision taken in October 1956 proved vital to the development of a more active approach to European policy. At a meeting held on 9 October 1956 the second Inter-Party government decided that, acting under the direction of the Taoiseach, the secretaries of the Departments of External Affairs, Industry and Commerce, Agriculture, Finance and the Taoiseach should examine the probable effects on Ireland's interests of an association of member countries of the OEEC in a free trade area.[13] Chaired by T.K. Whitaker, the newly appointed Finance secretary, this was the genesis of the cross-departmental group that played such a key role in moving Irish economic policy away from a protectionist framework to one where interdependence with other European economies was assumed. This body was thus crucial to the linkage of foreign and economic policies which dominated Irish policymaking in the second half of the 1950s. Seven meetings were held before the Committee of Secretaries issued a memorandum on 18 January 1957. This report pointed out that when assessing the question of Ireland's participation in a free trade area, the government had to take into account not only the economic considerations which would arise, but also general considerations of national policy that would affect Ireland's participation in a movement towards the closer integration of the countries of Western Europe. The importance of these initial stirrings within Ireland over the formation of economic blocs in Europe was noted by the American embassy

---

12 For an analysis of Ireland at the United Nations, see Joseph Morrison Skelly, *Irish Diplomacy at the United Nations, 1945–1965: National Interests and the International Order* (Dublin, 1997). **13** NAI DT S 15281/D, interim report of the Committee of Secretaries, 18 January 1957.

in Dublin, which reported to Washington that 'the Irish are beginning to think about the problems associated with EFTA. The Taoiseach ... pointed out that Ireland could not hope to remain unaffected by the plan and advised interested organisations to study the plan'.[14] Indeed, the various moves towards European integration were actively followed by the main economic interest groups, with farmers' organisations, trade unions and business interests all adopting positions on both EFTA and the EEC.[15]

The issue of a free trade area eventually came into the open the following month when the Council of the OEEC initiated formal negotiations to establish one. Its objective was to create a region within which there would be no tariff barriers or other restrictions to trade, although EEC nations and the other countries within the proposed trading bloc would maintain protective defences against the rest of the world. As a member of the OEEC since 1948, Ireland participated in the EFTA negotiations during 1957 and 1958. Two points were of particular importance to the government: the future of tariffs on agricultural products; and the proposal to give special treatment to underdeveloped countries (later known as 'countries in the course of economic development') by extending the period during which tariffs might be eliminated and by providing financial assistance if required. Initially, these countries were to be Greece and Turkey; Ireland, though, hoped to be included in this category.

While the Irish realised that powerful trading blocs would change the economic landscape of Western Europe, it would be fair to say that the prospect of a European free trade area embracing the member countries of the OEEC was not initially viewed by Irish policymakers with any great enthusiasm, given that the dismantling of protection was seen as a serious threat to Irish industry. Furthermore, the removal of barriers to imports into Britain would eliminate Ireland's preferential position in that market *vis-à-vis* other OEEC countries. Yet the weakness and instability of the Irish economy after a generation of self-government, and the evident failure of traditional protectionist economic policies to achieve their declared objective, led many to question the validity of these policies and to seek effective alternatives. As Garret FitzGerald pointed out at the time: 'The emergence of the Free Trade Area plan, and its presentation to the Irish public, could scarcely have been more opportune ... and the interest, even excitement which this proposal has aroused throughout the country provides remarkable evidence of the existence of this new and receptive climate of opinion.'[16]

14 National Archives and Records Administration, Washington [hereafter NARA], Record Group [hereafter RG] 59, Box 3170, 740A/oo (W)/18–157, Dublin embassy to State Department, 18 January 1957. **15** Gary Murphy, 'Government, Interest Groups and the Irish move to Europe, 1957–1963', *Irish Studies in International Affairs*, vol. 8 (1997), pp 57–68. **16** Garret FitzGerald, 'Ireland and the Free Trade Area', *Studies*, vol. xlv, no. 181 (Spring 1957), p. 19.

Three working parties were set up by the Council of the OEEC in March 1957: Working Party 21, which would deal with the general constitution of the proposed free trade area; Working Party 22, which would address the special position of agriculture; and Working Party 23 to consider the position of countries in the course of economic development. It was to the latter group that the Irish government turned its attention. As T.K. Whitaker has pointed out: 'it was taken as granted by Irish policy makers, particularly in Finance, from an early stage that economics and politics were mixed in a European context. We realised that serious issues had to be faced on both fronts when we first debated entering EFTA'.[17]

While domestic economic considerations remained paramount, there was now a foreign element to national economic policymaking. Although the Irish were worried about developments within EFTA, the fact that they were involved in the discussions at all showed the degree to which economic policy had become bound up with foreign policy. Thus it was the economic problems faced by Ireland within a rapidly changing European economic environment which dominated the Committee of Secretaries' January memorandum. While acknowledging that the establishment of the free trade zone was intended to secure the economic benefits of a unified market of 250 million people, the memorandum noted that this, of itself, would not ensure that individual countries would share proportionately in the expected benefits. It was also uncertain as to whether investment and readaptation funds would be established for the purpose of assisting any member countries which would otherwise suffer through having to fulfil the obligations of membership.

Whether Ireland joined or not, the formation of a free trade area would have profound implications for the Irish economy, necessitating a fundamental reappraisal of economic policies. The government, therefore, was forced to consider not merely the effects – favourable and unfavourable – of the advent of a free trade area on the economy, but also the question of whether participation in such a zone, or the adoption of some different policy, would best promote the expansion of the economy in the future.

After a lengthy analysis of the major sectors of the national economy it became clear that Industry and Commerce and Agriculture were the most fearful regarding Ireland's position. Industry and Commerce came to the following conclusion:

> As regards a large section of existing industries, the Department of Industry and Commerce can see no prospect of their survival, even as suppliers of the home market, except with permanent protection. The

---

[17] Author's interview with T.K. Whitaker 16 May 1994. Dr Whitaker was secretary of the Department of Finance between 1956 and 1969 and had served in Finance since 1938.

Department of Industry and Commerce can see no prospect of a significant expansion of industrial exports from Ireland to the continental part of the Free Trade Area even if we were members of the Area and could thus enter this market without any tariff barriers.[18]

Agriculture interpreted events in much the same light and saw 'little prospect of a significant expansion of agricultural exports from Ireland to the continental part of the Free Trade Area even if we were members of the Area and agricultural products were freely traded by all members other than Britain'.[19]

Ultimately, the Committee's report drew attention to the dangers inherent in the state of the economy:

> Ireland has reason not merely to be worried about the setting up of a Free Trade Area but about her future economic and political prospects generally. It is obvious that we can avoid economic stagnation and continuous loss of population only by making the most strenuous and urgent efforts to raise the efficiency and volume of production both in agriculture and in industry. If a Free Trade Area is established and we had to accept from the start the full obligations of membership, those existing industries which need permanent protection (and therefore could not adjust themselves over the transitional period) would go to the wall. Few new industries could be established in the absence of a protective shield and a guaranteed home market.[20]

While this report has come in for scathing historical criticism for its negativity and paucity of thinking, it must be noted that the fact that Irish policymakers were actually engaging in a debate about Europe at all is what is most important.[21] The negative tones are not unusual nor should they be read as so. Industry and Commerce undoubtedly felt a loyalty to those industries that had survived, and even prospered, under protection, while Agriculture was obviously very wary of any continental trading bloc that would have the potential to interfere with Ireland's special trading position with Britain. It was the question of a period of adjustment that was crucial to any proposed Irish application; despite the dire warnings about Ireland's future, one avenue that was going to be explored was the European option.

---

18 NAI DT S 15281/D, interim report of the committee of secretaries, appendix from the Department of Industry and Commerce, 18 January 1957. **19** Ibid., appendix from the Department of Agriculture. **20** Ibid., interim report. **21** Brian Girvin, *Between Two Worlds: Politics and Economy in Independent Ireland* (Dublin, 1989), pp 191–2; J.J. Lee, 'Economic Development in Historical Perspective', in John F. McCarthy (ed.), *Planning Ireland's Future: The Legacy of T.K. Whitaker* (Dublin, 1990), p. 121.

THE NEGOTIATION PROCESS

This was the position the Irish delegation was to take to the meeting of the Council of the OEEC, fixed for 12 February 1957. At a Cabinet meeting four days previously, it was decided to issue a formal statement voicing general approval of the idea of a free trade area:

> In accordance with her general attitude to movements by European countries towards closer economic association, Ireland welcomes the proposal to form a European Free Trade Area. While her attitude to the question of participating in an area will, as in the case of other countries, be determined in the light of consideration of her own national interests, Ireland views with sympathy this latest movement towards closer association among European countries and wishes the proposal every success.[22]

J.J. McElligott, at this stage Governor of the Central Bank, supported a more active approach to Europe and in early 1957, on behalf of the board of the Central Bank, he went on record in favour of Ireland joining EFTA. He noted that:

> taking the long view, the board was of the opinion that it would not be in the best interests of this country to remain aloof from the mainstream of European economic development and that the disadvantages which would result from failure to join the proposed Free Trade Area were likely to outweigh the temporary adjustments necessary in our economy consequent on a decision to join.[23]

It is significant that at this point even McElligott was of the opinion that the country's economy could not operate in isolation. He had overseen the preeminence of protection in his role as secretary of the Department of Finance between 1927 and 1953. As such, he can be seen as the architect of an economic policy that he was now to some extent renouncing. Sean Cromien, a Department of Finance official, recalls that McElligott's support for EFTA can in many ways be linked to the fact that he was 'a sponsor of Whitaker and he was open to ideas like EFTA, as philosophically he would have seen it as a classic free trade idea. I think also he had reached the conclusion that protectionism had had its day and a new economic philosophy had to be put into place'.[24] Whitaker, for

---

22 NAI DT CAB 7/183, 8 February 1957. **23** Quoted in Maurice Moynihan, *Currency and Central Banking in Ireland, 1922–60* (Dublin, 1975), pp 438–9. **24** Author's interview with Sean Cromien, 31 October 1995. Mr Cromien served in Finance from 1952 to 1994. He was appointed secretary in 1987.

his part, emphasised the need for closer association with some larger economic unit, arguing that:

> it would be a sad commentary on our industrial and agricultural policy over the last thirty years if we could now choose only between two alternatives of (a) continuing to fall behind other countries in material progress, with an unabated outflow of emigrants, or (b) economic reintegration with the United Kingdom. Whatever difficulties it may involve, the European Free Trade Area offers us a better prospect than either of those alternatives and we should hesitate long before we would decide to stay out. At the moment it is obviously the right policy to try to secure the most favourable terms of membership.[25]

At the first meeting of Working Party 23, held on 18 March 1957, two days before Ireland went to the polls for a general election, the government indicated that they would be submitting a claim for special treatment. This was based on the belief that the aim of EFTA should be to establish conditions which would enable every member of the OEEC to enter the area without fear of serious damage to its economic fabric. This Ireland would be unable to do unless she received special treatment within the zone. In the meantime, a vigorous debate was going on within the principal departments about the route to be taken.

Fianna Fáil returned to office with an overall majority after the election. Lemass was reappointed as Minister for Industry and Commerce and chaired the committee of ministers to whom the Whitaker committee reported. He immediately took a keen interest in the development of the EFTA proposals. A month previously J.C.B. MacCarthy, secretary of Industry and Commerce, had advanced the view that the Irish government:

> could offer to submit ourselves for examination (say in three years time and at successive three year intervals) and to accept the results of such examinations. It was also possible that in the last resort we might be able to agree to make an initial reduction of, say, 10 per cent in our tariffs, subject to exemption for certain sensitive industries, provided the choice was left to us.[26]

This was significant, because it showed that Industry and Commerce officials were not content to let things drift in the policy area. Although MacCarthy's tone is hesitant, and a number of years later he would argue bitterly with Whitaker about protection,[27] he also realised that association with some sort of

---

25 Quoted in Maher, *The Tortuous Path*, p. 67. **26** NAI DT S 15281/F, committee of secretaries, ninth meeting, comments of J.C.B. MacCarthy, 12 March 1957. **27** NAI DF F

trading bloc might have some benefit for Irish industry. In April the government decided to submit a memorandum to Working Party 23 which would include:

> an intimation to the effect that Ireland is willing to submit herself to independent examination, at suitable intervals, by the appropriate institutions of the Free Trade Area and to assume obligations of membership when it has been established, as a result of such examination, that her economy has attained a better relationship with the economies of those member countries of the Area which are at present more highly industrialised than Ireland.[28]

Still, the Irish Ambassador in Paris, William Fay, who was chairman of Working Party 23, urged the government to present its submission in a more 'optimistic' fashion. He suggested the application should note that Ireland welcomed the idea of the creation of a large free market that might at last provide a solid basis for the development of Irish industry through exports. He argued that the submission should declare that such development was, 'up to now, frustrated by the limits of the small home market', but that the creation of a free trade zone would enable Ireland 'to compete with the best in Europe and thus make a substantial contribution to the success of the free trade area'.[29] Eventually, the theme of Ireland's memorandum submitted to the Working Party in May was that she could not hope to share in the benefits of a free trade area unless the obligations of membership were modified so as not to deprive the country of its freedom to protect its industries over an extended transitional period.[30] Thus the government made it clear that it was 'most anxious to avail of external capital for the financing of national development' and confirmed its interest in any proposals that would be formulated for the creation of financial institutions in the free trade area.[31]

* * *

Fine Gael, back in opposition, had developed its own views on EFTA and circulated a private memorandum on Ireland's prospects within a European trading bloc, which turned up in trade union records.[32] This document noted that the cre-

---

121/15/59, Reasons for Reducing Protection. **28** NAI DT CAB 8/5, European Free Trade Area, 9 April 1957. **29** NAI DT S 15281/G, Fay to Cremin, 15 April 1957. **30** NAI DT S 15281/J, Memorandum of Government to OEEC, Working Party 23, 11 May 1957. **31** NAI DT S 15281/J, European Free Trade Area, 13 July 1957. **32** NAI ICTU, Box 41(Part 1), 7331, Fine Gael memorandum on EFTA, 23 January 1958. The memorandum was not intended to indicate official Fine Gael policy, but was prepared by a committee of experts on behalf of its research and information centre.

ation of a common customs barrier would profoundly affect the whole pattern of Irish external trade. Like other commentators, however, the party foresaw the transition from a highly protected industrial framework to an open one as having a considerable effect on Irish industrial production and employment. While the immediate danger to Irish industry could not be exaggerated, Fine Gael estimated that any drop in employment in one sector could be compensated by increases in others. They also claimed that between 1954 and 1957, a period when they were in government, 25 per cent of total national income was contributed by the industrial sector; any fall off in this figure could only be detrimental to the national economy if free trade led to a significant number of industries folding. Only 187,000 people, or 16 per cent of the labour force, were employed in manufacturing activities, and the Central Statistics Office estimated that one third of these industries would be affected by a gradual reduction in tariffs.

Thirty years of protection, however, had increased the numbers employed in manufacturing by less than 60,000. Furthermore, this figure included industries not affected by protection, such as grain milling, baking, construction engineering, electrical construction and newspaper production. Thus the labour increases in industries manufacturing some protected goods could be put at no more that 50,000, or 4 per cent of the working population. Fine Gael saw this as proof that the advent of free trade would certainly not lead to large scale unemployment in the country. It would, though, be necessary to have a period in which protected industries could prepare themselves to meet fair competition from abroad. It had been conclusively proved, they argued, that the way to full employment was not to be found in protection, since it was becoming increasingly recognised that the small size of the Irish market had hindered Irish manufacturers from obtaining the benefits of the economies of large scale production. Expansion of productivity and employment in Irish industry could be achieved only by securing access to a larger market, which could be found in a free trade zone:

> The onus of proof must be on those who argue that we should not join EFTA or be associated in some way with the EEC. With chronic unemployment, large scale emigration and a sluggish rate of industrial and agricultural expansion, nobody can be satisfied with the present framework of our economy. The prospect of increased exports bringing with them higher agricultural earnings and production, and greater supplies of foreign exchange to help finance domestic development, is one not lightly to be turned down. The Free Trade Area may not contain a magic formula to heal all our economic ills. But for a country so economically sick as Ireland is, it may easily point the way to a remedy, and should certainly not make our situation any worse.[33]

33 Ibid.

While Fine Gael was thus marketing itself as more European in its outlook than the Fianna Fáil government, some OEEC officials had doubts about the wisdom of Ireland categorising itself with Greece and Turkey. J.F. Cahan, secretary-general of the OEEC, told an audience at University College Dublin in May 1958 that Ireland was not underdeveloped in the sense that Greece and Turkey were. He went on to castigate the pessimistic mindset that prevailed in Ireland:

> I have heard a certain amount of rather pessimistic comment since I arrived. People who say that Ireland can never develop; that there is no hope. I think that it is desirable, from time to time, that one should sit down and count one's blessings before abandoning oneself to this kind of black despair.[34]

For Cahan, the free trade region offered a challenge to the less developed countries. Ireland, he argued, was not underdeveloped, but less developed. He contended that Ireland should draft a programme 'of what it is that you think you ought to achieve in the way of development in the next five or next ten years'. Cahan explicitly proclaimed that Irish policymakers should attempt to foresee progress, set themselves targets, judge as time advanced how near these targets were to being achieved and not leave it to the 'Good God or the whim of the moment' in deciding how development was to take place. He went on to argue that the Irish government should look to Europe in its search for economic progress, within which the OEEC would do all in its power to help. This assistance, however, would have to be linked with indigenous growth: 'we, who are outsiders, can give you help, but it will be useless unless you put your own backs into it as well'.[35]

Moreover, some British policymakers were asking if it was worth including such underdeveloped countries as Ireland at all. Otto Clarke, a Treasury official, maintained that they 'would be more trouble than they were worth'.[36] Indeed, the placing of Ireland, Greece and Turkey in their own working party from the start of the negotiations could well be taken as a sign of their importance or, more correctly, their lack of importance within the whole structure of EFTA thinking. Irish ambitions to enter such an area, though, received a dent from a different source when, in late 1958, the negotiations for a free trade area were dramatically suspended after France vetoed the project. From the outset, the French were suspicious of British motives in excluding agriculture and

---

34 Cahan's lecture is reprinted in *Studies* as J.F. Cahan, 'Ireland's Role in a Free Trade Area', vol. xlvii, no. 186 (Summer 1958), pp 122–30. **35** Ibid., p. 130. **36** Quoted in Richard Lamb, *The Macmillan Years, 1957–1963: The Emerging Truth* (London, 1995), p. 113.

eventually decided that their own best interests lay within the EEC, not the EFTA.

Almost immediately after this failure seven members of the OEEC started secret negotiations to form a free trade area among themselves. In June 1959 these talks came into the open, and six months later the Stockholm Convention establishing EFTA was ready for signing. The Irish government was not invited to the preliminary discussions held in February 1959, probably because the seven nations did not want to be encumbered with the kind of problems associated with Ireland during the OEEC negotiations. In Ireland the prospect of sudden isolation gave cause for concern in some official circles, particularly within Finance. *Economic Development*, Whitaker's seminal policy document of 1958, had proclaimed in its first chapter that 'Sooner or later, protection will have to go and the challenge of free trade be accepted. There is really no other choice for a country wishing to keep pace materially with the rest of Europe'.[37] Now, however, the European option seemed less attainable than ever.

Nonetheless, for Lemass the European dimension to economic policy remained at the hub of government thinking. This was noted by the American embassy in Dublin, which commented in August 1959:

> Although Ireland has demonstrated in the UN that it has a wide interest in foreign affairs that do not directly affect the interests of Ireland, the country has failed to show a realistic interest in foreign affairs that do have a direct bearing on its progress. In this regard the opposition ... have been most critical of the Taoiseach's failure to cope with Ireland's interest in European markets ... it appears that the necessity of foreign cooperation is being brought home to Lemass and that he now realises that he must deviate from his government's policy of indifferent isolation and take an active role in establishing a place for Ireland in the European trade pattern.[38]

This was also true at an administrative level. Finance emphasised the dismantling of protection and the evolution of an export-led external economic policy. Thus the thought of being outside any of the major European trading blocks was anathema to them. At this junction the Irish government had two alternatives in its quest to protect its interests. One was to seek participation in EFTA and thus secure a seat at subsequent negotiations. The other course was to work for closer economic relations with Britain. Notwithstanding the view of

37 T.K. Whitaker, *Economic Development* (Dublin, 1958), p. 1. **38** NARA RG 59 Box 3170, 740A/00 (W)/6–859, Dublin embassy to State Department, 6 August 1959.

the Americans that Lemass had recognised that Ireland's long term future lay within Europe, the second course was adopted in recognition of the preponderant place still occupied by Britain in Ireland's external trading relations. The government decided that since three-quarters of Irish exports were going to Britain and Northern Ireland, it should explore the possibility of building on the preferential arrangements of 1938 and 1948 before turning to Europe in its efforts to expand Irish exports and develop the economy.

Whether Ireland joined EFTA or not, it seemed quite clear that her prosperity still depended on the agricultural economy. While membership of EFTA would subject Irish manufacturers to unfettered competition, it would provide new markets for farmers (although their prime target was still the EEC). Faced with the options of embarking on a process of accession to EFTA or of negotiating free trade agreements with Britain alone, the government came down in favour of the latter when it turned its attention to the possibility of acceding to GATT. Irish interest in the free trade area had naturally stemmed from the prospect of greatly expanded agricultural exports. The government had informed the Council of the OEEC in early 1960 that its trade returns showed that the trade balance with non-sterling member countries was extremely unfavourable – in roughly the proportions of three to one. This position, it noted, had 'recently become more serious by reason of the emergence among our partners in this Organisation of two trading groups, EFTA and the EEC'.[39]

When agriculture was not going to be included in the EFTA context, Irish policymakers felt that they had no option but to revert to the old formula of negotiating independent trade agreements with the United Kingdom. Britain, meanwhile, was beginning to cast her own eyes towards the EEC, and ultimately the EEC was to become the prime focus of Irish economic policy. As Tadhg Ó Cearbhaill, who as assistant secretary in the Department of the Taoiseach was intimately involved in the EFTA negotiations, recalled:

> In the end we were not that enthusiastic, as there was a feeling within government at the time that the whole concept of Europe would come right in the end and it was within a larger unified EEC that we wanted to be associated. Lemass was very much of that view. Policy was directed with that in mind.[40]

---

[39] NAI DFA 348/69/II, statement by Irish representative at OEEC Council, 14 January 1960.
[40] Author's interview with Tadhg Ó Cearbhaill, 23 November 1995. Mr Ó Cearbhaill served as private secretary to three Ministers for Industry and Commerce and later worked as assistant secretary in the Department of the Taoiseach.

CONCLUSION

Although the Irish government reverted to traditional norms in its attitude to the development of trading blocs in Europe, there can be little doubt that the EFTA negotiations did mark the beginning of a wider perspective to Irish foreign and economic policymaking. While the EEC was to take precedence in the early 1960s, the EFTA negotiations which preceded it did open up the possibility that the European option was the way forward for Ireland.

Nevertheless, there were still many in the administrative framework who doubted the wisdom of fully entering a European trading bloc. Con Cremin, by this time secretary of External Affairs, saw Ireland's relationship with both European trading groups in June 1960 in the following terms when suggesting to the deputy secretary of Industry and Commerce a reply to a Dáil query about Ireland's refusal to join EFTA:

> It is probable that in our circumstances association would be the most appropriate formula having regard particularly to the fact that we could not accept the full obligations of either instrument nor accord that degree of reciprocity which would be required for full membership. The terms of association on our part with either group would have to safeguard the special trading relationship between this country and Britain which is provided for in the Anglo–Irish Trade Agreements. Such association would be considered primarily as a means of enabling us to share in the benefits of a general European settlement of trade and economic relations on terms which would take account of our own economic circumstances.[41]

The premise that Ireland initially seek association rather than full membership of an economic group suggested that any future EEC negotiations would be tortuous. In many respects, Cremin's view is symptomatic of a general caution in the Department of External Affairs towards European events in this period. Lemass' relationship with his External Affairs Minister, Frank Aiken, was problematic, and Aiken played little role in formulating European policy.[42] It was Lemass, as Fianna Fáil Taoiseach, and Whitaker, as secretary of Finance, who led the way towards the wider perspective to Europe in the late 1950s. External Affairs' attitude towards the European question was reactive.

Nevertheless, the decision to examine membership in EFTA and the EEC had important consequences for both economic and foreign policy. The entire

---

[41] NAI DT S 16877/B, Cremin to Connolly, deputy secretary, Department of Industry and Commerce, 18 June 1960. [42] Horgan, *Seán Lemass*, p. 193.

direction of Irish economic policy was opened up, became more closely focused on Europe and was thus critically interlinked with the state's foreign policy. This contrasted both with its previous isolationism and its relationship with Britain. While Britain's foreign policy intentions with regard to Europe were crucial to Ireland's own position, there was, nevertheless, a realisation within the government and the broader policymaking community by the close of the 1950s that Ireland could not ignore wider events in Western Europe.

Irish Neutrality and the First Application for Membership of the EEC, 1961–3

Dermot Keogh

INTRODUCTION

On 31 July 1961 Ireland applied for full membership of the European Economic Community.[1] More than a year later, the Fianna Fáil Taoiseach, Seán Lemass, informed Dáil Éireann on 30 October 1962 that the European Council had agreed to the opening of negotiations on the Irish application for membership of the Community under Article 237 of the Treaty of Rome, and those negotiations were to begin on a date to be fixed by agreement between the Irish government and the six EEC governments.[2] But General de Gaulle's veto of British membership in January 1963 was issued before Ireland had reached the point of formally opening negotiations with the 'Six'.[3]

Seán Lemass' government had to overcome two significant obstacles in order to achieve what might have been regarded by a number of contemporaries as a preliminary and very modest policy goal. First, Dublin was obliged to demonstrate to the Six that the Irish economy was robust enough to withstand the shock of entry into an open market. Second – and this was to prove the more difficult obstacle – a neutral Ireland which had refused to join the North Atlantic Treaty Organisation in 1949 was forced to demonstrate its willingness in principle to participate in a future political and defence union, even if the evolution of that Community might ultimately involve Ireland having to join NATO.

This chapter will briefly describe the historical background to the application for entry into the EEC and outline the course of the discussions between Dublin and the Six. It will lay particular emphasis on the Irish government's

---

[1] For background to developments in Ireland, see Denis. J. Maher, *The Tortuous Path: The Course of Ireland's Entry into the EEC, 1948–1973* (Dublin, 1986), pp 51–117. [2] *Dáil Deb.*, 197, 3–4, 30 October 1962. [3] Britain had applied for membership on 10 August 1961 and opened negotiations on 8 November 1961; Denmark applied on the same date, 10 August, and were allowed to open negotiations on 30 November 1961; Norway applied on 30 April 1962 and began negotiations on 12 November 1962.

reaction to the 'shock' discovery that the country's policy of neutrality was perceived in Washington and in the capitals of the Six as being a major stumbling block to full membership of the Community. That was to produce a fundamental reappraisal of Irish neutrality, as leading Irish politicians and senior civil servants were brought face-to-face with the realities and responsibilities of EEC membership.

LEMASS AND THE POLITICS OF EUROPEAN INTEGRATON

At the age of 60 Seán Lemass succeeded Eamon de Valera as Taoiseach in 1959.[4] A veteran of the 1916 rising and a founder-member of Fianna Fáil in 1926, he had played a central role for over twenty years at ministerial level in the development of national economic policy.[5] His assumption of the position of Taoiseach in June 1959 coincided with the culmination of a debate in senior political and administrative circles concerning the future of the traditional Fianna Fáil policy of economic protectionism.

The First Programme of Economic Expansion covering the period 1959 to 1963 was based on a study by the secretary of the Department of Finance, Dr T.K. Whitaker, entitled *Economic Development*, which had been completed in early 1958 and published under his own name in November of that year. The strategy was to increase Irish agricultural production and look for markets in the higher priced continental food market. The plan was also to attract foreign capital for investment in employment-intensive manufacturing export industries.[6]

Ireland, after long deliberations, did not join the European Free Trade Area (EFTA). A trade agreement with Britain, to which over seventy percent of her exports still went, was signed in 1960.[7] The country's application for EEC membership in July 1961 signalled the end of the policy of economic protectionism which had been introduced by Eamon de Valera when Fianna Fáil first came to power in 1932.

But, as Dublin was also to discover very soon, the preservation of another 'orthodoxy' – neutrality – was the subject of intense suspicion in the Commission and among the Six, all of which were members of NATO. Foreign policy was not an area in which Lemass had much direct involvement during his political career. That changed abruptly in mid 1961. Up to that point he had left

---

4 Dermot Keogh, *Twentieth-Century Ireland: Nation and State* (Dublin, 1994), p. 241 ff. **5** Michael O'Sullivan, *Seán Lemass: A Biography* (Dublin, 1994), pp 150–5. **6** Richard Breen, et al., *Understanding Contemporary Ireland: State, Class and Development in the Republic of Ireland* (Dublin, 1990), p. 38. **7** This was replaced by the Anglo–Irish Free Trade Area Agreement on 14 December 1965: see James F. Meenan, *The Irish Economy since 1922* (Liverpool, 1970), pp 79–80.

almost all matters relating to that portfolio in the hands of the Tánaiste and Minister for External Affairs, Frank Aiken.[8] The latter, a veteran republican and founder-member of Fianna Fáil, was as doctrinaire as Lemass was heterodox. While Lemass adjusted his thinking to take account of new international developments, Aiken's foreign policy remained dominated by radical nationalism. After Fianna Fáil's return to power in 1957 he concentrated his energies on Ireland's multilateral relations within the United Nations, spending a number of months each year living in New York.[9]

Dr Conor Cruise O'Brien, who was on the diplomatic staff of the Irish mission to the UN in the late 1950s,[10] viewed Aiken as 'an old and close associate of de Valera's' aspiring 'to play a similar part in the United Nations to Mr de Valera's in the League [of Nations]'.[11] O'Brien identified Aiken's UN policy as moving from one of relative independence from Washington from 1957 to one of being 'solidly riveted to the United States' in the 1960s.[12]

Aiken, in contrast to Lemass' Atlanticist position in the early 1960s, displayed at the UN the same independence of thought and action which had been characteristic of Eamon de Valera's stance at the League of Nations in the 1930s. He was outspoken on such questions as decolonisation, anti-apartheid and non-proliferation. In 1957 he caused fury in the State Department when – contrary to what had been reported by the United States embassy in Dublin – Ireland changed its vote on China. Dublin had been counted as a safe vote in blocking the entry of mainland China into the UN. In that year Ireland voted in favour of a discussion on the representation of China, and Henry Cabot Lodge, the American envoy to the UN, phoned the State Department: 'The F[oreign] M[inister] of Ireland is going nuts'. The Irish head of mission at the UN, Frederick Boland, had opposed the change in policy. Many years later he wrote: 'Well, we brought down a ton of bricks', describing the reaction within the United States.[13] That example of volatile behaviour at the UN between 1957 and 1960 did not build up a repository of goodwill towards Ireland in the State Department.[14]

---

8 Aiken, born in 1898, had served as Minister for Defence from 1932 to 1939; Minister for the Coordination of Defensive Measures, 1939 to 1945; Minister for Finance, 1945 to 1948; and Minister for External Affairs, 1951 to 1954, and 1957 to 1969.   **9** See Conor Cruise O'Brien, 'Ireland in International Affairs', in Owen Dudley Edwards (ed.), *Conor Cruise O'Brien Introduces Ireland* (London, 1969), pp 130–4; Con Cremin told me that when he was Irish representative at the UN in the 1960s, Aiken used to dine most nights with his family.   **10** Mr Liam Cosgrave, a future Taoiseach between 1973 and 1977, was Minister for External Affairs between 1954 and 1957. Irish–American relations were handled with sensitivity towards Washington's global positions during that period. Ireland was admitted to the UN in 1955.   **11** O'Brien, 'Ireland in International Affairs', p. 129.   **12** Ibid., p. 132; a comprehensive account of Conor Cruise O'Brien's diplomatic experiences may be found in *To Katanga and Back: A UN Case History* (London, 1962).   **13** Dermot Keogh, *Twentieth-Century Ireland: Nation and State* (Dublin, 1994), pp 235–6.   **14** The older serving officers in the State Department would

Neither did Aiken receive any praise in Washington for his support of Ireland's military neutrality. Although Fianna Fáil had not been in power at the time when Dublin refused an invitation in 1949 to join NATO, he accepted the retrospective rationale of the then Minister for External Affairs, Seán MacBride, that partition – the division of the island between North and South – was an impediment to membership.[15] In reality, MacBride had attempted to barter Irish membership of the Alliance in return for a *démarche* by Washington on partition.[16] That tactic failed.[17] The consequence of that action was that Ireland, a strongly anti-communist country, hyper-sensitive about its own military vulnerability in the 1950s, remained outside NATO.[18] Shortly after de Valera retired and was replaced by Lemass in 1959 sensitivity about Ireland's possible membership of a military alliance was secondary to the achievement of full EEC membership.

THE 1961 IRISH APPLICATION – THE ROLE OF THE POLICY OF NEUTRALITY

Aiken was given very little opportunity in the early 1960s to display either his maverick foreign policy instincts or his Euroscepticism. The Taoiseach played the lead role in the country's bid for EEC entry from 1961 to 1963. The Department of External Affairs was represented in the application process by its secretary, Con Cremin, by Ambassador Hugh McCann in London, by Ambassador Frank Biggar in Brussels and by Denis McDonald in Paris. The secretary of the Department of Finance, Dr T.K. Whitaker, together with Cremin, were the most important voices in the inter-departmental committee which was set up in Dublin to monitor and advise on the progress of the application.[19]

Although submitted on 31 July 1961, the German Vice-Chancellor and Minister for Economics, Professor Ludwig Erhard, informed Dublin that the Irish application would be placed before the Council of Ministers at their next meeting in September.[20] While the British and Danes were given permission to

---

have remembered – or the folklore would have supplied – details of Aiken's celebrated face-to-face confrontation with President Roosevelt during World War II. Aiken had refused to leave the room when the interview ended. Roosevelt's aides brought in the President's tea. When Aiken still refused to leave, Roosevelt overturned his tray onto the floor and the noise brought aides and bodyguards rushing into the room. Aiken then left: personal interview with Frank Aiken, March 1977. **15** Keogh, *Twentieth-Century Ireland*, pp 193. **16** Ibid., pp 194. **17** Ibid., pp 192–3. **18** Ibid., pp 203–8; here I provide an examination of the elaborate emergency planning in Ireland in the early 1950s. This was based on the hypothesis that the Cold War was inevitably going to turn into open conflict between East and West. **19** I base this judgement on a review of the files in the Departments of Finance, Taoiseach, Foreign Affairs and the State Department records in the National Archives and Records Administration, College Park, Maryland. **20** Maher, *The Tortuous Path*, p. 137.

proceed to the negotiation stage, the Council agreed to await the opinion of the Commission before making a decision on the Irish case. It was felt that there was a need to study whether Ireland, in view of her 'special circumstances', would be in a position to fulfil the economic and political commitments under the Treaty of Rome.[21]

Following the Council of Minister's meeting, Erhard informed Lemass by letter that the member states of the Six wished to have an 'exchange of views' with him in Brussels to discuss 'the special problems' raised by the application.[22] Aware of the need for further information, the Taoiseach sent both Cremin and Dr Whitaker on a tour of the capitals of the Six in late September to sound out official opinion on the Irish application.[23] After a round of discussions in Brussels, both men concluded that the 'political aspects can prove very important for the Council of Ministers. There is a tendency to group countries by categories and we are generally put in the same category as Sweden, Switzerland and Austria. Denmark and Britain, on the other hand, are classified in the NATO group.[24] In Bonn both men were made aware that the most Dublin could hope for was associate membership. It also came as no surprise to the two officials to learn that there was considerable scepticism in Bonn and in other member states about the *bona fides* of a non-NATO member's willingness to play a constructive role in the future defence of a political community.[25] The two diplomats reported the following in the context of their discussion in Germany:

> Acceptance by a potential member of the over-riding nature of the political objectives of the Community is, of course, essential. This is not, however, enough. Danger threatens Western Europe now and only if the Community is united and ready to defend what it has, can it hope to have the opportunity to move forward to its ideals. The countries joined in NATO have a defensive alliance. While there are reasons for our being outside NATO up to this – and membership of NATO has not been defined as a condition of membership of the Community – nevertheless the Community would expect a new member to make an effective, positive contribution, whether through NATO or otherwise, to the preservation of the existing foundations for advance towards the ideal of European unity.[26]

Ireland's decision to seek membership of the EEC, according to the two officials, had raised very sensitive issues concerning Ireland's commitment to the

---

21 Ibid., p. 142. **22** Ibid., p. 142. **23** NAI DT S 16877/Q/61. **24** NAI DT S 16877/Q/61, Whitaker/Cremin report, 26 September 1961, p. 25. **25** T.K. Whitaker interview, Dublin, July 1996. **26** NAI DT S 16877/Q/61, Whitaker/Cremin report, 26 September 1961, p. 40.

defence of Western Europe. European defence, while not in any strict sense part of the Treaty of Rome, was very much part of the wider policy debate on the future of Europe. Ireland could not afford to stand back from that debate, according to both Cremin and Whitaker.

THE IRISH APPLICATION AND THE UNITED STATES

The two senior Irish envoys had toured the capitals during the first three weeks in September and had written a fifty-eight-page report on their findings. The message did not bring much comfort to Lemass and his cabinet colleagues. In Washington, meanwhile, Dublin discovered that one very senior member of the Kennedy administration was quite hostile to the idea of Ireland's full membership of the EEC. The Under-Secretary for Economic Affairs, George Ball, did little to disguise his hostility. That was revealed when Joseph Sweeney, officer-in-charge of United Kingdom and Irish Affairs at the State Department,[27] had a 'free and easy' off-the-record conversation with Ambassador T.J. Kiernan on 13 November 1961. The ambassador reported to Dublin that:

> Starkly stated, the position is: (i) The present prospect, as seen by the State Department, is that Ireland's application for membership will be rejected; (ii) The United States' attitude is definitely not to favour neutrals, like Sweden and Ireland, as associate members; (iii) The US policy is formed by Under-Secretary of State, George W. Ball ... and he is frankly working towards a greater Atlantic Alliance, 'with all the works', seeing the economic union as a means to a more solid defence-against-communism organisation than NATO has proved to be.[28]

The conversation, as reported above, then moved from the ambassadors office across the road to the male-only surroundings of the Cosmos Club. Kiernan asked whether Ball saw the EEC developing towards 'taking in' NATO. Sweeney replied 'Yes'. The ambassador continued to find out the basis of the hostility towards Ireland:

---

27 Sweeney, according to Ambassador Kiernan, was 'on intelligence duties' in Great Britain and Ireland during World War II and he 'is well-informed about Ireland, has followed developments with a considerable degree of sympathy, is conversant with the main body of Irish writing, and can read the Irish language with facility ... He has a good understanding of Irish politics and political parties: NAI DFA 313/2/H, Kiernan to Cremin, 14 November 1961. (This file and subsequent documents were kindly pointed out to me by Paula Wylie, who is working on a doctorate under my supervision on recognition and Irish foreign policy.) **28** Ibid., Kiernan to Cremin, 14 November 1961.

Since I understood from him that Mr. Ball is not too friendly to our application, I asked him whether this attitude had arisen as a result of remarks from representatives of other countries concerned, or how. He said that while the British attitude, as reported to him, had at first not been noticeably friendly to us, he was aware that this had changed; but that the German and Italian attitudes were against us. But the nub of the matter was, it seemed, our refusal to join NATO in the first instance, and our policy of neutrality at the UNO. Mr Ball sees membership of the EEC as being properly confined to countries which are not, and do not profess to be, neutral. This would exclude us.

As to the way forward, Sweeney's own view was that while it could not be expected that Ireland would make it understood that the country would now apply for membership of NATO:

we still have to make it clear beyond doubt that we are prepared to accept the responsibilities of future developments of the EEC which would be political, would most likely involve our coming into the open from non-alignment and might very well involve a measure of military co-operation.

The man to influence was, according to Sweeney, George Ball: 'He said that the danger is that when the papers reach the President, fixed attitudes will have become frozen and our case will be under the ice, so that the issue will not be before the President.'

Kiernan, who had read Whitaker and Cremin's report of their trip to the capitals of the Six, briefed Sweeney about the Irish position: 'I told him that I understood that we accepted the full political implications of membership no matter how they should unfold in the future. I felt he still had doubts in regard to our attitude towards defence even hypothetically'. Sweeney wanted the Irish to move slowly so that he could take the matter away with him and discuss it with the heads of the European Division. Ball, who was going on a tour of the EEC capitals in December, might be approached with an *aide-memoire* followed by a request to be seen by Kiernan: 'A word from Washington can go a long way towards removing difficulties in Europe', the ambassador wrote to Cremin.[29]

---

29 Sweeney did not encourage the ambassador, nor was Kiernan enthusiastic, to look for an immediate meeting with Ball or with senior officials in the State Department. The ambassador wrote: 'I know these formal meetings very well and they make little impression on currently-formed and officially-orthodox views'. Neither would a note be, in Sweeney's view, be very productive as the 'reply would be checked by so many officials that it would be no more than evasive acknowledgement': ibid.

But those plans were disrupted by the news which reached Washington on 14 November that Aiken had independently requested a meeting three days later with Ball in Paris, where both were attending a meeting of the OECD. This came as a surprise as much to Sweeney as to Ambassador Kiernan. A State Department official further told Kevin Rush, chargé d'affaires in the Irish embassy, that he had concentrated his energies in the short time available before the meeting in trying to ensure that Ball would approach it 'at least with an open mind and would adopt a "fluid" position'. Rush was warned that:

> a confrontation at such a high level might have unfortunate consequences because of the lack of sufficient 'briefing' on either side. He said it was a great pity that there had not been time to put to better use your [Kiernan's] very valuable initiative of yesterday in explaining, in detail, the basis of our approach to the Common Market question.[30]

Kiernan briefed Ambassador McDonald in Paris about the delicate situation in a midnight telephone conversation on 16 November – the night before the Aiken/Ball meeting. Kiernan said bluntly that 'Mr Ball is unsympathetic towards us', having a difficult and 'grim' approach. He further told McDonald that two officials in the State Department had done a certain amount of work on the Irish voting record at the UN to show Ball that an independent attitude tended to help American policy and they 'had also used the argument of the effects on us of the rejection of our application and the grave economic repercussions this would have'. Kiernan had been informed that Ball had moved from 'a closed to an open mind'. He told McDonald that the talks between Aiken and Ball ought to be considered as preliminary and that it might be necessary for the Taoiseach to go to Washington to explain matters. If it proved impossible to move Ball from his antagonistic position toward Ireland, Kiernan said that 'it might be necessary to go as far as the White House'. However, it was important to ensure that the talks between Aiken and Ball would 'keep the doors open'.[31]

Both the American and Irish records of the meeting reveal that Ball and Aiken remained reserved. The Irish Ambassador in Paris, Denis McDonald, reported:

> At this point Mr Ball opened up the question of our EEC application ... The Minister said we had done so, believing that we could fulfil the political and economic obligations called for by membership. In regard to the political aspect, the Minister remarked that Ireland's difficulty

---

30 Ibid., Rush to Kiernan, 14 November 1961.   **31** Ibid., minute by McDonald, Paris, of a telephone conversation with Kiernan, Washington, at midnight on 16 November, 1961.

about entering the NATO Pact was, of course, well known and related to the partition problem. We believed that if Britain and ourselves were to enter the EEC as full members, the tariff problem between the North and the South would tend to disappear with a corresponding trend towards unity of political aims which would be good for both parts of Ireland. It was not clear what we would be required to do under the heading of defence, but felt that the partition problem might have taken on a different complexion before we would be relied upon to take a decision on a common defence policy.[32]

Aiken added that Ireland had always been in favour of European unity and in particular of rapprochement between the French and the Germans.

The American report of the conversation revealed that Ball had let Aiken do almost all of the talking. The Minister for External Affairs replied to Ball that Ireland was prepared to face the political and economic consequences of membership:

> Ireland's attitude towards Europe had evolved considerably since World War II days. He recalled that, while some sectors of Irish opinion at that time wish[ed] to take advantage of England's difficulties, the Irish Government had made it clear that Ireland would not be a base for attacks on the UK. He thought that the UK attitude on the partition question was 'beginning to come around' and that the disappearance of the customs border in Northern Ireland would help eventually to wipe out the political division. He felt the latter would come about before political integration in Europe reached a point where the question of the political division would be barrier to effective Irish participation.[33]

Nothing was decided at the meeting.

DR WHITAKER, IRISH POLICY AND NATO

Conscious of the nascent opposition in Washington and the ambivalence in the capitals of the Six towards Irish membership of the EEC, Lemass used every

---

32 Ibid., McDonald to Cremin, 17 November 1961. **33** National Archives and Records Administration, College Park, Maryland, General Records of the Department of State (Records regarding UK negotiations with the EEC, 1961/62), folder: Ireland/EEC negotiations, Box 1, memorandum of conversation between Aiken, McDonald, Ball and Tuthill, Head of American Permanent Delegation to OECD, 17 November 1961. A memorandum on the Irish position on the EEC, possibly written by Sweeney, was sent to Ball in advance of the meeting, but it was not on file.

major public occasion in the weeks remaining in 1961 to emphasise the totality of Ireland's commitment to Europe. He spoke to the Cork Chamber of Commerce on 11 November of the great economic progress enjoyed by Ireland in recent years and welcomed the prospect of the immediate political obligations of membership of the community being authoritatively defined. Although not a member of NATO, Lemass said that Ireland was not unwilling to participate in the movement for European integration.[34] The Taoiseach gave many similar speeches throughout the country in 1962 in the course of which he emphasised Ireland's willingness to play her role in the future defence of Europe.[35]

Intensive discussions continued at the most senior level in the civil service in preparation for the planned visit of Lemass to Brussels in January 1962. As the Taoiseach's presentation to the Six was being drafted, the issue of Ireland and NATO became a focus of attention amongst the relevant departmental secretaries. That exchange of views continued over Christmas and the issues were set out in a letter on 4 January from the secretary of the Taoiseach's office to departmental secretaries who were to meet Lemass the following morning. Before that meeting, Whitaker presented his observations to the Minister for Finance. The five-page minute addressed the issues in a frank manner: 'We have applied for membership of the EEC because it would be economic disaster for us to be outside the Community if Britain is in it', was his opening sentence. He advised his minister that if Ireland wished to protect her economic future, her independence and her influence in the rest of the world:

> we should not ourselves raise obstacles to being admitted as members of the EEC. To say that we would withdraw our application if membership of NATO were insisted upon would be extremely unfortunate. Nobody has yet told us that this is a condition of membership of the EEC. On the other hand, nobody so loves us as to want us in the EEC on our own terms. The Community have difficulties enough without adding those introduced by a 'contrary' new member who will bring the Community no particular benefits but will inflict on it additional problems including (as they might well view it) this tiresome 40-year old squabble with Britain. We would just be playing into the hands of those who would rather see us blackball ourselves than have the trouble themselves of doing it.[36]

He warned his minister against placing Ireland in a position where she was seen to be using the Community 'as a lever' against Britain: 'It would be a natural reaction to say in effect "no one asked you to apply and we would be happy to

---

34 Maher, *The Tortuous Path*, p. 144. **35** See the text of the speeches in the various parts of the file NAI DT S 16877. **36** NAI DT S 16877/61, Whitaker minute, 5 January 1961.

be rid of you, your agricultural surpluses, your industrial difficulties and your unintelligible attitude towards NATO."'

Whitaker pointed out that it was well to remember that 'it is our own propaganda which has given such an artificial significance to NATO in relation to Partition'. He then called into question the basis of Ireland's historical rationale for non-membership of NATO:

> There is, in fact, no necessary incompatibility between joining NATO and maintaining our stand on partition. Indeed, as I shall show later, quite the contrary would be the case if we were members of the EEC as well. The attitude that was taken towards NATO in 1949, and which perforce has been maintained since, does not bear very close examination.

Whitaker then outlined the original policy and argued that there was 'diminishing likelihood of its being effective as time goes on'. He was referring to the following line of argument:

> The attitude that we took towards NATO in 1949, and which perforce has been maintained since, does not bear very close examination. It is clear that the rejection in 1949 of the invitation from the United States Government to take part in the preparatory talks aimed at a North Atlantic Treaty took place in a mood of annoyance with the Ireland Bill and also in the belief, induced perhaps by Churchill's growls, that we were important to an Atlantic alliance and could use this as a means of getting the Americans to bring pressure to bear on Britain to end Partition. The Americans never professed to see the relevance of our Partition objection and the leverage didn't work.

Whitaker argued that it was not clear that Ireland could rationalise its attitude in the light of the NATO treaty itself. Ireland did not even take part in the preliminary discussions setting up the alliance:

> To the governments of Western Europe it may seem that we have refused to take part in the defence of the West simply because of our dispute with Britain over Partition. Do we wish it to be understood that we would not stir a finger to help the Six Counties if they were attacked by Russia or, more generally, that we would think it a matter of national principle to remain uncommitted and unhelpful if Russia attacked Western Europe? We say we agree with the aims of the North Atlantic Treaty and are not ideologically neutral. But are these not in danger of being regarded as empty professions when effect is deliberately not given to them because of preoccupation with a national problem which we have lived with for 40 years?

Whitaker argued that being a member of the EEC if Britain got in was the best hope available of eventual reunification of Ireland. 'We stand to gain nothing', he argued, 'from a continued refusal to join NATO, particularly if this is coupled with isolation from the European Economic Community'. He felt that the right course in approaching the attempt to gain membership was not 'by any action of ours to provoke a situation in which membership of NATO may be presented as a preliminary condition of membership of the EEC'. It was more important to be positive and as unqualified as possible in acceptance of the political objectives of the Community:

> It is no good ignoring the fact that common foreign policy and common defensive measures are essential to the preservation of any organised community. If we cannot accept this, we have no business applying for membership ... We need not conclude as yet that participation in NATO will be a *sine qua non* of membership of the community – other arrangements for common defence may conceivably be made. But, if, having got in as members without being put to the NATO fence, it later becomes clear that this is the forum in which common defence arrangements will be settled, surely we would be acting most unreasonably and short sightedly in raising Partition as a reason for non-participation.

Whitaker urged the deletion from the Lemass draft text of the reference to the 'principle of neutrality'. To do so would make the country liable to be classed in the same category as Switzerland and the other declared neutrals, that is, not eligible for EEC membership and not even qualified for associate membership. Whitaker won the policy argument

CHANGING THE PERCEPTION OF IRELAND AS A NEUTRAL

Great care was paid in the intervening weeks to the drafting of the text for Lemass' speech on 18 January 1962 in Brussels. This was a comprehensive statement of the Irish position. Keen to counteract the view that Ireland was unwilling to join fully in a political union, Lemass told the meeting:

> While Ireland did not accede to the North Atlantic Treaty, we have always agreed with the general aim of the Treaty. The fact that we did not accede to it was due to the special circumstances and does not qualify in any way our acceptance of the ideal of European unity and of the conception, embodied in the Treaty of Rome and the Bonn Declaration of 18 July last, of the duties, obligations and responsibilities which European unity would impose.[37]

---

[37] Maher, *The Tortuous Path*, pp 375–6 [Maher reproduces the entire text].

Not content that his message was strong enough, it is commonly believed[38] that Lemass instructed the Minister for Lands, Micheál Ó Moráin, to make a speech on neutrality and European defence in Claremorris, County Mayo on 5 February 1962:

> It had been made quite clear by the Taoiseach on different occasions that a policy of neutrality here in the present world division between communism and freedom was never laid down by us or indeed ever envisaged by our people. Neutrality in this context is not a policy to which we would even wish to appear committed ... I mention this to emphasise that we are entering negotiations for membership of the EEC without any pre-committed attitude, political or otherwise. Our whole history and cultural tradition and outlook has been bound up with that of Europe for past ages. We have, I believe, a full part to play in this day and age in the integration and development of a United States of Europe, and towards this end it may be necessary for us to share any political decisions for the common good.[39]

While the two speeches may have helped assuage fears in Washington and on the continent, the comments about NATO had rekindled fears among backbenchers in Dáil Éireann about a possible compromise of Irish neutrality.

Aware of the upcoming debate in Dáil Éireann, Dr Whitaker spoke by phone to Nicholas Nolan, his counterpart in the Department of the Taoiseach. The secretary of the Department of Finance said that if the political dimension of the EEC became the subject of internal controversy it would not escape the notice of Brussels. He suggested that Lemass table a motion that Dáil Éireann approved of his 18 January statement in Brussels.[40] Whitaker was told that the idea would be put to the Taoiseach.[41] Lemass did not follow that advice exactly. However, he did read the Bonn Declaration onto the record of the House before he faced a barrage of hostile questions in Dáil Éireann on 14 February. Lemass faced further questions on 15, 21, 22 and 28 February. The exchanges were robust.[42] Much of the questioning on the 14th unhelpfully focused on Irish membership of NATO and on neutrality. Lemass, trying to avoid having to accept the full content of Ó Moráin's 5 February speech in public, argued as strongly as political prudence would allow:

38 In a hierarchical and tightly disciplined party like Fianna Fáil it was unthinkable for, of all ministers, the Minister for Lands to make a speech on neutrality and defence without being instructed to do so by the Taoiseach. **39** See text of speech delivered in Conway's Hotel, Claremorris, on 5 February 1962: NAI DT S 17246/A/62. **40** See minute on file: NAI DT S 17246/A/62. **41** Ibid., Whitaker to Nolan, 10 February 1962. **42** *Dáil Deb.*, 193, 1–23, 75–6, 14 February 1962 and 193, 139–74, 15 February 1962; Lemass answered further questions on 21 February; 22 February and 28 February.

> I say in this regard that it would be highly undesirable that remarks made here should give the impression in Europe that there is a public opinion in this county which regards membership of NATO as something discreditable. The view of the Government in that regard has been made clear. We think the existence of NATO is necessary for the preservation of peace and for the defence of the countries of Western Europe, including this country. Although we are not members of NATO, we are in full agreement with its aims.[43]

In answer to a further question, Lemass said:

> The Bonn Declaration ... indicated the desire of the members of the European Economic Community to welcome as members other European states which shared their political aims. A Committee was set up to define these political aims. The Declaration made it clear that the aims would include the organisation of consultation and co-operation in the field of foreign policy.
> Mr McGilligan: And defence?
> The Taoiseach: It is, I think reasonable to assume that foreign policy includes defence.[44]

The gravity of the Irish position was evident at the regular meeting on 14 February of the secretaries of government departments – after the Dáil debate on EEC membership cited above. Cremin commented on a recent report from the Irish ambassador in Paris which he had circulated. McDonald had spoken to the director of Economic Affairs at the *Quai d'Orsay*, Olivier Wormser: 'according to the impression he formed', said Cremin, 'Mr Wormser's attitude to our application was negative'.[45] Whitaker sought the immediate preparation of a paper on the political implications of Irish membership of the EEC, not only in relation to NATO, but also to include matters such as the surrender of sovereignty to Community institutions. Cremin undertook to have a comprehensive document drafted on the political implications of membership.

In the face of further bad news about the Irish application from London, Whitaker wrote to Cremin on 1 March stressing the importance of the need to be seen to be holding one's nerve: 'It is impolitic to rush them when they have other and more pressing preoccupations. If rushed, they may take up the position suggested by the most negatively-minded member, this being the line of least resistance.'[46] He suggested that it was better in the circumstances to main-

---

[43] Ibid., 193, 6–8, 14 February 1962. [44] Ibid., 193, 13, 14 February 1962. [45] NAI DT S 17246/A/62, minutes of meeting of departmental secretaries, 14 February 1962. [46] Ibid., Whitaker to Cremin, 1 March 1962.

tain a 'dignified calm' and to take action through the Irish ambassadors in Brussels and Paris. A meeting of departmental secretaries on the same day (1 March) agreed with the Whitaker line.⁴⁷ Whitaker, worried by the divisions within Dáil Éireann on membership of NATO, told his fellow secretaries that they had to keep clear:

> in our minds that, while membership of NATO may not be a *sine qua non* for entry into the EEC, we would be committed to participate in the common defence arrangements and foreign policy of the Community. While European Ministers would, no doubt, understand political difficulties presented by a name or by certain formalities, he thought there was considerable danger that our present attitude would be understood in Community circles to mean that we could not join in any defence system with Britain.

Whitaker returned to the suggestion that he had made at an earlier meeting: he felt that it was time to 'straighten these matters out by means of an objective, logical statement on the political implications of membership of the EEC'.

Meanwhile, on the evening of 2 March Ambassador McDonald delivered an Irish statement to Couve de Murville, the French Foreign Minister. He read the note 'with a great show of concentration'. McDonald recorded that his attitude was 'friendly but non-committal'. On balance the ambassador found that his manner 'was objective and perhaps encouraging rather than anything to the contrary'. Couve de Murville suggested that perhaps the best thing would be for the Six to give something to the Irish government which could be passed on to the public after the discussions which were to take place on 6 March. The French Foreign Minister agreed that if the suggestion was agreeable to the Taoiseach the ambassador would not have to do anything more.⁴⁸ Cremin wrote to Whitaker on 6 March that Lemass regarded Couve de Murville's suggestion as 'reasonable', as did the other secretaries.⁴⁹

But the meeting of the Council did not advance the Irish case. Couve de Murville sent a senior French official on 13 March to tell Frank Biggar in Brussels that the Council was of the view that it did not have sufficient information on Ireland and had requested further clarification on certain points. The Council suggested that a meeting should take place between senior government officials and the heads of the permanent representations. But due to the heavy schedule of that group, a meeting could not take place until 11 May. Biggar, disappointed at the outcome of the Council meeting, inquired whether Ireland would be given the questions in advance. That was agreed.⁵⁰

47 Ibid., minutes of departmental secretaries' meeting, 1 March 1962. 48 Ibid., MacDonald to Cremin, 3 March 1962. 49 Ibid., Cremin to Whitaker, 6 March 1962. 50 Ibid., Biggar to

Dublin shared Biggar's disappointment. But as Couve de Murville had promised Ambassador McDonald, it gave the Irish government something positive to report in the press. It provided Whitaker and his colleagues with an opportunity to accelerate the preliminary stages leading to negotiations.

SHIFTING GROUND ON QUESTIONS OF EUROPEAN DEFENCE

Whitaker, it will be remembered, had called for the publication of a logical statement on the contentious aspects of the Irish application – as much for continental and American consumption as for the domestic audience. The Taoiseach had told the Dáil on 5 March, in relation to the traditional explanation given for Ireland's refusal to join NATO, that he had not read article 4 of its charter until recently:

> When I did read it, however, and came across this article which had been interpreted over the years as implying that accession to the Treaty would involve some implication in relation to Partition, some undertaking to do nothing about Partition, I began to ask myself was it wise in the national interest that we should persist in forcing that interpretation of the Treaty Article.[51]

That paragraph echoed the advice – quote above – tendered by Whitaker to the Minister for Finance on 5 January.

Interviewed on national television on 15 March by Dr Garret FitzGerald, who was to become Minister for Foreign Affairs in the 1970s and Taoiseach in the 1980s, Lemass gave full assurance regarding the Irish position:

> On the more general aspect, the government supports the whole conception of Western European integration, the idea of a continental union which Pope Pius XII advocated. We want Ireland to participate in this great development as we see it – with full equality of status – not as any sort of poor relation or, less still, as a reluctant partner. We are a European country geographically and historically. Our future will be affected decisively, for good or ill, by everything that happens in Europe. Personally, I regard this coming together of Western European countries as the greatest, most hopeful event of this century, and enormous in its potential for good, not merely for the peoples of Europe but for the whole world.[52]

Cremin, 13 March 1962. **51** Maher, *The Tortuous Path*, p. 151. **52** NAI DT S17246/D/62, transcript of Lemass interview with Dr Garret FitzGerald, 15 March 1962.

When FitzGerald asked Lemass about the coordination of foreign policy, defence and cultural matters, he replied: 'Yes, indeed, it is clear that without full and unreserved acceptance of these obligations, membership will not be conceded to any country.' FitzGerald then asked about the significance of NATO, and Lemass replied:

> The Treaty of Rome contains no reference to NATO. It is concerned only with economic arrangements. Nevertheless, we had to take note of the fact that the existing members of EEC, and other applicants for membership, are all in NATO. The question which we had to consider was whether the fact that we are not members could lead to misunderstanding of our attitude to the whole concept of European integration, or whether it might affect adversely the attitude of one or more member of EEC to our application, without it being even mentioned perhaps in the formal negations. It was for this reason that I decided, in my opening statement in Brussels, to refer to the fact that we are not members of NATO, to explain that this did not mean that we are not in agreement with the general aims of NATO, but was due to special circumstances, and to stress that it implied no lack of enthusiasm or support for the idea of European unity. There is, however, no reason to think that our non-membership of NATO will be a decisive factor affecting our admission to the community.[53]

Lemass followed up that statement with a number of public speeches. Opening a French festival in Dublin on 26 April, he spoke of the traditional friendship between France and Ireland in the presence of the French Minister for Industry and Commerce, Maurice Bokanowski: 'These relations will, I am convinced, grow closer in the years ahead, both because they correspond to mutual interests and because the European Economic Community is bound to bring all the countries of Western Europe much nearer together'.[54]

Later that day Lemass addressed a conference organised by the Institute of Public Administration, which trained Irish civil servants:

> Nor is there any tolerable alternative to which we can turn if our nerve should fail us when we measure the problems of membership. Declining to face the challenge of the new age, choosing to remain an isolated unit

---

[53] A journalist colleague of FitzGerald's, Desmond Fisher, had interviewed Walter Hallstein around that time. While he declined to speak explicitly about Ireland and NATO, he did have the following observations to make. He said 'the nature of neutrality has changed'. He said that the art of diplomacy was not to act in a way that would win the next war but would rather ensure that there would be no war. [54] See text on NAI DT S 17246/F/62.

on the fringe of a unified Europe – what I have already described as a sort of Red Indian Reservation – would not ensure any tolerable future and the price in the economic, moral and social decay of our country would be just as heavy.[55]

The cumulative impact of those speeches was designed to assuage further any fears on the continent and in Washington that Ireland would not live up to her responsibilities in an evolving Community.

On 4 May 1962 the departmental secretaries met to prepare the final text of the answers which had been sent to Dublin from Brussels on 18 April.[56] Led by Whitaker, the Irish delegation met the permanent representatives on 11 May.[57] The delegation delivered their answers and Whitaker answered many of the supplementary questions. They returned home confident that they had advanced the Irish case.[58]

While the various speeches on NATO and European defence by Lemass may have been read with interest in the foreign ministries of the Six, they were having an opposite impact on certain sectors of domestic political opinion. The Taoiseach was subjected to a series of questions on the progress of the application in Dáil Éireann.[59] The leader of the Labour Party, Brendan Corish, asked him on 2 May about a statement made by the Lord Mayor of Dublin and Fianna Fáil deputy, Robert Briscoe, that Ireland would grant military bases to the United States in return for Northern Ireland. Noel Browne and Jack McQuillan asked about allowing NATO naval and rocket bases in Ireland. Lemass denied that there was any truth in either of the queries. He dismissed Briscoe's speech.[60] The quality of debate in Dáil Éireann on the EEC application in 1962 remained quite abysmal.

ADMISSION TO NEGOTIATIONS ... BUT AT A DATE TO BE DETERMINED

The attitude of George Ball towards Irish entry into the EEC had remained unhelpful throughout the year. His hostility to neutral Ireland, if anything, grew as the months progressed. His casual remark that Ireland would enjoy associate

---

55 Ibid. **56** NAI DT S 17246/G/62, meeting of departmental secretaries, 4 May 1962. **57** Ibid., text of communiqué, 12 May 1962. **58** An eighteen-page memorandum was prepared for the government. It reviewed the progress of the application to date and it also provided details and an analysis of the consultations in Brussels on 11 May: ibid., 24 May 1962. **59** See text of Dáil Éireann questions and answers: NAI DT S 17246/H/62. **60** *Dáil deb.*, 195, 4–6, 2 May 1962.

membership of the Community, at best, prompted Lemass to be interviewed by the *New York Times* on 16 July 1962:

> We recognise that a military commitment will be an inevitable consequence of our joining the Common Market and ultimately we would be prepared to yield even the technical label of neutrality. We are prepared to go into this integrated Europe without any reservations as to how far this will take us in the field of foreign policy and defence.[61]

Lemass could not make Irish intentions any clearer. However, he found it necessary in early September to go over old ground when he addressed a group of visiting continental journalists. Referring to the decision in 1949 not to join NATO, he said: 'Nevertheless, they [the Irish government] made it quite clear that they were in full agreement with the aims of the NATO agreement, and at Brussels I reiterated that agreement with its aims and referred to the special circumstances which had resulted in our non-membership of NATO'.[62] He assured them that Ireland was strongly pro-Western in her foreign policy outlook:

> We do not wish, in the conflict between the free democracies and the communist empire, to be thought of as a neutral. We are not neutral and do not wish to be regarded as such, even though we have not got specific commitments of a military kind under any international agreement.

On the possible failure of the British application, Lemass replied:

> We did not make our application for membership of the European Community conditional on the success of the British application as Denmark and Norway have done. If the negotiations with Britain should fail we would, nevertheless, wish to pursue our application provided it was economically possible for us to do so.

Before George Ball's intervention, the departmental secretaries had been informed by Cremin at a meeting on 3 July that the Irish permanent representatives to the Six had given a favourable opinion on the Irish application. Cremin would arrange to meet the ambassadors from the member states to convey to them the Irish hope that the Council would deal favourably with the application at its meeting on 23 July and that Ireland would then proceed to formal negotiations. He would emphasise to the ambassadors that Dublin had refrained from pressing its case to date because the government was conscious of the pre-

---

61 Quoted in Keogh, *Twentieth-Century Ireland*, pp 246–7. **62** See the *Irish Press* and the *Irish Times*, 6 September 1962.

occupations of the Council, but the point had now been reached where further delay in proceedings to the negotiation stage would occasion disappointment and misrepresentation in the public mind.[63]

At the same meeting, Whitaker said that if the Council accepted the Irish application in principle there would probably be a formal meeting at ministerial level to open the negotiations, which would then proceed at deputy level with a further meeting at ministerial level at the end of the negotiations. He felt that it was unlikely that the government would be confronted by negotiations in September. More probably, he said, they would commence in October, but as the notice might be short it would be desirable to be fully prepared.

Contrary to what was expected in Dublin, no decision was taken to admit Ireland to negotiations by the Council in July. That was due substantially, in the eyes of the Department of External Affairs, to French requests for further clarifications from the Commission.[64]

In response, the Irish government mounted in the late summer and early autumn a major media and diplomatic campaign to help change perceptions of the country in the capitals of the Six and in Washington. Lemass concluded the initiative with a tour of the capitals of EEC member states in October 1962. Great emphasis was laid on trying to remove French doubts about the Irish case. Later that month the Council took the decision to admit Ireland to negotiations at a date to be determined in the future.[65] Ireland never got to the negotiating table in 1962.

CONCLUSION

The first application for membership of the EEC provided Lemass with a number of lessons in foreign policy realism. It was a shock for the government to realise how Ireland was perceived in Washington and in the capitals of the Six. In his memoirs, which were published in 1982, George Ball commented adversely about the policies of the European neutrals during the 1960s:

> Ireland, Denmark and Norway could, if they wished, join the European Community, accepting the same political commitments as other members; but Sweden, Switzerland, and Austria claimed that would compromise their neutrality. They wanted it both ways, demanding the chimeri-

[63] NAI DT S 17246/K/62, departmental secretaries meeting, 3 July 1962. [64] See Dermot Keogh, '"The Diplomacy of 'Dignified Calm:" An Analysis of Ireland's Application for Membership of the EEC, 1961–1963', *Journal of European Integration History*, vol. 3, no. 1 (1997), pp 81–101. [65] In order to break the logjam, Lemass had undertaken visits to Brussels, Rome, Paris and Bonn in October 1962. His shuttle diplomacy had the desired impact.

cal benefits of the community without assuming its burdens. In my view, Sweden and Switzerland defined 'neutrality' to suit their own purposes, and I had no sympathy for such casuistry.[66]

It may have been a lapse of memory on his part not to place Ireland among the neutrals. More likely it revealed his view that Irish neutrality was as ambivalent as it was contradictory, and her place was within the Atlantic Alliance. Although not prepared to force the issue, Washington made its views known through Ball, and John F. Kennedy's presence in the White House did not alter that stance.

Although the defence question was not part of the EEC treaties in 1962, Ireland's application raised certain sensitivities in the governments of the member states. A neutral during World War II, Ireland was the first non-member of NATO to seek membership. In response to the challenge for clarification, Lemass made a radical change in Irish policy towards NATO. Questioning the basis for rejection in 1949, he became very sympathetic to the arguments as outlined by Whitaker on 5 January 1962. His speeches reflected his conversion and his rhetoric became more explicit as the year progressed. In response to Ball, he went very far towards dismantling the country's traditional opposition to membership of military alliances.

Lemass, a foreign policy realist, was influenced by another major consideration. He was also innovative in his approach to Anglo–Irish relations. Cooperation between Dublin and London had been close – intimate may be a better word – throughout the entire application process. In Brussels, Biggar had very good relations with his British counterparts. The Irish ambassador in London, Hugh McCann, was given access to high level briefings on the progress of the British case.

Lemass' two principal foreign policy goals were to secure Irish membership of the EEC and to normalise the relationship between Britain and Ireland. That, in turn, meant improving relations between Dublin and Belfast – a relationship which had been neglected and allowed to fester practically without interruption since the 1925. Therefore, he was not prepared to allow matters of secondary consideration, such as eventual Irish membership of NATO or a Western European defence alliance, impede the achievement of his primary goals.

---

66 George Ball, *The Past has another Pattern: Memoirs* (New York, 1984), p. 219.

National Interests and International Mediation: Ireland's South Tyrol Initiative at the United Nations, 1960–1

Joseph Morrison Skelly

NATIONAL INTERESTS AND IRISH FOREIGN POLICY

Ireland's foreign policy is driven by the pursuit of Irish national interests. In this respect, Ireland is just like all other states. But most politicians and pundits, and even some analysts, have discounted this fundamental organising principle of Irish statecraft. They have preferred to assign other motives to it, including Christian morality, Irish cultural sensibilities or the country's supposed historical uniqueness. In the spring of 1956, for instance, the Taoiseach, John A. Costello, submitted a lengthy memorandum to his cabinet delineating the foreign policy guidelines of the second Inter-Party government. Its central thesis, he insisted, was that 'while we cannot muster big battalions, our moral influence is, or at least could be, considerable'.[1] Accordingly, it was vital to wield this authority within the wider world 'so as to strengthen the Christian civilisation of which Ireland is a part'.

Unconvinced by such assertions, historians of Irish foreign policy have recently begun to challenge the standard interpretations about its origins by concentrating on its real provenance: Irish national interests.[2] Several important developments have facilitated their efforts: the solid foundation built by a select group of earlier scholars; systematic access to original Irish diplomatic sources; a new international perspective at home. Yet there is still a lingering public and professional reluctance to apply the concept of *raison d'état* to the analysis of Irish foreign policy. This trend is quite misleading, for small states, just like their

---

[1] NAI DT S 13750/C, 30 April 1956. [2] Michael Kennedy, *Ireland and the League of Nations, 1919–46: International Relations, Diplomacy and Politics* (Dublin, 1996), p. 16; Joseph Morrison Skelly, *Irish Diplomacy at the United Nations, 1945–65: National Interests and the International Order* (Dublin, 1997), *passim;* Ronan Fanning, 'Small States, Large Neighbours: Ireland and the United Kingdom', *Irish Studies in International Affairs*, vol. 9 (1998), *passim;* Eunan O'Halpin, *Defending Ireland: The Irish State and its Enemies since 1922* (Oxford, 1999); in this volume, Gerard Keown, 'Taking the World Stage: Creating an Irish Foreign Policy in the 1920s' and Ronan Fanning, *'Raison d'État* and the Evolution of Irish Foreign Policy'.

larger neighbours, assiduously protect their interests in the international system. They do so by exercising some of the many options available to them: strong bilateral relationships, overlapping alliances, neutrality, non-alignment, economic agreements, trade pacts and so on. It is true that small states do not attain all of their objectives, for their leverage, just like that of larger states, is circumscribed by the very nature of the international order. But by no means do their limited capabilities *vis-à-vis* the great powers signify that failure in the pursuit of foreign policy aims is a foregone conclusion.

Now, the preceding analysis does not diminish the utility of ethics, or principles, in the formulation and execution of national foreign policies, for surely they have a part to play – and a very significant one. But relative to interests, their place recedes into the background. In his magisterial history of World War II Winston Churchill draws upon New Testament imagery to define the relationship between interests and ethics in the conduct of foreign affairs:

> Religion and virtue alike lend their sanctions to meekness and humility, not only between men but between nations. How many wars have been precipitated by firebrands! How many misunderstandings which led to wars could have been avoided by temporising! How often have countries fought cruel wars and then after a few years of peace found themselves not only friends, but allies!
>
> The Sermon on the Mount is the last word in Christian ethics. Everyone respects the Quakers. Still, it is not on these terms that Ministers assume their responsibilities of guiding states. Their duty is first so to deal with other nations as to avoid strife and war and to eschew aggression in all its forms, whether for nationalistic or ideological objects. But the safety of the state, the lives and freedom of their own fellow-countrymen, to whom they owe their position, make it right and imperative in the last resort, or when a final and definite conviction has been reached, that the use of force should not be excluded. If the circumstances are such as to warrant it, force may be used. And if this is so it should be used under the conditions which are most favourable.[3]

Churchill's scriptural exegesis regarding international politics remains valid even in the wake of NATO's intervention in Kosovo in early 1999. Contrary to the conclusions drawn by many utopian analysts, Wilsonian rhetoric was employed throughout this conflict not simply to describe a humanitarian response, but in a *realpolitik* fashion, namely, to legitimise an intervention driven by one of NATO'S fundamental *geostrategic* interests: the need to prevent instability along the Kosovar-Albanian frontier from engulfing the southern rim of

---

3 Winston Churchill, *The Second World War: Volume I: The Gathering Storm* (London, 1948), pp 250-1.

Balkans, especially Greece and Turkey. And the underlying international principle at work in Kosovo – interests – applies to Ireland. Consequently, those scholars who assess Irish foreign policy without paying heed to the ascendancy of national interests over idealistic intentions will arrive at erroneous conclusions about its nature and conduct.

* * *

International organisations have long served as platforms from which small states have pursued their objectives. Several of the essays in this volume attest to their immediate relevance to Irish statecraft. The United Nations is no exception in this regard. Once Ireland joined in 1955 (after being denied admission by a Soviet veto in the Security Council since 1946), Irish policymakers immediately grasped that it was a forum in which the state could successfully further some of its political aims, strengthen its long-standing bilateral relationships throughout Europe and North America, establish friendships with the emerging nations of Africa and Asia and carve out a significant niche within the international community. It was also a place where Ireland could, indirectly at least, further its economic goals by building on its positive relations with its current – and future – trading partners.

And like all nations, but especially the smaller states, Ireland constantly guarded another fundamental interest at the United Nations: the integrity of the international order. This was not an altruistic policy, but an overriding national objective, for history reveals how the descent of a stable world system into chaos asymmetrically harms small states. These countries have thus traditionally viewed the UN as instrumental in safeguarding their security interests. Ireland certainly does. As Seán Lemass, who was Taoiseach from 1959 until 1966, once asserted:

> If national self-interest is the fundamental motive force in international affairs, it is most assuredly, in the case of the small nations, that national self-interest and the interests of the United Nations as a whole, as defined in the United Nations Charter and the Universal Declaration of Human Rights, are most closely aligned.[4]

During its first decade of UN membership, Ireland contributed to the stability of the world order – its 'international' national interest – in creative ways. It promoted the rule of law; defended human rights; opposed colonialism in Africa and Asia; encouraged a relaxation of Cold War tensions; participated in UN peacekeeping missions; and sponsored a nuclear non-proliferation initiative

---

4 Sean Lemass, 'Small States in International Organizations', in A. Schou and A.O. Brundtland (eds), *Small States in International Relations* (Uppsala, 1971), pp 115–16.

that directly led to the Nuclear Non-Proliferation Treaty of 1968.[5] Quite relevant to this chapter, Ireland often engaged in diplomatic mediation, first as a member of the 'fire brigade' (a constellation of centrist delegations often called upon to resolve contentious colonial debates) and later as one of the 'middle powers' (the group of moderate states that led most peacekeeping operations). Membership in these UN clubs often overlapped, and those countries most closely associated with them included the Scandinavian states, Canada, Ireland, Tunisia, Malaysia and other middle-of-the-road Afro-Asian nations.

Irish officials at the United Nations were also sensitive to two interrelated interests germane to our discussion: partition and the rights of minorities. But in a sharp departure from the disastrous 'sore thumb' strategy pursued at the Council of Europe in the late 1940s and early 1950s, they never formally raised partition in the General Assembly.[6] Like their predecessors at the League of Nations,[7] Irish diplomats correctly grasped that the UN was an inappropriate forum for airing this grievance.

By no means, however, did Irish representatives abandon the question of partition wholesale. Instead, they addressed it in a mature diplomatic fashion. In several cases – Cyprus, Korea, Vietnam, Germany, West New Guinea, Algeria – the Irish delegation argued against partition as an expedient for resolving political conflicts. With Northern Irish Catholics in mind, it defended the rights of minorities in Tibet and elsewhere. And it adopted a liberal interpretation of Article 2.7 of the Charter (which precludes UN interference in the domestic affairs of member states) so as not to undermine any future, although at that time unlikely, move to raise partition in the Assembly.[8]

But pursuing a diplomatic agenda at the United Nations was never a straightforward task, because Ireland constantly had to reconcile many competing interests – a challenge it must also meet today in the wider international system. Irish statecraft at the UN thus demanded an endless weighing up of objectives, intentions, possibilities and constraints. In this context, when a dispute between Austria and Italy over South Tyrol arose in the General Assembly in 1960 many of Ireland's interests collided, including its wish to maintain

---

5 See Joseph Morrison Skelly, *Irish Diplomacy at the United Nations, 1945–65: National Interests and the International Order* (Dublin, 1997). **6** Patrick Keatinge, *A Place Among the Nations: Issues of Irish Foreign Policy* (Dublin, 1978), p. 113. **7** See Michael Kennedy, *Ireland and the League of Nations, 1919–46: International Relations, Diplomacy and Politics* (Dublin, 1996), pp 254–5; and, in this collection, Gerard Keown, 'Taking the World Stage: Creating an Irish Foreign Policy in the 1920s'. **8** Article 2.7 of the UN Charter reads: 'Nothing contained in the present Charter shall authorize the United Nations to intervene in matters which are essentially within the domestic jurisdiction of any state or shall require the Members to submit such matters to settlement under the present Charter; but this principle shall not prejudice the application of enforcement measures under Chapter VII.'

friendly relations with two of its European neighbours, its commitment to minority rights and its desire to increase foreign trade. The Irish delegation was forced to balance these and other priorities when determining its final stand. To their credit, Irish diplomats did not shy away from this delicate task, but actually mediated a sophisticated solution to the simmering conflict in South Tyrol. They evinced their diplomatic skills in the formidable arena of multilateral statecraft. The Irish delegation, in short, protected Ireland's national interests by engaging in a sustained round of international mediation.

AUSTRIAN NATIONALS IN THE ITALIAN STATE

The Italian alpine province of South Tyrol (also Bolzano or Alto Adige) is located just south of the Austrian border, near the Brenner Pass. Approximately two-thirds of its 250,000 inhabitants are German-speaking Austrians. It was part of the Austro-Hungarian Empire until the end of World War I. After this conflict the Triple Entente awarded it to Italy, which had entered the war coveting the region, but paid a heavy price – over 700,000 soldiers killed – to secure this and other territorial concessions from the Triple Alliance. During the inter-war years, Mussolini's fascist government pursued a policy of Italianisation by resettling thousands of Italian workers in the area and discriminating against the Austrian majority.

Despite this record, and the latent potential for ethnic tension in the province, the Allies insisted that South Tyrol remain under Italian control after World War II had ended. They supervised the drafting of the Gruber–de Gasperi Agreement (often called the Paris Agreement), which was signed by the Austrian and Italian foreign ministers in Paris on 5 September 1946. Under the terms of this treaty Austria reaffirmed Italy's sovereignty over the province. In exchange, Italy promised to protect the civil rights of the Austrian inhabitants in South Tyrol and in the bilingual border towns of the neighbouring Trento region, to safeguard their 'ethnic character and cultural and economic development' and to grant a measure of legislative and executive autonomy to the province.[9]

In the late 1950s friction developed between Italy and Austria over the implementation of the Gruber-de Gasperi Agreement. Italy asserted that they were scrupulously observing it. Austria, on the other hand, charged that by uniting

---

9 For a review of the background to this issue, see Antony Alcock, *The History of the South Tyrol Question* (London, 1970); Antony Alcock, 'The South Tyrol Package Agreement of 1969 and its Effect on Ethnic Relations in the Province of Bolzano', *Irish Studies in International Affairs*, vol. 1, no. 3 (1982); George A. Carbone and Mario Toscano (eds), *Alto Adige–South Tyrol: Italy's Frontier with the German World* (London, 1975).

the provinces of South Tyrol and Trento into a new administrative region, Italy had created an artificial zone with a manufactured Italian majority that cancelled out the original Austrian majority in South Tyrol. Austria also claimed that a smouldering sense of injustice felt by the German-speaking inhabitants, and widespread discrimination in education, housing and government appointments, accounted for the rise of a violent Austrian nationalist movement in South Tyrol and in the adjacent Tyrol region of Austria. On several occasions the Austrian government called on its Italian counterpart to discuss the crisis, but to no avail.

IRISH DIPLOMACY, AUSTRIA AND SOUTH TYROL

By the summer of 1960 Austria was considering bringing the South Tyrol dispute before the General Assembly, which was due to open in September. But before making a final decision the Austrian foreign ministry sought the advice of Ireland's Minister for External Affairs, Frank Aiken, for whom it had great respect owing to his independent stance at the UN. Ireland faced a diplomatic challenge, though, since many of its interests intersected across this one issue. For starters, it did not wish to see relations deteriorate between two European nations with which it was on very friendly terms. It was also sympathetic to Austria and Italy due to its expanding trade with both countries. On the other hand, Irish policymakers empathised with Italy for several reasons. With the partition of Ireland in mind, they understood its wish to address the last vestiges of the foreign occupation of its national territory. They likewise shared the Italian state's desire to ensure that its borders were coterminous with the surrounding natural frontiers: the entire island in Ireland's case; the Alps in Italy's case. Finally, one year later Iveagh House would be even more sensitive to Italy's position due to its potential impact on Ireland's recently submitted application to join the European Economic Community (EEC).

Other considerations tilted the Irish diplomatic scales in favour of Austria. As a long-standing matter of policy, the Irish delegation upheld the right of all member states to raise any issue in the General Assembly, no matter how controversial; this guideline accounted, in part, for its controversial backing of a discussion of the representation of China in the UN.[10] Consequently, Ireland backed in principle Austria's wish to discuss South Tyrol. It later supported Austria in practice once Italy's military allies subtly tried to prevent a non-NATO delegation – representing a small, neutral European country, no less – from challenging a NATO member in the Assembly. As Dr Conor Cruise O'Brien, who at the time was a counsellor in the Department of External Affairs

---

10 Skelly, *Irish Diplomacy at the United Nations*, chapter 2, *passim*.

and a senior member of Ireland's UN delegation, recalls, 'the idea that a non-member of NATO should be precluded from raising an issue because the county appealed against was a member of NATO was inherently uncongenial to Ireland, since it did not belong to NATO'.[11] Iveagh House's commitment to the discussion of all issues in the General Assembly also fused with another parallel to partition to incline the Irish diplomatic calculus towards Austria. This particular link to partition, however, was dissimilar from those congruities that encouraged Irish sympathy for Italy: it was motivated not by traces of foreign occupation nor by natural frontiers, but by people. Sensitive to the status of the Catholic minority in Northern Ireland, Iveagh House fully appreciated the Austrian government's wish to safeguard the rights of the German-speaking minority in South Tyrol. By the same token, Ireland endorsed Austria's desire to discuss South Tyrol, because at some future – although at that stage unlikely – date the Irish delegation might decide to raise the plight of the Catholic minority in Northern Ireland at the UN, and it was thus essential to defend the principle that minority rights could be debated in the Assembly.

* * *

Unfazed by this diplomatic minefield, Frank Aiken agreed to consult with the Austrian government, and on 15 June its ambassador to Ireland, Dr A.F. Rotter, met with Aiken to explain why his country wanted to bring South Tyrol before the United Nations. According to a summary of their conversation, Austria hoped that the General Assembly would adopt a resolution requesting the International Court of Justice at the Hague (ICJ) to consider the issue and to present an advisory opinion to the next session of the Assembly.[12] It favoured this *modus operandi* for several reasons. According to the procedural rules of the ICJ, if the Assembly asked it to investigate a matter it was required to do so forthwith, whereas if a government did so the ICJ was under no obligation to act immediately and often waited several years to do so. What's more, Rotter asserted, 'the fact that the request would emanate from the UN would give this procedure a political colour which would be entirely absent from an independent reference to the Hague and would, as it were, put the case under the umbrella of the UN'. That is to say, bringing South Tyrol within the ambit of the United Nations would internationalise it, broaden its scope and hopefully compel Italy to enter into bilateral negotiations.

Frank Aiken appreciated Rotter's remarks, but he was also well aware of Italian sensibilities. The Italian government obviously objected to a debate on South Tyrol in the General Assembly. It denied the UN's right to intervene in its own domestic affairs, basing its opposition on a strict interpretation of Article

---

11 Conor Cruise O'Brien, *Memoir: My Life and Themes* (Dublin, 1998), p. 196. 12 NAI DFA 428/14, 16 June 1960.

2.7 of the Charter. Italy also believed that an Assembly debate would only exacerbate the dispute. Further, it considered the question to be a purely legal one. The Italian government had already offered to submit the matter to the International Court of Justice on its own, without outside interference from the UN. Italy, in short, favoured a limited, juridical handling of the matter, as opposed to a political approach, since this narrow strategy would not bring outside political pressure to bear upon it.[13]

Cognisant of both sides of this issue, Aiken wisely opted to remain neutral at this early phase of the proceedings. He told Dr Rotter that South Tyrol was a problem that certainly 'all members of the UN and, in particular, countries like Ireland, which entertain very friendly relations with both Austria and Italy, would like to see solved both in the general interest and in the interest of better relations between those two countries'.[14] Nonetheless, he preferred not 'to pronounce definitely on the question at this stage'.

At the same time, Aiken did offer, 'on a friendly, informal basis', some procedural advice to Dr Rotter should his government decide to raise South Tyrol at the UN. He stressed that it was 'extremely important' that the Austrians consider the language of both the official request for inscription of the item on the Assembly's agenda and the resolution they eventually tabled. Ireland's experience in raising Tibet the previous year had demonstrated that many countries wished to see Article 2.7 of the Charter strictly applied, so it was 'most important to ensure that the item is so worded as not immediately to come up against' this clause. It would be essential, for instance, to make sure that the inscription request did not 'refer specifically to the Italian Tyrol'. Since this area was within Italy's domestic jurisdiction it would seize upon this wording to block a debate, and many delegations would 'rally to this view'. It 'would be wiser', Aiken opined, to refer simply to the Gruber-de Gasperi Agreement of 5 September 1946, 'an agreement between two countries and one which, therefore, on the face of it may be raised by one of them at the UN.' With regard to a resolution itself, Aiken counselled pragmatism – and a touch of diplomatic humility:

> The best line to take would be to request both sides to negotiate. This would seem to be a legitimate request for which a number of countries would be prepared to vote. Equally, such a request should not embarrass the Italian government, and it is very important that one should not ask the Assembly to adopt a text which would embarrass the Italian government or which might call for steps in relation to this problem which the Italian government could not take. It is necessary to bear in mind not only the relative strength or weakness of the government concerned, but

13 *United Nations Yearbook, 1960*, pp 176–8. **14** NAI DFA 428/14, 16 June 1960.

also the prospects of seeming to impose something which would indispose the Italian people on whom the government has to depend. A request for negotiations between Austria and Italy should give moral satisfaction to the former without seriously offending the latter. On the other hand, a resolution seeking the opinion of the [International] Court might not succeed, as many countries do not like the idea of outside bodies being asked to pronounce on the behaviour of one of their number.

Dr Rotter sincerely appreciated Aiken's sage observations – excellent advice, in fact, that was corroborated by future events. Still, he alluded to Austria's own difficulties in drafting a suitable resolution. Italy would probably contend that the Gruber-de Gasperi Agreement had been scrupulously observed and thus negotiations were unnecessary. More pressing, the Austrian delegation had 'to take account of opinion in South Tyrol and to try to achieve something which will keep the more extreme elements there quiet', especially those people now calling for 'self-determination'. Aiken listened attentively, but did not commit himself either way. He did ask Dr Rotter to keep him closely apprised of Austria's unfolding plans.

The spirit of Frank Aiken's advice to Rotter was appreciated in the Austrian foreign ministry, but only to a certain extent. Its request that the item be placed on the Assembly's agenda, lodged at the UN in late June, was couched in moderate language: it referred only to 'the problem of the Austrian minority in Italy' and not to the Italian region of South Tyrol itself. The concomitant explanatory memorandum focused on the Gruber-de Gasperi Agreement, as Aiken had counselled. But, in language aimed at the Austrian domestic audience, it also alluded to the pressing need for autonomy and self-government in the region.[15] Regardless of the exact diplomatic wording employed, the early signs in New York did not bode well for Austria. Andrew Cordier, executive assistant to Dag Hammarskjöld, told Frederick H. Boland, Ireland's ambassador to the United Nations, that 'the majority of the delegations deplored the decision of the Austrian government to bring the issue to the UN at all'.[16]

IRISH–ITALIAN RELATIONS

Italy, meanwhile, launched its own diplomatic offensive. It first appealed to its NATO allies, whose support was forthcoming. Besides their natural inclination to back a fellow member of the alliance, NATO member states were acutely

15 *United Nations Yearbook, 1960*, p. 176. **16** NAI DFA PMUN X/44, 6 July 1960.

aware of the strategic value of South Tyrol: Italy's possession of it extended NATO's border up to the imposing frontier of the Alps, a reassuring proposition should Soviet armies ever stream across neutral Austria.

Italy also sought Ireland's assistance. On 11 July Enrico Martino, the Italian ambassador in Dublin, explained his government's policy to T.J. Horan, assistant secretary in the Department of External Affairs. Italian officials regarded the Alto Adige (the Italian term for South Tyrol) 'as an integral part of … the national territory, which now extends right up to the Alps', the natural barrier between Italy and Austria.[17] They were also disturbed by growing calls for South Tyrolian self-determination and 'could in no circumstances countenance such a demand', which would merely be a first step towards unification with Austria. Martino, in fact, was at pains to refute a recent leader in the *Irish Independent* erroneously asserting that Austria had every 'right to demand the return of her lost province', just as Ireland had the right 'to demand the return of the six counties'. A parallel between the six counties and the Alto Adige certainly existed, he said, but it favoured his government: Italy's 'right to insist on her territorial integrity' was as legitimate as the Irish 'desire to see the six counties reincorporated into Ireland', which, like the Italian peninsula, was 'a geographically homogenous unit'. The Italian government, accordingly, believed that the dispute should be settled via bilateral negotiations and 'without reference to the United Nations'. Failing this, there was 'always the International Court at the Hague'. In reply to Martino, Horan said that Iveagh House was 'not yet prepared to express any views on this subject', but he would forward a summary of their conversation to Frank Aiken, who was away on leave. In keeping with standard Irish policy he did mention that it was unlikely Ireland would oppose a discussion of the item in the Assembly.

Martino called again at Iveagh House on 25 August; obviously, his superiors in Rome were growing more and more anxious. During a meeting with Conor Cruise O'Brien, the Italian envoy requested the Department of External Affairs to oppose the inscription of South Tyrol on the Assembly's agenda, because the UN was not competent to debate it and a discussion would only serve 'to envenom the dispute and further disturb relations between Austria and Italy'.[18] O'Brien echoed Ireland's policy as expressed in Horan's earlier conversation with Martino and Aiken's with Rotter: 'the problem was a very difficult one for Ireland, involving as it did a conflict between two countries with which we had historical ties of friendship and culture'; Ireland would not oppose the inscription of the item on the agenda; and since the Irish delegation had 'always upheld a liberal interpretation of Article 2.7', it could not accept the argument 'that the Assembly was not competent to discuss this question'. O'Brien assured Martino, though, that if a debate took place Ireland's 'voice would be heard, if at all, on

17 Ibid., 11 July 1960. **18** NAI DFA 428/14, 26 August 1960.

the side of moderation and that we would resist any efforts to inflame passions on the problem'.

Dr O'Brien forwarded a review of his conversation with Martino to Frank Aiken, who agreed with his colleague's conclusions. In early September Aiken circulated a memorandum to the government summarising the entire issue and delineating Ireland's policy.[19] Iveagh House preferred that the case be settled via bilateral negotiations. If this option faltered, 'the proper course for the Irish delegation to adopt, both on general grounds and by reference to the potential implications of the problem for partition, would appear to be to work for a settlement satisfactory to both sides'. Should this prove impossible, Ireland's 'general attitude in relation to other issues, and again the implications for the problem of partition, should lead us to vote for the inscription of the item on the agenda'. If it was inscribed and a substantive debate ensued, the Irish delegation would encourage 'the two parties to seek a settlement in accordance with the principles of the Charter and in a spirit of mutual tolerance and respect for the rights of the individual'. Finally, the memorandum recommended that Ireland abstain on any vote by reason of its 'friendship for the two countries and in the hope that the discussion will bring about an improvement'.

* * *

In late September the UN Steering Committee approved the inscription of the South Tyrol question on the Assembly's agenda. Just beforehand the Italian delegation had dropped its opposition to a discussion of the issue, but, hoping to restrict the course of the ensuing debate, did manage to revise the wording of the item to read: 'The Status of the German-speaking Element in the Province of Bolzano (Bozen); Implementation of the Paris Agreement of 5 September 1946'. Italian officials, meanwhile, continued to lobby their Irish counterparts. Enrico Martino kept up his frenetic pace by visiting Con Cremin, the secretary of the Department of External Affairs, in late September, but their conversation traversed across familiar diplomatic terrain.[20]

On 5 October Cremin and Seán Lemass, both of whom had stopped over in Rome while returning from independence celebrations in Nigeria, had a much more important meeting with Antonio Segni, the Italian Foreign Minister. According to Cremin's summary of the discussion, Segni stressed persistent themes. South Tyrol fell 'within the natural boundaries of Italy', which had been 'asserted in arms on a number of occasions', including during World War I, when Italy 'lost 700,000 men'. The Italian government thus held 'the view that the frontiers in the North are final'. In addition, the current dispute was 'a purely legal one', and Italy had properly 'suggested that it be referred to the obvious authority in such a matter, *viz.*, the World Court at the Hague'.

19 NAI DT S 16051/A, 7 September 1960. **20** NAI DFA PMUN X/44, 19 September 1960.

Lemass, for his part, told Segni that Ireland was 'very sorry to see a quarrel between two countries for each of which we entertain feelings of cordial friendship brought before the United Nations and argued there in public'. He hoped that the impending debate would 'be as free as possible from recrimination and fruitless controversy and that the two parties can, between them, reach a mutually satisfactory solution'. He also sympathised with Segni's remarks about 'the natural frontiers of Italy, saying that this is a principle to which we subscribe and which we would like to see applied' in Ireland. He thus accepted 'the Italian thesis on this particular point'. Still, 'any suggestion of unequal treatment for minorities is one which evokes keen sympathy in Ireland, having regard to the position of [Catholics in] the six counties', and was something 'to which the government could not be indifferent'. Lemass 'hoped that Signor Segni would recognise the dilemma in which we thus find ourselves – between support for acceptance of natural frontiers and alleged discrimination against minorities'. In conclusion, he said that the Irish delegation 'could not reasonably oppose the Italian thesis when the matter is discussed in New York and gave an assurance to Signor Segni to this effect'.

When Con Cremin arrived back in Dublin he sent a report of Lemass' conversation with Segni (which Lemass himself had read and approved) to Frank Aiken, who was in New York. In a covering letter Cremin emphasised that the 'line taken by the Taoiseach in the conversation and the assurance he gave to Signor Segni ... was naturally consistent with the memorandum on this subject' that Aiken had circulated to the government in early September, a report that Cremin and Lemass had discussed 'prior to going to the Villa Madana', the site of their meeting with Segni.[21] In his reply to Cremin, Aiken wrote that 'Signor Segni made a good case for himself on the boundary issue. I am also glad that the Taoiseach spoke so strongly on the ill-treatment-of-minorities question'.[22]

Nevertheless, the upshot of Lemass' assurance to Segni – Ireland 'could not reasonably oppose the Italian thesis' – was that Ireland would *abstain* if a resolution came to a vote that challenged the natural frontiers of Italy and also asserted the rights of minorities. As future events would reveal, the Italians misinterpreted Lemass' remarks to mean that Ireland would automatically vote with Italy *against* any motion that questioned its borders. But the Taoiseach had made it perfectly clear that Ireland could not oppose outright such a resolution if it also upheld minority rights. Perhaps the exact meaning of Lemass' nuanced position was lost in translation.

THE SPECIAL POLITICAL COMMITTEE

In mid October the Special Political Committee finally took up the South Tyrol question. It first considered a draft resolution circulated by the Austrian delega-

21 NAI DFA 428/14, 10 October 1960. 22 Ibid., 13 October 1960.

tion that referred to the Austrian minority in the region and the self-determination of the province.²³ This measure thus bore hardly any resemblance to the wording under which the issue had been inscribed. It also exceeded the aims Austrian diplomats had outlined in their discussions with Irish officials: its reference to the *Austrian* as opposed to the 'German-speaking' – minority smacked of irredentism; and by making no reference at all to the 1946 Gruber–de Gasperi Agreement it was implicitly trying to supersede it and undermine the constitutional arrangements outlined in it.

High-level officials in Iveagh House were sceptical about the motion's implications. In a minute to Conor Cruise O'Brien, who was in New York, Con Cremin reported that the reaction in Dublin 'to the draft Austrian resolution was that it went very far by reference to the 1946 Agreement; and it, of course, went much further than [Dr Rotter] had given the Minister to understand in their conversation in June last'.²⁴ The members of the Irish delegation concurred. At a meeting on 15 October they 'agreed that the terms of the Austrian draft resolution prejudged the issue completely in Austria's favour and that it was not likely to attract wide support'.²⁵ They also discussed Ireland's intervention in the debate and concluded that it should be governed by the principles that Irish officials had enunciated in their conversations with Austrian and Italian diplomats and that Frank Aiken had set out in his informational memorandum to the government. In his own report to Cremin, Dr O'Brien accurately noted that while 'these principles are reasonably clear, the question of wording remains important'.²⁶ It was essential to support 'the principle of negotiations between the parties' without denying 'the possible usefulness, in certain circumstances, of discussions of such problems by the United Nations' as minority rights. The Irish delegation, in fact, 'could scarcely do so consistent with our stand on other matters'.

* * *

As the debate in the Special Political Committee got underway, officials in the Italian foreign ministry grew extremely nervous about Ireland's intentions: it is likely that rumours circulating in the Viennese press that Ireland would support the Austrian line had unsettled them. On several occasions in mid October Enrico Martino sought up-to-the-minute clarifications from Con Cremin. During a conversation on 13 October, he relayed a direct message from Antonio Segni: the Italian foreign minister feared that Ireland might 'vote against Italy, which would be in contrast to the "favourable" attitude' the Taoiseach had expressed to him in Rome.²⁷ Cremin assured Martino that this was not the case: Lemass' remarks to Segni 'could be held to be "favourable" to Italy in a negative

---

23 *United Nations Yearbook, 1960*, p. 176. **24** NAI DFA 313/36/3, 24 October 1960. **25** Ibid., 15 October 1960. **26** NAI DFA PMUN X/44, 20 October 1960. **27** Ibid., 14 October 1960.

sense', that is to say, they committed Ireland 'only to abstention rather than to a vote in favour' of Italy. Martino grudgingly accepted Cremin's explanation, but asked him to confirm Ireland's position with Lemass and Aiken. One week later Cremin, who labelled Martino's attitude 'tendentious', informed the Italian envoy that both the Taoiseach and Aiken agreed with his interpretation of the Lemass–Segni meeting: Ireland would abstain on any resolution Italy opposed, but they could not vote with Italy against a text if it also championed minority rights.[28]

Italy's apprehensiveness was unwarranted, however. By 24 October it was clear that the Austrian draft was headed for defeat in the Special Political Committee. During the debate, various Austrian spokesmen had presented a rather confused case, with large parts of their argument leaning in the direction of self-determination and frontier revision. Their motion had garnered no support in the Committee, not even from the Soviet bloc, which feared undermining the Italian Communist Party on such a sensitive national issue. Italy, contrariwise, had argued its case with considerable force and had made a strong impression. It was backed by the members of NATO, the Latin American bloc and even many of the Afro–Asian nations.[29]

INTERNATIONAL MEDIATION

All the same, most delegations realised that a humiliating defeat of Austria at the United Nations would not resolve the dispute in South Tyrol. Such an outcome would actually polarise the communities in the region and exacerbate ethnic tensions. It was no surprise, then, that hints of a compromise started circulating in the corridors. Attention soon focused on the Irish delegation, whose mediation efforts on several other occasions, especially during controversial colonial debates, were greatly appreciated. On 24 October Conor Cruise O'Brien cabled Con Cremin with the news that the 'possibility now exists that we may cosponsor, with Cyprus, a compromise resolution designed to attract unanimous support'.[30] Its operative part would simply 'invite the parties to conduct negotiations on the implementation of the [Gruber-de Gasperi] Agreement'. The Austrians, O'Brien noted, were agreeable to this formula, because they realised that their own motion would fail. The Italians had expressed interest, but were awaiting instructions from Rome. Both the Irish and Cypriot representatives, meanwhile, had made it clear that unless a text could be found that was acceptable to both countries they would not put forward a resolution.

Alas, on the following day, 25 October, O'Brien reported to Cremin that the joint compromise proposal had run into the sand. The Italian government had

---

28 NAI DFA 428/14, 21 October 1960. **29** *United Nations Yearbook, 1960*, pp 176–8; NAI DFA PMUN X/44, 20 October 1960. **30** NAI DFA 428/14, 24 October 1960.

insisted on adding an additional operative paragraph 'requiring the parties, in the event of failure of the negotiations, to refer their differences to the International Court and abide by the Court's decision', but the restrictive nature of this clause was unacceptable to Austria.[31] O'Brien recounted, though, that diplomats from both Austria and Italy had expressed their 'understanding of [the Irish] position and gratitude for our efforts'. But several moderate delegations in the Committee believed that Italy had 'made [a] serious mistake in rejecting [an] innocuous text suggested by us and insisting on a text which represents, in effect, the Italian position', and the final result might prove to be 'less favourable to Italy than unanimity on our text would have been'. O'Brien expected more draft resolutions to follow and thus advised Cremin that 'in this confused and rapidly changing situation we will probably not be able to seek specific instructions covering all votes. As a general rule, however, we propose to abstain on controversial clauses and amendments and to support only uncontroversial clauses, such as a clause inviting the parties to negotiate'.

Later that same day two more resolutions appeared in the Special Political Committee. Austria submitted a revised version of its original motion, but, according to an update the Irish delegation cabled to Dublin, Italy rejected it, because it still contained 'unacceptable' elements, especially a request that the Secretary General remain seized of the matter, which implied 'some form of continuous UN intervention in the problem'.[32] Four Latin American countries also proposed a motion sympathetic to Italy, which was supported by nearly all of the members of NATO, including the United States. Yet it was unpalatable to Austria, because by confining the problem entirely to the implementation of the Gruber-de Gasperi Agreement and referring explicitly to the International Court of Justice it validated the Italian thesis, namely, that South Tyrol was solely a legal question.[33]

* * *

It became apparent the next day (26 October) that most of the delegations faced a very difficult vote. The worst-case scenario was still a ballot leading to a 'victory' for one side and a 'humiliation' for the other. To avoid this unsatisfactory diplomatic outcome, and its deleterious consequences for stability in South Tyrol, the Irish delegation resumed its own efforts to forge a suitable compromise measure. Frank Aiken was responsible for this bold, but risky, decision. He was well aware that Italy might interpret it unfavourably, but, as a report filed by Conor Cruise O'Brien makes clear, he believed it was worth taking a chance for several reasons. It was consistent with the Irish delegation's 'general role at the UN to press for compromise solutions wherever suitable opportunities presented themselves', and, in this case, it had become clear 'that unless Ireland was

31 Ibid., 25 October 1960.   **32** Ibid., 28 October 1960.   **33** *United Nations Yearbook, 1960*, p. 178.

prepared to take the initiative no compromise move would take place'.[34] The Minister felt, too, that the delegation 'could not, consistent with the requirements of our general position at the UN and of our own problem [of partition], seek to refuse any nation a hearing at the United Nations'. In the same vein, Aiken was unsettled by a subtle diplomatic implication of Italy's position *vis-à-vis* the partition of Ireland. Its approach to the South Tyrol dispute, which 'might be called "the Court, the whole Court, and nothing but the Court"', was quite rigid, and Aiken did not wish to be seen endorsing a narrow, legalistic strategy that precluded broader political options in the future. He 'had in mind here the Boundary Agreement [of 1925] and the various suggestions for juridical settlement of issues in dispute' between Britain and Ireland.

Against this background, the Irish delegation and eleven other cosponsors submitted a new draft to the Special Political Committee urging Austria and Italy to conduct negotiations without delay on the implementation of the Gruber–de Gasperi Agreement and, if these proved unsatisfactory, inviting them to seek a solution 'by other peaceful means of their own choice'.[35] Intriguingly, one of the cosponsors was Denmark. The Irish delegation had secured the support of this NATO member by drawing the link between South Tyrol and Schleswig–Holstein, the former Danish province surrendered to Prussia after the Danish and Austro–Prussian Wars. The Italian delegation, meanwhile, relayed its displeasure with this latest proposal to Irish officials: the draft did not specifically identify the International Court of Justice as a 'peaceful' means of resolving the dispute.[36]

Conor Cruise O'Brien, nevertheless, proceeded apace and effectively introduced the resolution on behalf of its twelve cosponsors. In a balanced, persuasive speech he first queried Italy's objections to bringing South Tyrol before the Assembly, particularly its contention that Article 2.7 of the UN Charter obviated a discussion of this matter: outweighing this one clause was the Charter as a whole, which gave delegations 'not only the right, but the duty, to discuss such problems as may be brought before us which endanger friendly relations between states or concern the human rights of distinctive groups'.[37] The UN's non-NATO members did not miss the subtext of his remarks, namely, that they should defend the right of other non-NATO delegations to raise questions in the Assembly.[38] Simultaneously, O'Brien recognised the legitimacy of Italy's interests: the twelve cosponsors of the resolution did not consider it 'desirable or helpful for the Assembly to lay down the exact lines' on which negotiations between Italy and Austria should proceed and, therefore, could not approve the draft resolutions submitted by Austria, which were 'considerably more specific' than was warranted.

Many delegations reacted warmly to O'Brien's remarks. The speech's positive reception neutralised any lingering Italian resistance to a fair-minded settle-

---

34 NAI DFA 428/14, 28 October 1960. **35** *United Nations Yearbook, 1960*, p. 178. **36** NAI DFA 428/14/II, 26 October 1960. **37** Ibid. **38** O'Brien, *Memoir*, p. 197.

ment. In fact, at the end of O'Brien's intervention the Italian delegate on the Special Political Committee exclaimed to one of his colleagues: 'It is Caporetto!' – a reference to Austria's stunning defeat of Italy during World War I.[39] Perhaps the sentiment behind this outburst explains why Antonio Segni, who was in New York, requested Enrico Martino to relay his reservations about the address (and Ireland's stance) to Seán Lemass, who patiently explained to the Italian representative – yet again – that the Irish government was not pursuing an unfriendly policy towards Italy.[40]

* * *

Since Italy could no longer resist the growing calls for a compromise, what remained was to finalise the details. The Irish delegation set to work with the cosponsors of the twelve-power draft and the Latin American resolution to hammer out a final motion. This text, ultimately cosponsored by eighteen delegations, was presented to the Special Political Committee on 27 October. It urged Italy and Austria 'to resume negotiations with a view to finding a solution for all differences relating to the implementation of the Paris Agreement of 5 September 1946' and recommended that if these talks were inconclusive they 'should give favourable consideration to the possibility of seeking a solution of their differences by any of the means provided in the Charter of the United Nations, including recourse to the International Court of Justice, or any other peaceful means of their own choice'.[41] Dr O'Brien later recalled that the cosponsors found it possible to craft a resolution that satisfied all parties: one that did not 'exclude any possible means of settling the difference, while conceding to the Italian position a specific mention of the International Court of Justice, although not as the only means of settling the dispute'.[42] Later that same day the Special Political Committee approved the resolution by acclamation. Afterwards, Frank Aiken phoned Con Cremin at his home in Dublin to say that the entire issue had been satisfactorily resolved; he also paid special tribute to Conor Cruise O'Brien for steering the item through the debates.[43]

IRELAND VINDICATED

On 31 October the General Assembly unanimously adopted the eighteen-power resolution on South Tyrol. Ireland's mediation of this thorny issue was widely appreciated. Dr O'Brien informed Dublin that the 'general feeling in the [Special Political] Committee as regards the line of action taken by the Irish delegation is undoubtedly favourable. Many delegations that did not look forward

39 Quoted in ibid., p. 197. **40** NAI DFA 428/14, 28 October 1961. **41** General Assembly Resolution 1497 (XV). **42** NAI DFA 428/14, 28 October 1960. **43** Ibid.

to a vote ... were very grateful for our efforts', a feeling that was also shared by officials working in the UN Secretariat.⁴⁴

But what about Austria and Italy? The Austrian Foreign Minister, Bruno Kriesky, told the Irish delegation that the outcome 'opened up possibilities for the moderate elements in both Italy and Austria' and even hinted that Austria might agree to refer the matter to the International Court of Justice.⁴⁵ The Austrian Deputy Foreign Minister, Franz Gschnitzer, told the press in his country that 'it was particularly the Irish and Danish delegates who demonstrated, in truly excellent declarations, their comprehension for minority problems'.⁴⁶ Referring to Conor Cruise O'Brien, he said that 'we owe particular gratitude to the Irish representative who, in a splendid manner and with personal courage, worked for the definitive solution incorporated in the final resolution'.

The official Italian line towards Ireland fluctuated for several months. Immediately after the General Assembly approved the compromise motion Italy's permanent representative to the UN, Egidio Ortona, publicly lauded its sponsors.⁴⁷ Other Italian diplomats in New York were less sanguine in their private conversations. According to O'Brien, they still would have preferred a decisive voting victory and so bore a slight grudge against Ireland. Yet on 29 October Enrico Martino called on Con Cremin 'to express the thanks of his government for the attitude of [the Irish] delegation in connection with this resolution'; a few days later Cremin informed Lemass of the Italian diplomat's new-found gratitude.⁴⁸ But it seems to have waned within a few months. During a conversation with Cremin on 23 March 1961, Martino mentioned that Denmark's cosponsorship of the final resolution had perturbed Rome.⁴⁹ The Italian foreign ministry had expected more support from a fellow NATO member and had spoken to Denmark on the subject. Apart from a brief reference to Ireland's role, Martino made no direct comment on its involvement in this issue, although he may have been dropping a subtle hint. Paolo Mussa, the Italian chargé d'affaires in Dublin, was more straightforward during a conversation several months later with Paul Keating, a second secretary in Iveagh House. Mussa indicated that his government had initially 'been upset, through a misunderstanding of our motives, by the activities of [the Irish] delegation at the last session' of the Assembly, but it now realised that its intentions were 'purely conciliatory'.⁵⁰

THE SIXTEENTH GENERAL ASSEMBLY

In the months following the passage of the UN resolution bilateral talks between Italy and Austria finally commenced. But by the summer of 1961 these

44 Ibid. **45** NAI DFA PMUN J/50/60, 29 October 1960. **46** *Tyroler Tageszeitung*, 5 November 1960. **47** *United Nations Yearbook, 1960*, p. 178. **48** NAI DT S 4831/B, 31 October, 1 November 1960. **49** Ibid., 23 March 1961. **50** NAI DFA 428/14/II, 13 July 1961.

negotiations had broken down, and new acts of violence further complicated Austro–Italian relations. In response, Austria once again requested that South Tyrol be inscribed on the agenda of the General Assembly, which was due to convene in September.[51]

On 11 September 1961 Arthur Zidek, the press attaché in the Austrian embassy in Paris, called on Frank Aiken in Dublin to secure Ireland's support once again. Aiken, according to a transcript of the meeting, was rightly hesitant: he doubted whether Austria's 'interests would be served by the tabling of another resolution on South Tyrol'.[52] Not only would there be other large and important issues before the Assembly but, as Aiken wisely pointed out, 'it would be difficult to get a resolution tabled or passed as good as the resolution that was passed on this subject last year'. He recommended, instead, that the Austrian delegation 'ask a number of people like ourselves to mention the matter in our speeches'.

Aiken proffered this sound diplomatic counsel not only with Austria's interests in mind, but Ireland's and the UN's as well. When Sean Ronan (who had assumed Conor Cruise O'Brien's duties in Iveagh House after the latter's appointment as Dag Hammarskjöld's representative in Katanga) forwarded a summary of Aiken's discussion with Zidek to Freddie Boland in New York, he recorded the Minister's personal reflections in an accompanying minute. Aiken believed that the 'tabling of a resolution on this item during the coming session would be likely to stir up a lot of emotion and create difficulties for states friendly to both parties'.[53] Ireland was just such a country, and Aiken correctly wished to avoid a self-induced diplomatic headache. This does not mean that he had abandoned Austria. To the contrary, he grasped that superfluous United Nations resolutions often did more harm than good and even detracted from the legitimacy of the organisation itself.

On the same day that he had spoken with Zidek, Aiken circulated a memorandum outlining the Assembly's agenda to the government. This document included a section on South Tyrol. The relevant passage stated that the Irish delegation's 'attitude will be that of previous years': it would vote 'for the admission of the item to the agenda' and would then 'persuade both countries to reconcile their differences in a friendly and constructive manner which will have due regard to the basic rights and interests of the people of South Tyrol'.[54] The advice Aiken had given to Zidek strongly suggests that he did not want the issue to arise at the UN; the contents of this memorandum indicate that if it did Ireland was again prepared to play a conciliatory role.

---

51 *United Nations Yearbook, 1961*, p. 140. 52 NAI DFA PMUN X/44, 13 September 1961. 53 Ibid. 54 NAI DT S 16051/C, 11 September 1961.

IRELAND AND THE EUROPEAN ECONOMIC COMMUNITY

Like Frank Aiken, Seán Lemass was unenthusiastic about the prospect of renewed Irish intervention in the South Tyrol dispute. In contrast to the previous year, a vital consideration now bulked large in the latter's political calculations: on 31 July 1961 Ireland had submitted its official application for membership in the European Economic Community (EEC).[55] A new economic variable thus had to be factored into the Irish diplomatic equation. So, two days after reading Aiken's memorandum on the UN slate, Lemass forwarded a personal note to his cabinet colleague requesting him 'to give some further consideration' to several items.[56] Apropos of South Tyrol, the Taoiseach did 'not think it wise to take any initiative on this subject'. He conceded that the two parties had drawn parallels to the partition of Ireland: the Italians claimed that they were 'dealing with a residual effect of foreign occupation of Italian soil, just as we are in the Northeast'; while the Austrians argued that a similarity existed on other grounds, namely, the rights of minorities. Lemass thought, nonetheless, that it was best for Ireland to maintain a low profile at the UN. Why? He reminded Aiken that 'having regard to our vital interests in retaining Italian goodwill during the EEC negotiations, it is very important that we should not come into any conflict with them on the Tyrol question at this time'.

Lemass was not overreacting, he was just being sensible. After all, he was quite familiar with the mixed sentiments Ireland's intervention in the South Tyrol dispute at the UN the previous year had generated in Rome. Surely he recalled Enrico Martino's frenetic visit in the midst of Ireland's efforts to forge a compromise resolution. He had also read a report of Con Cremin's late-March meeting with Martino, wherein the Italian ambassador had expressed his consternation over Denmark's role.[57] What's more, the Italian government was still sensitive about this issue: on 23 September, one week after Lemass had corresponded with Aiken, a foreign ministry official in Rome told Thomas V. Commins, Ireland's ambassador to Italy, that if South Tyrol arose in the Assembly he trusted 'that the Irish government's attitude toward the Italian position would not be negative', a position that 'would hardly be consistent with what he hoped would be our friendly association with the Common Market'.[58]

The rest of Lemass' cabinet shared his cautious approach. After finally considering Aiken's UN memorandum on 24 October the government 'informally agreed that we should keep out of the discussion on the question of South Tyrol'.[59] A consensus had emerged at the highest official levels against taking any unnecessary diplomatic risks while Ireland's EEC application was on the line.

---

55 For a review of the background to Ireland's EEC application, see Dennis Maher, *The Tortuous Path* (Dublin, 1986). **56** NAI DT S 16051/C, 13 September 1961. **57** NAI DT S 4831/B, 27 March, 1961. **58** NAI DFA 313/8/F, 28 September 1961. **59** NAI DT S 16051/C, 24 October 1961.

This conclusion is quite significant on two interconnected counts. Contrary to the assertions of previous scholars, it is now clear that Irish policymakers were fully attentive to the interrelationship between economic and political foreign policies. By the same token, Seán Lemass and Frank Aiken did not pursue divergent aims in Dublin and in New York, but reconciled their own priorities with Ireland's overall national interests.[60]

* * *

In late November the Special Political Committee turned to the question of South Tyrol for a second time, but discussions between Italy and Austria soon stalled. At this point, Antonio Segni, of all people, personally requested the Irish delegation to craft a settlement. He was cognisant of the delegation's mediation the previous year, its unbiased attitude, its influence in the Assembly and the Irish government's desire to evince its goodwill towards Italy in the context of its aspiration to join the EEC.[61] Accordingly, Ireland and several other delegations drafted a resolution calling 'for further efforts between the two parties concerned to find a solution' congruous with the motion passed in 1960, which the General Assembly unanimously adopted.[62] The process was not nearly as tortuous as the previous year, since Austria, realising that the patience of the other delegations was wearing thin, readily agreed to a compromise formula.

This turn of events certainly was ironic. Whereas Seán Lemass had first advised against entanglement in the South Tyrol dispute out of fear of upsetting Italy, the Italians, seizing on Ireland's wish to demonstrate its *bona fides*, encouraged them to intervene in a friendly manner. Indeed, the Italians were quite pleased with Ireland's contribution. On 5 December Baron Winspeare, the new Italian ambassador, called on Frank Aiken in Iveagh House 'to express the appreciation of his government for the attitude [the Irish delegation] had taken on the South Tyrol problem'.[63] Officials in Rome were 'very happy with the outcome and grateful for the way in which [Ireland] had helped to prevent the item being treated in a contentious manner and generating unnecessary "heat"'. Lemass surely welcomed the Italian envoy's remarks when informed of them the following day.[64]

NATIONAL INTERESTS AND INTERNATIONAL MEDIATION

After South Tyrol's appearance at the United Nations in 1960–1 the search for a solution to this issue reverted to bilateral negotiations between Austria and Italy.

60 See, for example, Trevor Salmon, *Unneutral Ireland: An Ambivalent and Unique Security Policy* (Oxford, 1989); Paul Sharp, *Irish Foreign Policy and the European Community* (Aldershot, 1990).   **61** NAI DFA 428/14/II, 15, 21, 23 November 1961.   **62** General Assembly Resolution 1661 (XVI).   **63** NAI DT S 4831/B, 5 December 1961.   **64** NAI DT S 16137/K, 6 December 1961.

The two countries finally signed an accord in 1969 that has maintained stability in the region until today.[65] Thus in retrospect, Ireland's arbitration of the South Tyrol dispute in the General Assembly, with the assistance of Cyprus and several other likeminded delegations, proved to be quite beneficial. It demonstrated the efficacy of the United Nations in limited circumstances. It prevented this bilateral issue from becoming a persistent, time-consuming regional or international one. And it released an important diplomatic safety valve: it allowed Austria to state its case; Italy to preserve its principles; and both governments to demonstrate to their respective domestic audiences that they were addressing the issue in a forthright manner.

This successful round of international mediation speaks well for Irish statecraft. So does the fact that while successfully walking across this diplomatic tightrope Ireland was able to further its own objectives. Its relationships with Austria and Italy were strengthened; its application for membership in the EEC did not suffer from Italian rancour; its international reputation was enhanced; and its commitment to minority rights was asserted, a precedent that proved helpful when the Irish government briefly addressed the Northern Ireland crisis in the Security Council in 1969.[66] The Irish delegation, in sum, crafted a diplomatic settlement that strengthened not only the international order, but its own national interests as well.

---

65 Alcock, 'The South Tyrol Package Agreement of 1969', pp 50–1. **66** See Cornelius Cremin, 'Northern Ireland at the United Nations: August/September, 1969', *Irish Studies in International Affairs*, vol. 1, no. 2 (1980).

Raison d'État and the Evolution of Irish Foreign Policy

Ronan Fanning

> It is a basic law of power politics that any weak State, incapable of defending itself by its own strength (whether its weakness is the result of incomplete development, lack of physical resources or internal confusion), is in danger of becoming a passive object, a hunting ground, a region of low political pressure, into which the winds of power may blow from neighbouring territories and cause a storm to get up.
>
> Friedrich Meinecke, *Machiavellism: The Doctrine of Raison d'État and its Place in Modern History* (London, 1957), p. 420.

Desmond Williams,[1] my mentor and predecessor as Professor of Modern History at University College Dublin, introduced me as an undergraduate to Meinecke's work on the doctrine of *raison d'état*, the pursuit of the supreme national interest. Historians of the school[2] to which Desmond Williams belonged have long applied this doctrine to their consideration of the foreign policy of great powers. It is much less commonplace for historians – especially historians living and working in large states – to apply that doctrine to understanding the foreign policy of small states.

Desmond Williams was not so afflicted. Although he never lectured formally on Irish foreign policy during his years in University College Dublin – no legislation on Irish national archives was enacted in his time and none of the records of the Department of Foreign Affairs (External Affairs from 1922 until 1971) had yet been released – his conviction about the primacy of political and diplomatic history, reflected in a brilliant series of lectures on the balance of power to his final year undergraduates, imbued him with an abiding interest in a subject about which he knew more than any other Irish historian of his generation.

---

[1] An earlier draft of this essay was delivered as the 1995 Desmond Williams Memorial Lecture.
[2] This included Hedley Bull, Herbert Butterfield (then Regius Professor of History at the University of Cambridge), Michael Howard (subsequently Regius Professor of History at the University of Oxford), Kenneth Thompson, Adam Watson and Martin Wight: see the preface to Herbert Butterfield and Martin Wight (eds), *Diplomatic Investigations: Essays in the Theory of International Politics* (London, 1966), pp 11–13.

His profound understanding of Irish foreign policy was reinforced, moreover, by close personal friendships with many of the most senior diplomats in the Irish foreign service; these included secretaries of the department such as Freddie Boland, Con Cremin, Hugh McCann, Paul Keating and, in a later generation, Sean Donlon, Noel Dorr and Dermot Gallagher – many of whom I also met through the generosity of Desmond's legendary hospitality at the Stephen's Green Club. He was also a close personal friend of Garret FitzGerald, whom he advised with remarkable frankness upon the strengths and weaknesses of the officials in his department when he became Minister for Foreign Affairs in 1973.[3]

Although the ill-health that dogged him throughout his life meant that Desmond Williams' publications were all too few, he put the inside knowledge of the realities of Irish foreign policy gleaned from such friendships to invaluable use in a handful of pioneering essays and articles, most notably in an essay published in 1979, where he wrote that:

> states are never wholly free in relation to the policy which they follow. Policy is limited because no state can act against the general philosophy and moral belief of its people and ... because that state must observe the limits circumscribing it – geographic, economic and ideological situations in the world. What states are really free to do is always subject to some restrictions and constraint. Therefore, two principal points arise for a small state; policy cannot be a single, grand design and freedom of action is limited.[4]

In the case of independent Ireland, as in the case of all small states, those limitations upon freedom of action are rooted in *raison d'état* . 'The success of a policy of *raison d'état*', Henry Kissinger has observed, 'depends above all on the ability to assess power relationships'.[5] It might equally be said that the success of a historian of foreign policy depends above all on the ability to assess the changes, the seismic shifts in power relationships. The object of this essay is to discuss how such changes – in particular, changes in Anglo–Irish relations since Britain is the state with which Ireland has always had its most significant power relationship – have shaped the evolution of Irish foreign policy.

* * *

The seminal text enunciating how *raison d'état* would shape Irish foreign policy after independence is Eamon de Valera's 1920 interview for the *Westminster Gazette* in response to the charge that Irish independence would pose a threat to

---

3 Information from Dr Garret FitzGerald. 4 T.D. Williams, 'Irish Foreign Policy, 1949–69', in J.J. Lee (ed.), *Ireland 1945–70* (Dublin, 1979), p. 137. 5 Henry Kissinger, *Diplomacy* (London, 1994), p. 63.

British security. Why, he asked, did the British not make provision for Irish security as the Americans had done under the Monroe doctrine? Why, in particular, did the British not do with Ireland as the Americans had done with Cuba when they safeguarded themselves 'from the possible use of the island of Cuba as a base for attack by a foreign power' by stipulating that the Cuban government 'shall never enter into any treaty or other compact with any foreign power or powers which will impair or tend to impair the independence of Cuba'.

The premature publication of extracts from the *Westminster Gazette* interview in the New York *Globe* on the previous day (6 February 1920), where it was described as a 'withdrawal by the official head of the Irish Republic of the demand that Ireland be set free to decide her own international relations', embarrassed de Valera, who was vilified by his Irish American opponents for allegedly betraying Irish sovereignty by suggesting that an independent Ireland would not be free to conduct an entirely independent foreign policy.[6]

Such criticisms missed the point. Although de Valera's commitment to the *theory* of sovereignty was absolute, the significance of his Cuban declaration is that it demonstrates how he conducted foreign policy on the basis of *realpolitik* even before Ireland achieved in practice the independence to which it laid claim in theory. No one realised earlier than de Valera that the traditional Irish revolutionary readiness to enter into alliances with Britain's enemies – whether in the shape of Spain under Philip II, of Napoleonic France or of the Kaiser's Germany – would run counter to an independent Ireland's national interest. The Cuban declaration serves as a prescient blueprint of how foreign policy would then be constrained:

> With a free Ireland, the *preservation* of its independence would be as strong a moving force as the *recovery* of its independence has been a moving force in every generation since the coming of the Normans.
>
> An independent Ireland would see everything to lose in losing its independence – in passing under the yoke of any foreign power whatsoever. An independent Ireland would see its own independence in jeopardy the moment it saw the independence of Britain seriously threatened. Mutual self-interest would make the people of these two islands, if both [were] independent, the closest possible allies in a moment of real danger to either.
>
> … Ireland, deprived of its freedom by Britain – in dependence, and persecuted because it is not satisfied to remain in dependence – is impelled by every natural instinct and force to see hope in the downfall of Britain and hope, not fear, in every attack on Britain. Whereas, in an independent Ireland, the tendency would be all the other way.[7]

---

6 The Earl of Longford and Thomas P. O'Neill, *Eamon de Valera* (London, 1970), p. 103. **7** Press statement issued by Eamon de Valera in New York, February 1920, published in

That passage goes to the heart of the dilemma of those responsible for framing foreign policy since the foundation of the state. The main elements of that dilemma are best put in the shape of three questions:

How can a state in the infancy of its independence escape the constraints imposed upon its foreign policy by traditional antagonisms and inhibitions which were an essential part, and remain an inescapable legacy, of its struggle for independence?

How can a small state in the adolescence of its independence pursue a foreign policy genuinely independent of a neighbouring great power or powers?

How can a newly independent state become mature enough about its independence to pursue policies of interdependence, if and when such policies become appropriate?

Or, to put it another way, the history of Irish foreign policy falls naturally into three themes or movements: first, the escape from dependence and the assertion of independence; second, the extension and affirmation of independence; third, the transition from independence to interdependence.

The themes are largely, but not entirely, sequential; indeed, they can sometimes seem inextricably interwoven. Affirmations of independence and acknowledgements of interdependence, in particular, can surface simultaneously in Irish responses to particular international circumstances. The way in which, ever since we joined the European Community in 1973, our commitment to military neutrality has run hand in hand with our commitment to European integration is a classic case in point.

Although the term interdependence did not enjoy its current vogue in 1920, the fascination of de Valera's Cuban declaration is that one can there see in embryo his theory of Anglo–Irish interdependence; a theory which he more fully elaborated during the Anglo–Irish negotiations of 1938 and which he put into effect by his benevolent neutrality towards the Allies during World War II. The core of the theory was that an independent Ireland would be free to purse an independent foreign policy only insofar as that policy did not represent a threat to Britain's vital strategic interests.

As de Valera put it in his open letter to President Woodrow Wilson in October 1920, 'Ireland is quite ready *by treaty* [my italics] to ensure England's safety and legitimate security against the danger of foreign powers seeking to use Ireland as a basis of attack against her'.[8] The achievement of Irish independence would not redress the unequal balance of power between the two islands, and the prospect of an alliance between an independent Ireland and an enemy of Britain would only provoke the British to threaten that hard-won independence. 'We have no enemies but England. She would never permit us other allies', wrote

---

Maurice Moynihan (ed.), *Speeches and Statements by Eamon de Valera, 1917–73* (Dublin, 1973), pp 31–4. **8** Ibid., p. 41.

Erskine Childers in a review of Irish defence policy during the preparations for the Anglo–Irish negotiations in July 1921. Citing the precedents of Switzerland, Belgium and Luxembourg, Childers made the case that guaranteed neutrality 'is the best status we can aim at, though no doubt hard to attain'.[9]

In this sense neutrality was the outer limit of how independent of British foreign policy Irish foreign policy could become and neutrality is, of course, the most notable characteristic of Irish foreign policy in all three phases of its evolution from dependence to independence to interdependence. When we were dependent upon Britain, neutrality was the policy to which we aspired; when we became independent, neutrality was the policy we practised; when we became interdependent, military neutrality remained a core value of Irish foreign policy.

In 1913, for example, Roger Casement, whose career in the Foreign Office made him Sinn Féin's first foreign policy expert, pseudonymously published an article on 'Ireland, Germany and the Next War' which put the attractions of neutrality for Irish revolutionaries in stark, if grandiose, terms: 'Ireland, already severed by a sea held by German warships, and temporarily occupied, might well be permanently and irrevocably severed from Great Britain, and with common assent erected into a neutralised, independent European state under international guarantees'.[10] James Connolly, another of the more internationally minded Irish revolutionaries, was similarly attracted by neutrality and, in 1914, became President of the Irish Neutrality League, which espoused neutrality as the most appropriate Irish policy towards the Great War.

The case for neutrality was advanced by the Irish representatives in a submission to the sub-committee on naval and air defence at the outset of the Anglo–Irish Treaty negotiations in 1921:

> It is in Britain's interest that Ireland should be completely satisfied and friendly and that on this basis there should be willing and amicable association and mutual intercourse for all peaceful purposes. Neutralisation will be the surest means of effecting this end.
>
> The strategical interests of Great Britain would, we urge, also be satisfied by this solution ...
>
> Ireland does not in any sense block the road to England. It is not denied that the use of her coasts are an additional convenience to the British Admiralty, but this convenience is not vital and cannot be set against the grave disadvantage of curtailing the status of Ireland and thus making her people feel unsatisfied.[11]

---

9 Ronan Fanning, Michael Kennedy, Dermot Keogh and Eunan O'Halpin (eds), *Documents on Irish Foreign Policy: Volume 1, 1919–1922* (Dublin, 1998) [hereafter cited as *DIFP*], pp 242–3. 10 Patrick Keatinge, *A Place among Nations: Issues of Irish Foreign Policy* (Dublin, 1978), pp 38–9. 11 *DIFP*, 18 October 1921, pp 279–81.

Arthur Griffith stressed that 'Ireland would want *to be free to be neutral* [my italics] in the event of war declared by Britain'; Michael Collins echoed de Valera's doctrine of interdependence by arguing that the 'compensating point' for the British, if they were fighting a war in which Ireland remained neutral, was that 'a country refusing to recognise Ireland's neutrality would make Ireland an enemy'.[12] But their proposal on the 'League of Nations and USA guaranteeing Irish freedom' fell on deaf ears.[13]

Again, however, it was de Valera who best expressed such thinking in his proposed alternative treaty, more commonly known as 'Document No 2':

> That, so far as her resources permit, Ireland shall provide for her own defence by sea, land and air, and shall repel by force any attempt by a foreign power to violate the integrity of her soil and territorial waters, or to use them for any purpose hostile to Great Britain and the other associated States of the Commonwealth.[14]

In other words, de Valera offered to embody in the 1921 treaty the concept of Anglo–Irish interdependence which he had formulated in 1920: a guarantee that Irish territory would never provide a base for Britain's enemies. Irish neutrality, the preferred foreign policy option of all Irish governments since 1922, has been defined as 'the ultimate expression of independence';[15] but the aspiration to neutrality in pre-independent Ireland embodied in Document No 2 was also a first expression of interdependence.

The British perspective was very different. Having just emerged victorious from a terrible war in which their control of the Atlantic had been seriously challenged by German submarines, the Admiralty was not prepared to relinquish their Irish resources, but instead insisted upon 'the importance of the geopolitical unity of the British Isles and the special strategic imperative that differentiated Ireland from other Dominions'. An annex to the Treaty – providing for the Admiralty's retention of harbour defence and aviation facilities at Berehaven, Queenstown [Cobh] and Lough Swilly – embodied 'the dichotomy between the geopolitical unity of the British Isles and the new geographical configuration of the United Kingdom'.[16]

* * *

---

12 Keith Middlemas (ed.), *Thomas Jones' Whitehall Diary* (London, 1971), vol. 3, pp 121, 143 (entries for 11, 24 October 1921).   **13** *DIFP*, Griffith to de Valera, 24 October 1921, p. 291.   **14** De Valera first made the proposal to a secret session of Dáil Éireann on 14 December 1921: for the full text, see *DIFP*, pp 362–70.   **15** F.S.L. Lyons, *Ireland since the Famine* (London, 1973 edt.), p. 554.   **16** G.R. Sloan, *The Geopolitics of Anglo–Irish Relations in the Twentieth Century* (London, 1997), p. 178. The title of Dr Sloan's book is somewhat misleading; although it provides a compelling analysis of Britain's strategic interest in Ireland since the Middle Ages, it takes no account of Irish geopolitical perspectives: see my review in *Journal of the Royal Institute for Defence Studies*, no. 143 (1998), p. 76.

Once independence had been achieved, the first problem for the makers of Irish foreign policy was less a matter of *what* foreign policy might be pursued and more a matter of *whether* the infant Irish Free State could establish *any* foreign policy truly independent of Britain. If the first government of the Irish Free State were to prove that the Treaty conferred what Michael Collins described as the freedom to achieve freedom, then they had to prove their ability to take foreign policy decisions in the face of British objections. Hence, for example, their decision to apply to join the League of Nations on 17 April 1923; hence their registration of the Treaty as an international agreement with the League on 11 July 1924; and hence the appointment of a minister plenipotentiary in Washington on 7 October 1924 when the Irish Free State became the first Dominion to be diplomatically accredited in its own right to the United States. In general, however, the reverence of the first Irish Free State governments for a treaty for which they had fought and won a civil war tended to dampen their appetite for extravagant affirmations of independence.

In December 1931 the Irish permanent delegate to the League of Nations telegraphed Dublin for authority to pursue a line 'based on principle but well seasoned with the sauce of realism'.[17] His phrase might well have served as an epigraph for Eamon de Valera when he assumed power three months later on a platform of dismantling the Treaty and breaking the British connection. De Valera's decision to retain the External Affairs portfolio in his own hands, moreover, testified to his belief in the maxim that all policy was foreign policy. De Valera's purpose, outlined in a speech in 1933, was to remove all the forms and symbols 'out of keeping with Ireland's right as a sovereign nation',[18] and article 1 of the 1937 constitution affirmed, *inter alia*, the nation's 'inalienable, indefeasible, and sovereign right … to determine its relations with other nations'. Yet, however much the British resented de Valera's dismantling the Treaty and expanding the limits of Irish independence, resentment never turned into resistance. The abolition of the oath of allegiance, the External Relations Act of 1936, the 1937 Constitution (which made Ireland a republic in all but name and as independent of Britain and the Commonwealth as de Valera wanted) – all alike were the results of unilateral decisions taken by Irish governments which British governments chose to ignore rather than to resist.

The British, in short, were relatively indifferent to Irish affirmations of the right to pursue an entirely independent foreign policy for as long as they posed no threat to vital British interests. But Irish neutrality became of more than academic interest when the prospect of another European war with an Atlantic

---

17 Michael Kennedy, '"Principle Well Seasoned with the Sauce of Realism": Seán Lester, Joseph Walshe and the Definition of the Irish Free State's Policy towards Manchuria', *Irish Studies in International Affairs*, vol. 6 (1995), p. 90. **18** Moynihan, *Speeches and Statements by Eamon de Valera*, p. 237.

dimension again focused British as well as Irish attention on the strategic interdependence of the two islands. The strategic nightmare of an unfriendly Ireland on her western flank in the event of war with Hitler's Germany persuaded the British military establishment to accept the force of the argument advanced by the Irish representatives during the Treaty negotiations: that British strategic assets in Ireland were 'not vital and cannot be set against the grave disadvantage of curtailing the status of Ireland and thus making her people feel unsatisfied'. In May 1936 the Committee of Imperial Defence unanimously endorsed a memorandum from the Chiefs of Staff stating that, 'provided improved relations are assured, and despite the risks involved, it would be desirable to offer to hand over the complete responsibility of the defences of the reserved ports to the Irish Free State'.[19] A year before Neville Chamberlain became Prime Minister, the door was thereby opened for him to apply his appeasing instincts to Anglo–Irish relations.

When the Chiefs of Staff met to consider a request from Chamberlain's cabinet for an estimate of the strategic significance of the ports if war came, the Chief of the Imperial General Staff, Lord Gort, concluded that it would be 'an almost intolerable situation if Ireland were hostile' and estimated that it would take at least one British army division to defend each port; Admiral Chatfield stressed that the prospect of German submarines or aircraft obtaining bases in Ireland 'must never be allowed to happen'; and Sir Cyril Newall, the Chief of the Air Staff, concluded that the loss of the Irish ports 'would be a nuisance but their importance was not sufficient to warrant the extensive effort necessary to hold them against a hostile Ireland'.[20] The upshot was the Anglo–Irish Defence Agreement of 25 April 1938 which, as de Valera put it, by handing over the Treaty ports to the Irish state 'recognises and finally establishes Irish sovereignty over the twenty-six counties and the territorial seas'.[21] In 1949 Pandit Nehru, the Prime Minister of another newly independent Dominion, asked the Indian parliament: 'What does independence consist of? It consists fundamentally and basically of foreign relations. That is the test of independence.'[22] World War II was the moment when Ireland, like so many other states, had to sit that test, for only then did the British perceive the exercise of Irish independence as a potential threat to their own national interest.

The threat became acute with the fall of France in June 1940; it eased when the German armies swept east and invaded Russia in June 1941; and it eased further when the Americans entered the war in December 1941. The threat was two-fold. Germany, aware of Ireland's lack of air-cover and tiny army, might invade as a backdoor to Britain. The British, on the other hand, isolated during

---

19 Quoted in Paul Canning, *British Policy Towards Ireland, 1921–1941* (Oxford, 1985), p. 185. **20** Ibid., pp 196–7. **21** Moynihan, *Speeches and Statements by Eamon de Valera*, p. 346. **22** Quoted in *Times Literary Supplementary*, 25 January 1980, p. 77.

the Battle of Britain and the first phase of the Battle of the Atlantic in 1940–1 and now led by Winston Churchill, who had passionately resisted the return of the ports in 1938, wanted Irish bases and might be tempted to invade to get them.

After the fall of France the prospect that Britain might soon suffer the same fate threatened the survival of that Irish independence of which neutrality was the visible expression. 'An independent Ireland that is interested in maintaining its own independence', declared de Valera in his Dáil speech on the 1938 agreements, 'is interested in seeing a strong shield between her and the dangers of the Continent'.[23] The fall of France exposed the frailty of de Valera's British shield. The national interest in the interdependence of these islands thereafter demanded that Ireland do all in its power to ensure that Britain was not defeated.

The result, as the British Dominions Secretary, Lord Cranborne, told his cabinet colleagues in February 1945 as the war in Europe was drawing to a close, was that de Valera's government was willing to give Allies '*any* facilities which would not be regarded as *overtly* prejudicing their attitude to neutrality' [my italics]. Cranborne appended a remarkable fourteen-point list which included the close liaison between Irish and British military authorities to plan against a possible German invasion of Ireland; similar co-operation between Irish and British intelligence services; the Irish government's silent acquiescence in the wishes of the thousands of their citizens who fought in the Allied forces; and the establishment in February 1945 of a radar station on Irish territory for use against the latest form of German submarine warfare.[24]

The Americans were even warmer in their private praise of the Irish contribution to the Allied cause. The wartime history of the OSS, the American intelligence service which predated the CIA, recorded the 'substantial results in intelligence' produced by the Irish government's 'clear cooperation' and the Pentagon recommended that three of the highest ranking officers in the Irish Army (the Chief of Staff, Deputy Chief of Staff and Chief of the Army Air Corps) be awarded the American Legion of Merit for 'exceptionally meritorious and outstanding services to the US'.[25]

Although the recommendation was never implemented because the State Department realised how it would embarrass the Irish government, it bears out the point that the purposes of Irish neutrality in World War II were both expressionist and preservationist. Neutrality may well have been, in F.S.L. Lyons' phrase, the ultimate expression of independence and of what he has also

---

[23] Moynihan, *Speeches and Statements by Eamon de Valera*, p. 352. [24] See Ronan Fanning, *Independent Ireland* (Dublin, 1983), pp 124–5, for a fuller account. [25] See Ronan Fanning, 'Irish Neutrality – an Historical Review', *Irish Studies in International Affairs*, vol. 1, no. 3 (1982), p. 35.

described as Ireland's 'almost total isolation from the rest of mankind' in a famous passage likening Ireland during the Emergency to the denizens of Plato's cave.[26] This was the face of neutrality presented to the Irish public 'behind the Green Curtain'[27] of censorship, and de Valera's visit to the German legation to offer his condolences on the news of Hitler's death was but its most grotesque manifestation. De Valera's gesture corroded the realism of Irish foreign policy and horrified Joe Walshe and Freddie Boland, his most senior officials in the Department of External Affairs.[28] But by then, as the Allied armies swept ever closer to Berlin, the preservationist purpose – that is to say, Ireland's assistance to the Allies to preserve Ireland's independence from the nightmare of a German victory – had become irrelevant. De Valera could now afford the expressionist luxury of gratuitously offending the British and the Americans by paying his condolences to an aghast Minister Hempel because, and only because, Germany had been defeated.

World War II was the crucible in which Irish and British assumptions about dependence, independence and interdependence were forged and, sometimes, reforged in quite different shapes. De Valera's practice of Irish neutrality throughout World War II at once embodied both his concept of independence and his concept of interdependence. Publicly, de Valera's strict adherence to an absolutely even-handed neutrality, such as his highly publicised visit to the German legation, was indeed the ultimate expression of independence. Privately, the secret assistance to the Allies was at once the ultimate expression and the outer limit of de Valera's commitment to interdependence.

There were two reasons, both rooted in *raison d'état*, why it was necessary that Irish support of the Allies remain shrouded in secrecy. First, because any public departure from neutrality would expose Irish cities to German air raids or other retaliation. Second, because, in Desmond Williams' phrase, 'no state can act against the general philosophy and moral belief of its people'. For de Valera to have publicly abandoned neutrality would have been to risk outraging the belief in the general philosophy of neutrality which he himself had created and cultivated so successfully since 1920. Desmond Williams has also pointed out that there was an intrinsic merit in 'the secrecy within which de Valera shrouded his ultimate intentions and wishes', because it enabled both belligerent blocs to interpret his statements 'according to their desires and in a sense favourable to themselves. De Valera in fact appears never to have told any one, even in his cabinet, everything that was in his mind'.[29]

26 Lyons, *Ireland since the Famine*, pp 554, 557–8. **27** The phrase is Seán O'Faoláin's: John Bowman, *De Valera and the Ulster Question, 1917–1973* (Oxford, 1982), p. 255. **28** Dermot Keogh, *Twentieth-Century Ireland* (Dublin, 1994), p. 157. **29** Desmond Williams, 'Ireland and the War', in Kevin B. Nowlan and T. Desmond Williams (eds), *Ireland in the War Years and After, 1939–51* (Dublin, 1969), p. 26. None of the records released by the National Archives since then contradict this assessment.

The virulence of British denunciations of Irish neutrality, notwithstanding Ireland's comprehensive support for the Allies, is largely explicable in terms of what the Austrian historian, Gerald Stourzh, has identified as twin paradoxes of the foreign policy of neutral states: the 'affinity paradox' and the 'credibility paradox'. The affinity paradox rests on Machiavelli's axiom in *The Prince* that:

> your friends want you to be allies, [but] your enemies want you to be neutral. In other words, neutrality will satisfy a potentially more hostile power or power bloc more than a potentially friendlier power or power bloc. Powers with whom for whatever reasons close ties of sympathy exist may be disappointed or even irritated that the neutral state pursues merely a neutral policy ... The credibility paradox consists in the fact that permanent neutrality strictly speaking is but a means to secure the end, independence. As a means, it may, like all other means, be abandoned in favour of other means better apt to secure the end, independence.[30]

The British response to Irish neutrality in World War II offers a classic illustration of the affinity paradox; in particular, the response of one man, Winston Churchill, whose influence was paramount in disseminating an overwhelmingly negative perception of Irish neutrality throughout the English-speaking world. 'Of all the neutrals Switzerland has the greatest right to distinction', wrote Churchill; 'she has been a democratic State, standing for freedom in self-defence among her mountains, and in thought, in spite of race, largely on our side'. Of Sweden, another of Germany's neutral neighbours, Churchill likewise wrote that 'the choice was a profitable neutrality or subjugation' and that she was blameless if she did not share British perceptions.[31] Ireland, as a Dominion and as Britain's nearest neutral neighbour, in stark contrast, had no right to be neutral. Legally, Churchill declared in October 1939, Ireland was 'At War but Skulking'; Irish neutrality was incompatible 'with her position under the Crown. Unlike other Dominions which were separated from us by thousands of miles, Eire was an integral part of the British Isles'.[32]

The affinity paradox and the British inability to come to terms with the reality of Irish independence when put into practice in time of war provoked an

---

30 Gerald Stourzh, 'Some Reflections on Permanent Neutrality', in August Schou and Arne Olav Brundtland (eds), *Small States in International Relations* (Nobel Symposium 17, Stockholm, 1971), p. 90. This passage is based on Ronan Fanning, 'Neutral Ireland?', *An Cosantóir*, 49, 9 (September, 1989), pp 45–8.   **31** Winston Churchill, *The Second World War* (London, Reprint Society edt., 1948), *Volume 6, Triumph and Tragedy*, appendix C, p. 565 and *Volume 1, The Gathering Storm*, p. 486.   **32** See Robert Fisk, *In Time of War: Ireland, Ulster and the Price of Neutrality, 1939–45* (London, 1983), pp 103, 107.

enduringly bitter British resentment of Irish neutrality of which a 1941 poem by Dorothy Sayers (better known as the author of the detective stories featuring Lord Peter Wimsey) is a particularly pungent example. Two stanzas of the nine-stanza poem, entitled 'The Burden of Ireland', will suffice to give its flavour:

> O never trouble Ireland, for she may sleep sound
> While the reek of blood and burning goes up from English ground.
> She lies down lightly with a smile upon her lips,
> Her bulwarks built of English bones and the wreck of English ships ....
>
> Say only of Catholic Ireland that she remained at home
> When the Pagan and apostate set heel on the neck of Rome,
> When the Cross lay under the fylfot, bowed down to the axe and rod,
> And the dirty English Protestant went out to die for God.[33]

The Irish practice of neutrality has also earned the opprobrium of certain political scientists, most notably in Professor Trevor Salmon's *Unneutral Ireland: an Ambivalent and Unique Security Policy*. Professor Salmon argues that the Irish 'variant of neutrality' is at odds with 'a conceptual analysis aimed at identifying the true nature of neutrality and the meaning of non-alignment' as embodied in 'the practice of three well-established European neutrals, Austria, Sweden, and Switzerland'.[34] *Pace* Professor Salmon, the historical reality is that the security policy of every neutral state is as ambivalent and unique as its national interest demands.

That reality is well expressed in Raymond Aron's maxim that 'in any inter-state system a small power usually tends to identify its "national interest" with its physical or political and moral survival, or both; consequently, depending on various geographical or military considerations, it seeks refuge in neutrality, abstention or alliance with the great powers'.[35] Ireland's physical survival dictated what was in effect a secret alliance with the British and Americans throughout World War II. Political and moral survival dictated public adherence to the ideal of an even-handed neutrality. Geographical considerations – 'Ireland's "extremely comfortable geo-strategic position" as an island lying on the western extremity of continental Europe'[36] – made Ireland the least vulnerable of European small states to the depredations of Hitler's war-machine.

---

33 John Colville, *The Fringes of Power: Downing Street Diaries, 1939–1955* (London, 1985), pp 327–8. Colville had served on Churchill's staff and, forty years after the war, he was still embittered enough to lard his footnote to the poem with a reference to the Irish Government's 'craven neutrality'. **34** Trevor Salmon, *Unneutral Ireland: An Ambivalent and Unique Security Policy* (Oxford, 1989), p. 2. **35** Raymond Aron, *The Imperial Republic: The United States and the World, 1945–1973* (London, 1974), p. 256. **36** Ronan Fanning,

Neutrality, in other words, is often no more than the most appropriate mode for the expression of the national interest of small states which need 'to make a particular effort to explain their foreign policy position as a shared experience of all neutral countries'. Neutrality, a Finnish scholar has argued, 'is pursued not so much as a strategy of security as a strategy for sovereignty, autonomy and identity'. The Finns adopted policy positions 'strictly on the basis of what seemed to be in the national interest, not on ideological or normative grounds'.[37] So, too, with the Irish experience in World War II, which serves as a good example of the phenomenon whereby 'a policy of neutrality, if taken seriously, tends to become more and more identified with the end of foreign policy (and) may tend to become the state's *raison d'être*'.[38]

* * *

If Ireland's close cooperation with the Allies during World War II marked the zenith of the realist tradition in Irish foreign policy, the conduct of foreign policy under Seán MacBride as Minister for External Affairs and John A. Costello as Taoiseach in the Inter-Party government of 1948–51 – in particular, certain of the circumstances surrounding the enactment of the Republic of Ireland Bill in 1948 and the rejection of the invitation to join NATO in 1949 – marked its nadir. Indeed, the rabidly anglophobic MacBride's very first words to the secretary of the Department of External Affairs when he arrived at Iveagh House – 'Mr Boland, give me a list of all the British agents working in your department'[39] – proved an appropriate overture for the surrealist interlude that was to follow.

MacBride, who had been chief of staff of the IRA as recently as 1936 and whose Clann na Poblachta party, founded in 1946, sought to outflank Fianna Fáil on its republican front, had no time for the interdependent realism of de Valera's External Relations Act. Neither had Costello (who had been the leading Fine Gael speaker in the 1936 Dáil debate on the External Relations Bill which he had dismissed as a semantic nonsense); nor had the Tánaiste, William Norton (who had led his party's opposition to the Bill in that same debate in an endeavour to demonstrate that Labour were better republicans than Fianna Fáil).

Whatever else divided them, all parties in the rag-bag 1948–51 government shared a common impulse to make an affirmation of independence as resound-

---

'Neutrality, Identity and Security: The Example of Ireland', in Werner Bauwens, *et al.* (eds), *Small States and the Security Challenge in the New Europe* (London, 1996), p. 147.   **37** Perti Joenniemi, 'The Form and Content of Finnish Neutrality: An Interpretation of the Underlying Assumptions', paper presented to a conference on Europe's neutrals at the Woodrow Wilson International Center for Scholars, Washington D.C., 19–21 November 1986.   **38** Paul Schroeder, speaking at the Washington conference.   **39** So Freddie Boland told Desmond Williams: Keogh, *Twentieth-Century Ireland*, pp 186 and 424 (n. 8).

ing as the Fianna Fáil affirmations of the thirties. By this stage de Valera, on the other hand, had proved his point and saw no need for reaffirmations. Although World War II left Ireland strangely isolated, de Valera was never an isolationist by choice. 'So far are we from desiring isolation', he had told the *Daily Herald* as long ago as April 1919, 'that our whole struggle is to get Ireland out of the cage in which the selfish statecraft of England would confine her ... to get her recognised as a free unit in a world league of nations'.[40] The end of World War II marked the end of that struggle. Asked by Churchill in 1953 if he would have taken Ireland out of the Commonwealth, de Valera's answer was an unequivocal 'no':

> he had no objection ever to Ireland being a member of the Commonwealth . What he had an objection to was an Oath of Allegiance to the King as King of the Commonwealth (as India did later) ... he had come to the conclusion that the Commonwealth was a very useful association for us because the Commonwealth countries (especially Canada, Australia and New Zealand) had a strong interest in Ireland.[41]

The surrealist simplicities of the Inter-Party government's foreign policy – 'Jack Costello', remarked Freddie Boland, 'had about as much notion of diplomacy as I have of astrology'[42] – were in stark contrast to de Valera's constructive ambiguities. The merits of the decision to sever all ties with the Commonwealth are debatable; not so the absurdity of Costello's gratuitously offending British and Canadians alike by announcing the decision in Ottawa. So, too, with MacBride's naive conclusion that the invitation to join NATO offered a golden opportunity 'to trade off Irish membership for a *démarche* on partition', a proposition which the more realistic Boland briskly dismissed as 'rubbish'.[43] And so it proved. When the Irish responded 'that they would be delighted to join provided we could get the British to give them back the six Northern counties', recalled one of the State Department officials involved in drawing up the North Atlantic pact, 'we simply replied, in effect, that "it's been nice knowing you" and that was that'.[44]

Yet even MacBride's foreign policy was occasionally tinged by the realist tradition. An ardent anti-communist (notwithstanding his being awarded the Lenin Peace Prize in later life), as the Cold War deepened he twice tried in vain (in 1950 and in 1951) to negotiate 'a bilateral treaty of defence' with American President Harry Truman to protect Ireland against 'communistic invasion'.[45]

---

40 Michael Kennedy, *Ireland and the League of Nations, 1919–46* (Dublin, 1996), p. 18. **41** Keogh, *Twentieth-Century Ireland*, pp 190–1. **42** Ibid. **43** Ibid., p. 192. **44** Transcript, Theodore Achilles Oral History Interview, 13 November 1972, p. 62, Truman Presidential Library. **45** See Ronan Fanning, 'The United States and Irish participation in NATO: The

Those negotiations, like Ireland's cooperation with the Allies in World War II, were conducted in the deepest secrecy and without the knowledge of the Dáil, let alone the Irish public.

* * *

The foreign policy of Costello's second Inter-Party government (1954–7) – which MacBride declined to join and in which Liam Cosgrave, then a relatively junior party colleague of Costello, served as Minister for External Affairs – witnessed something of a return to realism. Cosgrave, who had served as an officer in the Irish Army during World War II, endorsed a request from Allen Dulles (the director of the CIA and brother of John Foster Dulles, the American Secretary of State) for 'the re-establishment of liaison between our respective intelligence services'.[46]

After Ireland was finally admitted to the United Nations in 1955 it also fell to Cosgrave to present the framework of Ireland's UN policy in his 'three principles' speech to the Dáil in July 1956. The first principle merely called for fidelity to the UN Charter; the second stressed maintaining 'a position of independence, judging the various questions on which we have to adopt an attitude or cast a vote strictly on their merits in a just and disinterested way' and avoiding 'becoming associated with particular blocs or groups as far as possible'; and the third declared that:

> It must be our constant concern – indeed our moral responsibility – to do whatever we can as a member of the United Nations to preserve the Christian civilisation of which we are a part, and with that end in view to support wherever possible those powers principally responsible for the defence of the free world in their resistance to the spread of Communist power and influence.

Ireland, insisted Cosgrave, belonged 'to the great community of states, made up of the United States of America, Canada and Western Europe' and it was in Ireland's 'national interest that this group of states should remain strong and united'.[47]

The clear tension between the second, non-aligned or neutralist principle and the third, anti-Communist and pro-Western principle mirrored the tension between the idealist tradition in Irish foreign policy (with its emphasis on neutrality as an expression of independence) and the realist tradition (with its emphasis on co-operation with the British and Americans).

Debate of 1950', *Irish Studies in International Affairs*, vol. 1, no. 1 (1979), pp 38–48. **46** See Keogh, *Twentieth-Century Ireland* , pp 230–1. **47** Joseph Morrison Skelly, *Irish Diplomacy at the United Nations, 1945–1965* (Dublin, 1997), p. 37; also Fanning, *Independent Ireland*, p. 202.

It is now clear that Cosgrave's speech was, in fact, the product of a foreign policy initiative launched by Costello in the shape of a memorandum submitted to the Cabinet on 18 May 1956 following a visit to the United States. No longer encumbered by the unreconstructed republicanism of MacBride, Costello had joined the realist camp, and Cosgrave's speech merely endorsed the advice of the secretary of his department, Seán Murphy, on endeavouring 'to apply the principles which the Taoiseach has already formulated'. For Costello, the anti-communist principle had become paramount. Ireland should do nothing 'which by subtracting from the power of America and Britain would relatively strengthen the power of Russia', proclaimed his cabinet memorandum of 30 April 1948. Our policy must 'not be merely anti-British or else we shall come to be completely discounted … We must recognise in our relations with America that America cannot have Irish friendship at the risk of division with Britain.[48] 'The primary consideration for us', he told the Dáil on 11 July 1956 in a speech which unsurprisingly prompted a letter of congratulations from the Catholic Archbishop of Dublin, John Charles McQuaid, 'must be to see that the forces of atheistic communism are repelled and that we do not allow ourselves to become tools to serve communist imperialist initiatives, no matter how carefully they may be camouflaged'.[49]

* * *

The pendulum swung the other way, however, when Frank Aiken returned to Iveagh House as Minister for External Affairs in de Valera's last government in 1957 – he retained that portfolio until he retired to the backbenches in 1969. Aiken's abortive 1941 mission to the United States in search of military and economic aid had compounded his anglophobia with anti-Americanism;[50] it was Aiken, for example, who urged de Valera to disregard the advice of his officials not pay his condolences at the German legation when Hitler died. It was Aiken whom de Valera chose as his successor as Minister for External Affairs in 1951 and it was Aiken who, more than any other Minister for External Affairs, used the UN as a platform for Irish affirmations of independence. The most celebrated example was the so-called China vote on 23 September 1957 when, despite American outrage, Ireland backed the ultimately unsuccessful proposal seeking to inscribe the issue of Chinese representation at the UN on the General Assembly's agenda. Aiken's China policy gave offence to those who espoused the realist tradition in Irish foreign policy, such as Costello, who argued that the expenditure associated with Irish membership of the United Nations and 'foreign affairs generally can only be justified if it enables us to make a useful moral contribution in world affairs, and to obtain and secure the friendship of those nations who may assist in advancing our material interests'.[51]

48 NAI DT S 13750/C. **49** NAI DFA 422/11/29. **50** Skelly, *Irish Diplomacy at the United Nations*, p. 95. **51** Cathal Dowling, 'Irish Policy on the Representation of China at the

Aiken, instead, placed Ireland's UN policies firmly in the context of her struggle to escape from British domination and he advised the General Assembly that the Irish 'know what imperialism is and what resistance to it involves'; the UN, he argued, was 'an agent for the liquidation of imperialism in all parts of the world'.[52]

But Aiken's taste for affirmations of independence ran counter to the instincts of Seán Lemass, whose long-overdue tenure of office as Taoiseach from 1959 to 1966 witnessed the reaffirmation of the realist tradition. Unlike any former head of government, Lemass' abiding and predominant interest was in economic policy; that meant the primacy of economic interdependence in foreign policy. It found expression in his drive to improve Irish–American relations with a view to attracting American companies to Ireland. Such was the Irish public's adulation for John Fitzgerald Kennedy, moreover, when he became the first Irish American Catholic President in 1960, that even the mildest anti-American gesture was likely to incur the wrath of Irish voters, and the Irish delegation at the UN never challenged 'anything ... that the Kennedy administration did'.[53]

Lemass' pragmatic realism was likewise apparent in his quest for cross-border economic cooperation at his 1965 North–South summits with Terence O'Neill and in the Anglo–Irish Free Trade Agreement of the same year; and it found expression, above all, in the Europeanisation of Irish foreign policy consequent upon the decision progressively to dismantle protectionist barriers.

It was the 1961 decision to join the European Economic Community which laid bare as nothing had done before the idealist/realist tension between neutrality as an affirmation of independence and the Irish commitment to European integration as an expression of interdependence. Lemass, always impatient with the pieties of neutrality – he once complained to one of his most senior officials that the linkage between partition and neutrality had never been discussed by de Valera's cabinet[54] – forced the pace. When an inter-governmental working party was asked to reconcile the continued Irish refusal to join NATO with positive Irish support for the ideal of European unity, Con Cremin, the secretary of the Department of External Affairs, procrastinated, saying in his best mandarin that the matter was 'being discussed at the highest level'. Lemass would have none of it and demanded a formula as a matter of urgency. The Cremin formula, duly delivered within forty-eight hours to a Saturday morning meeting of the working party a week before Christmas, is a fascinating testament to the strength of the realist tradition in Irish foreign policy:

United Nations, 1957–9', *Irish Studies in International Affairs*, vol. 7 (1996), p. 92. **52** Skelly, *Irish Diplomacy at the United Nations*, p. 125. **53** Conor Cruise O'Brien, *Memoir: My Life and Themes* (Dublin, 1998), p. 99. **54** Private information.

It is true we are not a member of the North Atlantic Treaty Organisation. This is not due to any lack of sympathy with the basic objective of NATO – quite the contrary – but to the fact that membership would put us under an obligation not only to respect, but even to defend the territorial integrity of the countries party to the Treaty, whereas it is a fundamental aspiration of the Irish people to see the unity of our country restored. *Our non-participation in NATO is thus not an expression of any principle of neutrality* [my italics], nor does it weaken in any way our positive attitude towards the ideal of European unity.[55]

Having secured his Iveagh House flank, Lemass unequivocally advised the EEC's Council of Ministers in Brussels on 18 January 1962 that, 'while Ireland did not accede to the North Atlantic Treaty, we have always agreed with the general aims of that treaty'.[56] Lemass went ever further in the *New York Times* in July 1962, where he was quoted as recognising that:

a military commitment will be an inevitable consequence of our joining the Common Market and ultimately we would be prepared to yield even the technical label of neutrality. We are prepared to go into this integrated Europe without any reservation as to how far this will take us in the field of foreign policy and defence.[57]

Lemass practised what he preached during the Cuban missile crisis when, as the CIA reminded Kennedy on the eve of his Irish visit, that 'the Irish were most cooperative with the United States Government and searched all [Soviet] Bloc air traffic transiting Shannon'.[58] That secret assistance was all of a piece with the secret assistance rendered the Allies in World War II by de Valera's government

---

[55] NAI DFA CM 16. The final draft of the memorandum was diluted and reads: 'The fact that Ireland feels debarred ... from seeking membership of NATO should not be understood to mean that she is, or wishes to be regarded as, neutral in the great conflict which today divides the world into two opposing camps. The position of the Irish Government is today, as it was in 1949, one of agreement with the aims of the NATO Treaty, and they regret the persistence of the circumstances which preclude the consideration of participating therein. Ireland has declared herself to be unequivocally on the side of the Western democracies and nobody could seriously suggest that in any circumstances she could ever be otherwise than on that side. We are very willing to participate in the development of the political objectives of the Community by way of a Western European confederation. We recognise that confederation must involve the obligation to discuss the co-ordination of external policy and of defence measures and must be inspired by a readiness to agree on common aims': NAI DT S 14291/B/61 (copy on NAI DT S 16877/W). [56] Skelly, *Irish Diplomacy at the United Nations*, p. 209. [57] See D.J. Maher, *The Tortuous Path: The Course of Ireland's Entry into the EEC* (Dublin, 1986), p. 152. [58] Keogh, *Twentieth-Century Ireland*, p. 251.

and with the close links on counter-espionage and communist activities which Irish military intelligence maintained in the fifties with both MI5 and the CIA.[59]

What, then, is the significance of the events of 1961–2? Simply this: that although Ireland did not finally accede to the EEC until 1 January 1973, the evidence now available reveals that, notwithstanding the Euroscepticism of Eamon de Valera and Frank Aiken, the debate within the Irish foreign policy establishment about the tension between the independence enshrined in neutrality and the interdependence enshrined in the EEC had by then already been effectively resolved. Irish foreign policy has since remained wedded to the realism of interdependence.[60]

---

59 See Eunan O'Halpin, *Defending Ireland: The Irish State and its Enemies since 1922* (Oxford, 1999), pp 278–82. Professor O'Halpin's recently published 'gathering together of the various threads of what can broadly be called national security policy and activities' (ibid., p. viii) provides countless examples of how *raison d'état* has consistently shaped Irish defence and security policy since independence.   **60** See Fanning, 'Irish Neutrality – an Historical Review', p. 37, for subsequent affirmations from Jack Lynch and Aiken's successors in Iveagh House that Ireland has 'never been ideologically neutral'.

Select Bibliography

Aiken, Frank, *Ireland and the United Nations* (Dublin, 1957–63).
—, 'Can We Limit the Nuclear Club?', *Bulletin of the Atomic Scientist*, vol. 17, no. 7 (September, 1961).
Allen, Trevor, *The Storm Passed By: Ireland and the Battle of the Atlantic, 1941–42* (Dublin, 1996).
Arthur, Paul, 'Anglo–Irish Relations and the Northern Ireland Problem', *Irish Studies in International Affairs*, vol. 2, no. 1 (1985).
—, 'American Intervention in the Anglo–Irish Peace Process: Incrementalism or Interference?', *Cambridge Review of International Affairs*, vol. 11, no. 1 (1997).
Ashworth, Elizabeth De Boer. 'Thinking Globally, Suffering Locally – the Effects of International Trade Agreements on Ireland', *Irish Studies in International Affairs*, vol. 8 (1997).
Aughey, Arthur, 'Fukayama, the End of History and the Irish Question', *Irish Studies in International Affairs*, vol. 9 (1998).
Barcroft, Stephen. 'Irish Foreign Policy at the League of Nations, 1929–36', *Irish Studies in International Affairs*, vol. 1, no. 1 (1979).
Barton, Brian, 'The Impact of the War in Northern Ireland' in Girvin, Brian and Roberts, Geoffrey (eds) *Ireland and the Second World War* (Dublin, 1999).
Bowman, John, 'De Valera on Ulster, 1919–20: What he told America', *Irish Studies in International Affairs*, vol. 1, no. 1 (1979).
—, *De Valera and the Ulster Question, 1917–73* (Oxford, 1982).
Bowyer Bell, J., 'Ireland and the Spanish Civil War', *Studia Hibernica*, vol. 7 (1969).
Brown, Chris, 'Ireland's Foreign Policy in the Cold War', *Irish Studies in International Affairs*, vol. 10 (1999).
Brown, Tony, 'Internationalism and International Politics – the External Links of the Labour Party', *Irish Studies in International Affairs*, vol. 1, no. 2 (1980).
Canning, Paul, *British Policy towards Ireland, 1921–41* (Oxford, 1985).
Cochrane, Feargal, 'Progressive or Regressive? The Anglo–Irish Agreement as a Dynamic in the Northern Ireland Polity', *Irish Political Studies*, vol. 8 (1993).
Carroll, Francis. *American Opinion and the Irish Question, 1910–23* (Dublin, 1978).
—, 'Protocol and International Politics, 1928: The Secretary of State Goes to Ireland', *Éire-Ireland*, vol. 26, no. 4 (1991).
Carroll, Joseph T., *Ireland in the War Years* (Newton Abbott, 1975).
—, 'A French View of Irish Neutrality', *Etudes Irlandaises*, vol. 14, no. 2 (December 1989).
—, 'General de Gaulle and Ireland's EEC Application' in Joannon, Pierre (ed.) *De Gaulle and Ireland* (Dublin, 1991).
Carter, Carolle J., *The Shamrock and the Swastika: German Espionage in Ireland in World War II* (Palo Alto, 1977).
Chossudovsky, Evgeny, 'The Origins of the Treaty on the Non-Proliferation of Nuclear Weapons: Ireland's Initiative in the United Nations, 1958–61', *Irish Studies in International Affairs*, vol. 3, no. 2 (1990).
Collins, Stephen, *The Cosgrave Legacy* (Dublin, 1996).

Connolly, Jerome, 'Development Co-Operation: Options for Ireland', *Irish Studies in International Affairs*, vol. 1, no. 1 (1979).

Coombes, David (ed.), *Ireland and the European Communities: Ten Years of Membership* (Dublin, 1983).

Costello, John A., *Ireland in International Affairs* (Dublin, 1948).

Coughlan, Anthony, *The EEC: Ireland and the Making of a Superpower* (Dublin, 1979).

Cox, Michael, 'Bringing in the International: The IRA Ceasefire and the End of the Cold War', *International Affairs*, vol. 73, no. 4 (October, 1997).

—, 'Northern Ireland: The War that came in from the Cold', *Irish Studies in International Affairs*, vol. 9 (1998).

—, 'Thinking "Globally" about Peace in Northern Ireland', *Politics*, vol. 18, no. 1 (1998).

—, '"Cinderella at the Ball": Explaining the End of the War in Northern Ireland', *Millennium*, vol. 27, no. 2 (1998).

—, 'The War that came in from the Cold: Clinton and the Irish Question', *World Policy Journal*, vol. 16, no. 1 (Spring, 1999).

—, 'Friendly Relations', *Fortnight*, vol. 22, no. 369 (March/April, 1998).

Cox, Michael, Guelke, Adrian and Stephens, Fiona (eds), *The War that Came in from the Cold: Northern Ireland and the End of the Troubles* (Manchester, 2000).

Cremin, Cornelius, 'The United Nations Conference on the Law of the Sea', *Irish Studies in International Affairs*, vol. 1, no. 1 (1979).

—, 'Northern Ireland at the United Nations: August/September, 1969', *Irish Studies in International Affairs*, vol. 1, no. 2 (1980).

—, 'United Nations Peacekeeping Operations: An Irish Initiative, 1961-8', *Irish Studies in International Affairs*, vol. 1, no. 4 (1984).

Cronin, Mike, *The Blueshirts and Irish Politics* (Dublin, 1997).

Cronin, Sean, 'The Making of NATO and the Partition of Ireland', *Éire-Ireland*, vol. 20, no. 2 (1985).

—, *Washington's Irish Policy, 1916–1986: Independence, Partition, and Neutrality* (Dublin, 1987).

Davis, Troy, 'Diplomacy as Propaganda: The Appointment of T.A. Smiddy as Irish Free State Minister to the United States', *Éire-Ireland*, vol. 31, nos 3, 4 (Fall/Winter, 1996).

—, *Dublin's American Policy: Irish–American Diplomatic Relations, 1945–52* (Washington, 1998).

—, 'Anti-partitionism, Irish America and Anglo–American Relations, 1945–51' in Kennedy, Michael and Skelly, Joseph Morrison (eds), *Irish Foreign Policy, 1919–66: From Independence to Internationalism* (Dublin, 2000).

Dean, D.W., 'Final Exit? Britain, Eire, the Commonwealth and the Repeal of the External Relations Act, 1945–49', *Journal of Imperial and Commonwealth History*, vol. 20, no. 391–418 (1992).

Dempsey, George T., 'Mythmaking and Missing the Point: Largely Irish Perceptions of American Foreign Policy', *Irish Studies in International Affairs*, vol. 9 (1998).

Dillon, T.W.T., 'The Refugee Problem', *Studies*, vol. 28 (September 1939).

Dinan, Desmond, 'After the "Emergency": Ireland in the Post-War World, 1945–50', *Éire-Ireland*, vol. 24, no. 3 (Fall, 1989).

Ditchburn, Robert W., 'The Refugee Problem', *Studies*, vol. 28 (June 1939).

Dobrzynska-Cantwell, Krystyna, *An Unusual Diplomat* (London, 1998).

Doherty, Richard, *Clear the Way! A History of the 38th (Irish) Brigade, 1941–47* (Dublin, 1993).

—, *Irish Men and Women in the Second World War* (Dublin, 1999).

Dorr, Noel, 'Ireland at the United Nations: 40 Years On', *Irish Studies in International Affairs*, vol. 7 (1996).

Dowling, Cathal, 'Irish Policy on the Representation of China at the United Nations, 1957–59', *Irish Studies in International Affairs,* vol. 7 (1996).
Downey, James, *Them and Us: Britain, Ireland and the Northern Irish Question, 1969–82* (Dublin, 1983).
Doyle, John, 'Governance and Citizenship in Contested States: The Northern Ireland Peace Agreement as Internationalised Governance', *Irish Studies in International Affairs,* vol. 10 (1999).
Driscoll, Dennis, 'Is Ireland Really Neutral?' *Irish Studies in International Affairs,* vol. 1, no. 3 (1982).
Drudy, P.J. (ed.), *Ireland and Britain Since 1922* (Cambridge, 1986).
Drudy, P.J. and McAleese, D. (eds) *Ireland and the European Community* (Cambridge, 1983).
Duggan, John P., *Neutral Ireland and the Third Reich* (Dublin, 1989).
—, *A History of the Irish Army* (Dublin, 1991).
Dumbrell, John, 'The United States and the Northern Irish Conflict, 1969–94: From Indifference to Intervention', *Irish Studies in International Affairs,* vol. 6 (1995).
Dwyer, T. Ryle, *Irish Neutrality and the USA* (Dublin, 1977).
—, *Strained Relations: Ireland at Peace and the USA at War, 1941–45* (Dublin, 1988).
Fanning, Ronan, *The Irish Department of Finance, 1922–58* (Dublin 1978).
—, 'The United States and Irish Participation in NATO: The Debate of 1950', *Irish Studies in International Affairs,* vol. 1, no. 1 (1979).
—, 'London and Belfast's Response to the Declaration of the Republic of Ireland', *International Affairs,* vol. 58, no. 1 (1982).
—, 'Irish Neutrality – An Historical Perspective', *Irish Studies in International Affairs,* vol. 1, no. 3 (1982).
—, *Independent Ireland* (Dublin, 1983).
—, 'Anglo–Irish Relations – Partition and the British Dimension in Historical Perspective', *Irish Studies in International Affairs,* vol. 2, no. 1 (1985).
—, 'The Anglo–American Alliance and the Irish Application for Membership in the United Nations', *Irish Studies in International Affairs,* vol. 2, no. 2 (1986).
—, 'Irish Neutrality' in Bo Huldt and Atis Lejins (eds), *Neutrals in Europe: Ireland* (Stockholm, 1990).
—, 'Charles de Gaulle, 1946–58 – From Resignation to Return: The Irish Diplomatic Perspective' in Joannon, Pierre (ed.), *De Gaulle and Ireland* (Dublin, 1991).
—, 'Neutrality, Identity and Security: The Example of Ireland' in Bauwens, Werner, Cleese, Armand, Knudsen, Olav (eds), *Small States and the Security Challenge in the New Europe* (London and Washington, 1996).
—, 'Small States, Large Neighbours: Ireland and the United Kingdom', *Irish Studies in International Affairs,* vol. 9 (1998).
—, *'Raison d'État* and the Evolution of Irish Foreign Policy' in Kennedy, Michael and Skelly, Joseph Morrison, (eds), *Irish Foreign Policy, 1919–66: From Independence to Internationalism* (Dublin, 2000).
Fanning, Ronan, Kennedy, Michael, Keogh, Dermot and O'Halpin, Eunan, (eds) *Documents on Irish Foreign Policy: Volume I, 1919–22* (Dublin, 1998).
Farrell, Theo, '"The Model Army": Military Imitation and the Enfeeblement of the Irish Army, 1919–39', *Irish Studies in International Affairs,* vol. 8 (1997).
Fisk, Robert, *In Time of War: Ireland, Ulster and the Price of Neutrality, 1939–45* (Dublin, 1983).
FitzGerald, Garret. 'Political Implications of Irish Membership in the EEC', *Studies,* vol. 51 (1962).

—, *Towards a New Ireland* (Dublin, 1972).
—, *All in a Life* (Dublin, 1991)
—, 'The Origins, Development and Present Status of Irish "Neutrality"', *Irish Studies in International Affairs*, vol. 9 (1998).
FitzGerald, William, *Irish Unification and NATO* (Dublin, 1982).
Fitzpatrick, J.I., 'Ireland and the Free Trade Area', *Christus Rex*, vol. 12, no. 3 (July 1958)
Gallagher, Eamonn, 'Anglo–Irish Relations in the European Community', *Irish Studies in International Affairs*, vol. 2, no. 1 (1985).
Gallagher, Tom, 'Scotland and the Anglo–Irish Agreement: the Reaction of the Orange Order', *Irish Political Studies*, vol. 3 (1988).
Geiger, Till, 'The Enthusiastic Response of a Reluctant Supporter: Ireland and the Committee for European Economic Cooperation in 1947' in Kennedy, Michael and Skelly, Joseph Morrison (eds), *Irish Foreign Policy, 1919–66: From Independence to Internationalism* (Dublin, 2000).
Gillespie, Paul (ed.), *Britain's European Question: The Issues for Ireland* (Dublin, 1996).
—, 'Ireland in the New World Order: Interests and Values in the Irish Government's White Paper on Foreign Policy', *Irish Studies in International Affairs*, vol. 7 (1996).
Girvin, Brian, 'Ireland and the Marshall Plan: A Cargo Cult in the North Atlantic' in Griffiths, R.T. (ed.), *Explorations in OEEC History* (Paris, 1997).
—, 'The Politics of War in Ireland: Elections, Neutrality and Governing' in Girvin, Brian, Roberts, Geoffrey (eds), *Ireland and the Second World War* (Dublin, 1999).
Girvin, Brian and Roberts, Geoffrey (eds), *Ireland and the Second World War* (Dublin, 1999).
Goldstone, Katrina, '"Benevolent Helpfulness"? Ireland and the International Reaction to Jewish Refugees, 1933–39' in Kennedy, Michael and Skelly, Joseph Morrison (eds), *Irish Foreign Policy, 1919–66: From Independence to Internationalism* (Dublin, 2000).
Goodman, James, *Single Europe, Single Ireland? Uneven Development in Progress* (Dublin, 1999).
Gordenker, L., 'Conor Cruise O'Brien and the Truth About the United Nations', *International Organizations*, vol. 23, no. 4 (1969).
Guelke, Adrian, 'The American Connection to the Northern Ireland Conflict', *Irish Studies in International Affairs*, vol. 1, no. 4 (1984).
—, *Northern Ireland: The International Perspective* (Dublin, 1988).
—, The Peace Process in South Africa, Israel and Northern Ireland: A Farewell to Arms?', *Irish Studies in International Affairs*, vol. 5 (1994).
—, 'The United States, Irish Americans and the Northern Ireland Peace Process', *International Affairs*, vol. 72, no. 3 (1996).
Halliday, Fred, 'Irish Questions in International Perspective: A Personal View', *Irish Studies in International Affairs*, vol. 7 (1996).
Harkness, David, *The Restless Dominion: The Irish Free State and the British Commonwealth* (London, 1969).
—, 'Patrick McGilligan: Man of Commonwealth', *Journal of Imperial and Commonwealth History*, vol. 8, no. 1 (1979).
Harrison, Richard S., *Irish Anti-War Movements, 1824–1974* (Dublin, 1986).
Hayes-McCoy, G.A,. 'Irish Defence Policy, 1938–51', in Nowlan, K.B. and Williams, T.D. (eds), *Ireland in the War Years and After* (Dublin, 1969).
Heathcote, Nina, 'Ireland and the United Nations Operation in the Congo', *International Relations*, vol. 3, no. 11 (May, 1971).
Hederman, Miriam, *The Road to Europe: Irish Attitudes, 1948–61* (Dublin, 1983).

—, 'The Beginning of the Discussion on European Union in Ireland' in Lipgens, Walter and Loth, Wilfred (eds), *Documents on the History of European Integration: The Struggle for European Unity by Political Parties and Pressure Groups in Western European Countries, 1945–50* (Berlin, 1988).
Heffernan, Liz and Whelan, Anthony, 'Ireland, the United Nations and the Gulf War, *Irish Studies in International Affairs*, vol. 3, no. 3 (1991).
Hill, Ronald J. and O'Corcora, Michael, 'The Soviet Union in Irish Foreign Policy', *International Affairs*, vol. 58, no. 2 (1982).
Hill, Ronald J. and Marsh, Michael, *Modern Irish Democracy* (Dublin, 1993).
Holmes, Dennis and Holmes, Michael, *Ireland and India: Connections, Comparisons, Contrasts* (Dublin, 1997).
Holmes, Michael, 'A Friend of India? Ireland and the Diplomatic Relationship' in Holmes, Dennis and Holmes, Michael, *Ireland and India: Connections, Comparisons, Contrasts* (Dublin, 1997).
Horgan, John, *Sean Lemass: The Enigmatic Patriot* (Dublin, 1997).
—, 'Irish Foreign Policy, Northern Ireland, Neutrality and the Commonwealth: The Hisorical Roots of a Current Controversy', *Irish Studies in International Affairs*, vol. 10 (1999).
Ishizuka, Katsumi, 'Ireland and the Partnership for Peace', *Irish Studies in International Affairs*, vol. 10 (1999).
Joannon, Pierre (ed.), *De Gaulle and Ireland* (Dublin, 1991).
—, 'Charles de Gaulle and Ireland: A Return to the Sources' in Joannon, Pierre (ed.), *De Gaulle and Ireland* (Dublin, 1991).
Kavanagh, Cormac, 'Neutrality and the Volunteers: British and Irish Government Policy' in Girvin, Brian and Roberts, Geoffrey (eds), *Ireland and the Second World War* (Dublin, 1999).
Keatinge, Patrick, 'Ireland and the League of Nations', *Studies*, vol. 59 (1970).
—, 'Odd Man Out? Irish Neutrality and European Security', *International Affairs*, vol. 48 (1972).
—, *The Formulation of Irish Foreign Policy* (Dublin, 1973).
—, 'The Foreign Policy of the Irish Coalition Government', *World Today*, August, 1973.
—, *A Place Among the Nations: Issues of Irish Foreign Policy* (Dublin, 1978).
—, 'New Directions in Irish Foreign Policy', *Irish Studies in International Affairs*, vol. 1, no. 2 (1980).
—, 'Ireland and the World, 1957–82', Litton, F. (ed.), *Unequal Achievement* (Dublin, 1982).
—, 'An Odd Couple? Obstacles and Opportunities in Inter-State Political Cooperation between the Republic of Ireland and the United Kingdom' in Rea, Desmond (ed.), *Political Cooperation in Divided Societies: A Series of Papers Relevant to the Conflict in Northern Ireland* (Dublin, 1982).
—, 'The Europeanisation of Irish Foreign Policy' in Drudy, P.J. and McAleese, Dermot (eds), *Ireland and the European Community* (Cambridge, 1983).
—, 'Ireland: Neutrality in EPC' in Hill, Christopher (ed.), *National Foreign Policies and European Political Cooperation* (London, 1983).
—, *A Singular Stance: Irish Neutrality in the 1980s* (Dublin, 1984).
—, 'Ireland, Political Cooperation and the Middle East' in Allen, David and Pijpers, Alfred (eds), *European Foreign Policymaking and the Arab–Israeli Conflict* (The Hague, 1984).
—, 'Ireland and the Western European Union' in Tsakaloyannis, Panos (ed.) *The Reactivation of the Western European Union: The Effects on the EEC and its Institutions* (Maastricht, 1985).

—, 'Irish Neutrality and the European Community'. McSweeney, Bill (ed.), *Ireland and the Threat of Nuclear War* (Dublin, 1985).
—, 'Annual Review: Ireland's Foreign Policy', *Irish Studies in International Affairs*, vols 2–7 (1985–96).
—, *Towards a Safer Europe: Small State Security Policies and the European Union: Implications for Ireland* (Dublin, 1995).
—, *European Security: Ireland's Choices* (Dublin, 1996).
—, 'Ireland and European Security: Continuity and Change', *Irish Studies in International Affairs*, vol. 9 (1998).
Kelleher, John, V., 'Ireland ... Where Does She Stand?' *Foreign Affairs*, vol. 35, no. 3 (1957).
Kennedy, Denis, *The Widening Gulf* (Belfast, 1988).
Kennedy, Michael. 'The Irish Free State and the League of Nations, 1922–32: The Wider Implications', *Irish Studies in International Affairs*, vol. 3, no. 4 (1992).
—, '"Principle Well-Seasoned with the Sauce of Realism": Seán Lester, Joseph Walshe and the Definition of the Irish Free State's Policy towards Manchuria', *Irish Studies in International Affairs*, vol. 6 (1995).
—, '"Candour and Chicanery": The Irish Free State and the Geneva Protocol, 1924–25', *Irish Historical Studies*, vol. 29, no. 115 (May, 1995).
—, *Ireland and the League of Nations, 1919–46: International Relations, Diplomacy and Politics* (Dublin, 1996).
—, '"Civil servants Cannot be Politicians": The Professionalisation of the Irish Foreign Service, 1919–22', *Irish Studies in International Affairs*, vol. 8 (1997).
—, 'Prologue to Peacekeeping: Ireland and the Saar, 1934–35', *Irish Historical Studies*, vol. 30, no. 119 (May, 1997).
—, 'Towards Cooperation: Seán Lemass and North–South Economic Relations, 1956–65', *Irish Economic and Social History*, vol. 24 (1997).
—, '"Publishing a Secret History": The *Documents on Irish Foreign Policy* Project', *Irish Studies in International Affairs*, vol. 9 (1998).
—, 'Our Men in Berlin: Some Thoughts on Irish Diplomats in Germany, 1929–39', *Irish Studies in International Affairs*, vol. 10 (1999).
—, '"Mr Blythe, I Think, Hears From Him Occasionally": The Experiences of Irish Diplomats in Latin America, 1919–23' in Kennedy, Michael and Skelly, Joseph Morrison (eds), *Irish Foreign Policy, 1919–66: From Independence to Internationalism* (Dublin, 2000).
— and Skelly, Joseph Morrison (eds), *Irish Foreign Policy, 1919–66: From Independence to Internationalism* (Dublin, 2000).
— and Skelly, Joseph Morrison, 'The Study of Irish Foreign Policy from Independence to Internationalism' in Kennedy, Michael and Skelly, Joseph Morrison (eds), *Irish Foreign Policy, 1919–66: From Independence to Internationalism* (Dublin, 2000).
—, *Division and Consensus: The Politics of Cross-border Relations in Ireland 1919–69* (Dublin, 2000).
Keogh, Dermot, 'History of the Irish Department of External Affairs' in Steiner, Zara (ed.), *The Times Survey of Foreign Offices Around the World* (London, 1982).
—, 'De Valera, the Bishops and the Red Scare' in Murphy, John A., and O'Carroll, J.P. (eds), *De Valera and his Times* (Cork, 1983).
—, *The Vatican, the Bishops and Irish Politics, 1919–39* (Cambridge, 1986).
—, 'Jewish Refugees and Irish Government Policy in the 1930s and 1940s', *Remembering for the Future*, Conference Proceedings Oxford, 1988, vol. 1 (Oxford, 1988).
—, *Ireland and Europe, 1919–48: A Diplomatic and Political History* (Dublin, 1988); revised edition, *Ireland and Europe, 1919–1989* (Cork and Dublin, 1990).

—, 'Eamon de Valera and Hitler: An Analysis of International Reaction to the Visit to the German Minister, May 1945', *Irish Studies in International Affairs*, vol. 3, no. 1 (1989).
—, 'Profile of Joseph Walshe, Secretary of the Department of Foreign Affairs, 1922–46', *Irish Studies in International Affairs*, vol. 3, no. 2 (1990).
—, 'Ireland, the Vatican and the Cold War', *Irish Studies in International Affairs*, vol. 3, no. 3 (1991).
—, 'Ireland, de Gaulle and World War II' in Joannon, Pierre (ed.), *De Gaulle and Ireland* (Dublin, 1991).
—, *Twentieth-Century Ireland: Nation and State* (Dublin, 1994).
—, *Ireland and the Vatican: The Politics and Diplomacy of Church–State Relations, 1922–60* (Cork, 1995).
—, 'The Diplomacy of '"Dignified Calm": An Analysis of Ireland's Application for Membership of the EEC, 1961–1963', *Journal of European Integration History*, vol. 3, no. 1 (1997).
—, *Jews in Twentieth-Century Ireland: Refugees, Anti-Semitism and the Holocaust* (Cork, 1998).
—, 'Irish Neutrality and the First Application for Membership of the EEC, 1961–63' in Kennedy, Michael and Skelly, Joseph Morrison (eds), *Irish Foreign Policy, 1919–66: From Independence to Internationalism* (Dublin, 2000).
Keown, Gerard, 'Taking the World Stage: Creating an Irish Foreign Policy in the 1920s' in Kennedy, Michael and Skelly, Joseph Morrison (eds), *Irish Foreign Policy, 1919–66: From Independence to Internationalism* (Dublin, 2000).
King, Desmond S., 'The Interaction between Foreign and Domestic Policy in the 1979 European Elections in Ireland', *Irish Studies in International Affairs*, vol. 1, no. 3 (1982).
Lang, John Temple, 'The Proposed Treaty Setting Up the European Union: Constitutional Implications for Ireland and Comments on Neutrality', *Irish Studies in International Affairs*, vol. 2, no. 1 (1985).
Laffan, Brigid, 'The Consequences for Irish Foreign Policy' in Coombes, David, *Ireland in the European Communities: Ten Years of Membership* (Dublin, 1983).
—, *Ireland and South Africa: Irish Government Policy in the 1980s* (Dublin, 1988).
—, '"While you're over there in Brussels, Get us a Grant": The Management of the Structural Funds in Ireland', *Irish Political Studies*, vol. 5 (1989).
—, *Constitution Building in the European Union* (Dublin, 1996).
—, 'Constitutional Change in the European Union: The Small State–Large State Issue from Ireland's Perspective', *Irish Studies in International Affairs*, vol. 8 (1997).
Lemass, Seán, 'Small States in International Organizations' in Schou, A. and Brundtland, A.O. (eds), *Small States in International Relations* (Uppsala, 1971).
Lysaght, Charles, 'The Agreement on the Delimitation of the Continental Shelf between Ireland and the United Kingdom', *Irish Studies in International Affairs*, vol. 3, no. 2 (1990).
McCabe, Ian, *A Diplomatic History of Ireland, 1948–49: The Republic, the Commonwealth and NATO* (Dublin, 1991).
—, 'John Costello "Announces" the Repeal of the External Relations Act', *Irish Studies in International Affairs*, vol. 3, no. 4 (1992).
McCarron, Donal, *Step Together: The Story of Ireland's Emergency Army as Told by its Veterans* (Dublin, 1999).
McCaughren, Thomas, *The Peacemakers of Niemba* (Dublin, 1966).
McCullagh, David, *A Makeshift Majority: The First Inter-Party Government* (Dublin, 1998).
MacDonagh, Michael, 'Ireland's Attitude to External Affairs', *Studies*, vol. 48 (1959).
McDonald, Henry, *Irishbatt: The Story of Ireland's Blue Berets in the Lebanon* (Dublin, 1993).
McGarry, Fearghal, *Irish Politics and the Spanish Civil War* (Cork, 1999).

—, 'General O'Duffy, the National Corporate Party and the Irish Brigade' in Joost Augusteijn (ed.), *Ireland in the 1930s: New Perspectives* (Dublin, 1999).

McGinty, Roger, 'Almost Like Talking Dirty: Irish Security in Post-Cold War Europe', *Irish Studies in International Affairs*, vol. 6 (1995).

—, 'American Influences on the Northern Ireland Peace Process', *Journal of Conflict Studies*, vol. 17, no. 2 (1997).

—, 'Decommissioning and the Peace Process', *Irish Studies in International Affairs*, vol. 10 (1999).

McInnes, Colin and Kennedy-Pipes, Caroline, 'The British Army in Northern Ireland: The Peace Process and the End of the Cold War', *Irish Studies in International Affairs*, vol. 8 (1997).

MacKernan, Padraic, 'Ireland and European Political Cooperation', *Irish Studies in International Affairs*, vol. 1, no. 4 (1982).

McMahon, Deirdre, 'Ireland, the Dominions and the Munich Crisis', *Irish Studies in International Affairs*, vol. 1, no. 1 (1979).

—, '"A Transient Apparition": British Policy towards the de Valera Government', *Irish Historical Studies*, vol. 22, no. 88 (September, 1981).

—, *Republicans and Imperialists: Anglo–Irish Relations in the 1930s* (London, 1984).

—, 'A Larger and Noisier Southern Ireland: Ireland and the Evolution of Dominion Status in India, Burma and the Commonwealth, 1942–49' in Kennedy, Michael and Skelly, Joseph Morrison (eds), *Irish Foreign Policy, 1919–66: From Independence to Internationalism* (Dublin, 2000).

MacQueen, Norman, 'Ireland's Entry into the United Nations, 1946–56' in Gallagher, Thomas and O'Connell, James (eds), *Irish Contemporary Studies* (Manchester, 1983).

—, 'Frank Aiken and Irish Activism at the United Nations', *International History Review*, vol. 6, no. 2 (May, 1984).

McSweeney, Bill (ed.), *Ireland and the Threat of Nuclear War* (Dublin, 1985).

—, 'Identity, Interest and the Good Friday Agreement', *Irish Studies in International Affairs*, vol. 9 (1998).

Maguire, Maria, *A Bibliography of Published Works on Irish Foreign Relations, 1921–78* (Dublin, 1981).

Maher, Denis, *The Tortuous Path: The Course of Ireland's Entry into the EEC, 1948–73* (Dublin, 1986).

Manathunga, Catherine, 'The Evolution of Irish Disarmament Initiatives at the United Nations, 1957–61', *Irish Studies in International Affairs*, vol. 7 (1996).

Mangan, Colm, 'Plans and Operations', *Irish Sword*, vol. 19, nos 75, 76 (1993–94).

Manning, Maurice, *The Blueshirts* (Dublin, 1970).

Mansergh, Martin (ed.), *The Spirit of the Nation: The Speeches of Charles J. Haughey* (Cork and Dublin, 1986).

—, 'The Background to the Peace Process', *Irish Studies in International Affairs*, vol. 6 (1995).

Mansergh, Nicholas, 'Ireland: The Republic outside the Commonwealth', *International Affairs*, vol. 28, no. 3 (1952).

—, 'Ireland: External Relations, 1926–39' in MacManus, F. (ed.), *The Years of the Great Test* (Cork, 1967).

—, 'Irish Foreign Policy, 1945–55' in Nowlan, K.B. and Williams, T.D. (eds), *Ireland in the War Years and After* (Dublin, 1969).

—, *The Unresolved Question: The Anglo–Irish Settlement and its Undoing, 1912–72* (London, 1991).

—, *Nationalism and Independence: Selected Irish Papers* (Cork, 1997).

Matthews, Alan, 'European Union: The Economic Implications for Ireland', *Irish Studies in International Affairs*, vol. 2, no. 1 (1985).
Meehan, Elizabeth, 'British–Irish Relations in the Context of the European Union', *Review of International Studies* (1999).
Mitchell, Arthur, *Revolutionary Government in Ireland: Dáil Éireann, 1919–22* (Dublin, 1995).
Molohan, Cathy. *Germany and Ireland: Two Nations' Friendship* (Dublin, 1999).
Mulkeen, Thomas, 'Ireland at the UN'. *Éire-Ireland*, vol. 8, no. 1 (1973).
Murphy, Anna, 'Facing the Unknown: Ireland in an Expanding European Union', *Irish Studies in International Affairs*, vol. 10 (1999).
Murphy, Gary., 'Towards a Corporate State? Seán Lemass and the Realignment of Interest Groups in the Policy Process, 1948–64', *Administration*, vol. 47, no. 1 (Spring, 1996).
—, 'Government, Interests Groups and the Move to Europe, 1957–63', *Irish Studies in International Affairs*, vol. 8 (1997).
—, '"A Wider Perspective": Ireland's View of Western Europe in the 1950s', Kennedy, Michael and Skelly, Joseph Morrison (eds), *Irish Foreign Policy, 1919–66: From Independence to Internationalism* (Dublin, 2000).
Murphy, John A., *Ireland in the Twentieth Century* (Dublin, 1975).
Nowlan, K.B. and Williams, T.D. (eds), *Ireland in the War Years and After* (Dublin, 1969).
O'Brien, Conor Cruise, *To Katanga and Back: A UN Case Study* (London, 1962).
—, *Ireland, the United Nations, and Southern Africa* (Dublin, 1967).
—, 'Ireland in International Affairs' in Edwards, Owen Dudley (ed.), *Conor Cruise O'Brien Introduces Ireland* (Dublin, 1969).
—, 'Hands Off', *Foreign Policy*, vol. 37 (Winter 1979–80).
—, 'Liberty and Terrorism', *International Security*. vol. 2 (Fall 1997).
O'Brien, John, 'Australia and the Repeal of the External Relations Act' in Kiernan, Colm (ed.), *Australia and Ireland, 1788–1945* (Dublin, 1986).
O'Carroll, Donal, 'The Emergency Army', *Irish Sword*, vol. 19, nos 75, 76 (1993–94).
Ó Cearbhaill, Tadhg, 'Ireland in the ILO', *Irish Studies in International Affairs*, vol. 1, no. 2 (1980).
O'Clery, Conor, *The Greening of the White House* (Dublin, 1997).
O'Connor, Brian, *Ireland and the United Nations*, Tuairim pamphlet (Dublin, 1961).
Ó Dochartaigh, Niall, '"Sure its Hard to Keep up with the Splits Here": Irish American Responses to the Outbreak of Conflict in Northern Ireland, 1968–74', *Irish Political Studies*, vol. 10 (1995).
Ó Drisceoil, Donal, *Censorship in Ireland, 1939–45: Neutrality, Politics and Society* (Cork, 1996).
—, 'Censorship and Irish Perceptions of the War' in Girvin, Brian and Roberts, Geoffrey (eds), *Ireland and the Second World War* (Dublin, 1999).
O'Driscoll, Mervyn, 'The Political Economy of Irish–German Trade Relations, 1932–38', *Irish Studies in International Affairs*, vol. 10 (1999).
—, 'Inter-war Irish–German Diplomacy: Continuity, Ambiguity and Appeasement in Irish Foreign Policy' in Kennedy, Michael and Skelly, Joseph Morrison (eds), *Irish Foreign Policy, 1919–66: From Independence to Internationalism* (Dublin, 2000).
—, *Irish–German Relations* (Dublin, 2000).
O'Farrell, Patrick, *Ireland's British Question* (Dublin, 1975).
O'Grady, Joseph, 'Ireland, the Cuban Missile Crisis, and Civil Aviation: A Study in Applied Neutrality', *Éire-Ireland*, vol. 30, no. 3 (Fall, 1995).
O'Halloran, Clare, *Partition and the Limits of Irish Nationalism* (Dublin, 1987).

O'Halpin, Eunan, 'Intelligence and Security in Ireland, 1922–45'. *Intelligence and National Security,* vol. 5, no. 1 (1990).

—, 'Army, Politics and Society in Independent Ireland, 1932–45' in T.G. Fraser and Keith Jeffery (eds), *Men, Women and War: Historical Studies XVIII* (Dublin, 1993).

—, 'The Army and the Dáil' in Farrell, Brian (ed.), *The Creation of the Dáil* (Dublin, 1994).

—, '"According to the Irish Minister in Rome …", British Decrypts and Irish Diplomacy in the Second World War', *Irish Studies in International Affairs,* vol. 6 (1995).

—, 'The Army in Independent Ireland' in Bartlett, Thomas and Jeffrey, Keith (eds), *A Military History of Ireland* (Cambridge, 1996).

—, The Politics and Practice of Anglo–Irish Security Cooperation, 1939–45' in Girvin, Brian and Roberts, Geoffrey (eds), *Ireland and the Second World War* (Dublin, 1999).

—, *Defending Ireland: The Irish State and its Enemies since 1922* (Oxford, 1999).

—, '"Weird Prophecies": British Intelligence and Anglo–Irish Relations, 1932–33' in Kennedy, Michael and Skelly, Joseph Morrison (eds), *Irish Foreign Policy, 1919–66: From Independence to Internationalism* (Dublin, 2000).

O'Hara, Aidan, *I'll Live 'til I Die: The Story of Delia Murphy* (Leitrim, 1997).

Ó Muircheartaigh, Fíonán, *Ireland in the Coming Times: Essays to Celebrate T.K. Whitaker's 80 Years* (Dublin, 1997).

O'Neill, Helen, 'Annual Review: Ireland's Foreign Aid', *Irish Studies in International Affairs,* vols 5–10 (1994–9).

Ottonello, Paolo, 'Irish–Italian Diplomatic Relations in World War II: The Irish Perspective', *Irish Studies in International Affairs,* vol. 10 (1999).

Owen, Arwell Ellis, *The Anglo–Irish Agreement: The First Three Years* (Cardiff, 1994).

Parsons, Denis, 'Mobilisation and Expansion, 1939–40', *Irish Sword,* vol. 19, nos 75, 76 (1993–4).

Patterson, Robert, 'Ireland, Vichy and Post-Liberation France, 1938–50' in Kennedy, Michael and Skelly, Joseph Morrison (eds), *Irish Foreign Policy, 1919–66: From Independence to Internationalism* (Dublin, 2000).

Peck, John, *Dublin from Downing Street* (Dublin, 1978).

Prill, Felician, 'Sean Lester', *Studies,* vol. 49 (1960).

Raymond, Raymond J., 'Ireland in the European Recovery Program, 1947–53', *Oral History Project.* (Harry S. Truman Presidential Library, 1978).

—, 'American Public Opinion and Irish Neutrality, 1939–45', *Éire-Ireland,* vol. 18, no. 1 (1983).

—, 'Irish Neutrality: Ideology or Pragmatism?' *International Affairs,* vol. 60 (1984).

—, 'Ireland's 1949 NATO Decision: A Reassessment', *Éire-Ireland,* vol. 20, no. 3 (1985).

—, 'The Marshall Plan and Ireland' in Drudy, P.J. (ed.), *The Irish In America: Emigration, Assimilation, and Impact* (Cambridge, 1985).

—, 'David Gray, the Aiken Mission and Irish Neutrality', *Diplomatic History,* vol. 9 (1985).

Rees, Nicholas, 'Annual Review: Ireland's Foreign Relations', *Irish Studies in International Affairs,* vol. 8–10 (1997–9).

—, 'International Affairs: Principles and Practice' in Holmes, Dennis and Holmes, Michael, *Ireland and India: Connections, Comparisons, Contrasts* (Dublin, 1997).

Roberts, Geoffrey, 'Revising Neutrality: Historians and Ireland's War' in Girvin, Brian and Roberts, Geoffrey (eds), *Ireland and the Second World War* (Dublin, 1999).

Rosenberg, Joseph, 'The 1941 Mission of Frank Aiken to the United States: An American Perspective', *Irish Historical Studies,* vol. 22 (1980).

Salmon, Trevor, 'The Changing Nature of Irish Defense Policy', *The World Today,* vol. 35, no. 11 (1979).

—, 'Ireland: A Neutral in the Community?' *Journal of Common Market Studies,* vol. 20, no. 3 (1982).
—, *Unneutral Ireland: An Ambivalent and Unique Security Policy* (Oxford, 1989).
Sexton, Brendan, *Ireland and the Crown, 1922–36* (Dublin, 1989).
Sharp, Paul, 'External Challenges and Domestic Legitimacy: Ireland's Foreign Policy, 1983–87', *Irish Political Studies,* vol. 4 (1989).
—, *Irish Foreign Policy and the European Community* (Aldershot, 1990).
Sinnott, Richard, *Knowledge of the European Union in Irish Public Opinion: Sources and Implications* (Dublin, 1995.)
—, 'Ireland and the Diplomacy of Nuclear Non-Proliferation – the Politics of Incrementalism, *Irish Studies in International Affairs,* vol. 6 (1995).
Skelly, Joseph Morrison, 'Ireland, the Department of External Relations, and the United Nations, 1946–55: a New Look', *Irish Studies in International Affairs,* vol. 7 (1996).
—, *Irish Diplomacy at the United Nations, 1945–65: National Interests and the International Order* (Dublin, 1997).
—, and English, Richard (eds), *Ideas Matter: Essays in Honour of Conor Cruise O'Brien* (Dublin, 1998).
—, 'Appeasement in Our Time: Conor Cruise O'Brien's Analysis of the Irish Peace Process', *Irish Studies in International Affairs,* vol. 10 (1999).
—, 'National Interests and International Mediation: Ireland's South Tyrol Initiative at the United Nations, 1960–61' in Kennedy, Michael and Skelly, Joseph Morrison (eds), *Irish Foreign Policy, 1919–66: From Independence to Internationalism* (Dublin, 2000).
Skillen, Chris, 'Pravda's Provos: Russian and Soviet Manipulation of News from Ireland', *Irish Political Studies,* vol. 8 (1993).
Sloan, Geoffrey, *The Geopolitics of Anglo–Irish Relations in the Twentieth Century* (London, 1997).
—, 'Geopolitics and British Strategic Policy in Ireland: Issues and Interests', *Irish Studies in International Affairs,* vol. 8 (1997).
Smith, Raymond, *The Fighting Irish in the Congo* (Dublin, 1962).
—, *Under the Blue Flag* (Dublin, 1980).
Smylie, R.M., 'Unneutral Neutral Eire', *Foreign Affairs,* vol. 24 (1946).
Stephan, Enno, *Spies in Ireland* (London, 1963).
Storey, Andrew, 'Sectional Interests and Professed Ideas – An Assessment of the Irish Government's White Paper on Foreign Policy', *North–South Issues,* no. 20 (July 1996).
Sutherland, Peter, 'The Context of Neutrality: European Integration', *Studies,* vol. 81 (1992).
Tannam, Etain, 'The European Union and Business Cross-Border Cooperation: The Case of Northern Ireland and the Republic of Ireland', *Irish Political Studies,* vol. 11 (1996).
Tierney, William, 'Irish Writers and the Spanish Civil War', *Éire-Ireland,* vol. 7, no. 3 (1972).
Tonge, J.C., 'Irish Industry in the EFTA Era', *The Statist,* 19 March 1960.
Tonra, Ben, 'Ireland in European Political Cooperation: The Victory of Substance over Form', *Irish Political Studies,* vol. 9 (1994).
—, 'The Europeanisation of Irish Foreign Policy', *Irish Studies in International Affairs,* vol. 10 (1999).
Valiulis, Maryann, *Almost a Rebellion: The Irish Army Mutiny of 1924* (Cork, 1984).
Ward, Eilís, 'A Big Show-off to Show What We Could Do', *Irish Studies in International Affairs,* vol. 7 (1996).
Whelan, Bernadette, 'Ireland and the Marshall Plan, 1948–51', *Éire-Ireland,* vol. 24 (Fall, 1989).
—, 'Ireland and the Marshall Plan, 1948–51', *Irish Economic and Social History,* vol. 19 (1992).

—, Holmes, Michael and Rees, Nicholas, 'Irish Foreign Policy and the Third World: Voting in the UN General Assembly in the 1980s', *Trocaire Development Review* (Dublin, 1992).
—, Holmes, Michael and Rees, Nicholas (eds), *The Poor Relation: Irish Foreign Policy and the Third World* (Dublin, 1993).
— Holmes, Michael and Rees, Nicholas, 'Ireland and the Third World – A Historical Perspective', *Irish Studies in International Affairs*, vol. 5 (1994).
—, 'An Essay on Ireland and J. William Fulbright's Educational Vision', *Éire-Ireland*, vol. 31, nos 3, 4 (fall/winter, 1996).
—, *Ireland and the Marshall Plan, 1947–57* (Dublin, 2000).
—, 'Integration or Isolation? Ireland and the Invitation to Join the Marshall Plan' in Kennedy, Michael and Skelly, Joseph Morrison, (eds), *Irish Foreign Policy, 1919–66: From Independence to Internationalism* (Dublin, 2000).
White, Stephen, 'Ireland, Russia, Communism, Post-Communism', *Irish Studies in International Affairs*, vol. 8 (1997).
Williams, T.D., 'A Study in Neutrality', *The Leader*, 31 January, 1953.
—, 'Ireland and the War' in Nowlan, K.B. and Williams, T.D. (eds), *Ireland in the War Years and After* (Dublin, 1969).
—, 'Conclusion' in Nowlan, K.B. and Williams, T.D. (eds), *Ireland in the War Years and After* (Dublin, 1969).
—, 'Irish Foreign Policy, 1949–69' in Lee, Joseph (ed.), *Ireland, 1945–70* (Dublin, 1979).
Wilson, Andrew J., *Irish America and the Ulster Conflict, 1968–95* (Washington, D.C., 1995).
—, 'From the Beltway to Belfast: The Clinton Administration, Sinn Féin, and the Northern Ireland Peace Process', *New Hibernian Review*, vol. 1, no. 3 (Autumn, 1997).
Wright, Frank, *Northern Ireland: A Comparative Analysis* (Dublin, 1987).
Wylie, Paula, ' "The Virtual Minimum": Ireland's Decision for *De Facto* Recognition of Israel, 1947–49' in Kennedy, Michael and Skelly, Joseph Morrison (eds), *Irish Foreign Policy, 1919–66: From Independence to Internationalism* (Dublin, 2000).
Yeats, Michael B., *Cast a Cold Eye* (Dublin, 1999).
Young, Peter, 'Defence and the New Irish State', *Irish Sword*, vol. 19, nos 75, 76 (1993–4).

Notes on Contributors

Troy D. Davis is Assistant Professor of History at Stephen F. Austin State University in Nacogdoches, Texas. He received a PhD from Marquette University in 1992. He is the author of several articles on Irish and Irish American history. His book, *Dublin's American Policy: Irish–American Diplomatic Relations, 1945–52*, was published by Catholic University of America Press in 1998.

Ronan Fanning is Professor of Modern History at University College Dublin. He is an editor of the Documents on Irish Foreign Policy series and a founder-member of the Royal Irish Academy's National Committee for the Study of International Affairs. He was joint-editor of *Irish Historical Studies* from 1976 to 1987. He is the author of *The Irish Department of Finance* and *Independent Ireland* and co-editor of *Documents on Irish Foreign Policy: Volume I, 1919–22*. He has published scholarly articles in journals throughout Europe and North America and is a regular political columnist for the Irish *Sunday Independent*.

Till Geiger lectures in the Institute of European Studies at Queen's University Belfast and has held academic appointments at the London School of Economics and the University of Aberdeen, where he completed a PhD. He has written widely on post-World War II economic reconstruction, the Marshall Plan and western rearmament. He is currently working on a book entitled *Britain and the Economic Problem of the First Cold War*. His research on Ireland and the Marshall Plan forms part of a larger research project on the impact of American military aid on the Western European economy.

Katrina Goldstone is a researcher and scriptwriter. She received an MA in Modern Irish History from St Patrick's College Maynooth, where she specialised in Irish government policy towards Jewish refugees during World War II. She lectures and writes extensively on anti-Semitism, attitudes towards ethnic minorities and restrictive immigration practices. She frequently reviews books, plays and the arts for Irish radio and newspapers, including RTÉ, the *Irish Times* and the *Sunday Tribune*.

Patrick Keatinge has recently retired as Jean Monnet Professor of European Integration in the Department of Political Science, Trinity College Dublin. He was a founder-member of the Royal Irish Academy's National Committee for the Study of International Affairs, the Irish Association of Contemporary European Studies and the Institute of European Affairs. He has written widely on Irish and European foreign policy in numerous journals. His major publications include *The Formulation of Irish Foreign Policy*, *A Place Among the Nations: Issues in Irish Foreign Policy* and *A Singular Stance: Irish Neutrality in the 1980s*. During his tenure as Senior Research Fellow at the Institute of European Affairs he published, in 1996, the volume *European Security: Ireland's Choices*.

Michael Kennedy is Executive Editor of the Royal Irish Academy's Documents on Irish Foreign Policy series. Previously, he lectured in Modern and Irish History at Queen's University Belfast. He received a PhD from University College Dublin. He is the author of *Ireland and the League of Nations, 1919–46* and co-editor of *Documents on Irish Foreign Policy: Volume I, 1919–22*. He has published numerous articles on Irish diplomatic history and is currently completing a book on the politics of North–South relations in Ireland.

Dermot Keogh is Professor of History at University College Cork and an editor of the Documents on Irish Foreign Policy series. He has been a Fulbright Professor in California, Fellow of the Woodrow Wilson Center in Washington and Jean Monnet Professor of European Integration at University College Cork. He is the co-editor of *Documents on Irish Foreign Policy: Volume I, 1919–22* and the author of numerous books on Irish diplomatic and political history, including *Ireland and Europe, 1919–1989*, *Ireland and the Vatican: The Politics and Diplomacy of Church and State, 1922–1960*, *Twentieth-Century Ireland: Nation and State* and *Jews in Twentieth-Century Ireland: Refugees, Anti-Semitism and the Holocaust*.

Gerard Keown is a diplomat in the Irish Department of Foreign Affairs. He received a DPhil from the University of Oxford. His dissertation analysed the political origins of Irish diplomacy. He is currently completing a study of the development of Irish foreign policy during the early decades of Irish independence.

Deirdre McMahon lectures in the Department of History at Mary Immaculate College in Limerick. She received a PhD from Churchill College, Cambridge. She is the author of *Republicans and Imperialists: Anglo–Irish Relations in the 1930s*. She has published numerous articles on Irish history and Anglo–Irish relations and is currently writing a biography of Eamon de Valera.

Gary Murphy lectures in Government at Dublin City University. He was educated at University College Cork and Dublin City University, where he completed a PhD. He has published numerous articles on the history of the Irish state in *Administration, Irish Studies in International Affairs* and other journals and is review editor of *Irish Political Studies*. His forthcoming works include a biography of the Fianna Fáil politician Seán MacEntee and an edited volume of essays on the Seán Lemass era.

Mervyn O'Driscoll is College Lecturer in Modern European History at University College Cork and has taught at the University of Wolverhampton. He received a PhD from the University of Cambridge. His articles on international history, nuclear diplomacy and European integration have been widely published. He is also the author of the forthcoming volumes *Irish–German Relations, 1919–39* (Four Courts Press) and *Nuclear Issues and European Integration* (Macmillan).

Eunan O'Halpin is the Professor of Contemporary Irish History at Trinity College Dublin. He is also an editor of the Documents on Irish Foreign Policy series. His major works include *The Decline of the Union: British Government in Ireland, 1892–1920, Head of the Civil Service: A Study of Sir Warren Fisher* and *Defending Ireland: The Irish State and its Enemies since 1922*. He is a co-editor of *Documents on Irish Foreign Policy: Volume I, 1919–22* and is currently co-editing a study of Anglo–American security cooperation between 1914 and 1949.

Robert Patterson graduated from University College Cork in 1994 with an MA on the subject of 'Ireland and France: An Analysis of Diplomatic Relations, 1929–50'. He joined the Irish Department of Foreign Affairs as a Third Secretary in October 1995. He is currently posted to the Irish Embassy in London, having been seconded to the Finnish Foreign Ministry in Helsinki during its 1999 presidency of the European Union.

Joseph Morrison Skelly is Assistant Professor of History at the College of Mount Saint Vincent in New York and has taught at Fordham University and the Irish School of Ecumenics. He received a PhD from University College Dublin. He is the author of *Irish Diplomacy at the United Nations, 1945–65: National Interests and the International Order*, co-editor of *Ideas Matter: Essays in Honour of Conor Cruise O'Brien* and editor of the forthcoming *Collected Literary Criticism of Conor Cruise O'Brien* (Maunsel Press).

Bernadette Whelan is a lecturer in history in the Department of Government and Society at the University of Limerick. She received a PhD from University College Cork. Her book, *Ireland and the Marshall Plan, 1947–57*, is forthcoming from Four Courts Press, and she has written widely on Irish foreign policy and economic history in *Irish Studies in International Affairs*, *Éire-Ireland* and other journals.

Paula Wylie lectures in international relations and history at the University of North Carolina-Charlotte. She received an MA in International Relations from Boston University and is a PhD candidate in Modern History at University College Cork, where she is researching Ireland's diplomatic relations with non-recognised states, including Israel, East Germany and China. A native of Texas, she has spent ten years living and working in Europe and directs a consultancy firm in international business.

Index

Abyssinia, 85–6, 94
Acheson, Dean, 198, 203
Administration, 17
Aer Lingus, 145–6
Aiken, Frank, 24, 153, 218, 245, 263, 267–8, 272–3, 291–5, 297–302, 304, 305–6, 323–6
Albertas, H.E., 107
Alexander, A.V., 168
Algeria, 289
Algiers, 108
Aliens Act (1935) (Ireland), 118
Allesandri, Arturo, 49
Alphand, Charles, 36
Alphand, Hervé, 111
American Association for the Recognition of the Irish Republic, 194
American League for an Undivided Ireland, 194, 207
Amery, L.S., 155, 158–162, 165
Andrews, C.S. (Tod) 70
Anglo–American relations, 16, 21, 192–202, 204–8, 212
Anglo–Irish Agreements (1938), 91, 177, 178, 311, 315–7
Anglo–Irish relations, 16, 17, 19, 22, 24, 25–43, 61–73, 169, 205, 250, 264, 309–13
Anglo–Irish Trade Agreement (1960), 266
Anglo–Irish Free Trade Agreement (1965), 324
Anglo–Irish Treaty, 14, 21, 28, 32, 51, 55–8, 60, 62, 72–3, 77–8, 90, 155–6, 165, 181, 182, 191, 312, 314
Anglo–Irish War, 46–8, 51, 76–7, 96, 192, 202
Anti-Partition League, 194
Arbusch, Fay, 106
Archer, Liam, 133
Archer, Norman, 213
Argentina, 44, 46, 48–9, 51–5; Ireland establishes formal diplomatic relations with, 23, 59; Irish community in, 47, 51–4, 56–60
Attlee, Clement, 168, 173–4, 178, 183, 185, 187
Australia, 23, 63, 69, 136, 185, 188
Austria, 16, 127, 128, 133, 242, 269, 289–307, 319
Anschluss, 126, 130

Baldwin, Stanley, 62
Balfour Declaration, 160, 165
Ball, George, 270–3, 282–5
Barry, Colm, 235
Bayer, Abraham, 124
The Bell, 17
Belgium, 38, 242, 312
Benelux, 224, 229, 233–5
Bengal famine, 163
Ben Gurion, David, 143, 147
Bernadotte, Count Folke, 144, 146–7
Bernheim, Franz, 120–1
Bevin, Ernest, 197
Bewley, Charles, 16, 74–5, 77–8, 82–9, 92–5, 123, 131–2
Biggar, Francis, 268, 279–80
Binchy, Daniel, 74–5, 79, 80, 95
Birkenhead, Lord, 155–6
Blanche, Alfred, 35
Blythe, Ernest, 44, 48, 77
Bohlen, Charles, 203
Boland, Frederick H., 22, 23, 109, 111, 116, 134, 139–40, 146–51, 182, 188, 213, 216, 219, 228–39, 243, 245,248, 267, 294, 309, 320–1
Boland, Harry, 45, 49
Boland, H.P., 22
Bose, S.C., 156, 159, 163–4
Bonestal, Charles, 237
Bowman, John, 20
Brady, Carlos, 59

343

Brazil, 44–5, 49, 131
Brennan, Robert, 46–8, 51
Bretton Woods, 225
Briscoe, Robert, 77, 82, 87, 106, 122, 125, 142, 282
Britain (see also Anglo–Irish relations), ii, 16, 44, 52, 123, 261; and the EEC, 262, 264–5, 268–9, 276; and India, 155–91; and Israel, 147, 151; and Jewish immigration, 117–9, 128–9, 130, 134–6; and Palestine, 139, 143; relaxation of fifty-year rule on state papers, 19; Intelligence services and Ireland, 61–73; response to Irish neutrality, 318; and Marshall Plan, 216, 224, 234, 236–8
British Commonwealth, ii, 16, 18, 22, 25–43, 61–73,
Brook, Norman, 173, 179, 185, 186, 188
Brooke, Basil, 196–9
Browne, D.J., 89
Browne, Noel, 282
Brüning, Heinrich, 80, 81
Bryan, Dan, 133
Buckley, Donal, 45
Bulfin, Eamon, 44–8, 50, 52, 54, 58
Bullitt, William, 98
Bülow, Bernhard von, 87
Burma, 157, 159, 161–2, 167, 170, 182–3, 186; leaves the Commonwealth, 175–180

Cabot Lodge, Henry, 267
Cahan, J.F., 260
Canada, 26, 28, 63, 69, 114, 117, 135, 144, 185, 188, 199, 289; Irish relations with, 22
Capuchin Annual, 17
Casement, Roger, 76, 312
Cauvet-Duhamel, B.F., 107, 109
Committee on European Economic Co-operation, 203–22, 222–47
Celtic movements, 40
Censorship, 21, 23
Centre Party (Germany), 81, 84
Ceylon, 167, 170, 179
Chamberlain, Austen, 155
Chamberlain, Neville, 90, 91, 92, 315
Chapman, Vinton, 241–2
Chartres, John, 77, 78
Chatfield, Admiral, 315

Chelmsford, Lord, 155
Chifley, J.B., 185, 189
Childers, Erskine, 312
Chile, 44–5, 48–0, 55–60
China, 291
Christus Rex, 17
Church of Ireland Gazette, 39
Church of Ireland Jews Society, 129
Churchill, W.S., 61, 155–6, 158–63, 166–7, 178, 188, 287, 316, 318, 321
Clann na Poblachta, 143, 195, 209, 320
Clarke, Otto, 260
Clayton, William, 203, 236–8, 242
Clissman, Helmut, 88
Cold War, 219, 288; and Ireland, 24
Collins, Michael, 45–7, 57, 59, 77, 141, 313–4
Comite Argentino pro Libertad de Irlanda 52
Commins, T.V., 305
Committee on European Economic Co-operation (CEEC), 222–46
Communist Party (Ireland), 208–9
Congo, 18
Congress of Irish Unions, 209, 220
Congress Party, 157–62, 168, 172–3
Connolly, James, 312
Cordier, Andrew, 294
Corish, Brendan, 282
Cosgrave, Liam, 251–2, 322
Cosgrave, William T., 22, 39, 40–1, 62–3, 66–7, 71, 73
Costello, John A., 143, 181, 185–7, 190–1, 195, 286, 320–3
Council of Europe, 23, 249–50, 289
Couve de Murville, Maurice, 279, 280
Cox, Michael, 15
Cranborne, Lord, 316
Creech-Jones, Arthur, 177
Cremin, Con, 20, 22, 102, 105–6, 115, 128, 145–6, 153, 234, 239, 242–3, 263, 268–71, 278–9, 283, 296–9, 302–3, 305, 309, 324
Cremins, Francis T., 116, 122, 127
Cripps, Stafford, 160–2, 168, 180
Croft, William, 171
Cromien, Sean, 256
Crum, Erskine, 183
Cruise O'Brien, Conor, 18, 267, 291, 295–6, 298–9, 300–4

Cumann na nGaedheal, 28, 41, 65–6, 73, 82, 208
Cyprus, 289, 299, 307
Czechoslovakia, 27, 92, 94, 143, 144

Dáil Eireann (1919 – 22), 14, 25, 44, 45, 76
Dáil Loan, 45, 50–2, 54, 57
Danzig, 22, 92
Darblay, Jacques, 106
Darlan, Admiral, 107–8
Dawson, Geoffrey, 63, 66
de Gaulle, Charles, 97, 107–8, 110–13
Dehn, Georg von, 87–9
de Laforcade, M.F.X., 107–12
Denmark, 27, 105, 147, 233, 238–9, 242, 268, 269, 289, 301, 305
Department of Agriculture, 217, 250, 254–5
Department of Defence, 72
Department of External Affairs (Foreign Affairs from 1971), 14, 18, 20, 21–4, 31, 32, 57, 73, 113, 114, 250, 263, 317, 324; and the ERP, 214–7, 223, 229–30, 248; and Israel, 137–8, 144, 146, 147, 150, 152, 154; and Jewish refugees, 105, 122–5, 126–7, 130, 133; threats to future of, 96
Department of Finance, 19, 22, 24, 48, 215–7, 235–6, 250
Department of Industry and Commerce, 122–4, 133, 146, 217, 254–5
Department of Justice, 89, 122–7, 129, 130, 131, 133, 134, 140, 142
Department of the President, 22, 122
Department of the Taoiseach, 14, 20, 22, 144
de Valera, Eamon, 14, 18, 22, 23, 31, 34, 29, 41, 45–9, 61–7, 70, 73–4, 76, 82, 85–92, 94–5, 102–3, 112, 119–20, 122, 126–7, 133, 140–3, 161–2, 180–1, 191, 251, 267, 314, 316–7, 321, 324, 325–6; and anti-Partitionism, 194–5, 250; Cuban interview, 309–13; Economic policies, 266; visit to German Legation, 114, 205–6, 213, 317, 323; and India, 156, 158–9, 163–4, 168, 177–9, 182–4; and the Marshall Plan, 226, 232, 236, 239, 241–2, 244, 245, 246; approach to policy-making, 218, 221
Devlin, Denis, 15, 145
Dillon, James, 62, 218

Dillon, Theobald, 129
Dinan, Desmond, 222
Ditchburn, Robert, 131
Document number two, 41, 313
Documents on Irish Foreign Policy (See also Royal Irish Academy), 21
Donaldson, E.P., 169
Donlon, Seán, 309
Dorman Smith, Reginald, 162, 167, 176
Dorr, Noel, 20, 309
Drummond, Eric, 30
Duane, Cornelius, 77, 78
Duff, John E., 124, 125, 127, 131
Duggan, John, 20
Dulanty, John Whelan, 22, 23, 61, 62, 70, 90–1, 124, 125
Dulles, John F., 322
Dwyer, T. Ryle, 19

Eden, Anthony, 121
Egan, Frank, 44, 45, 48–51, 55–7, 60
Egypt, 37, 145, 152, 162
Erhard, Ludwig, 268, 269
Estonia, 27, 33
European customs union, 234–8
European Economic Community (See also European Union), iii, 16, 24, 250, 265–85
European Free Trade Area, 16, 253, 256–7, 260–3, 266–7
European Recovery Programme (Marshall Aid), 16, 23, 24, 222–46,
European Union (See also European Economic Community), ii, 15
Evian Conference, 116, 126–7
External association, 181, 182, 184, 191
External Relations Act (1936), 23, 157, 174, 181–2, 185–7, 189–90, 314, 320

Fanning, Ronan, ii, 13, 19, 20
Fay, William P., 258
Fianna Fáil, 37, 41, 64, 74, 82, 93, 143, 165, 166, 194, 208, 222, 247, 251, 257, 265, 320–1
Fine Gael, 251, 258–60
Finland, 27, 229, 236, 320
First Programme for Economic Expansion, 266

First World War, 27, 76
FitzGerald, Desmond, 22, 25, 27, 28, 30, 37, 40
FitzGerald, Garret, 253, 280–1, 309
Flanagan, Oliver, 142
Flannery, Edmund, 59
Food and Agriculture Organisation, 23
France, 16, 96, 147, 151, 261; *Comité Française de la Libération Nationale* (CFLN), 97, 109; Irish relations with, 22, 24, 25, 35, 69, 71, 96–115, 281; and Second World War, 23, 315; views on Ireland, 35–6; treatment of Jews in, 104–7; and Marshall Plan, 224, 229, 232–4, 236–8, 243; Vichy regime, 99–111, 114
Franks, Oliver, 197, 199, 229, 234–5, 237
Frazer, Peter, 185, 189

G2 (Irish Military Intelligence), 107, 133
Gaelic League, 53
Gallagher, Dermot, 309
Gandhi, Mahatma, 37, 159, 161–2, 164, 168
Garda Síochána, 64
GATT, 247, 262
Gaulle, Charles de, 265
Gavan Duffy, George, 33, 44, 56–9, 76–8
George V, 61–2
German–Irish Society, 76, 77
'German Plot' 162
Germany, 16, 74–95, 200, 203, 225, 229, 231–3, 236, 269, 289, 315–6; Irish relations with, 22, 35–6, 74–95, 312; Irish disapproval of reparations, 30; Position of Jews in, 74–94, 116–36; Weimar Republic, 74–9
Ginnell, Laurence, 55–60
Girvin, Brian, 222–3
Goebbels, Joesf, 86
Göring, Hermann, 83
Gordon-Walker, Patrick, 189–91
Gort, Lord, 315
Government Code and Cipher School (Britain), 67–72
Government of India Act (1935), 157, 173
Gray, David, 109, 110, 192, 200, 206, 210
Greece, 147, 215, 229, 260, 288
Green Pool, 250

Griffith, Arthur, 25, 37, 41, 45, 49, 313
Gruber-de Gasperi agreement (1946), 290, 293, 294, 298, 299, 301, 302

Hacha, Emil, 92
Hales, Donal, 47
Hales, Tom, 47
Hales, Sean, 47
Hammarskjöld, Dag, 229–30, 294
Hankinson, W.C., 251
Harkness, David, ii, 13, 18, 19
Hearne, John J., 22
Hempel, Edouard, 91, 317
Henderson, Arthur, 176
Henry, Paul, 40
Herzog, Chaim, 141, 142
Hindenburg, Paul von, 80, 82, 83
Hirschfield, Hans, 228–9
Hitler, Adolf, 75, 79–91, 114, 119, 319, 323
Hoare, Samuel, 156
Holy See (Vatican), 39, 100–1, 143, 147, 148, 149, 151, 152; Irish relations with, 22–3
Horan, T.J., 295
Huber, Max, 120
Hungary, 215

Iceland, 232
India, 21, 37, 155–91, 321
Inskip, Thomas, 91
Institute of European Affairs, 15
International Civil Aviation Organisation, 23
International Monetary Fund, 225
Inter-Party government (1948–51), 143, 181–2, 184–8, 195, 219, 222, 248–9, 251, 320–1
Inter-Party government (1954–7), 251–2, 286, 322–3
Iraq, 37
Ireland (selected aspects): Agricultural policy, 212; London agreement (December 1925), 301; Civil War, 21, 33, 175; and the Commonwealth 25–43, 61–73, 155–91; Defence policy and security policy, 32–3, 61–73, 91, 123–4, 313; Economic policy, 33, 177, 209–12, 216–7, 226–46, 247–64, 265–; and Europe,

222–46, 247–64, 265–85, 324–6; *Foreign policy*: Academic bodies dealing with, 19; Coded diplomatic traffic, 61–73; and EEC, 265–85, 250, 263–4, 305, 307, 311, 324–6; and European Coal and Steel Community, 250; Foreign diplomatic representatives in, 69–70; Historiography of, ii, iii, 13–21, 27, 222–3, 225, 246, 286–7; influence of religion on, 39–40, 138, 286; public discussion of, 18, 218–20; Minorities issues, 38, 116–36, 138, 140; Publishing on, 15, 20; Teaching of in universities, 15, 21, 308; and Western European Union, 250; relations with Austria, 286–307; relations with France 96–115; relations with Germany, 74–95; relations with Israel, 137–54; relations with Italy, 286–307; and the Marshall Plan, 203–21; and NATO, 273–7, 281, 285; Military neutrality of, 16, 20, 21, 23, 95, 133, 192, 204–5, 238, 244, 265–85, 287, 309–13, 316–20, 324–6; Partition (of Ireland), 38–9, 91, 185, 191, 192–202, 205–6, 219, 226–7, 249, 268, 289, 296; Provisional Government of (1922), 78; and United Nations, 213–4, 252, 322–4

Ireland Today, 17
Irish Bulletin, 46, 54, 77
Irish Christian Front, 94
Irish Committee for Austrian Relief, 129
Irish Co-ordinating Committee for Refugees, 128–32, 134
Irish diaspora, 33–5, 60
Irish Independent, 219
Irish Monthly, 17, 39
Irish Neutrality League, 312
Irish Press, 219
Irish Race Conference (Paris, 1922), 34, 54, 55
Irish Republican Army, 46, 47, 66, 70, 77, 320
Irish Situation Committee (Britain), 63, 65, 66, 67
Irish Statesman, 17
Irish Studies in International Affairs, 15, 20
Irish Trade Union Congress, 209, 220
Irish Times, 219

Ismay, General, 173–4, 178
Israel, 16, 137–54
Italy, 16, 22, 147, 203, 217–8, 224, 230, 237–8, 289–307

Jammet's Restaurant (Dublin), 113
Jewish refugees and Ireland, 16, 116–36
Jewish Standing Committee for Refugees, 129
Jinnah, M. A., 158, 164, 168, 172, 178
Johnson, Thomas, 41
John XXIII, 154
Jones, Thomas, 19, 62
Jowitt, Lord, 186–8

Keating, Paul, 303, 309
Keating, Sean 40
Keatinge, Patrick, ii, 13, 18, 19
Kell, Vernon, 64
Kellogg-Briand Pact (1928), 32
Kennan, George, 203, 237, 241
Kennedy, John F., 285, 324, 325
Kennedy, Michael, 93–4
Kennelly, Martin H., 199
Keogh, Dermot, ii, 13, 20, 118, 142
Kergoat, Marcel, 107
Khan, Liaquat Ali, 172, 189
Kiernan, T.J., 100, 270–2
Killearn, Lord, 177, 178
King, W. Mackenzie, 161, 185, 189
Kissinger, Henry, 309
Kohn, Leo, 28
Korea, 201, 289
Kriesky, Bruno, 303
Kristallnacht, 86, 118, 129, 135

Labour Party (Ireland), 208–9
Laithwaite, Gilbert, 155, 170, 187, 190
Lalouette, Roger, 109
Larkin, James, 112
Latin America, 21, 44–60, 299, 302
Laval, Pierre, 102
Law, Hugh, 36
The Leader, 17, 18
League of Nations, 16, 22, 23, 26–35, 55, 63, 69, 70–1, 76, 86, 90, 91, 120, 192, 200, 267, 289, 314

League of Nations Society of Ireland, 42, 122
Lee, Joseph, ii, 13, 15, 17, 233
Lemass, Seán, 14, 24, 41, 123, 126, 226–8, 230, 242, 243, 245, 251, 257, 261–3, 268, 325; and Irish membership of the EEC, 247, 265–6, 268–70, 273 85, 324–6; and the United Nations, 288, 296, 297, 298, 299, 302, 305, 306
Lester, Seán, 15, 22, 55, 69, 70, 120, 121
Lestocquoy, Eugene, 107
Ley, Robert, 83
Linlithgow, Lord, 155, 157, 159–63
Listowel, Lord, 172, 175–6, 188, 189
Little, Patrick J., 34, 52–5, 57
Lloyd George, David, 182
Lovett, Robert, 241
Lynch, Patrick, 216
Lyons, F.S.L., 316–7

MacBride, Seán 143, 144, 146, 147, 150, 152, 182, 185, 187–8, 195, 215, 247, 249–51, 268, 320–3
MacCarthy, J.C.B., 257
MacDonald, Malcolm, 156, 161, 177–8
MacDonald, Ramsay, 62, 63, 156
MacEntee, Séan, 258
Machiavelli, Nicolo, 318
Machtig, Eric 169, 170, 185
MacKernan, Padraic, 20
MacManus, Padraic, 52, 58–60
MacNeill, Eoin, 41
MacWhite, Eoin, 152
MacNeill, James, 63–4, 66
MacWhite, Michael, 15, 18, 55, 96
Maffey, John (Lord Rugby), 67, 109–10, 155, 181, 185–6, 188, 190, 192, 195, 200, 205
Maguire, W.J., 127
Malaya (Malaysia), 161, 162, 179, 289
Malcolm, Neil, 121
Malta, 39
Manchuria, 30
Mansergh, Nicholas, ii, 180–2, 185–6, 191
Marshall, George C., 195, 203, 215, 219
Marshall Plan, 200, 203–21, 247–9
Martino, Enrico, 295, 296, 299, 302, 303, 305
McCann, Hugh, 24, 268, 308

McCauley, Leo, 15, 74, 75, 80–2, 93, 119, 120
McDonald, Denis, 111, 268, 272, 278–80
McDonald, James, 121
McGilligan, Patrick, 22, 27, 32, 43, 71, 143
McElligott, J.J., 116, 216, 256
McEllin, John, 125
McGrath, George, 57
McLoughlin, Edward, 144–6
McMahon, Deirdre, 20, 63
McQuaid, John Charles, 323
McQuillan, Jack, 282
Meir, Golda, 154
Menon, V.P., 172, 190
Mexico, 39
Milward, Alan, 224, 225, 244
MI5, 64
MI6 (SIS), 65
Monnet Plan, 232
Monteath, David, 160, 170–1, 174, 175
Montivideo Convention (1933), 137
Morris-Jones, W.H., 179
Mountbatten, Lord Louis, 167, 172–4, 176–80, 182–4
Muintir na Tire, 220
Mulcahy, Richard, 185, 218
Munich agreement (1938), 90–1
Murphy, Gary, 222–3, 225, 244
Murphy, Séan, 15, 89, 96–106, 127, 109–15, 128, 323
Muslim League, 158–9, 171, 172
Mussolini, Benito, 82, 86, 91
Myrdal, Gunnar, 224

National Archives, iii, 14–5, 21
National Archives Act (1986), 14
National Committee for the Study of International Affairs (see also Royal Irish Academy), 19–20
National Labour (Ireland), 208–9
National University of Ireland, 36
Naval Disarmament, 29, 30, 34, 71
Nazi Party, 74, 79–94, 126, 129; Irish attitudes to, 75–6
Nehru, Jawaharlal, 158, 161, 171–3, 183–4, 187, 190, 315
Netherlands, 23, 147, 243
Neutrality, 133

New Zealand, 131, 185, 188
Newall, Cyril, 315
Nicaragua, 143
Nicholls, Jasper 45
Noel-Baker, Philip, 187–9
Nolan, Nicholas, 277
Non-proliferation treaty (1968), 289
North Atlantic Treaty Organisation (NATO), 23, 200, 247–8, 265, 269, 271, 274, 275, 277, 287, 291–2, 294, 299, 301, 320–1
Northern Ireland, iii, 32, 38–9, 65, 90, 158, 161, 172, 190, 193, 196–9, 200, 202, 206, 249, 285, 289, 307, 324
Norway, 27, 147, 229, 236, 238, 242, 289
Nowlan, Kevin B., 19
Nu, Thakin, 176
Nunan, Seán, 134
Nuremberg Laws, 121–2
Nuremberg Trials, 132

Oath of Allegiance, 62
O'Brien, Michael, 77
O'Ceallaigh, Sean T, 18, 96–7, 115
Ó Cearbhaill, Tadhg, 20, 262
O'Durnin, Mr., 45
O'Dwyer, William, 198–9
OEEC, 247, 249, 250, 253–7, 260, 262
O'Farrell, Patrick, 19
O'Hegarty, Diarmuid, 44, 47, 48
O'Hegarty, P.S., 42
O'Kelly de Gallagh, Count Gerald, 38, 98
Ó Moráin, Micheál, 277
O'Neill, Terence, 324
Opium Conference (1925), 30
Optional Clause dispute, 32
Ortona, Egidio, 303
O'Sullivan, Donal, 65
Ostroróg, Count Stanislas, 114, 148–9, 213
Ottawa Economic Conference, 63, 69

Pakenham, Frank (Lord Longford), 17
Pakistan, 158, 161, 168, 172, 178, 185, 189
Palestine, 139–43, 146–9
Papen, Franz von, 81, 84
Paraguay, 45, 55, 144
Paris Peace Conference, 14

Patel, V.J., 156
Peace by Ordeal, 17
Peck, John, 19
Peru, 55
Pétain, Marshall, 99–104, 107–8, 110
Peters, William, 63
Pethick-Lawrence, Lord, 167–8, 172
Philipson, Serge, 106
Philipson, Sophie, 106
Pius XI, 131, 208
Pius XII, 280
Plunkett, George Count 47, 48
Pokorny, Julius, 77
Poland, 97, 143
Portugal, 17, 105, 133, 203, 230, 232
Power, Nancy Wyse, 77, 78
Protocol for the Pacific Settlement of International Disputes (Geneva Protocol), 31–2

Quadragesimo Anno, 208, 215

Rance, Hubert, 175–8
Rau, B.N., 182, 187, 188
Raymond, R.J., 222–3, 232–3
Reading, Lord, 156
Red Cross, International Committee of the, 120
Redmond, John, 13–4
Riviere, Jean, 112–4
Robinson, Paschal, 87
Roche, Stephen, 125
Röhm, Ernst, 85
Ronan, Sean, 304
Roosevelt, F.D., 126
Rotter, A.F., 292–5, 298
Rosenberg, Alfred, 83
Royal Institute for International Affairs, 180
Royal Irish Academy, iii, 15, 19, 21
Rush, Kevin, 272
Ruttledge, P.J., 122, 126
Rynne, Michael, 22, 122, 149–50, 152–3

Saarland, 250
Salazar, Antonio, 17
Salmon, Trevor, 20, 319
Sang, Aung, 176

Saw, U, 159
Sayers, Dorothy, 319
Schonfield, Solomon, 126
Second World War, 97, 157, 314–6; and Ireland, 23, 126, 133–4, 319, 321, 325
Segni, Antonio, 296, 297, 298, 302, 306
Shamir, Yitzak, 141
Shertok, Moshe, 144, 150, 151
Simon, Lord John, 165
Simpson, Mr J., 49, 50
Singapore, 161, 177
Sinn Féin, 13, 25, 44, 54
Slim, General, 176
Smith, Patrick, 245
Smuts, J.C., 160–1, 189
Society of Friends, 128, 129
Society of Saint Vincent de Paul, 131
South Africa, 26, 53, 54, 63, 69, 117, 136, 189
South Tyrol, 289–307
Soviet Union, 23, 40, 86, 88, 143, 203, 238, 250
Spain, 39, 85, 86, 94, 147, 228
Statute of Westminster, 32, 61, 69, 165, 189
Sterling Area, 230
Stevenson, Adlai, 199
Stresemann, Gustav, 79
Studies, 17, 33
Sweden, 23, 105, 133, 147, 229–30, 233, 236, 238, 242, 269, 289, 318
Sweeney, Joseph, 270–2
Switzerland, 105, 133, 147, 217, 238, 242, 269, 312, 318, 319

Tardini, Monsignor Domenico, 147
Thomson, Basil, 72
Tibet, 289, 293
Tin Tut, U, 175
Tiso, Josep, 92
Treaty of Rome (1957), 265, 269–70
Trieste, 250
Truman Doctrine, 200
Truman, Harry S., 207, 321
Tunisia, 289
Turkey, 133, 215, 229, 260, 232, 288
Turnbull, F.F., 169

Ulster Irish Society of New York, 197

United Nations, 16, 18, 23, 24, 141, 142, 213–4, 238–9, 267, 272, 286–307
United Nations Economic Commission for Europe, 224, 229, 239
United Nations Relief and Reconstruction Administration, 232
United States, 14, 117, 143, 261; Irish relations with, 22, 26, 33–5, 37, 40, 45, 51, 69, 71, 192–202, 314, 324; British interception of diplomatic cables, 67, 71; Diplomatic telegrams to Ireland, 70–1; and post-war European recovery, 203–22, 222–46; and Irish membership of the EEC, 270–3, 284; views on Irish neutrality, 110, 204, 265, 268, 277, 316; relations with Ireland, 192–202, 253
University College Dublin, Archives Department, 20
Upper Silesia, 120
Uruguay, 55, 143

Valeri, Valerio, 98
Van der Beugel, Ernst, 223–5, 244, 246
Vietnam, 153, 289
Versailles, Treaty of, 74, 76, 90

Walshe, Joseph, 15, 18, 2–3, 39, 74, 85–8, 90–2, 94, 96–7, 100–4, 107–8, 110–15, 121–2, 125, 127, 131, 139–40, 147–9, 151, 164, 317
Warnock, William, 22, 83, 92, 144
Wavell, Archibald, 162–4, 168, 172
Weizmann, Chaim, 138, 143
Whaley, David, 235
Whelan, Bernadette, 223
Whitaker, T.K., 24, 219, 252, 254, 256, 263, 266, 268–71, 274–80, 282, 284, 285
White, Ivan, 231–2
Williams, T. Desmond, ii, 17, 18, 308–9, 317
Wilson, Woodrow, 192, 311
Winspeare, Baron, 306
Wirth, Joseph, 78
Witzthum, Marcus, 125
Wormser, Olivier, 278

Zaghlul, Said, 164, 168
Zetland, Lord Lawrence, 156